Praise for *Natural Language Processing with Transformers*

Pretrained transformer language models have taken the NLP world by storm, while libraries such as 🤗 Transformers have made them much easier to use. Who better to teach you how to leverage the latest breakthroughs in NLP than the creators of said library? *Natural Language Processing with Transformers* is a tour de force, reflecting the deep subject matter expertise of its authors in both engineering and research. It is the rare book that offers both substantial breadth and depth of insight and deftly mixes research advances with real-world applications in an accessible way. The book gives informed coverage of the most important methods and applications in current NLP, from multilingual to efficient models and from question answering to text generation. Each chapter provides a nuanced overview grounded in rich code examples that highlights best practices as well as practical considerations and enables you to put research-focused models to impactful real-world use. Whether you're new to NLP or a veteran, this book will improve your understanding and fast-track your development and deployment of state-of-the-art models.

—Sebastian Ruder, Google DeepMind

Transformers have changed how we do NLP, and Hugging Face has pioneered how we use transformers in product and research. Lewis Tunstall, Leandro von Werra, and Thomas Wolf from Hugging Face have written a timely volume providing a convenient and hands-on introduction to this critical topic. The book offers a solid conceptual grounding of transformer mechanics, a tour of the transformer menagerie, applications of transformers, and practical issues in training and bringing transformers to production. Having read chapters in this book, with the depth of its content and lucid presentation, I am confident that this will be the number one resource for anyone interested in learning transformers, particularly for natural language processing.

—Delip Rao, Author of Natural Language Processing *and* Deep Learning with PyTorch

Complexity made simple. This is a rare and precious book about NLP, transformers, and the growing ecosystem around them, Hugging Face. Whether these are still buzzwords to you or you already have a solid grasp of it all, the authors will navigate you with humor, scientific rigor, and plenty of code examples into the deepest secrets of the coolest technology around. From "off-the-shelf pretrained" to "from-scratch custom" models, and from performance to missing labels issues, the authors address practically every real-life struggle of a ML engineer and provide state-of-the-art solutions, making this book destined to dictate the standards in the field for years to come.

—*Luca Perrozzi, PhD, Data Science and Machine Learning Associate Manager at Accenture*

REVISED EDITION

Natural Language Processing with Transformers

Building Language Applications with Hugging Face

Lewis Tunstall, Leandro von Werra, and Thomas Wolf
Foreword by Aurélien Géron

Beijing • Boston • Farnham • Sebastopol • Tokyo

Natural Language Processing with Transformers

by Lewis Tunstall, Leandro von Werra, and Thomas Wolf

Published by O'Reilly Media, Inc., 1005 Gravenstein Highway North, Sebastopol, CA 95472.

O'Reilly books may be purchased for educational, business, or sales promotional use. Online editions are also available for most titles (*http://oreilly.com*). For more information, contact our corporate/institutional sales department: 800-998-9938 or *corporate@oreilly.com*.

Acquisitions Editor: Rebecca Novack
Development Editor: Melissa Potter
Production Editor: Katherine Tozer
Copyeditor: Rachel Head
Proofreader: Kim Cofer
Indexer: Potomac Indexing, LLC
Interior Designer: David Futato
Cover Designer: Karen Montgomery
Illustrator: Christa Lanz

February 2022: First Edition
May 2022: Revised Color Edition

Revision History for the Revised Edition

2022-05-27: First Release

See *http://oreilly.com/catalog/errata.csp?isbn=9781098136796* for release details.

978-1-098-13679-6

[LSI]

Table of Contents

Foreword

A miracle is taking place as you read these lines: the squiggles on this page are transforming into words and concepts and emotions as they navigate their way through your cortex. My thoughts from November 2021 have now successfully invaded your brain. If they manage to catch your attention and survive long enough in this harsh and highly competitive environment, they may have a chance to reproduce again as you share these thoughts with others. Thanks to language, thoughts have become airborne and highly contagious brain germs—and no vaccine is coming.

Luckily, most brain germs are harmless,[1] and a few are wonderfully useful. In fact, humanity's brain germs constitute two of our most precious treasures: knowledge and culture. Much as we can't digest properly without healthy gut bacteria, we cannot think properly without healthy brain germs. Most of your thoughts are not actually yours: they arose and grew and evolved in many other brains before they infected you. So if we want to build intelligent machines, we will need to find a way to infect them too.

The good news is that another miracle has been unfolding over the last few years: several breakthroughs in deep learning have given birth to powerful language models. Since you are reading this book, you have probably seen some astonishing demos of these language models, such as GPT-3, which given a short prompt such as "a frog meets a crocodile" can write a whole story. Although it's not quite Shakespeare yet, it's sometimes hard to believe that these texts were written by an artificial neural network. In fact, GitHub's Copilot system is helping me write these lines: you'll never know how much I really wrote.

The revolution goes far beyond text generation. It encompasses the whole realm of natural language processing (NLP), from text classification to summarization, translation, question answering, chatbots, natural language understanding (NLU), and

1 For brain hygiene tips, see CGP Grey's excellent video on memes (*https://youtu.be/rE3j_RHkqJc*).

more. Wherever there's language, speech or text, there's an application for NLP. You can already ask your phone for tomorrow's weather, or chat with a virtual help desk assistant to troubleshoot a problem, or get meaningful results from search engines that seem to truly understand your query. But the technology is so new that the best is probably yet to come.

Like most advances in science, this recent revolution in NLP rests upon the hard work of hundreds of unsung heroes. But three key ingredients of its success do stand out:

- The *transformer* is a neural network architecture proposed in 2017 in a groundbreaking paper called "Attention Is All You Need" (*https://arxiv.org/abs/1706.03762*), published by a team of Google researchers. In just a few years it swept across the field, crushing previous architectures that were typically based on recurrent neural networks (RNNs). The Transformer architecture is excellent at capturing patterns in long sequences of data and dealing with huge datasets—so much so that its use is now extending well beyond NLP, for example to image processing tasks.
- In most projects, you won't have access to a huge dataset to train a model from scratch. Luckily, it's often possible to download a model that was *pretrained* on a generic dataset: all you need to do then is fine-tune it on your own (much smaller) dataset. Pretraining has been mainstream in image processing since the early 2010s, but in NLP it was restricted to contextless word embeddings (i.e., dense vector representations of individual words). For example, the word "bear" had the same pretrained embedding in "teddy bear" and in "to bear." Then, in 2018, several papers proposed full-blown language models that could be pretrained and fine-tuned for a variety of NLP tasks; this completely changed the game.
- *Model hubs* like Hugging Face's have also been a game-changer. In the early days, pretrained models were just posted anywhere, so it wasn't easy to find what you needed. Murphy's law guaranteed that PyTorch users would only find TensorFlow models, and vice versa. And when you did find a model, figuring out how to fine-tune it wasn't always easy. This is where Hugging Face's Transformers library comes in: it's open source, it supports both TensorFlow and PyTorch, and it makes it easy to download a state-of-the-art pretrained model from the Hugging Face Hub, configure it for your task, fine-tune it on your dataset, and evaluate it. Use of the library is growing quickly: in Q4 2021 it was used by over five thousand organizations and was installed using `pip` over four million times per month. Moreover, the library and its ecosystem are expanding beyond NLP: image processing models are available too. You can also download numerous datasets from the Hub to train or evaluate your models.

So what more can you ask for? Well, this book! It was written by open source developers at Hugging Face—including the creator of the Transformers library!—and it shows: the breadth and depth of the information you will find in these pages is astounding. It covers everything from the Transformer architecture itself, to the Transformers library and the entire ecosystem around it. I particularly appreciated the hands-on approach: you can follow along in Jupyter notebooks, and all the code examples are straight to the point and simple to understand. The authors have extensive experience in training very large transformer models, and they provide a wealth of tips and tricks for getting everything to work efficiently. Last but not least, their writing style is direct and lively: it reads like a novel.

In short, I thoroughly enjoyed this book, and I'm certain you will too. Anyone interested in building products with state-of-the-art language-processing features needs to read it. It's packed to the brim with all the right brain germs!

— Aurélien Géron
November 2021, Auckland, NZ

Preface

Since their introduction in 2017, transformers have become the de facto standard for tackling a wide range of natural language processing (NLP) tasks in both academia and industry. Without noticing it, you probably interacted with a transformer today: Google now uses BERT to enhance its search engine by better understanding users' search queries. Similarly, the GPT family of models from OpenAI have repeatedly made headlines in mainstream media for their ability to generate human-like text and images.[1] These transformers now power applications like GitHub's Copilot (*https://copilot.github.com*), which, as shown in Figure P-1, can convert a comment into source code that automatically creates a neural network for you!

So what is it about transformers that changed the field almost overnight? Like many great scientific breakthroughs, it was the synthesis of several ideas, like *attention*, *transfer learning*, and *scaling up neural networks*, that were percolating in the research community at the time.

But however useful it is, to gain traction in industry any fancy new method needs tools to make it accessible. The 🤗 Transformers library (*https://oreil.ly/Z79jF*) and its surrounding ecosystem answered that call by making it easy for practitioners to use, train, and share models. This greatly accelerated the adoption of transformers, and the library is now used by over five thousand organizations. Throughout this book we'll guide you on how to train and optimize these models for practical applications.

1 NLP researchers tend to name their creations after characters in *Sesame Street*. We'll explain what all these acronyms mean in Chapter 1.

```
# Create a convolutional neural network to classify MNIST images in PyTorch.
class ConvNet(nn.Module):
    def __init__(self):
        super(ConvNet, self).__init__()
        self.conv1 = nn.Conv2d(1, 10, kernel_size=5)
        self.conv2 = nn.Conv2d(10, 20, kernel_size=5)
        self.conv2_drop = nn.Dropout2d()
        self.fc1 = nn.Linear(320, 50)
        self.fc2 = nn.Linear(50, 10)

    def forward(self, x):
        x = F.relu(F.max_pool2d(self.conv1(x), 2))
        x = F.relu(F.max_pool2d(self.conv2_drop(self.conv2(x)), 2))
        x = x.view(-1, 320)
        x = F.relu(self.fc1(x))
        x = F.dropout(x, training=self.training)
        x = self.fc2(x)
        return F.log_softmax(x, dim=1)
```

Figure P-1. An example from GitHub Copilot where, given a brief description of the task, the application provides a suggestion for the entire class (everything following `class` *is autogenerated)*

Who Is This Book For?

This book is written for data scientists and machine learning engineers who may have heard about the recent breakthroughs involving transformers, but are lacking an in-depth guide to help them adapt these models to their own use cases. The book is not meant to be an introduction to machine learning, and we assume you are comfortable programming in Python and has a basic understanding of deep learning frameworks like PyTorch (*https://pytorch.org*) and TensorFlow (*https://www.tensorflow.org*). We also assume you have some practical experience with training models on GPUs. Although the book focuses on the PyTorch API of 🤗 Transformers, Chapter 2 shows you how to translate all the examples to TensorFlow.

The following resources provide a good foundation for the topics covered in this book. We assume your technical knowledge is roughly at their level:

- *Hands-On Machine Learning with Scikit-Learn and TensorFlow*, by Aurélien Géron (O'Reilly)
- *Deep Learning for Coders with fastai and PyTorch*, by Jeremy Howard and Sylvain Gugger (O'Reilly)

- *Natural Language Processing with PyTorch*, by Delip Rao and Brian McMahan (O'Reilly)
- *The Hugging Face Course* (*https://oreil.ly/n3MaR*), by the open source team at Hugging Face

What You Will Learn

The goal of this book is to enable you to build your own language applications. To that end, it focuses on practical use cases, and delves into theory only where necessary. The style of the book is hands-on, and we highly recommend you experiment by running the code examples yourself.

The book covers all the major applications of transformers in NLP by having each chapter (with a few exceptions) dedicated to one task, combined with a realistic use case and dataset. Each chapter also introduces some additional concepts. Here's a high-level overview of the tasks and topics we'll cover:

- Chapter 1, *Hello Transformers*, introduces transformers and puts them into context. It also provides an introduction to the Hugging Face ecosystem.
- Chapter 2, *Text Classification*, focuses on the task of sentiment analysis (a common text classification problem) and introduces the `Trainer` API.
- Chapter 3, *Transformer Anatomy*, dives into the Transformer architecture in more depth, to prepare you for the chapters that follow.
- Chapter 4, *Multilingual Named Entity Recognition*, focuses on the task of identifying entities in texts in multiple languages (a token classification problem).
- Chapter 5, *Text Generation*, explores the ability of transformer models to generate text, and introduces decoding strategies and metrics.
- Chapter 6, *Summarization*, digs into the complex sequence-to-sequence task of text summarization and explores the metrics used for this task.
- Chapter 7, *Question Answering*, focuses on building a review-based question answering system and introduces retrieval with Haystack.
- Chapter 8, *Making Transformers Efficient in Production*, focuses on model performance. We'll look at the task of intent detection (a type of sequence classification problem) and explore techniques such a knowledge distillation, quantization, and pruning.
- Chapter 9, *Dealing with Few to No Labels*, looks at ways to improve model performance in the absence of large amounts of labeled data. We'll build a GitHub issues tagger and explore techniques such as zero-shot classification and data augmentation.

- Chapter 10, *Training Transformers from Scratch*, shows you how to build and train a model for autocompleting Python source code from scratch. We'll look at dataset streaming and large-scale training, and build our own tokenizer.
- Chapter 11, *Future Directions*, explores the challenges transformers face and some of the exciting new directions that research in this area is going into.

🤗 Transformers offers several layers of abstraction for using and training transformer models. We'll start with the easy-to-use pipelines that allow us to pass text examples through the models and investigate the predictions in just a few lines of code. Then we'll move on to tokenizers, model classes, and the `Trainer` API, which allow us to train models for our own use cases. Later, we'll show you how to replace the `Trainer` with the 🤗 Accelerate library, which gives us full control over the training loop and allows us to train large-scale transformers entirely from scratch! Although each chapter is mostly self-contained, the difficulty of the tasks increases in the later chapters. For this reason, we recommend starting with Chapters 1 and 2, before branching off into the topic of most interest.

Besides 🤗 Transformers and 🤗 Accelerate, we will also make extensive use of 🤗 Datasets, which seamlessly integrates with other libraries. 🤗 Datasets offers similar functionality for data processing as Pandas but is designed from the ground up for tackling large datasets and machine learning.

With these tools, you have everything you need to tackle almost any NLP challenge!

Software and Hardware Requirements

Due to the hands-on approach of this book, we highly recommend that you run the code examples while you read each chapter. Since we're dealing with transformers, you'll need access to a computer with an NVIDIA GPU to train these models. Fortunately, there are several free online options that you can use, including:

- Google Colaboratory (*https://oreil.ly/jyXgA*)
- Kaggle Notebooks (*https://oreil.ly/RnMP3*)
- Paperspace Gradient Notebooks (*https://oreil.ly/mZEKy*)

To run the examples, you'll need to follow the installation guide that we provide in the book's GitHub repository. You can find this guide and the code examples at *https://github.com/nlp-with-transformers/notebooks*.

We developed most of the chapters using NVIDIA Tesla P100 GPUs, which have 16GB of memory. Some of the free platforms provide GPUs with less memory, so you may need to reduce the batch size when training the models.

Conventions Used in This Book

The following typographical conventions are used in this book:

Italic
: Indicates new terms, URLs, email addresses, filenames, and file extensions.

`Constant width`
: Used for program listings, as well as within paragraphs to refer to program elements such as variable or function names, databases, data types, environment variables, statements, and keywords.

`Constant width bold`
: Shows commands or other text that should be typed literally by the user.

`Constant width italic`
: Shows text that should be replaced with user-supplied values or by values determined by context.

This element signifies a tip or suggestion.

This element signifies a general note.

This element indicates a warning or caution.

Using Code Examples

Supplemental material (code examples, exercises, etc.) is available for download at *https://github.com/nlp-with-transformers/notebooks*.

If you have a technical question or a problem using the code examples, please send email to *bookquestions@oreilly.com*.

This book is here to help you get your job done. In general, if example code is offered with this book, you may use it in your programs and documentation. You do not need to contact us for permission unless you're reproducing a significant portion of the code. For example, writing a program that uses several chunks of code from this book does not require permission. Selling or distributing examples from O'Reilly books does require permission. Answering a question by citing this book and quoting example code does not require permission. Incorporating a significant amount of example code from this book into your product's documentation does require permission.

We appreciate, but generally do not require, attribution. An attribution usually includes the title, author, publisher, and ISBN. For example: "*Natural Language Processing with Transformers* by Lewis Tunstall, Leandro von Werra, and Thomas Wolf (O'Reilly). Copyright 2022 Lewis Tunstall, Leandro von Werra, and Thomas Wolf, 978-1-098-13679-6."

If you feel your use of code examples falls outside fair use or the permission given above, feel free to contact us at *permissions@oreilly.com*.

O'Reilly Online Learning

For more than 40 years, *O'Reilly Media* has provided technology and business training, knowledge, and insight to help companies succeed.

Our unique network of experts and innovators share their knowledge and expertise through books, articles, and our online learning platform. O'Reilly's online learning platform gives you on-demand access to live training courses, in-depth learning paths, interactive coding environments, and a vast collection of text and video from O'Reilly and 200+ other publishers. For more information, visit *http://oreilly.com*.

How to Contact Us

Please address comments and questions concerning this book to the publisher:

O'Reilly Media, Inc.
1005 Gravenstein Highway North
Sebastopol, CA 95472
800-998-9938 (in the United States or Canada)
707-829-0515 (international or local)
707-829-0104 (fax)

We have a web page for this book, where we list errata, examples, and any additional information. You can access this page at *https://oreil.ly/nlp-with-transformers*.

Email *bookquestions@oreilly.com* to comment or ask technical questions about this book.

For news and information about our books and courses, visit *http://oreilly.com*.

Find us on Facebook: *http://facebook.com/oreilly*

Follow us on Twitter: *http://twitter.com/oreillymedia*

Watch us on YouTube: *http://youtube.com/oreillymedia*

Acknowledgments

Writing a book about one of the fastest-moving fields in machine learning would not have been possible without the help of many people. We thank the wonderful O'Reilly team, and especially Melissa Potter, Rebecca Novack, and Katherine Tozer for their support and advice. The book has also benefited from amazing reviewers who spent countless hours to provide us with invaluable feedback. We are especially grateful to Luca Perozzi, Hamel Husain, Shabie Iqbal, Umberto Lupo, Malte Pietsch, Timo Möller, and Aurélien Géron for their detailed reviews. We thank Branden Chan at deepset (*https://www.deepset.ai*) for his help with extending the Haystack library to support the use case in Chapter 7. The beautiful illustrations in this book are due to the amazing Christa Lanz (*https://christalanz.ch*)—thank you for making this book extra special. We were also fortunate enough to have the support of the whole Hugging Face team. Many thanks to Quentin Lhoest for answering countless questions on 🤗 Datasets, to Lysandre Debut for help on everything related to the Hugging Face Hub, Sylvain Gugger for his help with 🤗 Accelerate, and Joe Davison for his inspiration for Chapter 9 with regard to zero-shot learning. We also thank Sidd Karamcheti and the whole Mistral team (*https://oreil.ly/aOYLt*) for adding stability tweaks for GPT-2 to make Chapter 10 possible. This book was written entirely in Jupyter Notebooks, and we thank Jeremy Howard and Sylvain Gugger for creating delightful tools like fastdoc (*https://oreil.ly/yVCfT*) that made this possible.

Lewis

To Sofia, thank you for being a constant source of support and encouragement—without both, this book would not exist. After a long stretch of writing, we can finally enjoy our weekends again!

Leandro

Thank you Janine, for your patience and encouraging support during this long year with many late nights and busy weekends.

Thomas

I would like to thank first and foremost Lewis and Leandro for coming up with the idea of this book and pushing strongly to produce it in such a beautiful and accessible format. I would also like to thank all the Hugging Face team for believing in the mission of AI as a community effort, and the whole NLP/AI community for building and using the libraries and research we describe in this book together with us.

More than what we build, the journey we take is what really matters, and we have the privilege to travel this path with thousands of community members and readers like you today. Thank you all from the bottom of our hearts.

CHAPTER 1

Hello Transformers

In 2017, researchers at Google published a paper that proposed a novel neural network architecture for sequence modeling.[1] Dubbed the *Transformer*, this architecture outperformed recurrent neural networks (RNNs) on machine translation tasks, both in terms of translation quality and training cost.

In parallel, an effective transfer learning method called ULMFiT showed that training long short-term memory (LSTM) networks on a very large and diverse corpus could produce state-of-the-art text classifiers with little labeled data.[2]

These advances were the catalysts for two of today's most well-known transformers: the Generative Pretrained Transformer (GPT)[3] and Bidirectional Encoder Representations from Transformers (BERT).[4] By combining the Transformer architecture with unsupervised learning, these models removed the need to train task-specific architectures from scratch and broke almost every benchmark in NLP by a significant margin. Since the release of GPT and BERT, a zoo of transformer models has emerged; a timeline of the most prominent entries is shown in Figure 1-1.

1 A. Vaswani et al., "Attention Is All You Need" (*https://arxiv.org/abs/1706.03762*), (2017). This title was so catchy that no less than 50 follow-up papers (*https://oreil.ly/wT8Ih*) have included "all you need" in their titles!

2 J. Howard and S. Ruder, "Universal Language Model Fine-Tuning for Text Classification" (*https://arxiv.org/abs/1801.06146*), (2018).

3 A. Radford et al., "Improving Language Understanding by Generative Pre-Training" (*https://openai.com/blog/language-unsupervised*), (2018).

4 J. Devlin et al., "BERT: Pre-Training of Deep Bidirectional Transformers for Language Understanding" (*https://arxiv.org/abs/1810.04805*), (2018).

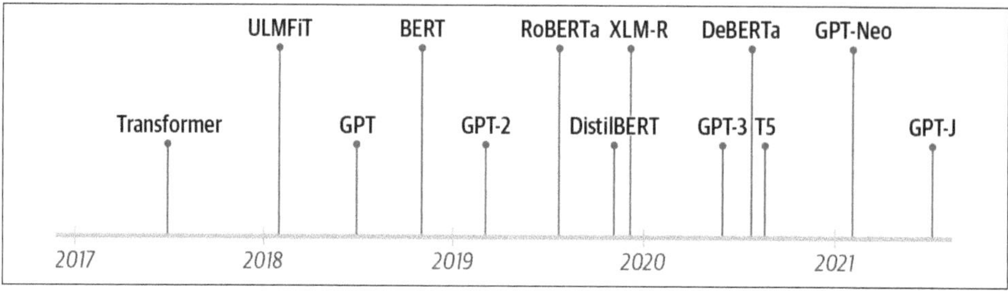

Figure 1-1. The transformers timeline

But we're getting ahead of ourselves. To understand what is novel about transformers, we first need to explain:

- The encoder-decoder framework
- Attention mechanisms
- Transfer learning

In this chapter we'll introduce the core concepts that underlie the pervasiveness of transformers, take a tour of some of the tasks that they excel at, and conclude with a look at the Hugging Face ecosystem of tools and libraries.

Let's start by exploring the encoder-decoder framework and the architectures that preceded the rise of transformers.

The Encoder-Decoder Framework

Prior to transformers, recurrent architectures such as LSTMs were the state of the art in NLP. These architectures contain a feedback loop in the network connections that allows information to propagate from one step to another, making them ideal for modeling sequential data like text. As illustrated on the left side of Figure 1-2, an RNN receives some input (which could be a word or character), feeds it through the network, and outputs a vector called the *hidden state*. At the same time, the model feeds some information back to itself through the feedback loop, which it can then use in the next step. This can be more clearly seen if we "unroll" the loop as shown on the right side of Figure 1-2: the RNN passes information about its state at each step to the next operation in the sequence. This allows an RNN to keep track of information from previous steps, and use it for its output predictions.

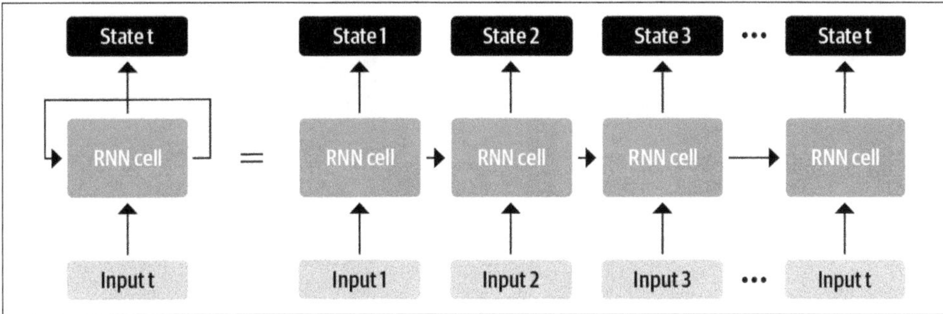

Figure 1-2. Unrolling an RNN in time

These architectures were (and continue to be) widely used for NLP tasks, speech processing, and time series. You can find a wonderful exposition of their capabilities in Andrej Karpathy's blog post, "The Unreasonable Effectiveness of Recurrent Neural Networks" (*https://oreil.ly/Q55o0*).

One area where RNNs played an important role was in the development of machine translation systems, where the objective is to map a sequence of words in one language to another. This kind of task is usually tackled with an *encoder-decoder* or *sequence-to-sequence* architecture,[5] which is well suited for situations where the input and output are both sequences of arbitrary length. The job of the encoder is to encode the information from the input sequence into a numerical representation that is often called the *last hidden state*. This state is then passed to the decoder, which generates the output sequence.

In general, the encoder and decoder components can be any kind of neural network architecture that can model sequences. This is illustrated for a pair of RNNs in Figure 1-3, where the English sentence "Transformers are great!" is encoded as a hidden state vector that is then decoded to produce the German translation "Transformer sind grossartig!" The input words are fed sequentially through the encoder and the output words are generated one at a time, from top to bottom.

5 I. Sutskever, O. Vinyals, and Q.V. Le, "Sequence to Sequence Learning with Neural Networks" (*https://arxiv.org/abs/1409.3215*), (2014).

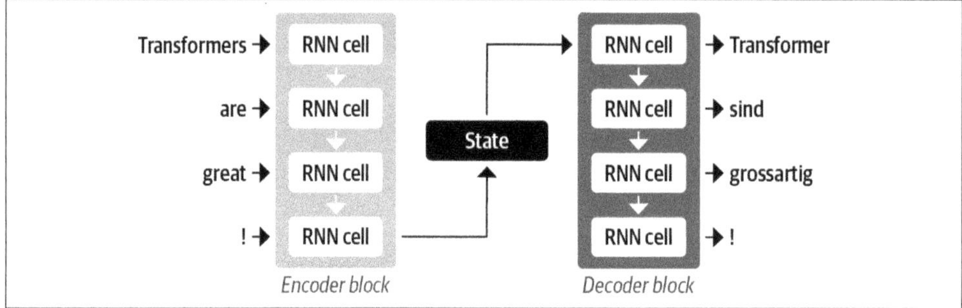

Figure 1-3. An encoder-decoder architecture with a pair of RNNs (in general, there are many more recurrent layers than those shown here)

Although elegant in its simplicity, one weakness of this architecture is that the final hidden state of the encoder creates an *information bottleneck*: it has to represent the meaning of the whole input sequence because this is all the decoder has access to when generating the output. This is especially challenging for long sequences, where information at the start of the sequence might be lost in the process of compressing everything to a single, fixed representation.

Fortunately, there is a way out of this bottleneck by allowing the decoder to have access to all of the encoder's hidden states. The general mechanism for this is called *attention*,[6] and it is a key component in many modern neural network architectures. Understanding how attention was developed for RNNs will put us in good shape to understand one of the main building blocks of the Transformer architecture. Let's take a deeper look.

Attention Mechanisms

The main idea behind attention is that instead of producing a single hidden state for the input sequence, the encoder outputs a hidden state at each step that the decoder can access. However, using all the states at the same time would create a huge input for the decoder, so some mechanism is needed to prioritize which states to use. This is where attention comes in: it lets the decoder assign a different amount of weight, or "attention," to each of the encoder states at every decoding timestep. This process is illustrated in Figure 1-4, where the role of attention is shown for predicting the third token in the output sequence.

6 D. Bahdanau, K. Cho, and Y. Bengio, "Neural Machine Translation by Jointly Learning to Align and Translate" (*https://arxiv.org/abs/1409.0473*), (2014).

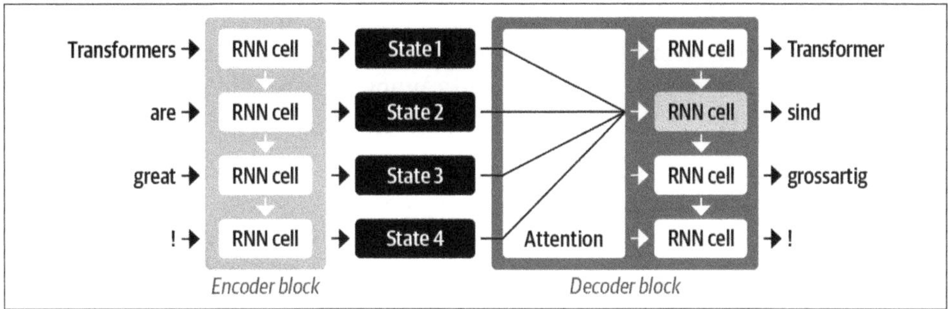

Figure 1-4. An encoder-decoder architecture with an attention mechanism for a pair of RNNs

By focusing on which input tokens are most relevant at each timestep, these attention-based models are able to learn nontrivial alignments between the words in a generated translation and those in a source sentence. For example, Figure 1-5 visualizes the attention weights for an English to French translation model, where each pixel denotes a weight. The figure shows how the decoder is able to correctly align the words "zone" and "Area", which are ordered differently in the two languages.

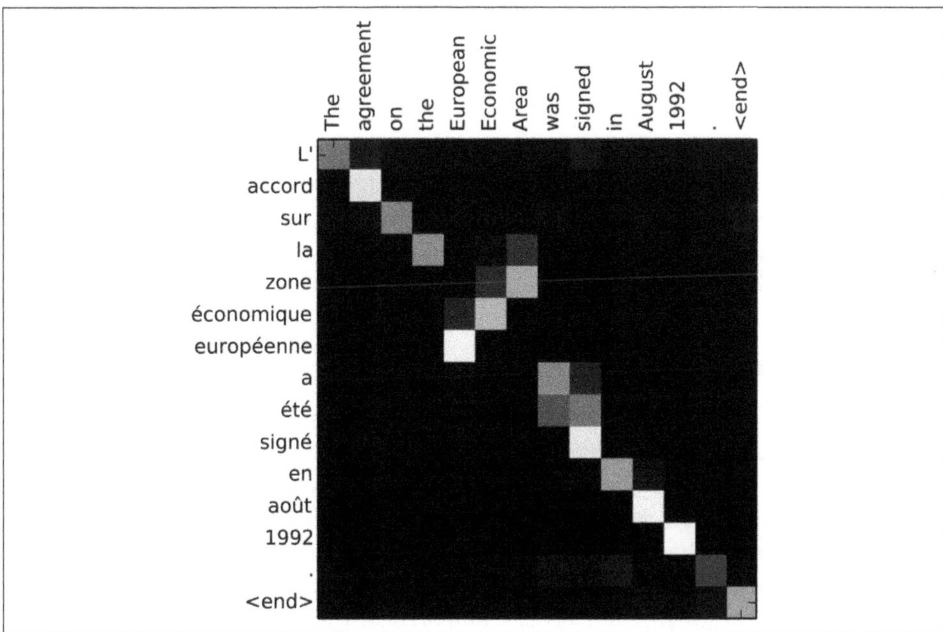

Figure 1-5. RNN encoder-decoder alignment of words in English and the generated translation in French (courtesy of Dzmitry Bahdanau)

Although attention enabled the production of much better translations, there was still a major shortcoming with using recurrent models for the encoder and decoder: the computations are inherently sequential and cannot be parallelized across the input sequence.

With the transformer, a new modeling paradigm was introduced: dispense with recurrence altogether, and instead rely entirely on a special form of attention called *self-attention*. We'll cover self-attention in more detail in Chapter 3, but the basic idea is to allow attention to operate on all the states in the *same layer* of the neural network. This is shown in Figure 1-6, where both the encoder and the decoder have their own self-attention mechanisms, whose outputs are fed to feed-forward neural networks (FF NNs). This architecture can be trained much faster than recurrent models and paved the way for many of the recent breakthroughs in NLP.

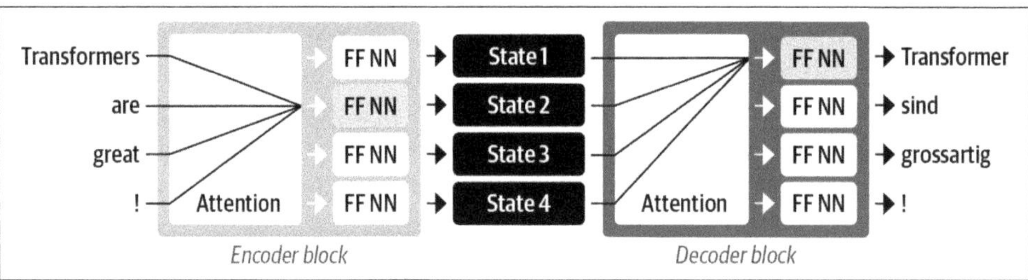

Figure 1-6. Encoder-decoder architecture of the original Transformer

In the original Transformer paper, the translation model was trained from scratch on a large corpus of sentence pairs in various languages. However, in many practical applications of NLP we do not have access to large amounts of labeled text data to train our models on. A final piece was missing to get the transformer revolution started: transfer learning.

Transfer Learning in NLP

It is nowadays common practice in computer vision to use transfer learning to train a convolutional neural network like ResNet on one task, and then adapt it to or *fine-tune* it on a new task. This allows the network to make use of the knowledge learned from the original task. Architecturally, this involves splitting the model into of a *body* and a *head*, where the head is a task-specific network. During training, the weights of the body learn broad features of the source domain, and these weights are used to initialize a new model for the new task.[7] Compared to traditional supervised learning, this approach typically produces high-quality models that can be trained much more

7 Weights are the learnable parameters of a neural network.

efficiently on a variety of downstream tasks, and with much less labeled data. A comparison of the two approaches is shown in Figure 1-7.

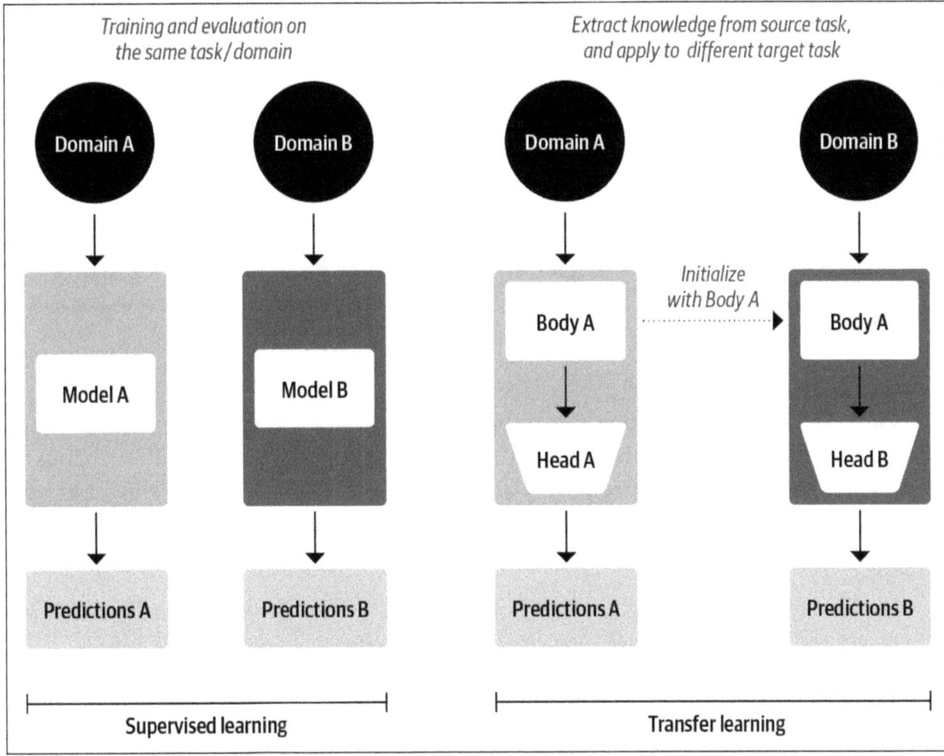

Figure 1-7. Comparison of traditional supervised learning (left) and transfer learning (right)

In computer vision, the models are first trained on large-scale datasets such as ImageNet (*https://image-net.org*), which contain millions of images. This process is called *pretraining* and its main purpose is to teach the models the basic features of images, such as edges or colors. These pretrained models can then be fine-tuned on a downstream task such as classifying flower species with a relatively small number of labeled examples (usually a few hundred per class). Fine-tuned models typically achieve a higher accuracy than supervised models trained from scratch on the same amount of labeled data.

Although transfer learning became the standard approach in computer vision, for many years it was not clear what the analogous pretraining process was for NLP. As a result, NLP applications typically required large amounts of labeled data to achieve high performance. And even then, that performance did not compare to what was achieved in the vision domain.

In 2017 and 2018, several research groups proposed new approaches that finally made transfer learning work for NLP. It started with an insight from researchers at OpenAI who obtained strong performance on a sentiment classification task by using features extracted from unsupervised pretraining.[8] This was followed by ULMFiT, which introduced a general framework to adapt pretrained LSTM models for various tasks.[9]

As illustrated in Figure 1-8, ULMFiT involves three main steps:

Pretraining
: The initial training objective is quite simple: predict the next word based on the previous words. This task is referred to as *language modeling*. The elegance of this approach lies in the fact that no labeled data is required, and one can make use of abundantly available text from sources such as Wikipedia.[10]

Domain adaptation
: Once the language model is pretrained on a large-scale corpus, the next step is to adapt it to the in-domain corpus (e.g., from Wikipedia to the IMDb corpus of movie reviews, as in Figure 1-8). This stage still uses language modeling, but now the model has to predict the next word in the target corpus.

Fine-tuning
: In this step, the language model is fine-tuned with a classification layer for the target task (e.g., classifying the sentiment of movie reviews in Figure 1-8).

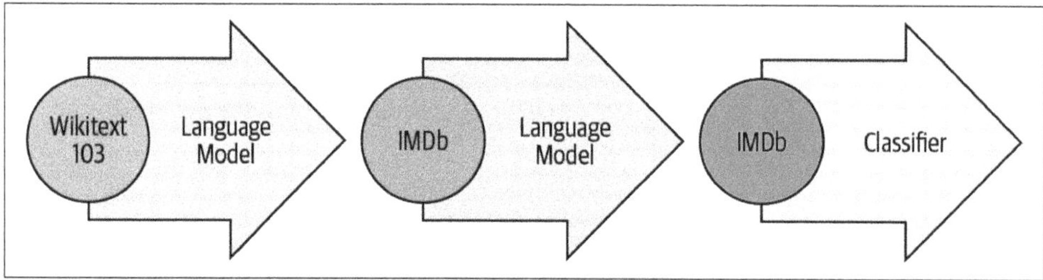

Figure 1-8. The ULMFiT process (courtesy of Jeremy Howard)

By introducing a viable framework for pretraining and transfer learning in NLP, ULMFiT provided the missing piece to make transformers take off. In 2018, two transformers were released that combined self-attention with transfer learning:

8 A. Radford, R. Jozefowicz, and I. Sutskever, "Learning to Generate Reviews and Discovering Sentiment" (*https://arxiv.org/abs/1704.01444*), (2017).

9 A related work at this time was ELMo (Embeddings from Language Models), which showed how pretraining LSTMs could produce high-quality word embeddings for downstream tasks.

10 This is more true for English than for most of the world's languages, where obtaining a large corpus of digitized text can be difficult. Finding ways to bridge this gap is an active area of NLP research and activism.

GPT

Uses only the decoder part of the Transformer architecture, and the same language modeling approach as ULMFiT. GPT was pretrained on the BookCorpus,[11] which consists of 7,000 unpublished books from a variety of genres including Adventure, Fantasy, and Romance.

BERT

Uses the encoder part of the Transformer architecture, and a special form of language modeling called *masked language modeling*. The objective of masked language modeling is to predict randomly masked words in a text. For example, given a sentence like "I looked at my `[MASK]` and saw that `[MASK]` was late." the model needs to predict the most likely candidates for the masked words that are denoted by `[MASK]`. BERT was pretrained on the BookCorpus and English Wikipedia.

GPT and BERT set a new state of the art across a variety of NLP benchmarks and ushered in the age of transformers.

However, with different research labs releasing their models in incompatible frameworks (PyTorch or TensorFlow), it wasn't always easy for NLP practitioners to port these models to their own applications. With the release of 🤗 Transformers (*https://oreil.ly/Z79jF*), a unified API across more than 50 architectures was progressively built. This library catalyzed the explosion of research into transformers and quickly trickled down to NLP practitioners, making it easy to integrate these models into many real-life applications today. Let's have a look!

Hugging Face Transformers: Bridging the Gap

Applying a novel machine learning architecture to a new task can be a complex undertaking, and usually involves the following steps:

1. Implement the model architecture in code, typically based on PyTorch or TensorFlow.
2. Load the pretrained weights (if available) from a server.
3. Preprocess the inputs, pass them through the model, and apply some task-specific postprocessing.
4. Implement dataloaders and define loss functions and optimizers to train the model.

11 Y. Zhu et al., "Aligning Books and Movies: Towards Story-Like Visual Explanations by Watching Movies and Reading Books" (*https://arxiv.org/abs/1506.06724*), (2015).

Each of these steps requires custom logic for each model and task. Traditionally (but not always!), when research groups publish a new article, they will also release the code along with the model weights. However, this code is rarely standardized and often requires days of engineering to adapt to new use cases.

This is where 🤗 Transformers comes to the NLP practitioner's rescue! It provides a standardized interface to a wide range of transformer models as well as code and tools to adapt these models to new use cases. The library currently supports three major deep learning frameworks (PyTorch, TensorFlow, and JAX) and allows you to easily switch between them. In addition, it provides task-specific heads so you can easily fine-tune transformers on downstream tasks such as text classification, named entity recognition, and question answering. This reduces the time it takes a practitioner to train and test a handful of models from a week to a single afternoon!

You'll see this for yourself in the next section, where we show that with just a few lines of code, 🤗 Transformers can be applied to tackle some of the most common NLP applications that you're likely to encounter in the wild.

A Tour of Transformer Applications

Every NLP task starts with a piece of text, like the following made-up customer feedback about a certain online order:

```
text = """Dear Amazon, last week I ordered an Optimus Prime action figure
from your online store in Germany. Unfortunately, when I opened the package,
I discovered to my horror that I had been sent an action figure of Megatron
instead! As a lifelong enemy of the Decepticons, I hope you can understand my
dilemma. To resolve the issue, I demand an exchange of Megatron for the
Optimus Prime figure I ordered. Enclosed are copies of my records concerning
this purchase. I expect to hear from you soon. Sincerely, Bumblebee."""
```

Depending on your application, the text you're working with could be a legal contract, a product description, or something else entirely. In the case of customer feedback, you would probably like to know whether the feedback is positive or negative. This task is called *sentiment analysis* and is part of the broader topic of *text classification* that we'll explore in Chapter 2. For now, let's have a look at what it takes to extract the sentiment from our piece of text using 🤗 Transformers.

Text Classification

As we'll see in later chapters, 🤗 Transformers has a layered API that allows you to interact with the library at various levels of abstraction. In this chapter we'll start with *pipelines*, which abstract away all the steps needed to convert raw text into a set of predictions from a fine-tuned model.

In 🤗 Transformers, we instantiate a pipeline by calling the `pipeline()` function and providing the name of the task we are interested in:

```
from transformers import pipeline

classifier = pipeline("text-classification")
```

The first time you run this code you'll see a few progress bars appear because the pipeline automatically downloads the model weights from the Hugging Face Hub (*https://oreil.ly/zLK11*). The second time you instantiate the pipeline, the library will notice that you've already downloaded the weights and will use the cached version instead. By default, the `text-classification` pipeline uses a model that's designed for sentiment analysis, but it also supports multiclass and multilabel classification.

Now that we have our pipeline, let's generate some predictions! Each pipeline takes a string of text (or a list of strings) as input and returns a list of predictions. Each prediction is a Python dictionary, so we can use Pandas to display them nicely as a `DataFrame`:

```
import pandas as pd

outputs = classifier(text)
pd.DataFrame(outputs)
```

	label	score
0	NEGATIVE	0.901546

In this case the model is very confident that the text has a negative sentiment, which makes sense given that we're dealing with a complaint from an angry customer! Note that for sentiment analysis tasks the pipeline only returns one of the `POSITIVE` or `NEGATIVE` labels, since the other can be inferred by computing `1-score`.

Let's now take a look at another common task, identifying named entities in text.

Named Entity Recognition

Predicting the sentiment of customer feedback is a good first step, but you often want to know if the feedback was about a particular item or service. In NLP, real-world objects like products, places, and people are called *named entities*, and extracting them from text is called *named entity recognition* (NER). We can apply NER by loading the corresponding pipeline and feeding our customer review to it:

```
ner_tagger = pipeline("ner", aggregation_strategy="simple")
outputs = ner_tagger(text)
pd.DataFrame(outputs)
```

	entity_group	score	word	start	end
0	ORG	0.879010	Amazon	5	11
1	MISC	0.990859	Optimus Prime	36	49

	entity_group	score	word	start	end
2	LOC	0.999755	Germany	90	97
3	MISC	0.556569	Mega	208	212
4	PER	0.590256	##tron	212	216
5	ORG	0.669692	Decept	253	259
6	MISC	0.498350	##icons	259	264
7	MISC	0.775361	Megatron	350	358
8	MISC	0.987854	Optimus Prime	367	380
9	PER	0.812096	Bumblebee	502	511

You can see that the pipeline detected all the entities and also assigned a category such as `ORG` (organization), `LOC` (location), or `PER` (person) to each of them. Here we used the `aggregation_strategy` argument to group the words according to the model's predictions. For example, the entity "Optimus Prime" is composed of two words, but is assigned a single category: `MISC` (miscellaneous). The scores tell us how confident the model was about the entities it identified. We can see that it was least confident about "Decepticons" and the first occurrence of "Megatron", both of which it failed to group as a single entity.

See those weird hash symbols (`#`) in the `word` column in the previous table? These are produced by the model's *tokenizer*, which splits words into atomic units called *tokens*. You'll learn all about tokenization in Chapter 2.

Extracting all the named entities in a text is nice, but sometimes we would like to ask more targeted questions. This is where we can use *question answering*.

Question Answering

In question answering, we provide the model with a passage of text called the *context*, along with a question whose answer we'd like to extract. The model then returns the span of text corresponding to the answer. Let's see what we get when we ask a specific question about our customer feedback:

```
reader = pipeline("question-answering")
question = "What does the customer want?"
outputs = reader(question=question, context=text)
pd.DataFrame([outputs])
```

	score	start	end	answer
0	0.631291	335	358	an exchange of Megatron

We can see that along with the answer, the pipeline also returned `start` and `end` integers that correspond to the character indices where the answer span was found (just like with NER tagging). There are several flavors of question answering that we will investigate in Chapter 7, but this particular kind is called *extractive question answering* because the answer is extracted directly from the text.

With this approach you can read and extract relevant information quickly from a customer's feedback. But what if you get a mountain of long-winded complaints and you don't have the time to read them all? Let's see if a summarization model can help!

Summarization

The goal of text summarization is to take a long text as input and generate a short version with all the relevant facts. This is a much more complicated task than the previous ones since it requires the model to *generate* coherent text. In what should be a familiar pattern by now, we can instantiate a summarization pipeline as follows:

```
summarizer = pipeline("summarization")
outputs = summarizer(text, max_length=45, clean_up_tokenization_spaces=True)
print(outputs[0]['summary_text'])
```

```
 Bumblebee ordered an Optimus Prime action figure from your online store in
Germany. Unfortunately, when I opened the package, I discovered to my horror
that I had been sent an action figure of Megatron instead.
```

This summary isn't too bad! Although parts of the original text have been copied, the model was able to capture the essence of the problem and correctly identify that "Bumblebee" (which appeared at the end) was the author of the complaint. In this example you can also see that we passed some keyword arguments like `max_length` and `clean_up_tokenization_spaces` to the pipeline; these allow us to tweak the outputs at runtime.

But what happens when you get feedback that is in a language you don't understand? You could use Google Translate, or you can use your very own transformer to translate it for you!

Translation

Like summarization, translation is a task where the output consists of generated text. Let's use a translation pipeline to translate an English text to German:

```
translator = pipeline("translation_en_to_de",
                      model="Helsinki-NLP/opus-mt-en-de")
outputs = translator(text, clean_up_tokenization_spaces=True, min_length=100)
print(outputs[0]['translation_text'])
```

```
Sehr geehrter Amazon, letzte Woche habe ich eine Optimus Prime Action Figur aus
Ihrem Online-Shop in Deutschland bestellt. Leider, als ich das Paket öffnete,
entdeckte ich zu meinem Entsetzen, dass ich stattdessen eine Action Figur von
```

```
Megatron geschickt worden war! Als lebenslanger Feind der Decepticons, Ich
hoffe, Sie können mein Dilemma verstehen. Um das Problem zu lösen, Ich fordere
einen Austausch von Megatron für die Optimus Prime Figur habe ich bestellt.
Anbei sind Kopien meiner Aufzeichnungen über diesen Kauf. Ich erwarte, bald von
Ihnen zu hören. Aufrichtig, Bumblebee.
```

Again, the model produced a very good translation that correctly uses German's formal pronouns, like "Ihrem" and "Sie." Here we've also shown how you can override the default model in the pipeline to pick the best one for your application—and you can find models for thousands of language pairs on the Hugging Face Hub. Before we take a step back and look at the whole Hugging Face ecosystem, let's examine one last application.

Text Generation

Let's say you would like to be able to provide faster replies to customer feedback by having access to an autocomplete function. With a text generation model you can do this as follows:

```
generator = pipeline("text-generation")
response = "Dear Bumblebee, I am sorry to hear that your order was mixed up."
prompt = text + "\n\nCustomer service response:\n" + response
outputs = generator(prompt, max_length=200)
print(outputs[0]['generated_text'])
```

```
Dear Amazon, last week I ordered an Optimus Prime action figure from your online
store in Germany. Unfortunately, when I opened the package, I discovered to my
horror that I had been sent an action figure of Megatron instead! As a lifelong
enemy of the Decepticons, I hope you can understand my dilemma. To resolve the
issue, I demand an exchange of Megatron for the Optimus Prime figure I ordered.
Enclosed are copies of my records concerning this purchase. I expect to hear
from you soon. Sincerely, Bumblebee.

Customer service response:
Dear Bumblebee, I am sorry to hear that your order was mixed up. The order was
completely mislabeled, which is very common in our online store, but I can
appreciate it because it was my understanding from this site and our customer
service of the previous day that your order was not made correct in our mind and
that we are in a process of resolving this matter. We can assure you that your
order
```

OK, maybe we wouldn't want to use this completion to calm Bumblebee down, but you get the general idea.

Now that you've seen a few cool applications of transformer models, you might be wondering where the training happens. All of the models that we've used in this chapter are publicly available and already fine-tuned for the task at hand. In general, however, you'll want to fine-tune models on your own data, and in the following chapters you will learn how to do just that.

But training a model is just a small piece of any NLP project—being able to efficiently process data, share results with colleagues, and make your work reproducible are key components too. Fortunately, 🤗 Transformers is surrounded by a big ecosystem of useful tools that support much of the modern machine learning workflow. Let's take a look.

The Hugging Face Ecosystem

What started with 🤗 Transformers has quickly grown into a whole ecosystem consisting of many libraries and tools to accelerate your NLP and machine learning projects. The Hugging Face ecosystem consists of mainly two parts: a family of libraries and the Hub, as shown in Figure 1-9. The libraries provide the code while the Hub provides the pretrained model weights, datasets, scripts for the evaluation metrics, and more. In this section we'll have a brief look at the various components. We'll skip 🤗 Transformers, as we've already discussed it and we will see a lot more of it throughout the course of the book.

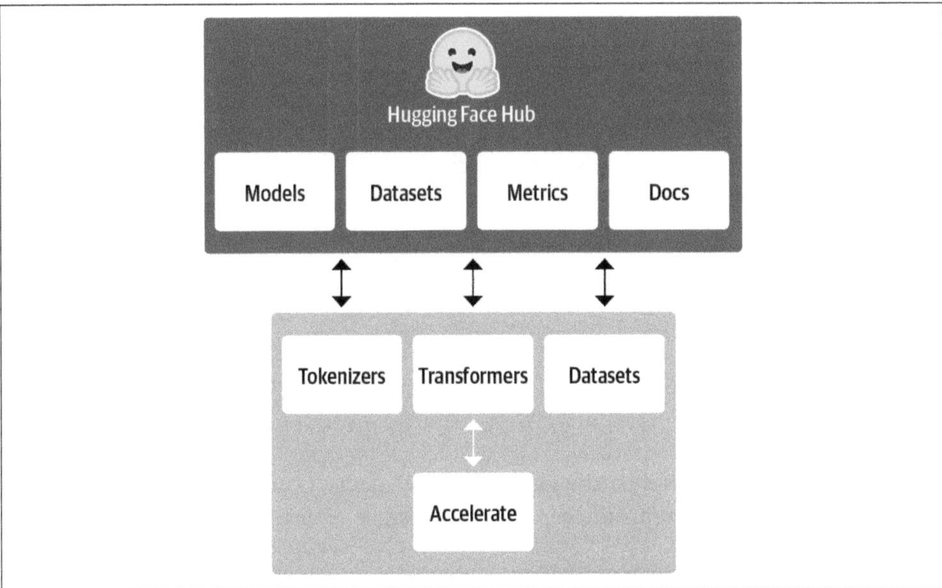

Figure 1-9. An overview of the Hugging Face ecosystem

The Hugging Face Hub

As outlined earlier, transfer learning is one of the key factors driving the success of transformers because it makes it possible to reuse pretrained models for new tasks. Consequently, it is crucial to be able to load pretrained models quickly and run experiments with them.

The Hugging Face Hub hosts over 20,000 freely available models. As shown in Figure 1-10, there are filters for tasks, frameworks, datasets, and more that are designed to help you navigate the Hub and quickly find promising candidates. As we've seen with the pipelines, loading a promising model in your code is then literally just one line of code away. This makes experimenting with a wide range of models simple, and allows you to focus on the domain-specific parts of your project.

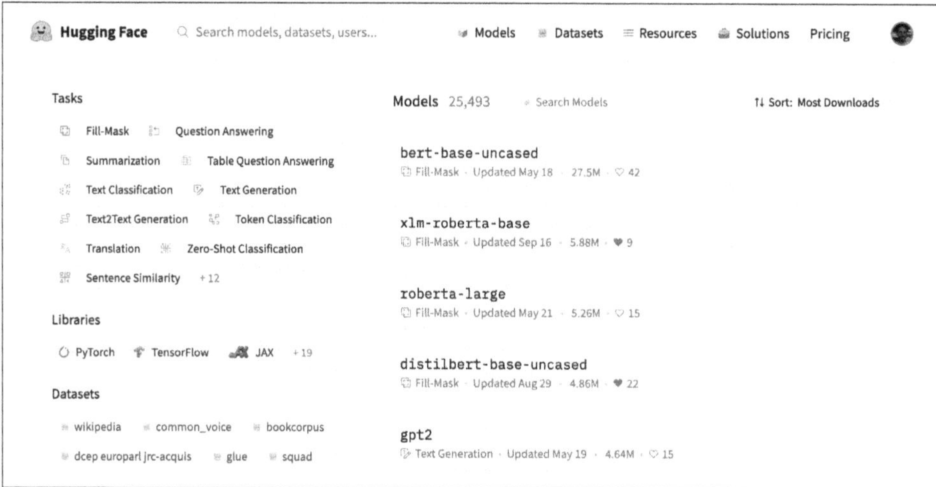

Figure 1-10. The Models page of the Hugging Face Hub, showing filters on the left and a list of models on the right

In addition to model weights, the Hub also hosts datasets and scripts for computing metrics, which let you reproduce published results or leverage additional data for your application.

The Hub also provides *model* and *dataset cards* to document the contents of models and datasets and help you make an informed decision about whether they're the right ones for you. One of the coolest features of the Hub is that you can try out any model directly through the various task-specific interactive widgets as shown in Figure 1-11.

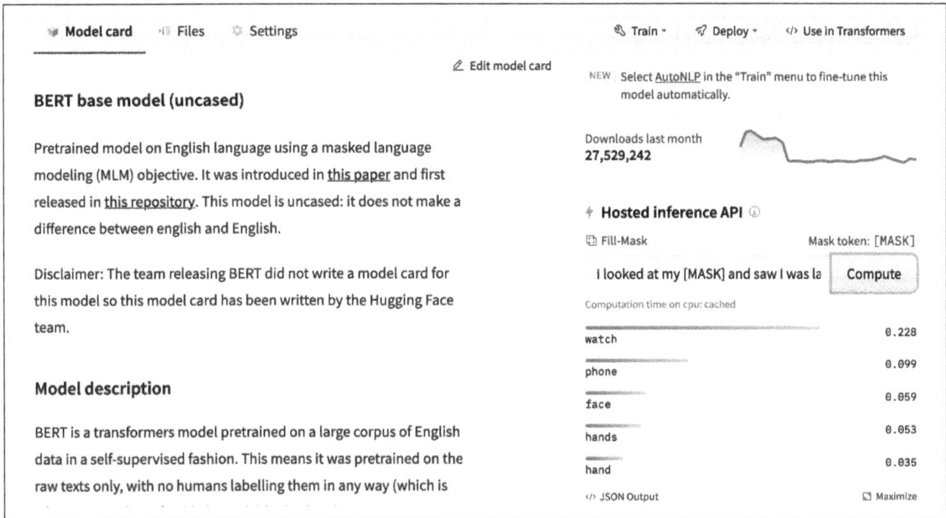

Figure 1-11. An example model card from the Hugging Face Hub: the inference widget, which allows you to interact with the model, is shown on the right

Let's continue our tour with 🤗 Tokenizers.

PyTorch (*https://oreil.ly/AyTYC*) and TensorFlow (*https://oreil.ly/JOKgq*) also offer hubs of their own and are worth checking out if a particular model or dataset is not available on the Hugging Face Hub.

Hugging Face Tokenizers

Behind each of the pipeline examples that we've seen in this chapter is a tokenization step that splits the raw text into smaller pieces called tokens. We'll see how this works in detail in Chapter 2, but for now it's enough to understand that tokens may be words, parts of words, or just characters like punctuation. Transformer models are trained on numerical representations of these tokens, so getting this step right is pretty important for the whole NLP project!

🤗 Tokenizers (*https://oreil.ly/Z79jF*) provides many tokenization strategies and is extremely fast at tokenizing text thanks to its Rust backend.[12] It also takes care of all the pre- and postprocessing steps, such as normalizing the inputs and transforming the model outputs to the required format. With 🤗 Tokenizers, we can load a tokenizer in the same way we can load pretrained model weights with 🤗 Transformers.

12 Rust (*https://rust-lang.org*) is a high-performance programming language.

We need a dataset and metrics to train and evaluate models, so let's take a look at 🤗 Datasets, which is in charge of that aspect.

Hugging Face Datasets

Loading, processing, and storing datasets can be a cumbersome process, especially when the datasets get too large to fit in your laptop's RAM. In addition, you usually need to implement various scripts to download the data and transform it into a standard format.

🤗 Datasets (*https://oreil.ly/959YT*) simplifies this process by providing a standard interface for thousands of datasets that can be found on the Hub (*https://oreil.ly/Rdhcu*). It also provides smart caching (so you don't have to redo your preprocessing each time you run your code) and avoids RAM limitations by leveraging a special mechanism called *memory mapping* that stores the contents of a file in virtual memory and enables multiple processes to modify a file more efficiently. The library is also interoperable with popular frameworks like Pandas and NumPy, so you don't have to leave the comfort of your favorite data wrangling tools.

Having a good dataset and powerful model is worthless, however, if you can't reliably measure the performance. Unfortunately, classic NLP metrics come with many different implementations that can vary slightly and lead to deceptive results. By providing the scripts for many metrics, 🤗 Datasets helps make experiments more reproducible and the results more trustworthy.

With the 🤗 Transformers, 🤗 Tokenizers, and 🤗 Datasets libraries we have everything we need to train our very own transformer models! However, as we'll see in Chapter 10 there are situations where we need fine-grained control over the training loop. That's where the last library of the ecosystem comes into play: 🤗 Accelerate.

Hugging Face Accelerate

If you've ever had to write your own training script in PyTorch, chances are that you've had some headaches when trying to port the code that runs on your laptop to the code that runs on your organization's cluster. 🤗 Accelerate (*https://oreil.ly/iRfDe*) adds a layer of abstraction to your normal training loops that takes care of all the custom logic necessary for the training infrastructure. This literally accelerates your workflow by simplifying the change of infrastructure when necessary.

This sums up the core components of Hugging Face's open source ecosystem. But before wrapping up this chapter, let's take a look at a few of the common challenges that come with trying to deploy transformers in the real world.

Main Challenges with Transformers

In this chapter we've gotten a glimpse of the wide range of NLP tasks that can be tackled with transformer models. Reading the media headlines, it can sometimes sound like their capabilities are limitless. However, despite their usefulness, transformers are far from being a silver bullet. Here are a few challenges associated with them that we will explore throughout the book:

Language
: NLP research is dominated by the English language. There are several models for other languages, but it is harder to find pretrained models for rare or low-resource languages. In Chapter 4, we'll explore multilingual transformers and their ability to perform zero-shot cross-lingual transfer.

Data availability
: Although we can use transfer learning to dramatically reduce the amount of labeled training data our models need, it is still a lot compared to how much a human needs to perform the task. Tackling scenarios where you have little to no labeled data is the subject of Chapter 9.

Working with long documents
: Self-attention works extremely well on paragraph-long texts, but it becomes very expensive when we move to longer texts like whole documents. Approaches to mitigate this are discussed in Chapter 11.

Opacity
: As with other deep learning models, transformers are to a large extent opaque. It is hard or impossible to unravel "why" a model made a certain prediction. This is an especially hard challenge when these models are deployed to make critical decisions. We'll explore some ways to probe the errors of transformer models in Chapters 2 and 4.

Bias
: Transformer models are predominantly pretrained on text data from the internet. This imprints all the biases that are present in the data into the models. Making sure that these are neither racist, sexist, or worse is a challenging task. We discuss some of these issues in more detail in Chapter 10.

Although daunting, many of these challenges can be overcome. As well as in the specific chapters mentioned, we will touch on these topics in almost every chapter ahead.

Conclusion

Hopefully, by now you are excited to learn how to start training and integrating these versatile models into your own applications! You've seen in this chapter that with just a few lines of code you can use state-of-the-art models for classification, named entity recognition, question answering, translation, and summarization, but this is really just the "tip of the iceberg."

In the following chapters you will learn how to adapt transformers to a wide range of use cases, such as building a text classifier, or a lightweight model for production, or even training a language model from scratch. We'll be taking a hands-on approach, which means that for every concept covered there will be accompanying code that you can run on Google Colab or your own GPU machine.

Now that we're armed with the basic concepts behind transformers, it's time to get our hands dirty with our first application: text classification. That's the topic of the next chapter!

CHAPTER 2

Text Classification

Text classification is one of the most common tasks in NLP; it can be used for a broad range of applications, such as tagging customer feedback into categories or routing support tickets according to their language. Chances are that your email program's spam filter is using text classification to protect your inbox from a deluge of unwanted junk!

Another common type of text classification is sentiment analysis, which (as we saw in Chapter 1) aims to identify the polarity of a given text. For example, a company like Tesla might analyze Twitter posts like the one in Figure 2-1 to determine whether people like its new car roofs or not.

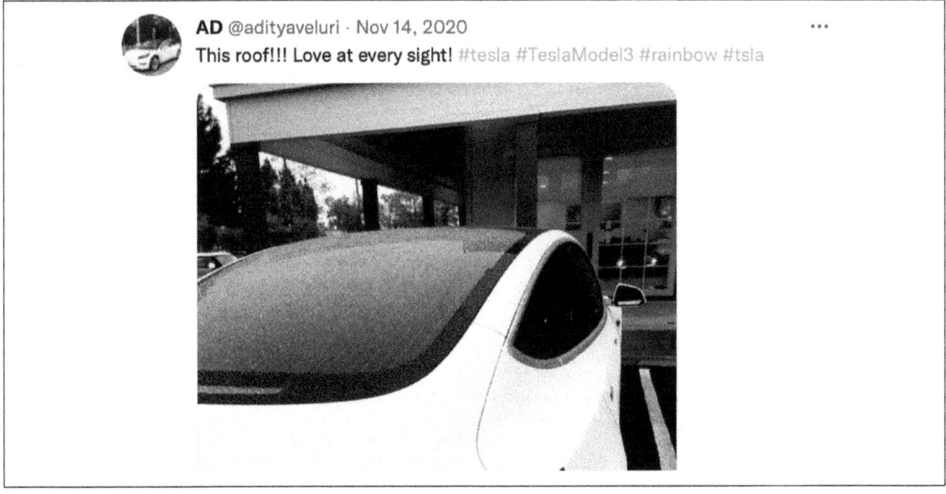

Figure 2-1. Analyzing Twitter content can yield useful feedback from customers (courtesy of Aditya Veluri)

Now imagine that you are a data scientist who needs to build a system that can automatically identify emotional states such as "anger" or "joy" that people express about your company's product on Twitter. In this chapter, we'll tackle this task using a variant of BERT called DistilBERT.[1] The main advantage of this model is that it achieves comparable performance to BERT, while being significantly smaller and more efficient. This enables us to train a classifier in a few minutes, and if you want to train a larger BERT model you can simply change the checkpoint of the pretrained model. A *checkpoint* corresponds to the set of weights that are loaded into a given transformer architecture.

This will also be our first encounter with three of the core libraries from the Hugging Face ecosystem: 🤗 Datasets, 🤗 Tokenizers, and 🤗 Transformers. As shown in Figure 2-2, these libraries will allow us to quickly go from raw text to a fine-tuned model that can be used for inference on new tweets. So, in the spirit of Optimus Prime, let's dive in, "transform, and roll out!"[2]

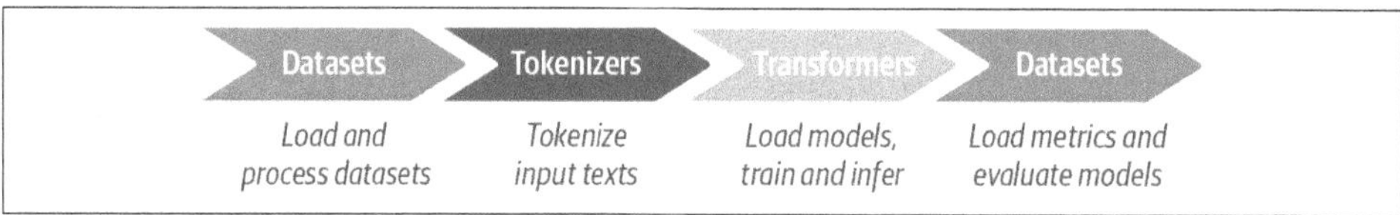

Figure 2-2. A typical pipeline for training transformer models with the 🤗 Datasets, 🤗 Tokenizers, and 🤗 Transformers libraries

The Dataset

To build our emotion detector we'll use a great dataset from an article that explored how emotions are represented in English Twitter messages.[3] Unlike most sentiment analysis datasets that involve just "positive" and "negative" polarities, this dataset contains six basic emotions: anger, disgust, fear, joy, sadness, and surprise. Given a tweet, our task will be to train a model that can classify it into one of these emotions.

1 V. Sanh et al., "DistilBERT, a Distilled Version of BERT: Smaller, Faster, Cheaper and Lighter" (*https://arxiv.org/abs/1910.01108*), (2019).

2 Optimus Prime is the leader of a race of robots in the popular Transformers franchise for children (and for those who are young at heart!).

3 E. Saravia et al., "CARER: Contextualized Affect Representations for Emotion Recognition," *Proceedings of the 2018 Conference on Empirical Methods in Natural Language Processing* (Oct–Nov 2018): 3687–3697, *http://dx.doi.org/10.18653/v1/D18-1404*.

A First Look at Hugging Face Datasets

We will use 🤗 Datasets to download the data from the Hugging Face Hub (*https://oreil.ly/959YT*). We can use the `list_datasets()` function to see what datasets are available on the Hub:

```
from datasets import list_datasets

all_datasets = list_datasets()
print(f"There are {len(all_datasets)} datasets currently available on the Hub")
print(f"The first 10 are: {all_datasets[:10]}")
```

```
There are 1753 datasets currently available on the Hub
The first 10 are: ['acronym_identification', 'ade_corpus_v2', 'adversarial_qa',
'aeslc', 'afrikaans_ner_corpus', 'ag_news', 'ai2_arc', 'air_dialogue',
'ajgt_twitter_ar', 'allegro_reviews']
```

We see that each dataset is given a name, so let's load the `emotion` dataset with the `load_dataset()` function:

```
from datasets import load_dataset

emotions = load_dataset("emotion")
```

If we look inside our `emotions` object:

```
emotions
```

```
DatasetDict({
    train: Dataset({
        features: ['text', 'label'],
        num_rows: 16000
    })
    validation: Dataset({
        features: ['text', 'label'],
        num_rows: 2000
    })
    test: Dataset({
        features: ['text', 'label'],
        num_rows: 2000
    })
})
```

we see it is similar to a Python dictionary, with each key corresponding to a different split. And we can use the usual dictionary syntax to access an individual split:

```
train_ds = emotions["train"]
train_ds
```

```
Dataset({
    features: ['text', 'label'],
    num_rows: 16000
})
```

which returns an instance of the Dataset class. The Dataset object is one of the core data structures in 🤗 Datasets, and we'll be exploring many of its features throughout the course of this book. For starters, it behaves like an ordinary Python array or list, so we can query its length:

```
len(train_ds)
```

```
16000
```

or access a single example by its index:

```
train_ds[0]
```

```
{'label': 0, 'text': 'i didnt feel humiliated'}
```

Here we see that a single row is represented as a dictionary, where the keys correspond to the column names:

```
train_ds.column_names
```

```
['text', 'label']
```

and the values are the tweet and the emotion. This reflects the fact that 🤗 Datasets is based on *Apache Arrow* (*https://arrow.apache.org*), which defines a typed columnar format that is more memory efficient than native Python. We can see what data types are being used under the hood by accessing the features attribute of a Dataset object:

```
print(train_ds.features)
```

```
{'text': Value(dtype='string', id=None), 'label': ClassLabel(num_classes=6,
names=['sadness', 'joy', 'love', 'anger', 'fear', 'surprise'], names_file=None,
id=None)}
```

In this case, the data type of the text column is string, while the label column is a special ClassLabel object that contains information about the class names and their mapping to integers. We can also access several rows with a slice:

```
print(train_ds[:5])
```

```
{'text': ['i didnt feel humiliated', 'i can go from feeling so hopeless to so
damned hopeful just from being around someone who cares and is awake', 'im
grabbing a minute to post i feel greedy wrong', 'i am ever feeling nostalgic
about the fireplace i will know that it is still on the property', 'i am feeling
grouchy'], 'label': [0, 0, 3, 2, 3]}
```

Note that in this case, the dictionary values are now lists instead of individual elements. We can also get the full column by name:

```
print(train_ds["text"][:5])
```

```
['i didnt feel humiliated', 'i can go from feeling so hopeless to so damned
hopeful just from being around someone who cares and is awake', 'im grabbing a
minute to post i feel greedy wrong', 'i am ever feeling nostalgic about the
fireplace i will know that it is still on the property', 'i am feeling grouchy']
```

Now that we've seen how to load and inspect data with 🤗 Datasets, let's do a few checks about the content of our tweets.

What If My Dataset Is Not on the Hub?

We'll be using the Hugging Face Hub to download datasets for most of the examples in this book. But in many cases, you'll find yourself working with data that is either stored on your laptop or on a remote server in your organization. 🤗 Datasets provides several loading scripts to handle local and remote datasets. Examples for the most common data formats are shown in Table 2-1.

Table 2-1. How to load datasets in various formats

Data format	Loading script	Example
CSV	`csv`	`load_dataset("csv", data_files="my_file.csv")`
Text	`text`	`load_dataset("text", data_files="my_file.txt")`
JSON	`json`	`load_dataset("json", data_files="my_file.jsonl")`

As you can see, for each data format, we just need to pass the relevant loading script to the `load_dataset()` function, along with a `data_files` argument that specifies the path or URL to one or more files. For example, the source files for the `emotion` dataset are actually hosted on Dropbox, so an alternative way to load the dataset is to first download one of the splits:

```
dataset_url = "https://www.dropbox.com/s/1pzkadrvffbqw6o/train.txt"
!wget {dataset_url}
```

If you're wondering why there's a `!` character in the preceding shell command, that's because we're running the commands in a Jupyter notebook. Simply remove the prefix if you want to download and unzip the dataset within a terminal. Now, if we peek at the first row of the *train.txt* file:

```
!head -n 1 train.txt
```

```
i didnt feel humiliated;sadness
```

we can see that here are no column headers and each tweet and emotion are separated by a semicolon. Nevertheless, this is quite similar to a CSV file, so we can load the dataset locally by using the `csv` script and pointing the `data_files` argument to the *train.txt* file:

```
emotions_local = load_dataset("csv", data_files="train.txt", sep=";",
                              names=["text", "label"])
```

Here we've also specified the type of delimiter and the names of the columns. An even simpler approach is to just point the `data_files` argument to the URL itself:

```
dataset_url = "https://www.dropbox.com/s/1pzkadrvffbqw6o/train.txt?dl=1"
emotions_remote = load_dataset("csv", data_files=dataset_url, sep=";",
                               names=["text", "label"])
```

which will automatically download and cache the dataset for you. As you can see, the `load_dataset()` function is very versatile. We recommend checking out the 🤗 Datasets documentation (*https://oreil.ly/Jodu4*) to get a complete overview.

From Datasets to DataFrames

Although 🤗 Datasets provides a lot of low-level functionality to slice and dice our data, it is often convenient to convert a `Dataset` object to a Pandas `DataFrame` so we can access high-level APIs for data visualization. To enable the conversion, 🤗 Datasets provides a `set_format()` method that allows us to change the *output format* of the `Dataset`. Note that this does not change the underlying *data format* (which is an Arrow table), and you can switch to another format later if needed:

```
import pandas as pd

emotions.set_format(type="pandas")
df = emotions["train"][:]
df.head()
```

	text	label
0	i didnt feel humiliated	0
1	i can go from feeling so hopeless to so damned...	0
2	im grabbing a minute to post i feel greedy wrong	3
3	i am ever feeling nostalgic about the fireplac...	2
4	i am feeling grouchy	3

As you can see, the column headers have been preserved and the first few rows match our previous views of the data. However, the labels are represented as integers, so let's use the `int2str()` method of the `label` feature to create a new column in our `DataFrame` with the corresponding label names:

```
def label_int2str(row):
    return emotions["train"].features["label"].int2str(row)

df["label_name"] = df["label"].apply(label_int2str)
df.head()
```

	text	label	label_name
0	i didnt feel humiliated	0	sadness
1	i can go from feeling so hopeless to so damned...	0	sadness

	text	label	label_name
2	im grabbing a minute to post i feel greedy wrong	3	anger
3	i am ever feeling nostalgic about the fireplac...	2	love
4	i am feeling grouchy	3	anger

Before diving into building a classifier, let's take a closer look at the dataset. As Andrej Karpathy notes in his famous blog post "A Recipe for Training Neural Networks" (*https://oreil.ly/bNayo*), becoming "one with the data" is an essential step for training great models!

Looking at the Class Distribution

Whenever you are working on text classification problems, it is a good idea to examine the distribution of examples across the classes. A dataset with a skewed class distribution might require a different treatment in terms of the training loss and evaluation metrics than a balanced one.

With Pandas and Matplotlib, we can quickly visualize the class distribution as follows:

```
import matplotlib.pyplot as plt

df["label_name"].value_counts(ascending=True).plot.barh()
plt.title("Frequency of Classes")
plt.show()
```

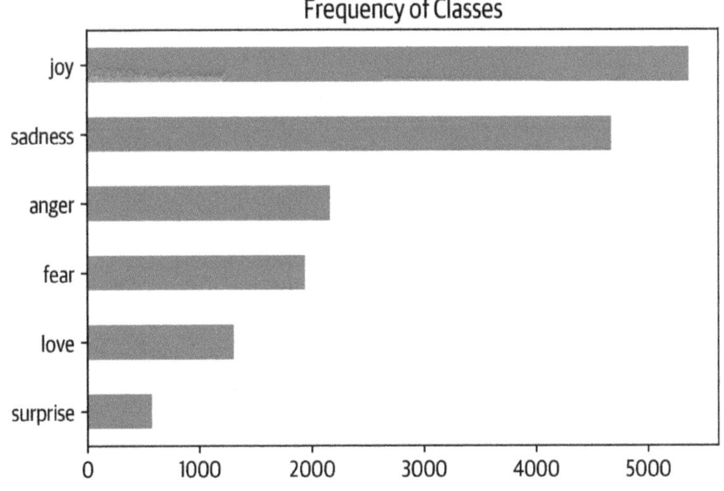

In this case, we can see that the dataset is heavily imbalanced; the `joy` and `sadness` classes appear frequently, whereas `love` and `surprise` are about 5–10 times rarer. There are several ways to deal with imbalanced data, including:

- Randomly oversample the minority class.
- Randomly undersample the majority class.
- Gather more labeled data from the underrepresented classes.

To keep things simple in this chapter, we'll work with the raw, unbalanced class frequencies. If you want to learn more about these sampling techniques, we recommend checking out the Imbalanced-learn library (*https://oreil.ly/5XBhb*). Just make sure that you don't apply sampling methods *before* creating your train/test splits, or you'll get plenty of leakage between them!

Now that we've looked at the classes, let's take a look at the tweets themselves.

How Long Are Our Tweets?

Transformer models have a maximum input sequence length that is referred to as the *maximum context size*. For applications using DistilBERT, the maximum context size is 512 tokens, which amounts to a few paragraphs of text. As we'll see in the next section, a token is an atomic piece of text; for now, we'll treat a token as a single word. We can get a rough estimate of tweet lengths per emotion by looking at the distribution of words per tweet:

```
df["Words Per Tweet"] = df["text"].str.split().apply(len)
df.boxplot("Words Per Tweet", by="label_name", grid=False,
          showfliers=False, color="black")
plt.suptitle("")
plt.xlabel("")
plt.show()
```

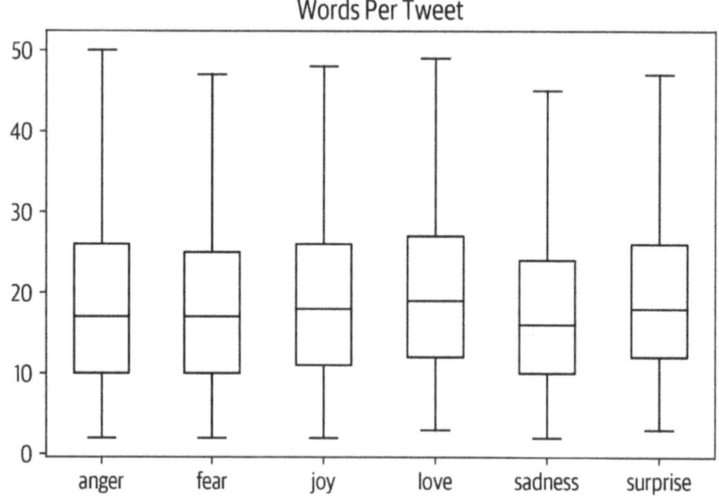

From the plot we see that for each emotion, most tweets are around 15 words long and the longest tweets are well below DistilBERT's maximum context size. Texts that are longer than a model's context size need to be truncated, which can lead to a loss in performance if the truncated text contains crucial information; in this case, it looks like that won't be an issue.

Let's now figure out how we can convert these raw texts into a format suitable for 🤗 Transformers! While we're at it, let's also reset the output format of our dataset since we don't need the `DataFrame` format anymore:

```
emotions.reset_format()
```

From Text to Tokens

Transformer models like DistilBERT cannot receive raw strings as input; instead, they assume the text has been *tokenized* and *encoded* as numerical vectors. Tokenization is the step of breaking down a string into the atomic units used in the model. There are several tokenization strategies one can adopt, and the optimal splitting of words into subunits is usually learned from the corpus. Before looking at the tokenizer used for DistilBERT, let's consider two extreme cases: *character* and *word* tokenization.

Character Tokenization

The simplest tokenization scheme is to feed each character individually to the model. In Python, `str` objects are really arrays under the hood, which allows us to quickly implement character-level tokenization with just one line of code:

```
text = "Tokenizing text is a core task of NLP."
tokenized_text = list(text)
print(tokenized_text)
```

```
['T', 'o', 'k', 'e', 'n', 'i', 'z', 'i', 'n', 'g', ' ', 't', 'e', 'x', 't', ' ',
'i', 's', ' ', 'a', ' ', 'c', 'o', 'r', 'e', ' ', 't', 'a', 's', 'k', ' ', 'o',
'f', ' ', 'N', 'L', 'P', '.']
```

This is a good start, but we're not done yet. Our model expects each character to be converted to an integer, a process sometimes called *numericalization*. One simple way to do this is by encoding each unique token (which are characters in this case) with a unique integer:

```
token2idx = {ch: idx for idx, ch in enumerate(sorted(set(tokenized_text)))}
print(token2idx)
```

```
{' ': 0, '.': 1, 'L': 2, 'N': 3, 'P': 4, 'T': 5, 'a': 6, 'c': 7, 'e': 8, 'f': 9,
'g': 10, 'i': 11, 'k': 12, 'n': 13, 'o': 14, 'r': 15, 's': 16, 't': 17, 'x': 18,
'z': 19}
```

This gives us a mapping from each character in our vocabulary to a unique integer. We can now use `token2idx` to transform the tokenized text to a list of integers:

```
input_ids = [token2idx[token] for token in tokenized_text]
print(input_ids)
```

```
[5, 14, 12, 8, 13, 11, 19, 11, 13, 10, 0, 17, 8, 18, 17, 0, 11, 16, 0, 6, 0, 7,
14, 15, 8, 0, 17, 6, 16, 12, 0, 14, 9, 0, 3, 2, 4, 1]
```

Each token has now been mapped to a unique numerical identifier (hence the name `input_ids`). The last step is to convert `input_ids` to a 2D tensor of one-hot vectors. One-hot vectors are frequently used in machine learning to encode categorical data, which can be either ordinal or nominal. For example, suppose we wanted to encode the names of characters in the *Transformers* TV series. One way to do this would be to map each name to a unique ID, as follows:

```
categorical_df = pd.DataFrame(
    {"Name": ["Bumblebee", "Optimus Prime", "Megatron"], "Label ID": [0,1,2]})
categorical_df
```

	Name	Label ID
0	Bumblebee	0
1	Optimus Prime	1
2	Megatron	2

The problem with this approach is that it creates a fictitious ordering between the names, and neural networks are *really* good at learning these kinds of relationships. So instead, we can create a new column for each category and assign a 1 where the category is true, and a 0 otherwise. In Pandas, this can be implemented with the `get_dummies()` function as follows:

```
pd.get_dummies(categorical_df["Name"])
```

	Bumblebee	Megatron	Optimus Prime
0	1	0	0
1	0	0	1
2	0	1	0

The rows of this `DataFrame` are the one-hot vectors, which have a single "hot" entry with a 1 and 0s everywhere else. Now, looking at our `input_ids`, we have a similar problem: the elements create an ordinal scale. This means that adding or subtracting two IDs is a meaningless operation, since the result is a new ID that represents another random token.

On the other hand, the result of adding two one-hot encodings can easily be interpreted: the two entries that are "hot" indicate that the corresponding tokens co-occur. We can create the one-hot encodings in PyTorch by converting `input_ids` to a tensor and applying the `one_hot()` function as follows:

```
import torch
import torch.nn.functional as F

input_ids = torch.tensor(input_ids)
one_hot_encodings = F.one_hot(input_ids, num_classes=len(token2idx))
one_hot_encodings.shape
```

```
torch.Size([38, 20])
```

For each of the 38 input tokens we now have a one-hot vector with 20 dimensions, since our vocabulary consists of 20 unique characters.

It's important to always set `num_classes` in the `one_hot()` function because otherwise the one-hot vectors may end up being shorter than the length of the vocabulary (and need to be padded with zeros manually). In TensorFlow, the equivalent function is `tf.one_hot()`, where the `depth` argument plays the role of `num_classes`.

By examining the first vector, we can verify that a 1 appears in the location indicated by `input_ids[0]`:

```
print(f"Token: {tokenized_text[0]}")
print(f"Tensor index: {input_ids[0]}")
print(f"One-hot: {one_hot_encodings[0]}")
```

```
Token: T
Tensor index: 5
One-hot: tensor([0, 0, 0, 0, 0, 1, 0, 0, 0, 0, 0, 0, 0, 0, 0, 0, 0, 0, 0, 0])
```

From our simple example we can see that character-level tokenization ignores any structure in the text and treats the whole string as a stream of characters. Although this helps deal with misspellings and rare words, the main drawback is that linguistic structures such as words need to be *learned* from the data. This requires significant compute, memory, and data. For this reason, character tokenization is rarely used in practice. Instead, some structure of the text is preserved during the tokenization step. *Word tokenization* is a straightforward approach to achieve this, so let's take a look at how it works.

Word Tokenization

Instead of splitting the text into characters, we can split it into words and map each word to an integer. Using words from the outset enables the model to skip the step of learning words from characters, and thereby reduces the complexity of the training process.

One simple class of word tokenizers uses whitespace to tokenize the text. We can do this by applying Python's `split()` function directly on the raw text (just like we did to measure the tweet lengths):

```
tokenized_text = text.split()
print(tokenized_text)
```

```
['Tokenizing', 'text', 'is', 'a', 'core', 'task', 'of', 'NLP.']
```

From here we can take the same steps we took for the character tokenizer to map each word to an ID. However, we can already see one potential problem with this tokenization scheme: punctuation is not accounted for, so `NLP.` is treated as a single token. Given that words can include declinations, conjugations, or misspellings, the size of the vocabulary can easily grow into the millions!

Some word tokenizers have extra rules for punctuation. One can also apply stemming or lemmatization, which normalizes words to their stem (e.g., "great", "greater", and "greatest" all become "great"), at the expense of losing some information in the text.

Having a large vocabulary is a problem because it requires neural networks to have an enormous number of parameters. To illustrate this, suppose we have 1 million unique words and want to compress the 1-million-dimensional input vectors to 1-thousand-dimensional vectors in the first layer of our neural network. This is a standard step in most NLP architectures, and the resulting weight matrix of this first layer would contain 1 million × 1 thousand = 1 billion weights. This is already comparable to the largest GPT-2 model,[4] which has around 1.5 billion parameters in total!

Naturally, we want to avoid being so wasteful with our model parameters since models are expensive to train, and larger models are more difficult to maintain. A common approach is to limit the vocabulary and discard rare words by considering, say, the 100,000 most common words in the corpus. Words that are not part of the vocabulary are classified as "unknown" and mapped to a shared `UNK` token. This means that we lose some potentially important information in the process of word tokenization, since the model has no information about words associated with `UNK`.

Wouldn't it be nice if there was a compromise between character and word tokenization that preserved all the input information *and* some of the input structure? There is: *subword tokenization*.

4 GPT-2 is the successor of GPT, and it captivated the public's attention with its impressive ability to generate realistic text. We'll explore GPT-2 in detail in Chapter 6.

Subword Tokenization

The basic idea behind subword tokenization is to combine the best aspects of character and word tokenization. On the one hand, we want to split rare words into smaller units to allow the model to deal with complex words and misspellings. On the other hand, we want to keep frequent words as unique entities so that we can keep the length of our inputs to a manageable size. The main distinguishing feature of subword tokenization (as well as word tokenization) is that it is *learned* from the pretraining corpus using a mix of statistical rules and algorithms.

There are several subword tokenization algorithms that are commonly used in NLP, but let's start with WordPiece,[5] which is used by the BERT and DistilBERT tokenizers. The easiest way to understand how WordPiece works is to see it in action. 🤗 Transformers provides a convenient `AutoTokenizer` class that allows you to quickly load the tokenizer associated with a pretrained model—we just call its `from_pretrained()` method, providing the ID of a model on the Hub or a local file path. Let's start by loading the tokenizer for DistilBERT:

```
from transformers import AutoTokenizer

model_ckpt = "distilbert-base-uncased"
tokenizer = AutoTokenizer.from_pretrained(model_ckpt)
```

The `AutoTokenizer` class belongs to a larger set of "auto" classes (*https://oreil.ly/h4YPz*) whose job is to automatically retrieve the model's configuration, pretrained weights, or vocabulary from the name of the checkpoint. This allows you to quickly switch between models, but if you wish to load the specific class manually you can do so as well. For example, we could have loaded the DistilBERT tokenizer as follows:

```
from transformers import DistilBertTokenizer

distilbert_tokenizer = DistilBertTokenizer.from_pretrained(model_ckpt)
```

When you run the `AutoTokenizer.from_pretrained()` method for the first time you will see a progress bar that shows which parameters of the pretrained tokenizer are loaded from the Hugging Face Hub. When you run the code a second time, it will load the tokenizer from the cache, usually at *~/.cache/huggingface*.

Let's examine how this tokenizer works by feeding it our simple "Tokenizing text is a core task of NLP." example text:

5 M. Schuster and K. Nakajima, "Japanese and Korean Voice Search," *2012 IEEE International Conference on Acoustics, Speech and Signal Processing* (2012): 5149–5152, *https://doi.org/10.1109/ICASSP.2012.6289079*.

```
encoded_text = tokenizer(text)
print(encoded_text)
```

```
{'input_ids': [101, 19204, 6026, 3793, 2003, 1037, 4563, 4708, 1997, 17953,
2361, 1012, 102], 'attention_mask': [1, 1, 1, 1, 1, 1, 1, 1, 1, 1, 1, 1, 1]}
```

Just as with character tokenization, we can see that the words have been mapped to unique integers in the `input_ids` field. We'll discuss the role of the `attention_mask` field in the next section. Now that we have the `input_ids`, we can convert them back into tokens by using the tokenizer's `convert_ids_to_tokens()` method:

```
tokens = tokenizer.convert_ids_to_tokens(encoded_text.input_ids)
print(tokens)
```

```
['[CLS]', 'token', '##izing', 'text', 'is', 'a', 'core', 'task', 'of', 'nl',
'##p', '.', '[SEP]']
```

We can observe three things here. First, some special `[CLS]` and `[SEP]` tokens have been added to the start and end of the sequence. These tokens differ from model to model, but their main role is to indicate the start and end of a sequence. Second, the tokens have each been lowercased, which is a feature of this particular checkpoint. Finally, we can see that "tokenizing" and "NLP" have been split into two tokens, which makes sense since they are not common words. The ## prefix in `##izing` and `##p` means that the preceding string is not whitespace; any token with this prefix should be merged with the previous token when you convert the tokens back to a string. The `AutoTokenizer` class has a `convert_tokens_to_string()` method for doing just that, so let's apply it to our tokens:

```
print(tokenizer.convert_tokens_to_string(tokens))
```

```
[CLS] tokenizing text is a core task of nlp. [SEP]
```

The `AutoTokenizer` class also has several attributes that provide information about the tokenizer. For example, we can inspect the vocabulary size:

```
tokenizer.vocab_size
```

```
30522
```

and the corresponding model's maximum context size:

```
tokenizer.model_max_length
```

```
512
```

Another interesting attribute to know about is the names of the fields that the model expects in its forward pass:

```
tokenizer.model_input_names
```

```
['input_ids', 'attention_mask']
```

Now that we have a basic understanding of the tokenization process for a single string, let's see how we can tokenize the whole dataset!

When using pretrained models, it is *really* important to make sure that you use the same tokenizer that the model was trained with. From the model's perspective, switching the tokenizer is like shuffling the vocabulary. If everyone around you started swapping random words like "house" for "cat," you'd have a hard time understanding what was going on too!

Tokenizing the Whole Dataset

To tokenize the whole corpus, we'll use the `map()` method of our `DatasetDict` object. We'll encounter this method many times throughout this book, as it provides a convenient way to apply a processing function to each element in a dataset. As we'll soon see, the `map()` method can also be used to create new rows and columns.

To get started, the first thing we need is a processing function to tokenize our examples with:

```
def tokenize(batch):
    return tokenizer(batch["text"], padding=True, truncation=True)
```

This function applies the tokenizer to a batch of examples; `padding=True` will pad the examples with zeros to the size of the longest one in a batch, and `truncation=True` will truncate the examples to the model's maximum context size. To see `tokenize()` in action, let's pass a batch of two examples from the training set:

```
print(tokenize(emotions["train"][:2]))

{'input_ids': [[101, 1045, 2134, 2102, 2514, 26608, 102, 0, 0, 0, 0, 0, 0, 0, 0,
0, 0, 0, 0, 0, 0, 0, 0], [101, 1045, 2064, 2175, 2013, 3110, 2061, 20625, 2000,
2061, 9636, 17772, 2074, 2013, 2108, 2105, 2619, 2040, 14977, 1998, 2003, 8300,
102]], 'attention_mask': [[1, 1, 1, 1, 1, 1, 1, 0, 0, 0, 0, 0, 0, 0, 0, 0, 0, 0,
0, 0, 0, 0, 0], [1, 1, 1, 1, 1, 1, 1, 1, 1, 1, 1, 1, 1, 1, 1, 1, 1, 1, 1, 1, 1,
1, 1]]}
```

Here we can see the result of padding: the first element of `input_ids` is shorter than the second, so zeros have been added to that element to make them the same length. These zeros have a corresponding `[PAD]` token in the vocabulary, and the set of special tokens also includes the `[CLS]` and `[SEP]` tokens that we encountered earlier:

Special Token	[PAD]	[UNK]	[CLS]	[SEP]	[MASK]
Special Token ID	0	100	101	102	103

Also note that in addition to returning the encoded tweets as `input_ids`, the tokenizer returns a list of `attention_mask` arrays. This is because we do not want the model to get confused by the additional padding tokens: the attention mask allows the model to ignore the padded parts of the input. Figure 2-3 provides a visual explanation of how the input IDs and attention masks are padded.

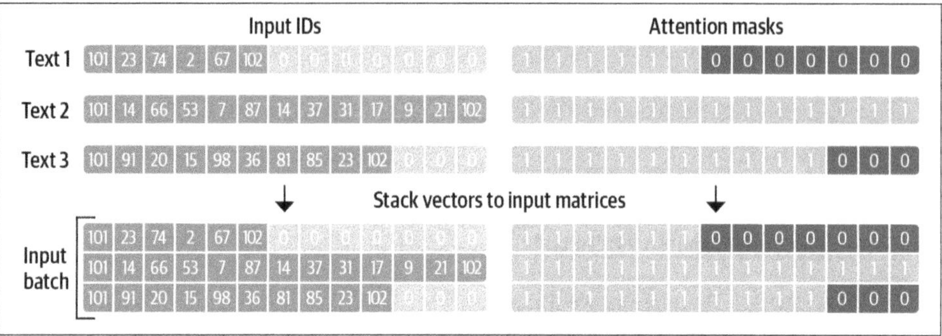

Figure 2-3. For each batch, the input sequences are padded to the maximum sequence length in the batch; the attention mask is used in the model to ignore the padded areas of the input tensors

Once we've defined a processing function, we can apply it across all the splits in the corpus in a single line of code:

```
emotions_encoded = emotions.map(tokenize, batched=True, batch_size=None)
```

By default, the `map()` method operates individually on every example in the corpus, so setting `batched=True` will encode the tweets in batches. Because we've set `batch_size=None`, our `tokenize()` function will be applied on the full dataset as a single batch. This ensures that the input tensors and attention masks have the same shape globally, and we can see that this operation has added new `input_ids` and `attention_mask` columns to the dataset:

```
print(emotions_encoded["train"].column_names)
```

```
['attention_mask', 'input_ids', 'label', 'text']
```

In later chapters, we'll see how *data collators* can be used to dynamically pad the tensors in each batch. Padding globally will come in handy in the next section, where we extract a feature matrix from the whole corpus.

Training a Text Classifier

As discussed in Chapter 1, models like DistilBERT are pretrained to predict masked words in a sequence of text. However, we can't use these language models directly for text classification; we need to modify them slightly. To understand what modifications are necessary, let's take a look at the architecture of an encoder-based model like DistilBERT, which is depicted in Figure 2-4.

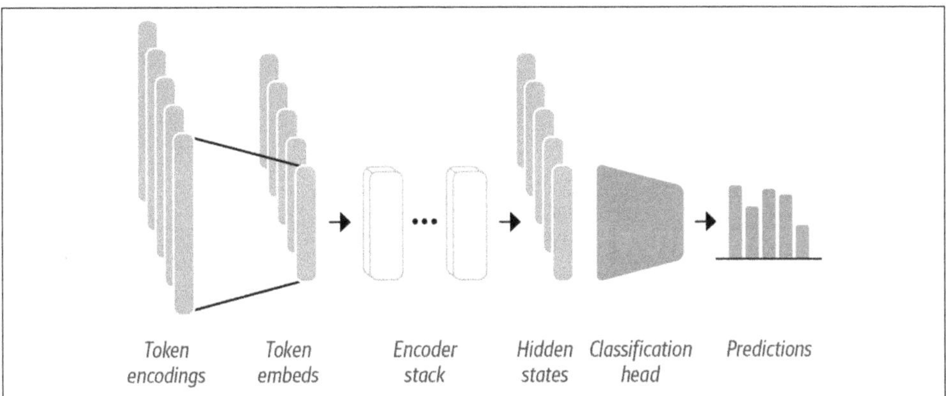

Figure 2-4. The architecture used for sequence classification with an encoder-based transformer; it consists of the model's pretrained body combined with a custom classification head

First, the text is tokenized and represented as one-hot vectors called *token encodings*. The size of the tokenizer vocabulary determines the dimension of the token encodings, and it usually consists of 20k–200k unique tokens. Next, these token encodings are converted to *token embeddings*, which are vectors living in a lower-dimensional space. The token embeddings are then passed through the encoder block layers to yield a *hidden state* for each input token. For the pretraining objective of language modeling,[6] each hidden state is fed to a layer that predicts the masked input tokens. For the classification task, we replace the language modeling layer with a classification layer.

In practice, PyTorch skips the step of creating one-hot vectors for token encodings because multiplying a matrix with a one-hot vector is the same as selecting a column from the matrix. This can be done directly by getting the column with the token ID from the matrix. We'll see this in Chapter 3 when we use the `nn.Embedding` class.

We have two options to train such a model on our Twitter dataset:

Feature extraction
: We use the hidden states as features and just train a classifier on them, without modifying the pretrained model.

6 In the case of DistilBERT, it's guessing the masked tokens.

Fine-tuning
: We train the whole model end-to-end, which also updates the parameters of the pretrained model.

In the following sections we explore both options for DistilBERT and examine their trade-offs.

Transformers as Feature Extractors

Using a transformer as a feature extractor is fairly simple. As shown in Figure 2-5, we freeze the body's weights during training and use the hidden states as features for the classifier. The advantage of this approach is that we can quickly train a small or shallow model. Such a model could be a neural classification layer or a method that does not rely on gradients, such as a random forest. This method is especially convenient if GPUs are unavailable, since the hidden states only need to be precomputed once.

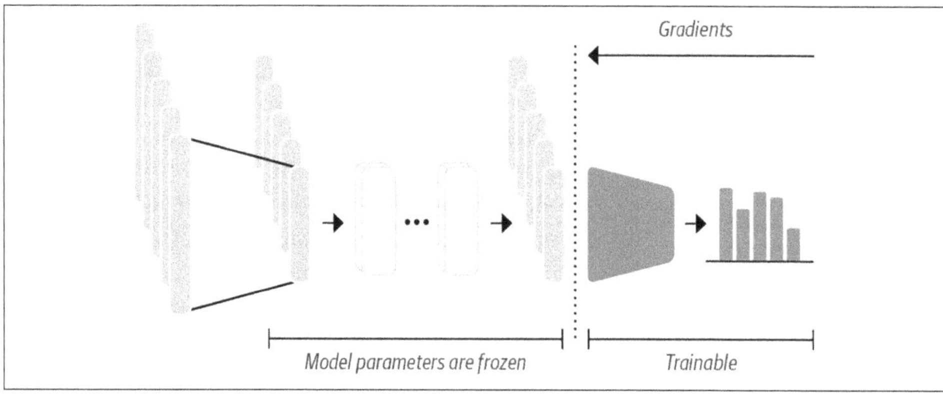

Figure 2-5. In the feature-based approach, the DistilBERT model is frozen and just provides features for a classifier

Using pretrained models

We will use another convenient auto class from 🤗 Transformers called `AutoModel`. Similar to the `AutoTokenizer` class, `AutoModel` has a `from_pretrained()` method to load the weights of a pretrained model. Let's use this method to load the DistilBERT checkpoint:

```
from transformers import AutoModel

model_ckpt = "distilbert-base-uncased"
device = torch.device("cuda" if torch.cuda.is_available() else "cpu")
model = AutoModel.from_pretrained(model_ckpt).to(device)
```

Here we've used PyTorch to check whether a GPU is available or not, and then chained the PyTorch `nn.Module.to()` method to the model loader. This ensures that the model will run on the GPU if we have one. If not, the model will run on the CPU, which can be considerably slower.

The `AutoModel` class converts the token encodings to embeddings, and then feeds them through the encoder stack to return the hidden states. Let's take a look at how we can extract these states from our corpus.

Interoperability Between Frameworks

Although the code in this book is mostly written in PyTorch, 🤗 Transformers provides tight interoperability with TensorFlow and JAX. This means that you only need to change a few lines of code to load a pretrained model in your favorite deep learning framework! For example, we can load DistilBERT in TensorFlow by using the `TFAutoModel` class as follows:

```
from transformers import TFAutoModel

tf_model = TFAutoModel.from_pretrained(model_ckpt)
```

This interoperability is especially useful when a model is only released in one framework, but you'd like to use it in another. For example, the XLM-RoBERTa model (*https://oreil.ly/OUMvG*) that we'll encounter in Chapter 4 only has PyTorch weights, so if you try to load it in TensorFlow as we did before:

```
tf_xlmr = TFAutoModel.from_pretrained("xlm-roberta-base")
```

you'll get an error. In these cases, you can specify a `from_pt=True` argument to the `TfAutoModel.from_pretrained()` function, and the library will automatically download and convert the PyTorch weights for you:

```
tf_xlmr = TFAutoModel.from_pretrained("xlm-roberta-base", from_pt=True)
```

As you can see, it is very simple to switch between frameworks in 🤗 Transformers! In most cases, you can just add a "TF" prefix to the classes and you'll get the equivalent TensorFlow 2.0 classes. When we use the `"pt"` string (e.g., in the following section), which is short for PyTorch, just replace it with `"tf"`, which is short for TensorFlow.

Extracting the last hidden states

To warm up, let's retrieve the last hidden states for a single string. The first thing we need to do is encode the string and convert the tokens to PyTorch tensors. This can be done by providing the `return_tensors="pt"` argument to the tokenizer as follows:

```
text = "this is a test"
inputs = tokenizer(text, return_tensors="pt")
print(f"Input tensor shape: {inputs['input_ids'].size()}")

Input tensor shape: torch.Size([1, 6])
```

As we can see, the resulting tensor has the shape [batch_size, n_tokens]. Now that we have the encodings as a tensor, the final step is to place them on the same device as the model and pass the inputs as follows:

```
inputs = {k:v.to(device) for k,v in inputs.items()}
with torch.no_grad():
    outputs = model(**inputs)
print(outputs)
```

```
BaseModelOutput(last_hidden_state=tensor([[[-0.1565, -0.1862,  0.0528,  ...,
-0.1188,  0.0662,  0.5470],
         [-0.3575, -0.6484, -0.0618,  ..., -0.3040,  0.3508,  0.5221],
         [-0.2772, -0.4459,  0.1818,  ..., -0.0948, -0.0076,  0.9958],
         [-0.2841, -0.3917,  0.3753,  ..., -0.2151, -0.1173,  1.0526],
         [ 0.2661, -0.5094, -0.3180,  ..., -0.4203,  0.0144, -0.2149],
         [ 0.9441,  0.0112, -0.4714,  ...,  0.1439, -0.7288, -0.1619]]],
       device='cuda:0'), hidden_states=None, attentions=None)
```

Here we've used the torch.no_grad() context manager to disable the automatic calculation of the gradient. This is useful for inference since it reduces the memory footprint of the computations. Depending on the model configuration, the output can contain several objects, such as the hidden states, losses, or attentions, arranged in a class similar to a namedtuple in Python. In our example, the model output is an instance of BaseModelOutput, and we can simply access its attributes by name. The current model returns only one attribute, which is the last hidden state, so let's examine its shape:

```
outputs.last_hidden_state.size()
```

```
torch.Size([1, 6, 768])
```

Looking at the hidden state tensor, we see that it has the shape [batch_size, n_tokens, hidden_dim]. In other words, a 768-dimensional vector is returned for each of the 6 input tokens. For classification tasks, it is common practice to just use the hidden state associated with the [CLS] token as the input feature. Since this token appears at the start of each sequence, we can extract it by simply indexing into outputs.last_hidden_state as follows:

```
outputs.last_hidden_state[:,0].size()
```

```
torch.Size([1, 768])
```

Now we know how to get the last hidden state for a single string; let's do the same for the whole dataset by creating a new hidden_state column that stores all these vectors. As we did with the tokenizer, we'll use the map() method of DatasetDict to extract all the hidden states in one go. The first thing we need to do is wrap the previous steps in a processing function:

```
def extract_hidden_states(batch):
    # Place model inputs on the GPU
    inputs = {k:v.to(device) for k,v in batch.items()
```

```
            if k in tokenizer.model_input_names}
    # Extract last hidden states
    with torch.no_grad():
        last_hidden_state = model(**inputs).last_hidden_state
    # Return vector for [CLS] token
    return {"hidden_state": last_hidden_state[:,0].cpu().numpy()}
```

The only difference between this function and our previous logic is the final step where we place the final hidden state back on the CPU as a NumPy array. The `map()` method requires the processing function to return Python or NumPy objects when we're using batched inputs.

Since our model expects tensors as inputs, the next thing to do is convert the `input_ids` and `attention_mask` columns to the `"torch"` format, as follows:

```
emotions_encoded.set_format("torch",
                            columns=["input_ids", "attention_mask", "label"])
```

We can then go ahead and extract the hidden states across all splits in one go:

```
emotions_hidden = emotions_encoded.map(extract_hidden_states, batched=True)
```

Notice that we did not set `batch_size=None` in this case, which means the default `batch_size=1000` is used instead. As expected, applying the `extract_ hidden_ states()` function has added a new `hidden_state` column to our dataset:

```
emotions_hidden["train"].column_names
```

```
['attention_mask', 'hidden_state', 'input_ids', 'label', 'text']
```

Now that we have the hidden states associated with each tweet, the next step is to train a classifier on them. To do that, we'll need a feature matrix—let's take a look.

Creating a feature matrix

The preprocessed dataset now contains all the information we need to train a classifier on it. We will use the hidden states as input features and the labels as targets. We can easily create the corresponding arrays in the well-known Scikit-learn format as follows:

```
import numpy as np

X_train = np.array(emotions_hidden["train"]["hidden_state"])
X_valid = np.array(emotions_hidden["validation"]["hidden_state"])
y_train = np.array(emotions_hidden["train"]["label"])
y_valid = np.array(emotions_hidden["validation"]["label"])
X_train.shape, X_valid.shape
```

```
((16000, 768), (2000, 768))
```

Before we train a model on the hidden states, it's good practice to perform a quick check to ensure that they provide a useful representation of the emotions we want to classify. In the next section, we'll see how visualizing the features provides a fast way to achieve this.

Visualizing the training set

Since visualizing the hidden states in 768 dimensions is tricky to say the least, we'll use the powerful UMAP algorithm to project the vectors down to 2D.[7] Since UMAP works best when the features are scaled to lie in the [0,1] interval, we'll first apply a `MinMaxScaler` and then use the UMAP implementation from the `umap-learn` library to reduce the hidden states:

```
from umap import UMAP
from sklearn.preprocessing import MinMaxScaler

# Scale features to [0,1] range
X_scaled = MinMaxScaler().fit_transform(X_train)
# Initialize and fit UMAP
mapper = UMAP(n_components=2, metric="cosine").fit(X_scaled)
# Create a DataFrame of 2D embeddings
df_emb = pd.DataFrame(mapper.embedding_, columns=["X", "Y"])
df_emb["label"] = y_train
df_emb.head()
```

	X	Y	label
0	4.358075	6.140816	0
1	-3.134567	5.329446	0
2	5.152230	2.732643	3
3	-2.519018	3.067250	2
4	-3.364520	3.356613	3

The result is an array with the same number of training samples, but with only 2 features instead of the 768 we started with! Let's investigate the compressed data a little bit further and plot the density of points for each category separately:

```
fig, axes = plt.subplots(2, 3, figsize=(7,5))
axes = axes.flatten()
cmaps = ["Greys", "Blues", "Oranges", "Reds", "Purples", "Greens"]
labels = emotions["train"].features["label"].names

for i, (label, cmap) in enumerate(zip(labels, cmaps)):
    df_emb_sub = df_emb.query(f"label == {i}")
    axes[i].hexbin(df_emb_sub["X"], df_emb_sub["Y"], cmap=cmap,
                   gridsize=20, linewidths=(0,))
```

7 L. McInnes, J. Healy, and J. Melville, "UMAP: Uniform Manifold Approximation and Projection for Dimension Reduction" (*https://arxiv.org/abs/1802.03426*), (2018).

```
    axes[i].set_title(label)
    axes[i].set_xticks([]), axes[i].set_yticks([])

plt.tight_layout()
plt.show()
```

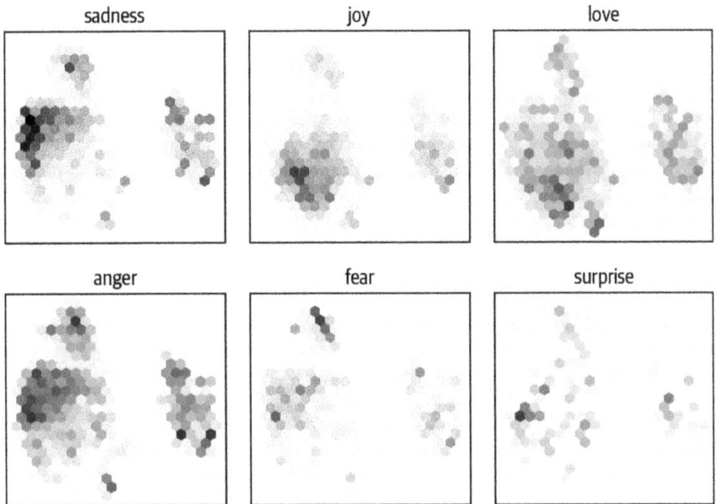

These are only projections onto a lower-dimensional space. Just because some categories overlap does not mean that they are not separable in the original space. Conversely, if they are separable in the projected space they will be separable in the original space.

From this plot we can see some clear patterns: the negative feelings such as `sadness`, `anger`, and `fear` all occupy similar regions with slightly varying distributions. On the other hand, `joy` and `love` are well separated from the negative emotions and also share a similar space. Finally, `surprise` is scattered all over the place. Although we may have hoped for some separation, this is in no way guaranteed since the model was not trained to know the difference between these emotions. It only learned them implicitly by guessing the masked words in texts.

Now that we've gained some insight into the features of our dataset, let's finally train a model on it!

Training a simple classifier

We've seen that the hidden states are somewhat different between the emotions, although for several of them there is no obvious boundary. Let's use these hidden states to train a logistic regression model with Scikit-learn. Training such a simple model is fast and does not require a GPU:

```
from                      import LogisticRegression

# We increase `max_iter` to guarantee convergence
lr_clf = LogisticRegression(max_iter=3000)
lr_clf.fit(X_train, y_train)
lr_clf.score(X_valid, y_valid)
```

```
0.633
```

Looking at the accuracy, it might appear that our model is just a bit better than random—but since we are dealing with an unbalanced multiclass dataset, it's actually significantly better. We can examine whether our model is any good by comparing it against a simple baseline. In Scikit-learn there is a `DummyClassifier` that can be used to build a classifier with simple heuristics such as always choosing the majority class or always drawing a random class. In this case the best-performing heuristic is to always choose the most frequent class, which yields an accuracy of about 35%:

```
from                import DummyClassifier

dummy_clf = DummyClassifier(strategy="most_frequent")
dummy_clf.fit(X_train, y_train)
dummy_clf.score(X_valid, y_valid)
```

```
0.352
```

So, our simple classifier with DistilBERT embeddings is significantly better than our baseline. We can further investigate the performance of the model by looking at the confusion matrix of the classifier, which tells us the relationship between the true and predicted labels:

```
from                     import ConfusionMatrixDisplay, confusion_matrix

def plot_confusion_matrix(y_preds, y_true, labels):
    cm = confusion_matrix(y_true, y_preds, normalize="true")
    fig, ax = plt.subplots(figsize=(6, 6))
    disp = ConfusionMatrixDisplay(confusion_matrix=cm, display_labels=labels)
    disp.plot(cmap="Blues", values_format=".2f", ax=ax, colorbar=False)
    plt.title("Normalized confusion matrix")
    plt.show()

y_preds = lr_clf.predict(X_valid)
plot_confusion_matrix(y_preds, y_valid, labels)
```

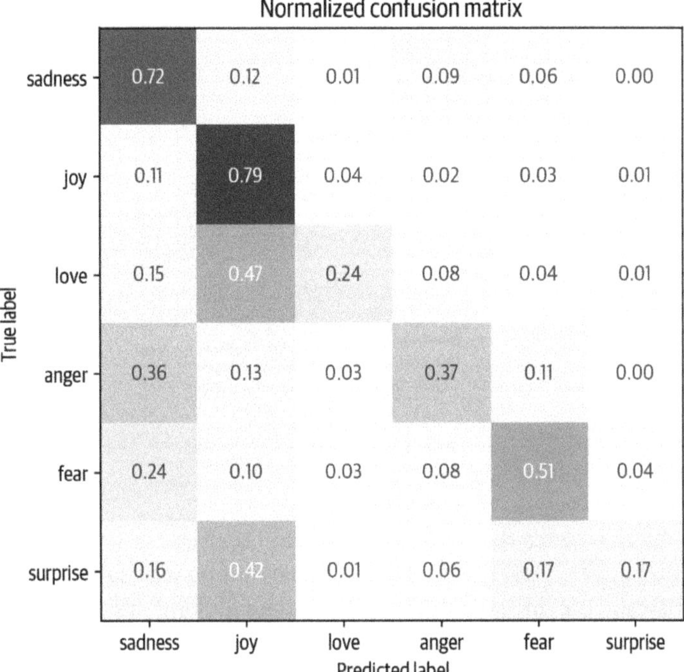

We can see that `anger` and `fear` are most often confused with `sadness`, which agrees with the observation we made when visualizing the embeddings. Also, `love` and `surprise` are frequently mistaken for `joy`.

In the next section we will explore the fine-tuning approach, which leads to superior classification performance. It is, however, important to note that doing this requires more computational resources, such as GPUs, that might not be available in your organization. In cases like these, a feature-based approach can be a good compromise between doing traditional machine learning and deep learning.

Fine-Tuning Transformers

Let's now explore what it takes to fine-tune a transformer end-to-end. With the fine-tuning approach we do not use the hidden states as fixed features, but instead train them as shown in Figure 2-6. This requires the classification head to be differentiable, which is why this method usually uses a neural network for classification.

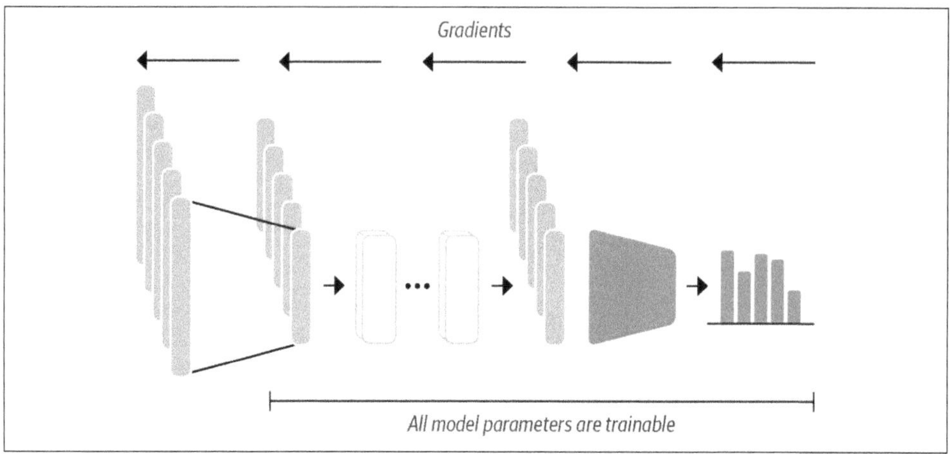

Figure 2-6. When using the fine-tuning approach the whole DistilBERT model is trained along with the classification head

Training the hidden states that serve as inputs to the classification model will help us avoid the problem of working with data that may not be well suited for the classification task. Instead, the initial hidden states adapt during training to decrease the model loss and thus increase its performance.

We'll be using the `Trainer` API from 🤗 Transformers to simplify the training loop. Let's look at the ingredients we need to set one up!

Loading a pretrained model

The first thing we need is a pretrained DistilBERT model like the one we used in the feature-based approach. The only slight modification is that we use the `AutoModelForSequenceClassification` model instead of `AutoModel`. The difference is that the `AutoModelForSequenceClassification` model has a classification head on top of the pretrained model outputs, which can be easily trained with the base model. We just need to specify how many labels the model has to predict (six in our case), since this dictates the number of outputs the classification head has:

```
from transformers import AutoModelForSequenceClassification

num_labels = 6
model = (AutoModelForSequenceClassification
         .from_pretrained(model_ckpt, num_labels=num_labels)
         .to(device))
```

You will see a warning that some parts of the model are randomly initialized. This is normal since the classification head has not yet been trained. The next step is to define the metrics that we'll use to evaluate our model's performance during fine-tuning.

Defining the performance metrics

To monitor metrics during training, we need to define a `compute_metrics()` function for the `Trainer`. This function receives an `EvalPrediction` object (which is a named tuple with `predictions` and `label_ids` attributes) and needs to return a dictionary that maps each metric's name to its value. For our application, we'll compute the F_1-score and the accuracy of the model as follows:

```
from sklearn.metrics import accuracy_score, f1_score

def compute_metrics(pred):
    labels = pred.label_ids
    preds = pred.predictions.argmax(-1)
    f1 = f1_score(labels, preds, average="weighted")
    acc = accuracy_score(labels, preds)
    return {"accuracy": acc, "f1": f1}
```

With the dataset and metrics ready, we just have two final things to take care of before we define the `Trainer` class:

1. Log in to our account on the Hugging Face Hub. This will allow us to push our fine-tuned model to our account on the Hub and share it with the community.
2. Define all the hyperparameters for the training run.

We'll tackle these steps in the next section.

Training the model

If you're running this code in a Jupyter notebook, you can log in to the Hub with the following helper function:

```
from huggingface_hub import notebook_login

notebook_login()
```

This will display a widget in which you can enter your username and password, or an access token with write privileges. You can find details on how to create access tokens in the Hub documentation (*https://oreil.ly/IRkN1*). If you're working in the terminal, you can log in by running the following command:

```
$ huggingface-cli login
```

To define the training parameters, we use the `TrainingArguments` class. This class stores a lot of information and gives you fine-grained control over the training and evaluation. The most important argument to specify is `output_dir`, which is where all the artifacts from training are stored. Here is an example of `TrainingArguments` in all its glory:

```
from transformers import Trainer, TrainingArguments

batch_size = 64
logging_steps = len(emotions_encoded["train"]) // batch_size
model_name = f"{model_ckpt}-finetuned-emotion"
training_args = TrainingArguments(output_dir=model_name,
                                  num_train_epochs=2,
                                  learning_rate=2e-5,
                                  per_device_train_batch_size=batch_size,
                                  per_device_eval_batch_size=batch_size,
                                  weight_decay=0.01,
                                  evaluation_strategy="epoch",
                                  disable_tqdm=False,
                                  logging_steps=logging_steps,
                                  push_to_hub=True,
                                  log_level="error")
```

Here we also set the batch size, learning rate, and number of epochs, and specify to load the best model at the end of the training run. With this final ingredient, we can instantiate and fine-tune our model with the `Trainer`:

```
from transformers import Trainer

trainer = Trainer(model=model, args=training_args,
                  compute_metrics=compute_metrics,
                  train_dataset=emotions_encoded["train"],
                  eval_dataset=emotions_encoded["validation"],
                  tokenizer=tokenizer)
trainer.train();
```

Epoch	Training Loss	Validation Loss	Accuracy	F1
1	0.840900	0.327445	0.896500	0.892285
2	0.255000	0.220472	0.922500	0.922550

Looking at the logs, we can see that our model has an F_1-score on the validation set of around 92%—this is a significant improvement over the feature-based approach!

We can take a more detailed look at the training metrics by calculating the confusion matrix. To visualize the confusion matrix, we first need to get the predictions on the validation set. The `predict()` method of the `Trainer` class returns several useful objects we can use for evaluation:

```
preds_output = trainer.predict(emotions_encoded["validation"])
```

The output of the `predict()` method is a `PredictionOutput` object that contains arrays of `predictions` and `label_ids`, along with the metrics we passed to the trainer. For example, the metrics on the validation set can be accessed as follows:

```
preds_output.metrics
```

```
{'test_loss': 0.22047173976898193,
 'test_accuracy': 0.9225,
 'test_f1': 0.9225500751072866,
 'test_runtime': 1.6357,
 'test_samples_per_second': 1222.725,
 'test_steps_per_second': 19.564}
```

It also contains the raw predictions for each class. We can decode the predictions greedily using `np.argmax()`. This yields the predicted labels and has the same format as the labels returned by the Scikit-learn models in the feature-based approach:

```
y_preds = np.argmax(preds_output.predictions, axis=1)
```

With the predictions, we can plot the confusion matrix again:

```
plot_confusion_matrix(y_preds, y_valid, labels)
```

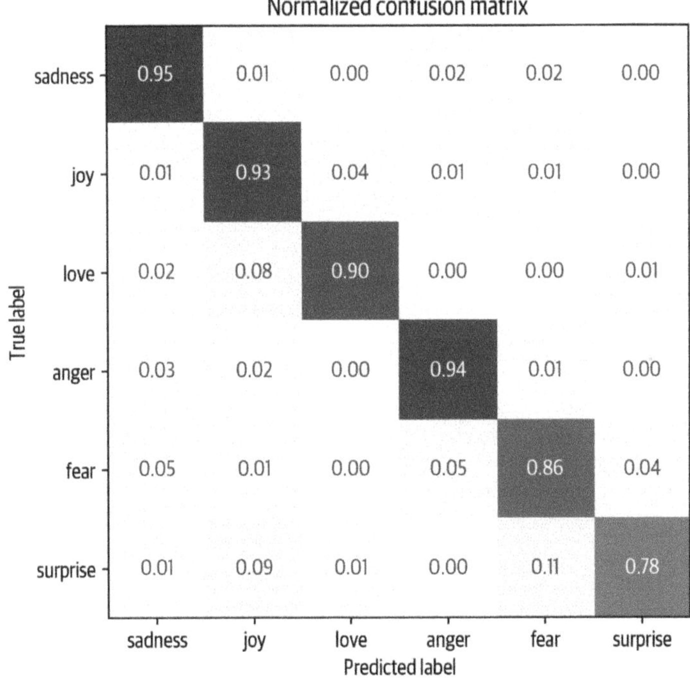

This is much closer to the ideal diagonal confusion matrix. The `love` category is still often confused with `joy`, which seems natural. `surprise` is also frequently mistaken for `joy`, or confused with `fear`. Overall the performance of the model seems quite good, but before we call it a day, let's dive a little deeper into the types of errors our model is likely to make.

Fine-Tuning with Keras

If you are using TensorFlow, it's also possible to fine-tune your models using the Keras API. The main difference from the PyTorch API is that there is no `Trainer` class, since Keras models already provide a built-in `fit()` method. To see how this works, let's first load DistilBERT as a TensorFlow model:

```
from transformers import TFAutoModelForSequenceClassification

tf_model = (TFAutoModelForSequenceClassification
            .from_pretrained(model_ckpt, num_labels=num_labels))
```

Next, we'll convert our datasets into the `tf.data.Dataset` format. Because we have already padded our tokenized inputs, we can do this conversion easily by applying the `to_tf_dataset()` method to `emotions_encoded`:

```
# The column names to convert to TensorFlow tensors
tokenizer_columns = tokenizer.model_input_names

tf_train_dataset = emotions_encoded["train"].to_tf_dataset(
    columns=tokenizer_columns, label_cols=["label"], shuffle=True,
    batch_size=batch_size)
tf_eval_dataset = emotions_encoded["validation"].to_tf_dataset(
    columns=tokenizer_columns, label_cols=["label"], shuffle=False,
    batch_size=batch_size)
```

Here we've also shuffled the training set, and defined the batch size for it and the validation set. The last thing to do is compile and train the model:

```
import tensorflow as tf

tf_model.compile(
    optimizer=tf.keras.optimizers.Adam(learning_rate=5e-5),
    loss=tf.keras.losses.SparseCategoricalCrossentropy(from_logits=True),
    metrics=tf.metrics.SparseCategoricalAccuracy())

tf_model.fit(tf_train_dataset, validation_data=tf_eval_dataset, epochs=2)
```

Error analysis

Before moving on, we should investigate our model's predictions a little bit further. A simple yet powerful technique is to sort the validation samples by the model loss. When we pass the label during the forward pass, the loss is automatically calculated and returned. Here's a function that returns the loss along with the predicted label:

```
from torch.nn.functional import cross_entropy

def forward_pass_with_label(batch):
    # Place all input tensors on the same device as the model
    inputs = {k:v.to(device) for k,v in batch.items()
```

```
            if k in tokenizer.model_input_names}

    with torch.no_grad():
        output = model(**inputs)
        pred_label = torch.argmax(output.logits, axis=-1)
        loss = cross_entropy(output.logits, batch["label"].to(device),
                             reduction="none")
    # Place outputs on CPU for compatibility with other dataset columns
    return {"loss": loss.cpu().numpy(),
            "predicted_label": pred_label.cpu().numpy()}
```

Using the `map()` method once more, we can apply this function to get the losses for all the samples:

```
# Convert our dataset back to PyTorch tensors
emotions_encoded.set_format("torch",
                            columns=["input_ids", "attention_mask", "label"])
# Compute loss values
emotions_encoded["validation"] = emotions_encoded["validation"].map(
    forward_pass_with_label, batched=True, batch_size=16)
```

Finally, we create a `DataFrame` with the texts, losses, and predicted/true labels:

```
emotions_encoded.set_format("pandas")
cols = ["text", "label", "predicted_label", "loss"]
df_test = emotions_encoded["validation"][:][cols]
df_test["label"] = df_test["label"].apply(label_int2str)
df_test["predicted_label"] = (df_test["predicted_label"]
                              .apply(label_int2str))
```

We can now easily sort `emotions_encoded` by the losses in either ascending or descending order. The goal of this exercise is to detect one of the following:

Wrong labels
: Every process that adds labels to data can be flawed. Annotators can make mistakes or disagree, while labels that are inferred from other features can be wrong. If it was easy to automatically annotate data, then we would not need a model to do it. Thus, it is normal that there are some wrongly labeled examples. With this approach, we can quickly find and correct them.

Quirks of the dataset
: Datasets in the real world are always a bit messy. When working with text, special characters or strings in the inputs can have a big impact on the model's predictions. Inspecting the model's weakest predictions can help identify such features, and cleaning the data or injecting similar examples can make the model more robust.

Let's first have a look at the data samples with the highest losses:

```
df_test.sort_values("loss", ascending=False).head(10)
```

text	label	predicted_label	loss
i feel that he was being overshadowed by the supporting characters	love	sadness	5.704531
i called myself pro life and voted for perry without knowing this information i would feel betrayed but moreover i would feel that i had betrayed god by supporting a man who mandated a barely year old vaccine for little girls putting them in danger to financially support people close to him	joy	sadness	5.484461
i guess i feel betrayed because i admired him so much and for someone to do this to his wife and kids just goes beyond the pale	joy	sadness	5.434768
i feel badly about reneging on my commitment to bring donuts to the faithful at holy family catholic church in columbus ohio	love	sadness	5.257482
i as representative of everything thats wrong with corporate america and feel that sending him to washington is a ludicrous idea	surprise	sadness	4.827708
i guess this is a memoir so it feels like that should be fine too except i dont know something about such a deep amount of self absorption made me feel uncomfortable	joy	fear	4.713047
i am going to several holiday parties and i can t wait to feel super awkward i am going to several holiday parties and i can t wait to feel super awkward a href http badplaydate	joy	sadness	4.704955
i felt ashamed of these feelings and was scared because i knew that something wrong with me and thought i might be gay	fear	sadness	4.656096
i guess we would naturally feel a sense of loneliness even the people who said unkind things to you might be missed	anger	sadness	4.593202
im lazy my characters fall into categories of smug and or blas people and their foils people who feel inconvenienced by smug and or blas people	joy	fear	4.311287

We can clearly see that the model predicted some of the labels incorrectly. On the other hand, it seems that there are quite a few examples with no clear class, which might be either mislabeled or require a new class altogether. In particular, `joy` seems to be mislabeled several times. With this information we can refine the dataset, which often can lead to as big a performance gain (or more) as having more data or larger models!

When looking at the samples with the lowest losses, we observe that the model seems to be most confident when predicting the `sadness` class. Deep learning models are exceptionally good at finding and exploiting shortcuts to get to a prediction. For this reason, it is also worth investing time into looking at the examples that the model is most confident about, so that we can be confident that the model does not improperly exploit certain features of the text. So, let's also look at the predictions with the smallest loss:

```
df_test.sort_values("loss", ascending=True).head(10)
```

text	label	predicted_label	loss
i feel try to tell me im ungrateful tell me im basically the worst daughter sister in the world	sadness	sadness	0.017331
im kinda relieve but at the same time i feel disheartened	sadness	sadness	0.017392
i and feel quite ungrateful for it but i m looking forward to summer and warmth and light nights	sadness	sadness	0.017400
i remember feeling disheartened one day when we were studying a poem really dissecting it verse by verse stanza by stanza	sadness	sadness	0.017461
i feel like an ungrateful asshole	sadness	sadness	0.017485
i leave the meeting feeling more than a little disheartened	sadness	sadness	0.017670
i am feeling a little disheartened	sadness	sadness	0.017685
i feel like i deserve to be broke with how frivolous i am	sadness	sadness	0.017888
i started this blog with pure intentions i must confess to starting to feel a little disheartened lately by the knowledge that there doesnt seem to be anybody reading it	sadness	sadness	0.017899
i feel so ungrateful to be wishing this pregnancy over now	sadness	sadness	0.017913

We now know that the `joy` is sometimes mislabeled and that the model is most confident about predicting the label `sadness`. With this information we can make targeted improvements to our dataset, and also keep an eye on the class the model seems to be very confident about.

The last step before serving the trained model is to save it for later usage. 🤗 Transformers allows us to do this in a few steps, which we'll show you in the next section.

Saving and sharing the model

The NLP community benefits greatly from sharing pretrained and fine-tuned models, and everybody can share their models with others via the Hugging Face Hub. Any community-generated model can be downloaded from the Hub just like we downloaded the DistilBERT model. With the `Trainer` API, saving and sharing a model is simple:

```
trainer.push_to_hub(commit_message="Training completed!")
```

We can also use the fine-tuned model to make predictions on new tweets. Since we've pushed our model to the Hub, we can now use it with the `pipeline()` function, just like we did in Chapter 1. First, let's load the pipeline:

```
from transformers import pipeline

# Change `transformersbook` to your Hub username
model_id = "transformersbook/distilbert-base-uncased-finetuned-emotion"
classifier = pipeline("text-classification", model=model_id)
```

Then let's test the pipeline with a sample tweet:

```
custom_tweet = "I saw a movie today and it was really good."
preds = classifier(custom_tweet, return_all_scores=True)
```

Finally, we can plot the probability for each class in a bar plot. Clearly, the model estimates that the most likely class is `joy`, which appears to be reasonable given the tweet:

```
preds_df = pd.DataFrame(preds[0])
plt.bar(labels, 100 * preds_df["score"], color='C0')
plt.title(f'"{custom_tweet}"')
plt.ylabel("Class probability (%)")
plt.show()
```

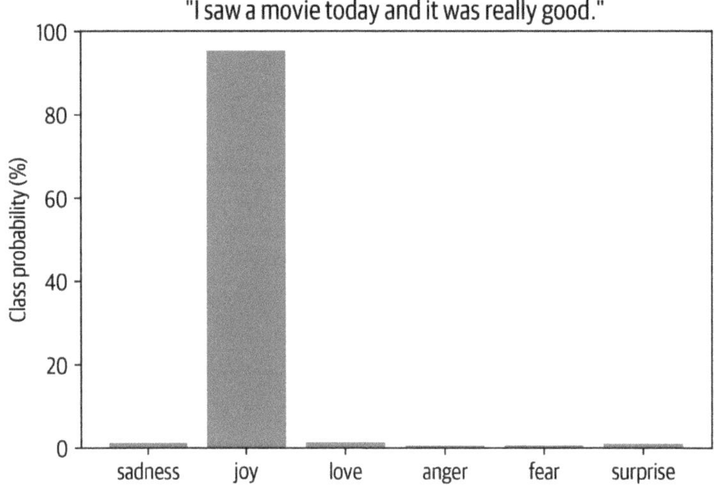

Conclusion

Congratulations, you now know how to train a transformer model to classify the emotions in tweets! We have seen two complementary approaches based on features and fine-tuning, and investigated their strengths and weaknesses.

However, this is just the first step in building a real-world application with transformer models, and we have a lot more ground to cover. Here's a list of challenges you're likely to experience in your NLP journey:

My boss wants my model in production yesterday!
: In most applications, your model doesn't just sit somewhere gathering dust—you want to make sure it's serving predictions! When a model is pushed to the Hub, an inference endpoint is automatically created that can be called with HTTP requests. We recommend checking out the documentation of the Inference API (*https://oreil.ly/XACF5*) if you want to learn more.

My users want faster predictions!
: We've already seen one approach to this problem: using DistilBERT. In Chapter 8 we'll dive into knowledge distillation (the process by which DistilBERT was created), along with other tricks to speed up your transformer models.

Can your model also do X?
: As we've alluded to in this chapter, transformers are extremely versatile. In the rest of the book we will be exploring a range of tasks, like question answering and named entity recognition, all using the same basic architecture.

None of my texts are in English!
: It turns out that transformers also come in a multilingual variety, and we'll use them in Chapter 4 to tackle several languages at once.

I don't have any labels!
: If there is very little labeled data available, fine-tuning may not be an option. In Chapter 9, we'll explore some techniques to deal with this situation.

Now that we've seen what's involved in training and sharing a transformer, in the next chapter we'll explore implementing our very own transformer model from scratch.

CHAPTER 3

Transformer Anatomy

In Chapter 2, we saw what it takes to fine-tune and evaluate a transformer. Now let's take a look at how they work under the hood. In this chapter we'll explore the main building blocks of transformer models and how to implement them using PyTorch. We'll also provide guidance on how to do the same in TensorFlow. We'll first focus on building the attention mechanism, and then add the bits and pieces necessary to make a transformer encoder work. We'll also have a brief look at the architectural differences between the encoder and decoder modules. By the end of this chapter you will be able to implement a simple transformer model yourself!

While a deep technical understanding of the Transformer architecture is generally not necessary to use 🤗 Transformers and fine-tune models for your use case, it can be helpful for comprehending and navigating the limitations of transformers and using them in new domains.

This chapter also introduces a taxonomy of transformers to help you understand the zoo of models that have emerged in recent years. Before diving into the code, let's start with an overview of the original architecture that kick-started the transformer revolution.

The Transformer Architecture

As we saw in Chapter 1, the original Transformer is based on the *encoder-decoder* architecture that is widely used for tasks like machine translation, where a sequence of words is translated from one language to another. This architecture consists of two components:

Encoder
: Converts an input sequence of tokens into a sequence of embedding vectors, often called the *hidden state* or *context*

Decoder
: Uses the encoder's hidden state to iteratively generate an output sequence of tokens, one token at a time

As illustrated in Figure 3-1, the encoder and decoder are themselves composed of several building blocks.

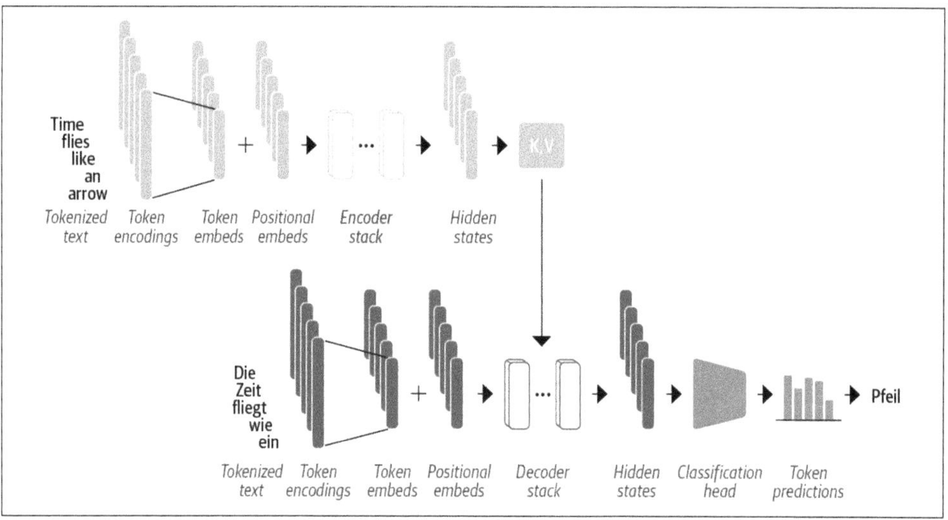

Figure 3-1. Encoder-decoder architecture of the transformer, with the encoder shown in the upper half of the figure and the decoder in the lower half

We'll look at each of the components in detail shortly, but we can already see a few things in Figure 3-1 that characterize the Transformer architecture:

- The input text is tokenized and converted to *token embeddings* using the techniques we encountered in Chapter 2. Since the attention mechanism is not aware of the relative positions of the tokens, we need a way to inject some information about token positions into the input to model the sequential nature of text. The token embeddings are thus combined with *positional embeddings* that contain positional information for each token.
- The encoder is composed of a stack of *encoder layers* or "blocks," which is analogous to stacking convolutional layers in computer vision. The same is true of the decoder, which has its own stack of *decoder layers*.
- The encoder's output is fed to each decoder layer, and the decoder then generates a prediction for the most probable next token in the sequence. The output of this step is then fed back into the decoder to generate the next token, and so on until a special end-of-sequence (EOS) token is reached. In the example from Figure 3-1, imagine the decoder has already predicted "Die" and "Zeit". Now it

gets these two as an input as well as all the encoder's outputs to predict the next token, "fliegt". In the next step the decoder gets "fliegt" as an additional input. We repeat the process until the decoder predicts the EOS token or we reached a maximum length.

The Transformer architecture was originally designed for sequence-to-sequence tasks like machine translation, but both the encoder and decoder blocks were soon adapted as standalone models. Although there are hundreds of different transformer models, most of them belong to one of three types:

Encoder-only
: These models convert an input sequence of text into a rich numerical representation that is well suited for tasks like text classification or named entity recognition. BERT and its variants, like RoBERTa and DistilBERT, belong to this class of architectures. The representation computed for a given token in this architecture depends both on the left (before the token) and the right (after the token) contexts. This is often called *bidirectional attention*.

Decoder-only
: Given a prompt of text like "Thanks for lunch, I had a…" these models will autocomplete the sequence by iteratively predicting the most probable next word. The family of GPT models belong to this class. The representation computed for a given token in this architecture depends only on the left context. This is often called *causal* or *autoregressive attention*.

Encoder-decoder
: These are used for modeling complex mappings from one sequence of text to another; they're suitable for machine translation and summarization tasks. In addition to the Transformer architecture, which as we've seen combines an encoder and a decoder, the BART and T5 models belong to this class.

In reality, the distinction between applications for decoder-only versus encoder-only architectures is a bit blurry. For example, decoder-only models like those in the GPT family can be primed for tasks like translation that are conventionally thought of as sequence-to-sequence tasks. Similarly, encoder-only models like BERT can be applied to summarization tasks that are usually associated with encoder-decoder or decoder-only models.[1]

1 Y. Liu and M. Lapata, "Text Summarization with Pretrained Encoder" (*https://arxiv.org/abs/1908.08345*), (2019).

Now that you have a high-level understanding of the Transformer architecture, let's take a closer look at the inner workings of the encoder.

The Encoder

As we saw earlier, the transformer's encoder consists of many encoder layers stacked next to each other. As illustrated in Figure 3-2, each encoder layer receives a sequence of embeddings and feeds them through the following sublayers:

- A multi-head self-attention layer
- A fully connected feed-forward layer that is applied to each input embedding

The output embeddings of each encoder layer have the same size as the inputs, and we'll soon see that the main role of the encoder stack is to "update" the input embeddings to produce representations that encode some contextual information in the sequence. For example, the word "apple" will be updated to be more "company-like" and less "fruit-like" if the words "keynote" or "phone" are close to it.

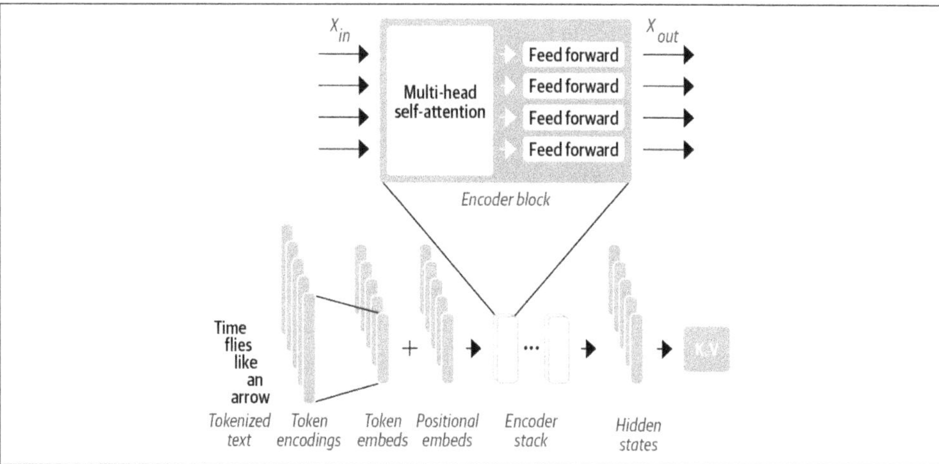

Figure 3-2. Zooming into the encoder layer

Each of these sublayers also uses skip connections and layer normalization, which are standard tricks to train deep neural networks effectively. But to truly understand what makes a transformer work, we have to go deeper. Let's start with the most important building block: the self-attention layer.

Self-Attention

As we discussed in Chapter 1, attention is a mechanism that allows neural networks to assign a different amount of weight or "attention" to each element in a sequence. For text sequences, the elements are *token embeddings* like the ones we encountered in Chapter 2, where each token is mapped to a vector of some fixed dimension. For example, in BERT each token is represented as a 768-dimensional vector. The "self" part of self-attention refers to the fact that these weights are computed for all hidden states in the same set—for example, all the hidden states of the encoder. By contrast, the attention mechanism associated with recurrent models involves computing the relevance of each encoder hidden state to the decoder hidden state at a given decoding timestep.

The main idea behind self-attention is that instead of using a fixed embedding for each token, we can use the whole sequence to compute a *weighted average* of each embedding. Another way to formulate this is to say that given a sequence of token embeddings $x_1, ..., x_n$, self-attention produces a sequence of new embeddings $x'_1, ..., x'_n$ where each x'_i is a linear combination of all the x_j:

$$x'_i = \sum_{j=1}^{n} w_{ji} x_j$$

The coefficients w_{ji} are called *attention weights* and are normalized so that $\sum_j w_{ji} = 1$. To see why averaging the token embeddings might be a good idea, consider what comes to mind when you see the word "flies". You might think of annoying insects, but if you were given more context, like "time flies like an arrow", then you would realize that "flies" refers to the verb instead. Similarly, we can create a representation for "flies" that incorporates this context by combining all the token embeddings in different proportions, perhaps by assigning a larger weight w_{ji} to the token embeddings for "time" and "arrow". Embeddings that are generated in this way are called *contextualized embeddings* and predate the invention of transformers in language models like ELMo.[2] A diagram of the process is shown in Figure 3-3, where we illustrate how, depending on the context, two different representations for "flies" can be generated via self-attention.

2 M.E. Peters et al., "Deep Contextualized Word Representations" (*https://arxiv.org/abs/1802.05365*), (2017).

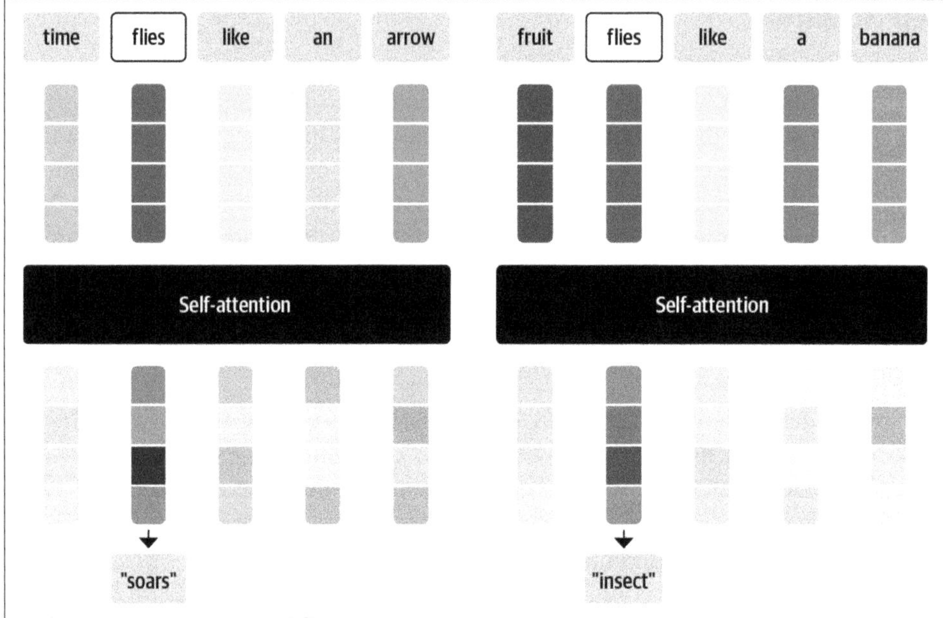

Figure 3-3. Diagram showing how self-attention updates raw token embeddings (upper) into contextualized embeddings (lower) to create representations that incorporate information from the whole sequence

Let's now take a look at how we can calculate the attention weights.

Scaled dot-product attention

There are several ways to implement a self-attention layer, but the most common one is *scaled dot-product attention*, from the paper introducing the Transformer architecture.[3] There are four main steps required to implement this mechanism:

1. Project each token embedding into three vectors called *query*, *key*, and *value*.
2. Compute attention scores. We determine how much the query and key vectors relate to each other using a *similarity function*. As the name suggests, the similarity function for scaled dot-product attention is the dot product, computed efficiently using matrix multiplication of the embeddings. Queries and keys that are similar will have a large dot product, while those that don't share much in common will have little to no overlap. The outputs from this step are called the *attention scores*, and for a sequence with n input tokens there is a corresponding $n \times n$ matrix of attention scores.

3 A. Vaswani et al., "Attention Is All You Need" (*https://arxiv.org/abs/1706.03762*), (2017).

3. Compute attention weights. Dot products can in general produce arbitrarily large numbers, which can destabilize the training process. To handle this, the attention scores are first multiplied by a scaling factor to normalize their variance and then normalized with a softmax to ensure all the column values sum to 1. The resulting $n \times n$ matrix now contains all the attention weights, w_{ji}.
4. Update the token embeddings. Once the attention weights are computed, we multiply them by the value vector $v_1, ..., v_n$ to obtain an updated representation for embedding $x_i' = \sum_j w_{ji} v_j$.

We can visualize how the attention weights are calculated with a nifty library called *BertViz* for Jupyter (*https://oreil.ly/eQK3I*). This library provides several functions that can be used to visualize different aspects of attention in transformer models. To visualize the attention weights, we can use the `neuron_view` module, which traces the computation of the weights to show how the query and key vectors are combined to produce the final weight. Since BertViz needs to tap into the attention layers of the model, we'll instantiate our BERT checkpoint with the model class from BertViz and then use the `show()` function to generate the interactive visualization for a specific encoder layer and attention head. Note that you need to click the "+" on the left to activate the attention visualization:

```
from transformers import AutoTokenizer
from bertviz.transformers_neuron_view import BertModel
from bertviz.neuron_view import show

model_ckpt = "bert-base-uncased"
tokenizer = AutoTokenizer.from_pretrained(model_ckpt)
model = BertModel.from_pretrained(model_ckpt)
text = "time flies like an arrow"
show(model, "bert", tokenizer, text, display_mode="light", layer=0, head=8)
```

From the visualization, we can see the values of the query and key vectors are represented as vertical bands, where the intensity of each band corresponds to the magnitude. The connecting lines are weighted according to the attention between the tokens, and we can see that the query vector for "flies" has the strongest overlap with the key vector for "arrow".

Demystifying Queries, Keys, and Values

The notion of query, key, and value vectors may seem a bit cryptic the first time you encounter them. Their names were inspired by information retrieval systems, but we can motivate their meaning with a simple analogy. Imagine that you're at the supermarket buying all the ingredients you need for your dinner. You have the dish's recipe, and each of the required ingredients can be thought of as a query. As you scan the shelves, you look at the labels (keys) and check whether they match an ingredient on your list (similarity function). If you have a match, then you take the item (value) from the shelf.

In this analogy, you only get one grocery item for every label that matches the ingredient. Self-attention is a more abstract and "smooth" version of this: *every* label in the supermarket matches the ingredient to the extent to which each key matches the query. So if your list includes a dozen eggs, then you might end up grabbing 10 eggs, an omelette, and a chicken wing.

Let's take a look at this process in more detail by implementing the diagram of operations to compute scaled dot-product attention, as shown in Figure 3-4.

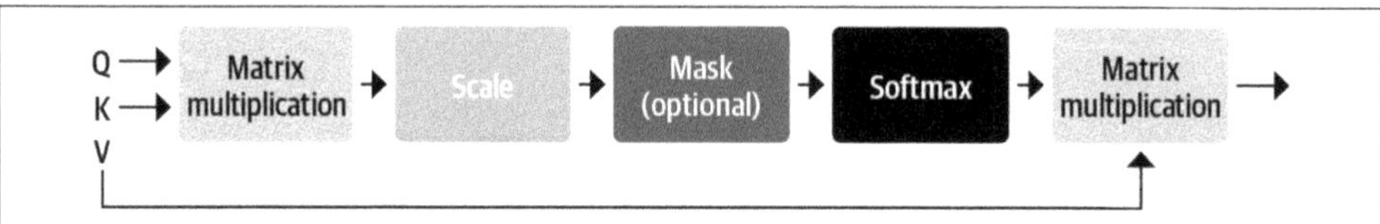

Figure 3-4. Operations in scaled dot-product attention

We will use PyTorch to implement the Transformer architecture in this chapter, but the steps in TensorFlow are analogous. We provide a mapping between the most important functions in the two frameworks in Table 3-1.

Table 3-1. PyTorch and TensorFlow (Keras) classes and methods used in this chapter

PyTorch	TensorFlow (Keras)	Creates/implements
`nn.Linear`	`keras.layers.Dense`	A dense neural network layer
`nn.Module`	`keras.layers.Layer`	The building blocks of models
`nn.Dropout`	`keras.layers.Dropout`	A dropout layer
`nn.LayerNorm`	`keras.layers.LayerNormalization`	Layer normalization
`nn.Embedding`	`keras.layers.Embedding`	An embedding layer
`nn.GELU`	`keras.activations.gelu`	The Gaussian Error Linear Unit activation function
`nn.bmm`	`tf.matmul`	Batched matrix multiplication
`model.forward`	`model.call`	The model's forward pass

The first thing we need to do is tokenize the text, so let's use our tokenizer to extract the input IDs:

```
inputs = tokenizer(text, return_tensors="pt", add_special_tokens=False)
inputs.input_ids
```

```
tensor([[ 2051, 10029,  2066,  2019,  8612]])
```

As we saw in Chapter 2, each token in the sentence has been mapped to a unique ID in the tokenizer's vocabulary. To keep things simple, we've also excluded the `[CLS]` and `[SEP]` tokens by setting `add_special_tokens=False`. Next, we need to create some dense embeddings. *Dense* in this context means that each entry in the embeddings contains a nonzero value. In contrast, the one-hot encodings we saw in Chapter 2 are *sparse*, since all entries except one are zero. In PyTorch, we can do this by using a `torch.nn.Embedding` layer that acts as a lookup table for each input ID:

```
from torch import nn
from transformers import AutoConfig

config = AutoConfig.from_pretrained(model_ckpt)
token_emb = nn.Embedding(config.vocab_size, config.hidden_size)
token_emb
```

```
Embedding(30522, 768)
```

Here we've used the `AutoConfig` class to load the *config.json* file associated with the `bert-base-uncased` checkpoint. In 🤗 Transformers, every checkpoint is assigned a configuration file that specifies various hyperparameters like `vocab_size` and `hidden_size`, which in our example shows us that each input ID will be mapped to one of the 30,522 embedding vectors stored in `nn.Embedding`, each with a size of 768. The `AutoConfig` class also stores additional metadata, such as the label names, which are used to format the model's predictions.

Note that the token embeddings at this point are independent of their context. This means that homonyms (words that have the same spelling but different meaning), like "flies" in the previous example, have the same representation. The role of the subsequent attention layers will be to mix these token embeddings to disambiguate and inform the representation of each token with the content of its context.

Now that we have our lookup table, we can generate the embeddings by feeding in the input IDs:

```
inputs_embeds = token_emb(inputs.input_ids)
inputs_embeds.size()
```

```
torch.Size([1, 5, 768])
```

This has given us a tensor of shape `[batch_size, seq_len, hidden_dim]`, just like we saw in Chapter 2. We'll postpone the positional encodings, so the next step is to create the query, key, and value vectors and calculate the attention scores using the dot product as the similarity function:

```
import torch
from math import sqrt

query = key = value = inputs_embeds
dim_k = key.size(-1)
scores = torch.bmm(query, key.transpose(1,2)) / sqrt(dim_k)
scores.size()
```

```
torch.Size([1, 5, 5])
```

This has created a 5×5 matrix of attention scores per sample in the batch. We'll see later that the query, key, and value vectors are generated by applying independent weight matrices $W_{Q,K,V}$ to the embeddings, but for now we've kept them equal for simplicity. In scaled dot-product attention, the dot products are scaled by the size of the embedding vectors so that we don't get too many large numbers during training that can cause the softmax we will apply next to saturate.

The `torch.bmm()` function performs a *batch matrix-matrix product* that simplifies the computation of the attention scores where the query and key vectors have the shape `[batch_size, seq_len, hidden_dim]`. If we ignored the batch dimension we could calculate the dot product between each query and key vector by simply transposing the key tensor to have the shape `[hidden_dim, seq_len]` and then using the matrix product to collect all the dot products in a `[seq_len, seq_len]` matrix. Since we want to do this for all sequences in the batch independently, we use `torch.bmm()`, which takes two batches of matrices and multiplies each matrix from the first batch with the corresponding matrix in the second batch.

Let's apply the softmax now:

```
import torch.nn.functional as F

weights = F.softmax(scores, dim=-1)
weights.sum(dim=-1)
```

```
tensor([[1., 1., 1., 1., 1.]], grad_fn=<SumBackward1>)
```

The final step is to multiply the attention weights by the values:

```
attn_outputs = torch.bmm(weights, value)
attn_outputs.shape
```

```
torch.Size([1, 5, 768])
```

And that's it—we've gone through all the steps to implement a simplified form of self-attention! Notice that the whole process is just two matrix multiplications and a softmax, so you can think of "self-attention" as just a fancy form of averaging.

Let's wrap these steps into a function that we can use later:

```
def scaled_dot_product_attention(query, key, value):
    dim_k = query.size(-1)
    scores = torch.bmm(query, key.transpose(1, 2)) / sqrt(dim_k)
    weights = F.softmax(scores, dim=-1)
    return torch.bmm(weights, value)
```

Our attention mechanism with equal query and key vectors will assign a very large score to identical words in the context, and in particular to the current word itself: the dot product of a query with itself is always 1. But in practice, the meaning of a word will be better informed by complementary words in the context than by identical words—for example, the meaning of "flies" is better defined by incorporating information from "time" and "arrow" than by another mention of "flies". How can we promote this behavior?

Let's allow the model to create a different set of vectors for the query, key, and value of a token by using three different linear projections to project our initial token vector into three different spaces.

Multi-headed attention

In our simple example, we only used the embeddings "as is" to compute the attention scores and weights, but that's far from the whole story. In practice, the self-attention layer applies three independent linear transformations to each embedding to generate the query, key, and value vectors. These transformations project the embeddings and each projection carries its own set of learnable parameters, which allows the self-attention layer to focus on different semantic aspects of the sequence.

It also turns out to be beneficial to have *multiple* sets of linear projections, each one representing a so-called *attention head*. The resulting *multi-head attention layer* is illustrated in Figure 3-5. But why do we need more than one attention head? The reason is that the softmax of one head tends to focus on mostly one aspect of similarity. Having several heads allows the model to focus on several aspects at once. For instance, one head can focus on subject-verb interaction, whereas another finds nearby adjectives. Obviously we don't handcraft these relations into the model, and they are fully learned from the data. If you are familiar with computer vision models you might see the resemblance to filters in convolutional neural networks, where one filter can be responsible for detecting faces and another one finds wheels of cars in images.

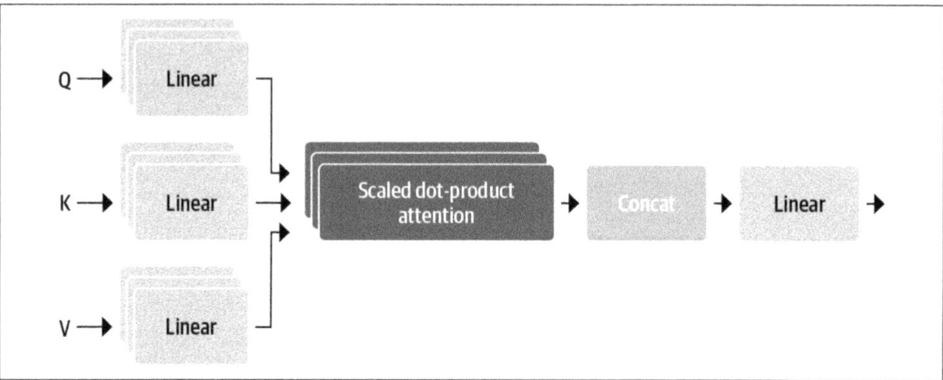

Figure 3-5. Multi-head attention

Let's implement this layer by first coding up a single attention head:

```
class AttentionHead(nn.Module):
    def __init__(self, embed_dim, head_dim):
        super().__init__()
        self.q = nn.Linear(embed_dim, head_dim)
        self.k = nn.Linear(embed_dim, head_dim)
        self.v = nn.Linear(embed_dim, head_dim)

    def forward(self, hidden_state):
        attn_outputs = scaled_dot_product_attention(
            self.q(hidden_state), self.k(hidden_state), self.v(hidden_state))
        return attn_outputs
```

Here we've initialized three independent linear layers that apply matrix multiplication to the embedding vectors to produce tensors of shape `[batch_size, seq_len, head_dim]`, where `head_dim` is the number of dimensions we are projecting into. Although `head_dim` does not have to be smaller than the number of embedding dimensions of the tokens (`embed_dim`), in practice it is chosen to be a multiple of `embed_dim` so that the computation across each head is constant. For example, BERT has 12 attention heads, so the dimension of each head is 768/12 = 64.

Now that we have a single attention head, we can concatenate the outputs of each one to implement the full multi-head attention layer:

```
class MultiHeadAttention(nn.Module):
    def __init__(self, config):
        super().__init__()
        embed_dim = config.hidden_size
        num_heads = config.num_attention_heads
        head_dim = embed_dim // num_heads
        self.heads = nn.ModuleList(
            [AttentionHead(embed_dim, head_dim) for _ in range(num_heads)]
        )
        self.output_linear = nn.Linear(embed_dim, embed_dim)
```

```
    def forward(self, hidden_state):
        x = torch.cat([h(hidden_state) for h in self.heads], dim=-1)
        x = self.output_linear(x)
        return x
```

Notice that the concatenated output from the attention heads is also fed through a final linear layer to produce an output tensor of shape `[batch_size, seq_len, hidden_dim]` that is suitable for the feed-forward network downstream. To confirm, let's see if the multi-head attention layer produces the expected shape of our inputs. We pass the configuration we loaded earlier from the pretrained BERT model when initializing the `MultiHeadAttention` module. This ensures that we use the same settings as BERT:

```
multihead_attn = MultiHeadAttention(config)
attn_output = multihead_attn(inputs_embeds)
attn_output.size()
```

```
torch.Size([1, 5, 768])
```

It works! To wrap up this section on attention, let's use BertViz again to visualize the attention for two different uses of the word "flies". Here we can use the `head_view()` function from BertViz by computing the attentions of a pretrained checkpoint and indicating where the sentence boundary lies:

```
from bertviz import head_view
from transformers import AutoModel

model = AutoModel.from_pretrained(model_ckpt, output_attentions=True)

sentence_a = "time flies like an arrow"
sentence_b = "fruit flies like a banana"

viz_inputs = tokenizer(sentence_a, sentence_b, return_tensors='pt')
attention = model(**viz_inputs).attentions
sentence_b_start = (viz_inputs.token_type_ids == 0).sum(dim=1)
tokens = tokenizer.convert_ids_to_tokens(viz_inputs.input_ids[0])

head_view(attention, tokens, sentence_b_start, heads=[8])
```

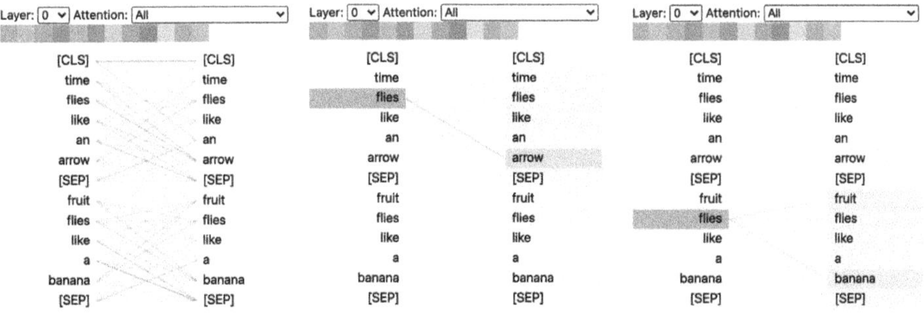

This visualization shows the attention weights as lines connecting the token whose embedding is getting updated (left) with every word that is being attended to (right). The intensity of the lines indicates the strength of the attention weights, with dark lines representing values close to 1, and faint lines representing values close to 0.

In this example, the input consists of two sentences and the `[CLS]` and `[SEP]` tokens are the special tokens in BERT's tokenizer that we encountered in Chapter 2. One thing we can see from the visualization is that the attention weights are strongest between words that belong to the same sentence, which suggests BERT can tell that it should attend to words in the same sentence. However, for the word "flies" we can see that BERT has identified "arrow" as important in the first sentence and "fruit" and "banana" in the second. These attention weights allow the model to distinguish the use of "flies" as a verb or noun, depending on the context in which it occurs!

Now that we've covered attention, let's take a look at implementing the missing piece of the encoder layer: position-wise feed-forward networks.

The Feed-Forward Layer

The feed-forward sublayer in the encoder and decoder is just a simple two-layer fully connected neural network, but with a twist: instead of processing the whole sequence of embeddings as a single vector, it processes each embedding *independently*. For this reason, this layer is often referred to as a *position-wise feed-forward layer*. You may also see it referred to as a one-dimensional convolution with a kernel size of one, typically by people with a computer vision background (e.g., the OpenAI GPT codebase uses this nomenclature). A rule of thumb from the literature is for the hidden size of the first layer to be four times the size of the embeddings, and a GELU activation function is most commonly used. This is where most of the capacity and memorization is hypothesized to happen, and it's the part that is most often scaled when scaling up the models. We can implement this as a simple `nn.Module` as follows:

```
class FeedForward(nn.Module):
    def __init__(self, config):
        super().__init__()
        self.linear_1 = nn.Linear(config.hidden_size, config.intermediate_size)
        self.linear_2 = nn.Linear(config.intermediate_size, config.hidden_size)
        self.gelu = nn.GELU()
        self.dropout = nn.Dropout(config.hidden_dropout_prob)

    def forward(self, x):
        x = self.linear_1(x)
        x = self.gelu(x)
        x = self.linear_2(x)
        x = self.dropout(x)
        return x
```

Note that a feed-forward layer such as `nn.Linear` is usually applied to a tensor of shape `(batch_size, input_dim)`, where it acts on each element of the batch dimension independently. This is actually true for any dimension except the last one, so when we pass a tensor of shape `(batch_size, seq_len, hidden_dim)` the layer is applied to all token embeddings of the batch and sequence independently, which is exactly what we want. Let's test this by passing the attention outputs:

```
feed_forward = FeedForward(config)
ff_outputs = feed_forward(attn_outputs)
ff_outputs.size()
```

```
torch.Size([1, 5, 768])
```

We now have all the ingredients to create a fully fledged transformer encoder layer! The only decision left to make is where to place the skip connections and layer normalization. Let's take a look at how this affects the model architecture.

Adding Layer Normalization

As mentioned earlier, the Transformer architecture makes use of *layer normalization* and *skip connections*. The former normalizes each input in the batch to have zero mean and unity variance. Skip connections pass a tensor to the next layer of the model without processing and add it to the processed tensor. When it comes to placing the layer normalization in the encoder or decoder layers of a transformer, there are two main choices adopted in the literature:

Post layer normalization
: This is the arrangement used in the Transformer paper; it places layer normalization in between the skip connections. This arrangement is tricky to train from scratch as the gradients can diverge. For this reason, you will often see a concept known as *learning rate warm-up*, where the learning rate is gradually increased from a small value to some maximum value during training.

Pre layer normalization
: This is the most common arrangement found in the literature; it places layer normalization within the span of the skip connections. This tends to be much more stable during training, and it does not usually require any learning rate warm-up.

The difference between the two arrangements is illustrated in Figure 3-6.

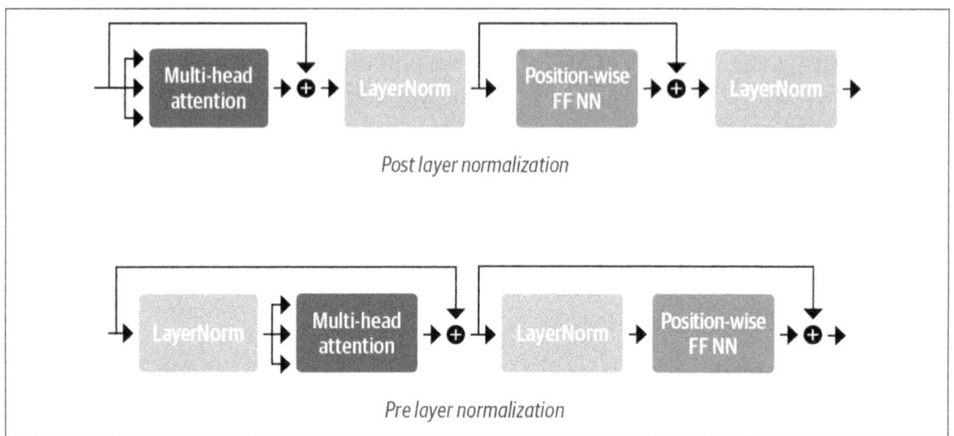

Figure 3-6. Different arrangements of layer normalization in a transformer encoder layer

We'll use the second arrangement, so we can simply stick together our building blocks as follows:

```
class TransformerEncoderLayer(nn.Module):
    def __init__(self, config):
        super().__init__()
        self.layer_norm_1 = nn.LayerNorm(config.hidden_size)
        self.layer_norm_2 = nn.LayerNorm(config.hidden_size)
        self.attention = MultiHeadAttention(config)
        self.feed_forward = FeedForward(config)

    def forward(self, x):
        # Apply layer normalization and then copy input into query, key, value
        hidden_state = self.layer_norm_1(x)
        # Apply attention with a skip connection
        x = x + self.attention(hidden_state)
        # Apply feed-forward layer with a skip connection
        x = x + self.feed_forward(self.layer_norm_2(x))
        return x
```

Let's now test this with our input embeddings:

```
encoder_layer = TransformerEncoderLayer(config)
inputs_embeds.shape, encoder_layer(inputs_embeds).size()
```

```
(torch.Size([1, 5, 768]), torch.Size([1, 5, 768]))
```

We've now implemented our very first transformer encoder layer from scratch! However, there is a caveat with the way we set up the encoder layers: they are totally invariant to the position of the tokens. Since the multi-head attention layer is effectively a fancy weighted sum, the information on token position is lost.[4]

Luckily, there is an easy trick to incorporate positional information using positional embeddings. Let's take a look.

Positional Embeddings

Positional embeddings are based on a simple, yet very effective idea: augment the token embeddings with a position-dependent pattern of values arranged in a vector. If the pattern is characteristic for each position, the attention heads and feed-forward layers in each stack can learn to incorporate positional information into their transformations.

There are several ways to achieve this, and one of the most popular approaches is to use a learnable pattern, especially when the pretraining dataset is sufficiently large. This works exactly the same way as the token embeddings, but using the position index instead of the token ID as input. With that approach, an efficient way of encoding the positions of tokens is learned during pretraining.

Let's create a custom `Embeddings` module that combines a token embedding layer that projects the `input_ids` to a dense hidden state together with the positional embedding that does the same for `position_ids`. The resulting embedding is simply the sum of both embeddings:

```
class Embeddings(nn.Module):
    def __init__(self, config):
        super().__init__()
        self.token_embeddings = nn.Embedding(config.vocab_size,
                                             config.hidden_size)
        self.position_embeddings = nn.Embedding(config.max_position_embeddings,
                                                config.hidden_size)
        self.layer_norm = nn.LayerNorm(config.hidden_size, eps=1e-12)
        self.dropout = nn.Dropout()

    def forward(self, input_ids):
        # Create position IDs for input sequence
        seq_length = input_ids.size(1)
        position_ids = torch.arange(seq_length, dtype=torch.long).unsqueeze(0)
        # Create token and position embeddings
        token_embeddings = self.token_embeddings(input_ids)
        position_embeddings = self.position_embeddings(position_ids)
        # Combine token and position embeddings
        embeddings = token_embeddings + position_embeddings
        embeddings = self.layer_norm(embeddings)
```

4 In fancier terminology, the self-attention and feed-forward layers are said to be *permutation equivariant*—if the input is permuted then the corresponding output of the layer is permuted in exactly the same way.

```
        embeddings = self.dropout(embeddings)
        return embeddings

embedding_layer = Embeddings(config)
embedding_layer(inputs.input_ids).size()
```

```
torch.Size([1, 5, 768])
```

We see that the embedding layer now creates a single, dense embedding for each token.

While learnable position embeddings are easy to implement and widely used, there are some alternatives:

Absolute positional representations
: Transformer models can use static patterns consisting of modulated sine and cosine signals to encode the positions of the tokens. This works especially well when there are not large volumes of data available.

Relative positional representations
: Although absolute positions are important, one can argue that when computing an embedding, the surrounding tokens are most important. Relative positional representations follow that intuition and encode the relative positions between tokens. This cannot be set up by just introducing a new relative embedding layer at the beginning, since the relative embedding changes for each token depending on where from the sequence we are attending to it. Instead, the attention mechanism itself is modified with additional terms that take the relative position between tokens into account. Models such as DeBERTa use such representations.[5]

Let's put all of this together now by building the full transformer encoder combining the embeddings with the encoder layers:

```
class TransformerEncoder(nn.Module):
    def __init__(self, config):
        super().__init__()
        self.embeddings = Embeddings(config)
        self.layers = nn.ModuleList([TransformerEncoderLayer(config)
                                     for _ in range(config.num_hidden_layers)])

    def forward(self, x):
        x = self.embeddings(x)
        for layer in self.layers:
            x = layer(x)
        return x
```

Let's check the output shapes of the encoder:

5 By combining the idea of absolute and relative positional representations, rotary position embeddings achieve excellent results on many tasks. GPT-Neo is an example of a model with rotary position embeddings.

```
encoder = TransformerEncoder(config)
encoder(inputs.input_ids).size()
```

```
torch.Size([1, 5, 768])
```

We can see that we get a hidden state for each token in the batch. This output format makes the architecture very flexible, and we can easily adapt it for various applications such as predicting missing tokens in masked language modeling or predicting the start and end position of an answer in question answering. In the following section we'll see how we can build a classifier like the one we used in Chapter 2.

Adding a Classification Head

Transformer models are usually divided into a task-independent body and a task-specific head. We'll encounter this pattern again in Chapter 4 when we look at the design pattern of 🤗 Transformers. What we have built so far is the body, so if we wish to build a text classifier, we will need to attach a classification head to that body. We have a hidden state for each token, but we only need to make one prediction. There are several options to approach this. Traditionally, the first token in such models is used for the prediction and we can attach a dropout and a linear layer to make a classification prediction. The following class extends the existing encoder for sequence classification:

```
class TransformerForSequenceClassification(nn.Module):
    def __init__(self, config):
        super().__init__()
        self.encoder = TransformerEncoder(config)
        self.dropout = nn.Dropout(config.hidden_dropout_prob)
        self.classifier = nn.Linear(config.hidden_size, config.num_labels)

    def forward(self, x):
        x = self.encoder(x)[:, 0, :] # select hidden state of [CLS] token
        x = self.dropout(x)
        x = self.classifier(x)
        return x
```

Before initializing the model we need to define how many classes we would like to predict:

```
config.num_labels = 3
encoder_classifier = TransformerForSequenceClassification(config)
encoder_classifier(inputs.input_ids).size()
```

```
torch.Size([1, 3])
```

That is exactly what we have been looking for. For each example in the batch we get the unnormalized logits for each class in the output. This corresponds to the BERT model that we used in Chapter 2 to detect emotions in tweets.

This concludes our analysis of the encoder and how we can combine it with a task-specific head. Let's now cast our attention (pun intended!) to the decoder.

The Decoder

As illustrated in Figure 3-7, the main difference between the decoder and encoder is that the decoder has *two* attention sublayers:

Masked multi-head self-attention layer
: Ensures that the tokens we generate at each timestep are only based on the past outputs and the current token being predicted. Without this, the decoder could cheat during training by simply copying the target translations; masking the inputs ensures the task is not trivial.

Encoder-decoder attention layer
: Performs multi-head attention over the output key and value vectors of the encoder stack, with the intermediate representations of the decoder acting as the queries.[6] This way the encoder-decoder attention layer learns how to relate tokens from two different sequences, such as two different languages. The decoder has access to the encoder keys and values in each block.

Let's take a look at the modifications we need to make to include masking in our self-attention layer, and leave the implementation of the encoder-decoder attention layer as a homework problem. The trick with masked self-attention is to introduce a *mask matrix* with ones on the lower diagonal and zeros above:

```
seq_len = inputs.input_ids.size(-1)
mask = torch.tril(torch.ones(seq_len, seq_len)).unsqueeze(0)
mask[0]
```

```
tensor([[1., 0., 0., 0., 0.],
        [1., 1., 0., 0., 0.],
        [1., 1., 1., 0., 0.],
        [1., 1., 1., 1., 0.],
        [1., 1., 1., 1., 1.]])
```

Here we've used PyTorch's `tril()` function to create the lower triangular matrix. Once we have this mask matrix, we can prevent each attention head from peeking at future tokens by using `Tensor.masked_fill()` to replace all the zeros with negative infinity:

```
scores.masked_fill(mask == 0, -float("inf"))
```

6 Note that unlike the self-attention layer, the key and query vectors in encoder-decoder attention can have different lengths. This is because the encoder and decoder inputs will generally involve sequences of differing length. As a result, the matrix of attention scores in this layer is rectangular, not square.

```
tensor([[[26.8082,    -inf,    -inf,    -inf,    -inf],
         [-0.6981, 26.9043,    -inf,    -inf,    -inf],
         [-2.3190,  1.2928, 27.8710,    -inf,    -inf],
         [-0.5897,  0.3497, -0.3807, 27.5488,    -inf],
         [ 0.5275,  2.0493, -0.4869,  1.6100, 29.0893]]],
       grad_fn=<MaskedFillBackward0>)
```

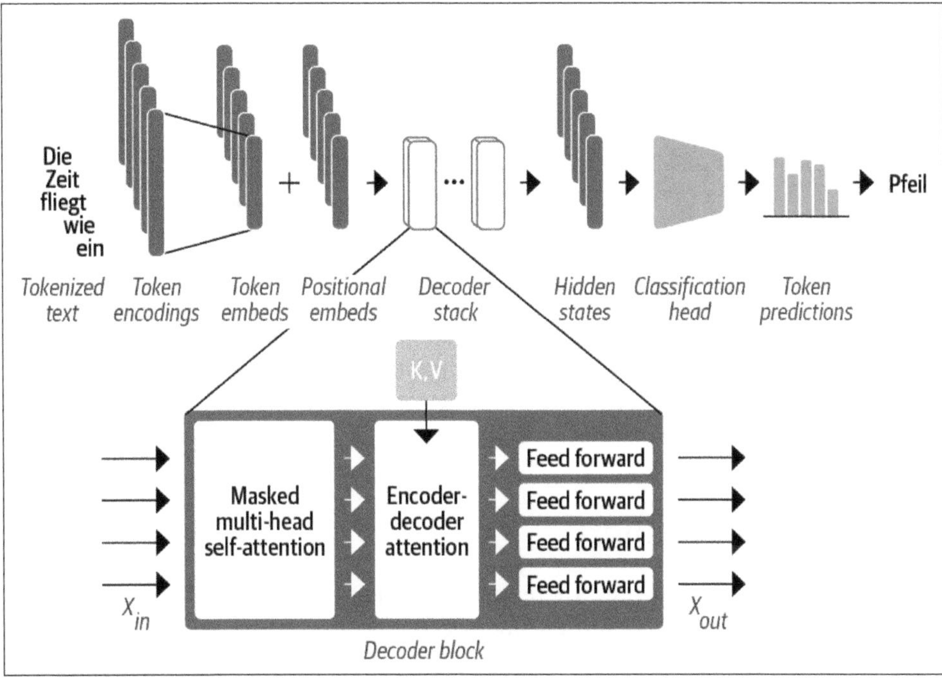

Figure 3-7. Zooming into the transformer decoder layer

By setting the upper values to negative infinity, we guarantee that the attention weights are all zero once we take the softmax over the scores because $e^{-\infty} = 0$ (recall that softmax calculates the normalized exponential). We can easily include this masking behavior with a small change to our scaled dot-product attention function that we implemented earlier in this chapter:

```
def scaled_dot_product_attention(query, key, value, mask=None):
    dim_k = query.size(-1)
    scores = torch.bmm(query, key.transpose(1, 2)) / sqrt(dim_k)
    if mask is not None:
        scores = scores.masked_fill(mask == 0, float("-inf"))
    weights = F.softmax(scores, dim=-1)
    return weights.bmm(value)
```

From here it is a simple matter to build up the decoder layer; we point the reader to the excellent implementation of minGPT (*https://oreil.ly/kwsOP*) by Andrej Karpathy for details.

We've given you a lot of technical information here, but now you should have a good understanding of how every piece of the Transformer architecture works. Before we move on to building models for tasks more advanced than text classification, let's round out the chapter by stepping back a bit and looking at the landscape of different transformer models and how they relate to each other.

Demystifying Encoder-Decoder Attention

Let's see if we can shed some light on the mysteries of encoder-decoder attention. Imagine you (the decoder) are in class taking an exam. Your task is to predict the next word based on the previous words (decoder inputs), which sounds simple but is incredibly hard (try it yourself and predict the next words in a passage of this book). Fortunately, your neighbor (the encoder) has the full text. Unfortunately, they're a foreign exchange student and the text is in their mother tongue. Cunning students that you are, you figure out a way to cheat anyway. You draw a little cartoon illustrating the text you already have (the query) and give it to your neighbor. They try to figure out which passage matches that description (the key), draw a cartoon describing the word following that passage (the value), and pass that back to you. With this system in place, you ace the exam.

Meet the Transformers

As you've seen in this chapter, there are three main architectures for transformer models: encoders, decoders, and encoder-decoders. The initial success of the early transformer models triggered a Cambrian explosion in model development as researchers built models on various datasets of different size and nature, used new pretraining objectives, and tweaked the architecture to further improve performance. Although the zoo of models is still growing fast, they can still be divided into these three categories.

In this section we'll provide a brief overview of the most important transformer models in each class. Let's start by taking a look at the transformer family tree.

The Transformer Tree of Life

Over time, each of the three main architectures has undergone an evolution of its own. This is illustrated in Figure 3-8, which shows a few of the most prominent models and their descendants.

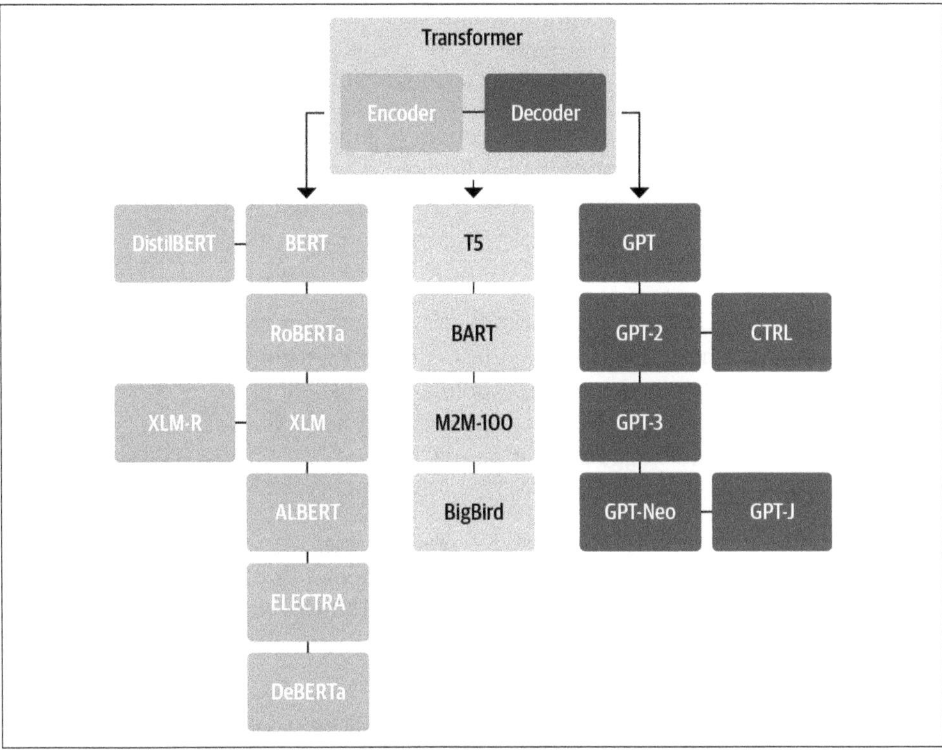

Figure 3-8. An overview of some of the most prominent transformer architectures

With over 50 different architectures included in 🤗 Transformers, this family tree by no means provides a complete overview of all the ones that exist: it simply highlights a few of the architectural milestones. We've covered the original Transformer architecture in depth in this chapter, so let's take a closer look at some of the key descendants, starting with the encoder branch.

The Encoder Branch

The first encoder-only model based on the Transformer architecture was BERT. At the time it was published, it outperformed all the state-of-the-art models on the popular GLUE benchmark,[7] which measures natural language understanding (NLU) across several tasks of varying difficulty. Subsequently, the pretraining objective and the architecture of BERT have been adapted to further improve performance. Encoder-only models still dominate research and industry on NLU tasks such as text

7 A. Wang et al., "GLUE: A Multi-Task Benchmark and Analysis Platform for Natural Language Understanding" (*https://arxiv.org/abs/1804.07461*), (2018).

classification, named entity recognition, and question answering. Let's have a brief look at the BERT model and its variants:

BERT
: BERT is pretrained with the two objectives of predicting masked tokens in texts and determining if one text passage is likely to follow another.[8] The former task is called *masked language modeling* (MLM) and the latter *next sentence prediction* (NSP).

DistilBERT
: Although BERT delivers great results, it's size can make it tricky to deploy in environments where low latencies are required. By using a technique known as knowledge distillation during pretraining, DistilBERT achieves 97% of BERT's performance while using 40% less memory and being 60% faster.[9] You can find more details on knowledge distillation in Chapter 8.

RoBERTa
: A study following the release of BERT revealed that its performance can be further improved by modifying the pretraining scheme. RoBERTa is trained longer, on larger batches with more training data, and it drops the NSP task.[10] Together, these changes significantly improve its performance compared to the original BERT model.

XLM
: Several pretraining objectives for building multilingual models were explored in the work on the cross-lingual language model (XLM),[11] including the autoregressive language modeling from GPT-like models and MLM from BERT. In addition, the authors of the paper on XLM pretraining introduced *translation language modeling* (TLM), which is an extension of MLM to multiple language inputs. Experimenting with these pretraining tasks, they achieved state-of-the-art results on several multilingual NLU benchmarks as well as on translation tasks.

XLM-RoBERTa
: Following the work of XLM and RoBERTa, the XLM-RoBERTa or XLM-R model takes multilingual pretraining one step further by massively upscaling the

---

8 J. Devlin et al., "BERT: Pre-Training of Deep Bidirectional Transformers for Language Understanding" (*https://arxiv.org/abs/1810.04805*), (2018).

9 V. Sanh et al., "DistilBERT, a Distilled Version of BERT: Smaller, Faster, Cheaper and Lighter" (*https://arxiv.org/abs/1910.01108*), (2019).

10 Y. Liu et al., "RoBERTa: A Robustly Optimized BERT Pretraining Approach" (*https://arxiv.org/abs/1907.11692*), (2019).

11 G. Lample, and A. Conneau, "Cross-Lingual Language Model Pretraining" (*https://arxiv.org/abs/1901.07291*), (2019).

training data.[12] Using the Common Crawl corpus (*https://commoncrawl.org*), its developers created a dataset with 2.5 terabytes of text; they then trained an encoder with MLM on this dataset. Since the dataset only contains data without parallel texts (i.e., translations), the TLM objective of XLM was dropped. This approach beats XLM and multilingual BERT variants by a large margin, especially on low-resource languages.

ALBERT
The ALBERT model introduced three changes to make the encoder architecture more efficient.[13] First, it decouples the token embedding dimension from the hidden dimension, thus allowing the embedding dimension to be small and thereby saving parameters, especially when the vocabulary gets large. Second, all layers share the same parameters, which decreases the number of effective parameters even further. Finally, the NSP objective is replaced with a sentence-ordering prediction: the model needs to predict whether or not the order of two consecutive sentences was swapped rather than predicting if they belong together at all. These changes make it possible to train even larger models with fewer parameters and reach superior performance on NLU tasks.

ELECTRA
One limitation of the standard MLM pretraining objective is that at each training step only the representations of the masked tokens are updated, while the other input tokens are not. To address this issue, ELECTRA uses a two-model approach:[14] the first model (which is typically small) works like a standard masked language model and predicts masked tokens. The second model, called the *discriminator*, is then tasked to predict which of the tokens in the first model's output were originally masked. Therefore, the discriminator needs to make a binary classification for every token, which makes training 30 times more efficient. For downstream tasks the discriminator is fine-tuned like a standard BERT model.

DeBERTa
The DeBERTa model introduces two architectural changes.[15] First, each token is represented as two vectors: one for the content, the other for relative position. By

12 A. Conneau et al., "Unsupervised Cross-Lingual Representation Learning at Scale" (*https://arxiv.org/abs/1911.02116*), (2019).

13 Z. Lan et al., "ALBERT: A Lite BERT for Self-Supervised Learning of Language Representations" (*https://arxiv.org/abs/1909.11942*), (2019).

14 K. Clark et al., "ELECTRA: Pre-Training Text Encoders as Discriminators Rather Than Generators" (*https://arxiv.org/abs/2003.10555*), (2020).

15 P. He et al., "DeBERTa: Decoding-Enhanced BERT with Disentangled Attention" (*https://arxiv.org/abs/2006.03654*), (2020).

disentangling the tokens' content from their relative positions, the self-attention layers can better model the dependency of nearby token pairs. On the other hand, the absolute position of a word is also important, especially for decoding. For this reason, an absolute position embedding is added just before the softmax layer of the token decoding head. DeBERTa is the first model (as an ensemble) to beat the human baseline on the SuperGLUE benchmark,[16] a more difficult version of GLUE consisting of several subtasks used to measure NLU performance.

Now that we've highlighted some of the major encoder-only architectures, let's take a look at the decoder-only models.

The Decoder Branch

The progress on transformer decoder models has been spearheaded to a large extent by OpenAI. These models are exceptionally good at predicting the next word in a sequence and are thus mostly used for text generation tasks (see Chapter 5 for more details). Their progress has been fueled by using larger datasets and scaling the language models to larger and larger sizes. Let's have a look at the evolution of these fascinating generation models:

GPT
: The introduction of GPT combined two key ideas in NLP:[17] the novel and efficient transformer decoder architecture, and transfer learning. In that setup, the model was pretrained by predicting the next word based on the previous ones. The model was trained on the BookCorpus and achieved great results on downstream tasks such as classification.

GPT-2
: Inspired by the success of the simple and scalable pretraining approach, the original model and training set were upscaled to produce GPT-2.[18] This model is able to produce long sequences of coherent text. Due to concerns about possible misuse, the model was released in a staged fashion, with smaller models being published first and the full model later.

CTRL
: Models like GPT-2 can continue an input sequence (also called a *prompt*). However, the user has little control over the style of the generated sequence. The

16 A. Wang et al., "SuperGLUE: A Stickier Benchmark for General-Purpose Language Understanding Systems" (*https://arxiv.org/abs/1905.00537*), (2019).

17 A. Radford et al., "Improving Language Understanding by Generative Pre-Training" (*https://openai.com/blog/language-unsupervised*), OpenAI (2018).

18 A. Radford et al., "Language Models Are Unsupervised Multitask Learners" (*https://openai.com/blog/better-language-models*), OpenAI (2019).

Conditional Transformer Language (CTRL) model addresses this issue by adding "control tokens" at the beginning of the sequence.[19] These allow the style of the generated text to be controlled, which allows for diverse generation.

GPT-3

Following the success of scaling GPT up to GPT-2, a thorough analysis on the behavior of language models at different scales revealed that there are simple power laws that govern the relation between compute, dataset size, model size, and the performance of a language model.[20] Inspired by these insights, GPT-2 was upscaled by a factor of 100 to yield GPT-3,[21] with 175 billion parameters. Besides being able to generate impressively realistic text passages, the model also exhibits few-shot learning capabilities: with a few examples of a novel task such as translating text to code, the model is able to accomplish the task on new examples. OpenAI has not open-sourced this model, but provides an interface through the OpenAI API (*https://oreil.ly/SEGRW*).

GPT-Neo/GPT-J-6B

GPT-Neo and GPT-J-6B are GPT-like models that were trained by EleutherAI (*https://eleuther.ai*), a collective of researchers who aim to re-create and release GPT-3 scale models.[22] The current models are smaller variants of the full 175-billion-parameter model, with 1.3, 2.7, and 6 billion parameters, and are competitive with the smaller GPT-3 models OpenAI offers.

The final branch in the transformers tree of life is the encoder-decoder models. Let's take a look.

The Encoder-Decoder Branch

Although it has become common to build models using a single encoder or decoder stack, there are several encoder-decoder variants of the Transformer architecture that have novel applications across both NLU and NLG domains:

19 N.S. Keskar et al., "CTRL: A Conditional Transformer Language Model for Controllable Generation" (*https://arxiv.org/abs/1909.05858*), (2019).

20 J. Kaplan et al., "Scaling Laws for Neural Language Models" (*https://arxiv.org/abs/2001.08361*), (2020).

21 T. Brown et al., "Language Models Are Few-Shot Learners" (*https://arxiv.org/abs/2005.14165*), (2020).

22 S. Black et al., "GPT-Neo: Large Scale Autoregressive Language Modeling with Mesh-TensorFlow" (*https://doi.org/10.5281/zenodo.5297715*), (2021); B. Wang and A. Komatsuzaki, "GPT-J-6B: A 6 Billion Parameter Autoregressive Language Model" (*https://github.com/kingoflolz/mesh-transformer-jax*), (2021).

T5

The T5 model unifies all NLU and NLG tasks by converting them into text-to-text tasks.[23] All tasks are framed as sequence-to-sequence tasks, where adopting an encoder-decoder architecture is natural. For text classification problems, for example, this means that the text is used as the encoder input and the decoder has to generate the label as normal text instead of a class. We will look at this in more detail in Chapter 6. The T5 architecture uses the original Transformer architecture. Using the large crawled C4 dataset, the model is pretrained with masked language modeling as well as the SuperGLUE tasks by translating all of them to text-to-text tasks. The largest model with 11 billion parameters yielded state-of-the-art results on several benchmarks.

BART

BART combines the pretraining procedures of BERT and GPT within the encoder-decoder architecture.[24] The input sequences undergo one of several possible transformations, from simple masking to sentence permutation, token deletion, and document rotation. These modified inputs are passed through the encoder, and the decoder has to reconstruct the original texts. This makes the model more flexible as it is possible to use it for NLU as well as NLG tasks, and it achieves state-of-the-art-performance on both.

M2M-100

Conventionally a translation model is built for one language pair and translation direction. Naturally, this does not scale to many languages, and in addition there might be shared knowledge between language pairs that could be leveraged for translation between rare languages. M2M-100 is the first translation model that can translate between any of 100 languages.[25] This allows for high-quality translations between rare and underrepresented languages. The model uses prefix tokens (similar to the special `[CLS]` token) to indicate the source and target language.

BigBird

One main limitation of transformer models is the maximum context size, due to the quadratic memory requirements of the attention mechanism. BigBird addresses this issue by using a sparse form of attention that scales linearly.[26] This

---

23 C. Raffel et al., "Exploring the Limits of Transfer Learning with a Unified Text-to-Text Transformer" (*https://arxiv.org/abs/1910.10683*), (2019).

24 M. Lewis et al., "BART: Denoising Sequence-to-Sequence Pre-Training for Natural Language Generation, Translation, and Comprehension" (*https://arxiv.org/abs/1910.13461*), (2019).

25 A. Fan et al., "Beyond English-Centric Multilingual Machine Translation" (*https://arxiv.org/abs/2010.11125*), (2020).

26 M. Zaheer et al., "Big Bird: Transformers for Longer Sequences" (*https://arxiv.org/abs/2007.14062*), (2020).

allows for the drastic scaling of contexts from 512 tokens in most BERT models to 4,096 in BigBird. This is especially useful in cases where long dependencies need to be conserved, such as in text summarization.

Pretrained checkpoints of all models that we have seen in this section are available on the Hugging Face Hub (*https://oreil.ly/EIOrN*) and can be fine-tuned to your use case with 🤗 Transformers, as described in the previous chapter.

Conclusion

In this chapter we started at the heart of the Transformer architecture with a deep dive into self-attention, and we subsequently added all the necessary parts to build a transformer encoder model. We added embedding layers for tokens and positional information, we built in a feed-forward layer to complement the attention heads, and finally we added a classification head to the model body to make predictions. We also had a look at the decoder side of the Transformer architecture, and concluded the chapter with an overview of the most important model architectures.

Now that you have a better understanding of the underlying principles, let's go beyond simple classification and build a multilingual named entity recognition model.

CHAPTER 4

Multilingual Named Entity Recognition

So far in this book we have applied transformers to solve NLP tasks on English corpora—but what do you do when your documents are written in Greek, Swahili, or Klingon? One approach is to search the Hugging Face Hub for a suitable pretrained language model and fine-tune it on the task at hand. However, these pretrained models tend to exist only for "high-resource" languages like German, Russian, or Mandarin, where plenty of webtext is available for pretraining. Another common challenge arises when your corpus is multilingual: maintaining multiple monolingual models in production will not be any fun for you or your engineering team.

Fortunately, there is a class of multilingual transformers that come to the rescue. Like BERT, these models use masked language modeling as a pretraining objective, but they are trained jointly on texts in over one hundred languages. By pretraining on huge corpora across many languages, these multilingual transformers enable *zero-shot cross-lingual transfer*. This means that a model that is fine-tuned on one language can be applied to others without any further training! This also makes these models well suited for "code-switching," where a speaker alternates between two or more languages or dialects in the context of a single conversation.

In this chapter we will explore how a single transformer model called XLM-RoBERTa (introduced in Chapter 3)[1] can be fine-tuned to perform named entity recognition (NER) across several languages. As we saw in Chapter 1, NER is a common NLP task that identifies entities like people, organizations, or locations in text. These entities can be used for various applications such as gaining insights from company documents, augmenting the quality of search engines, or simply building a structured database from a corpus.

1 A. Conneau et al., "Unsupervised Cross-Lingual Representation Learning at Scale" (*https://arxiv.org/abs/1911.02116*), (2019).

For this chapter let's assume that we want to perform NER for a customer based in Switzerland, where there are four national languages (with English often serving as a bridge between them). Let's start by getting a suitable multilingual corpus for this problem.

Zero-shot transfer or *zero-shot learning* usually refers to the task of training a model on one set of labels and then evaluating it on a different set of labels. In the context of transformers, zero-shot learning may also refer to situations where a language model like GPT-3 is evaluated on a downstream task that it wasn't even fine-tuned on.

The Dataset

In this chapter we will be using a subset of the Cross-lingual TRansfer Evaluation of Multilingual Encoders (XTREME) benchmark called WikiANN or PAN-X.[2] This dataset consists of Wikipedia articles in many languages, including the four most commonly spoken languages in Switzerland: German (62.9%), French (22.9%), Italian (8.4%), and English (5.9%). Each article is annotated with `LOC` (location), `PER` (person), and `ORG` (organization) tags in the "inside-outside-beginning" (IOB2) format (*https://oreil.ly/yXMUn*). In this format, a `B-` prefix indicates the beginning of an entity, and consecutive tokens belonging to the same entity are given an `I-` prefix. An `O` tag indicates that the token does not belong to any entity. For example, the following sentence:

> Jeff Dean is a computer scientist at Google in California

would be labeled in IOB2 format as shown in Table 4-1.

Table 4-1. An example of a sequence annotated with named entities

Tokens	Jeff	Dean	is	a	computer	scientist	at	Google	in	California
Tags	B-PER	I-PER	O	O	O	O	O	B-ORG	O	B-LOC

To load one of the PAN-X subsets in XTREME, we'll need to know which *dataset configuration* to pass the `load_dataset()` function. Whenever you're dealing with a dataset that has multiple domains, you can use the `get_dataset_config_names()` function to find out which subsets are available:

---

2 J. Hu et al., "XTREME: A Massively Multilingual Multi-Task Benchmark for Evaluating Cross-Lingual Generalization" (*https://arxiv.org/abs/2003.11080*), (2020); X. Pan et al., "Cross-Lingual Name Tagging and Linking for 282 Languages," *Proceedings of the 55th Annual Meeting of the Association for Computational Linguistics* 1 (July 2017): 1946–1958, *http://dx.doi.org/10.18653/v1/P17-1178*.

```
from datasets import get_dataset_config_names

xtreme_subsets = get_dataset_config_names("xtreme")
print(f"XTREME has {len(xtreme_subsets)} configurations")
```

```
XTREME has 183 configurations
```

Whoa, that's a lot of configurations! Let's narrow the search by just looking for the configurations that start with "PAN":

```
panx_subsets = [s for s in xtreme_subsets if s.startswith("PAN")]
panx_subsets[:3]
```

```
['PAN-X.af', 'PAN-X.ar', 'PAN-X.bg']
```

OK, it seems we've identified the syntax of the PAN-X subsets: each one has a two-letter suffix that appears to be an ISO 639-1 language code (*https://oreil.ly/R8XNu*). This means that to load the German corpus, we pass the `de` code to the `name` argument of `load_dataset()` as follows:

```
from datasets import load_dataset

load_dataset("xtreme", name="PAN-X.de")
```

To make a realistic Swiss corpus, we'll sample the German (`de`), French (`fr`), Italian (`it`), and English (`en`) corpora from PAN-X according to their spoken proportions. This will create a language imbalance that is very common in real-world datasets, where acquiring labeled examples in a minority language can be expensive due to the lack of domain experts who are fluent in that language. This imbalanced dataset will simulate a common situation when working on multilingual applications, and we'll see how we can build a model that works on all languages.

To keep track of each language, let's create a Python `defaultdict` that stores the language code as the key and a PAN-X corpus of type `DatasetDict` as the value:

```
from collections import defaultdict
from datasets import DatasetDict

langs = ["de", "fr", "it", "en"]
fracs = [0.629, 0.229, 0.084, 0.059]
# Return a DatasetDict if a key doesn't exist
panx_ch = defaultdict(DatasetDict)

for lang, frac in zip(langs, fracs):
    # Load monolingual corpus
    ds = load_dataset("xtreme", name=f"PAN-X.{lang}")
    # Shuffle and downsample each split according to spoken proportion
    for split in ds:
        panx_ch[lang][split] = (
            ds[split]
            .shuffle(seed=0)
            .select(range(int(frac * ds[split].num_rows))))
```

Here we've used the `shuffle()` method to make sure we don't accidentally bias our dataset splits, while `select()` allows us to downsample each corpus according to the values in `fracs`. Let's have a look at how many examples we have per language in the training sets by accessing the `Dataset.num_rows` attribute:

```
import pandas as pd

pd.DataFrame({lang: [panx_ch[lang]["train"].num_rows] for lang in langs},
             index=["Number of training examples"])
```

	de	fr	it	en
Number of training examples	12580	4580	1680	1180

By design, we have more examples in German than all other languages combined, so we'll use it as a starting point from which to perform zero-shot cross-lingual transfer to French, Italian, and English. Let's inspect one of the examples in the German corpus:

```
element = panx_ch["de"]["train"][0]
for key, value in element.items():
    print(f"{key}: {value}")
```

```
langs: ['de', 'de', 'de', 'de', 'de', 'de', 'de', 'de', 'de', 'de', 'de', 'de']
ner_tags: [0, 0, 0, 0, 5, 6, 0, 0, 5, 5, 6, 0]
tokens: ['2.000', 'Einwohnern', 'an', 'der', 'Danziger', 'Bucht', 'in', 'der',
'polnischen', 'Woiwodschaft', 'Pommern', '.']
```

As with our previous encounters with `Dataset` objects, the keys of our example correspond to the column names of an Arrow table, while the values denote the entries in each column. In particular, we see that the `ner_tags` column corresponds to the mapping of each entity to a class ID. This is a bit cryptic to the human eye, so let's create a new column with the familiar `LOC`, `PER`, and `ORG` tags. To do this, the first thing to notice is that our `Dataset` object has a `features` attribute that specifies the underlying data types associated with each column:

```
for key, value in panx_ch["de"]["train"].features.items():
    print(f"{key}: {value}")
```

```
tokens: Sequence(feature=Value(dtype='string', id=None), length=-1, id=None)
ner_tags: Sequence(feature=ClassLabel(num_classes=7, names=['O', 'B-PER',
'I-PER', 'B-ORG', 'I-ORG', 'B-LOC', 'I-LOC'], names_file=None, id=None),
length=-1, id=None)
langs: Sequence(feature=Value(dtype='string', id=None), length=-1, id=None)
```

The `Sequence` class specifies that the field contains a list of features, which in the case of `ner_tags` corresponds to a list of `ClassLabel` features. Let's pick out this feature from the training set as follows:

```
tags = panx_ch["de"]["train"].features["ner_tags"].feature
print(tags)
```

```
ClassLabel(num_classes=7, names=['O', 'B-PER', 'I-PER', 'B-ORG', 'I-ORG',
'B-LOC', 'I-LOC'], names_file=None, id=None)
```

We can use the `ClassLabel.int2str()` method that we encountered in Chapter 2 to create a new column in our training set with class names for each tag. We'll use the `map()` method to return a `dict` with the key corresponding to the new column name and the value as a `list` of class names:

```
def create_tag_names(batch):
    return {"ner_tags_str": [tags.int2str(idx) for idx in batch["ner_tags"]]}

panx_de = panx_ch["de"].map(create_tag_names)
```

Now that we have our tags in human-readable format, let's see how the tokens and tags align for the first example in the training set:

```
de_example = panx_de["train"][0]
pd.DataFrame([de_example["tokens"], de_example["ner_tags_str"]],
['Tokens', 'Tags'])
```

	0	1	2	3	4	5	6	7	8	9	10	11
Tokens	2.000	Einwohnern	an	der	Danziger	Bucht	in	der	polnischen	Woiwodschaft	Pommern	.
Tags	O	O	O	O	B-LOC	I-LOC	O	O	B-LOC	B-LOC	I-LOC	O

The presence of the `LOC` tags make sense since the sentence "2,000 Einwohnern an der Danziger Bucht in der polnischen Woiwodschaft Pommern" means "2,000 inhabitants at the Gdansk Bay in the Polish voivodeship of Pomerania" in English, and Gdansk Bay is a bay in the Baltic sea, while "voivodeship" corresponds to a state in Poland.

As a quick check that we don't have any unusual imbalance in the tags, let's calculate the frequencies of each entity across each split:

```
from collections import Counter

split2freqs = defaultdict(Counter)
for split, dataset in panx_de.items():
    for row in dataset["ner_tags_str"]:
        for tag in row:
            if tag.startswith("B"):
                tag_type = tag.split("-")[1]
                split2freqs[split][tag_type] += 1
pd.DataFrame.from_dict(split2freqs, orient="index")
```

	ORG	LOC	PER
validation	2683	3172	2893

	ORG	LOC	PER
test	2573	3180	3071
train	5366	6186	5810

This looks good—the distributions of the `PER`, `LOC`, and `ORG` frequencies are roughly the same for each split, so the validation and test sets should provide a good measure of our NER tagger's ability to generalize. Next, let's look at a few popular multilingual transformers and how they can be adapted to tackle our NER task.

Multilingual Transformers

Multilingual transformers involve similar architectures and training procedures as their monolingual counterparts, except that the corpus used for pretraining consists of documents in many languages. A remarkable feature of this approach is that despite receiving no explicit information to differentiate among the languages, the resulting linguistic representations are able to generalize well *across* languages for a variety of downstream tasks. In some cases, this ability to perform cross-lingual transfer can produce results that are competitive with those of monolingual models, which circumvents the need to train one model per language!

To measure the progress of cross-lingual transfer for NER, the CoNLL-2002 (*https://oreil.ly/nYd0o*) and CoNLL-2003 (*https://oreil.ly/sVESv*) datasets are often used as a benchmark for English, Dutch, Spanish, and German. This benchmark consists of news articles annotated with the same `LOC`, `PER`, and `ORG` categories as PAN-X, but it contains an additional `MISC` label for miscellaneous entities that do not belong to the previous three groups. Multilingual transformer models are usually evaluated in three different ways:

`en`
: Fine-tune on the English training data and then evaluate on each language's test set.

`each`
: Fine-tune and evaluate on monolingual test data to measure per-language performance.

`all`
: Fine-tune on all the training data to evaluate on all on each language's test set.

We will adopt a similar evaluation strategy for our NER task, but first we need to select a model to evaluate. One of the first multilingual transformers was mBERT, which uses the same architecture and pretraining objective as BERT but adds Wikipedia articles from many languages to the pretraining corpus. Since then, mBERT has been superseded by XLM-RoBERTa (or XLM-R for short), so that's the model we'll consider in this chapter.

As we saw in Chapter 3, XLM-R uses only MLM as a pretraining objective for 100 languages, but is distinguished by the huge size of its pretraining corpus compared to its predecessors: Wikipedia dumps for each language and 2.5 *terabytes* of Common Crawl data from the web. This corpus is several orders of magnitude larger than the ones used in earlier models and provides a significant boost in signal for low-resource languages like Burmese and Swahili, where only a small number of Wikipedia articles exist.

The RoBERTa part of the model's name refers to the fact that the pretraining approach is the same as for the monolingual RoBERTa models. RoBERTa's developers improved on several aspects of BERT, in particular by removing the next sentence prediction task altogether.[3] XLM-R also drops the language embeddings used in XLM and uses SentencePiece to tokenize the raw texts directly.[4] Besides its multilingual nature, a notable difference between XLM-R and RoBERTa is the size of the respective vocabularies: 250,000 tokens versus 55,000!

XLM-R is a great choice for multilingual NLU tasks. In the next section, we'll explore how it can efficiently tokenize across many languages.

A Closer Look at Tokenization

Instead of using a WordPiece tokenizer, XLM-R uses a tokenizer called SentencePiece that is trained on the raw text of all one hundred languages. To get a feel for how SentencePiece compares to WordPiece, let's load the BERT and XLM-R tokenizers in the usual way with 🤗 Transformers:

```
from transformers import AutoTokenizer

bert_model_name = "bert-base-cased"
xlmr_model_name = "xlm-roberta-base"
bert_tokenizer = AutoTokenizer.from_pretrained(bert_model_name)
xlmr_tokenizer = AutoTokenizer.from_pretrained(xlmr_model_name)
```

By encoding a small sequence of text we can also retrieve the special tokens that each model used during pretraining:

```
text = "Jack Sparrow loves New York!"
bert_tokens = bert_tokenizer(text).tokens()
xlmr_tokens = xlmr_tokenizer(text).tokens()
```

3 Y. Liu et al., "RoBERTa: A Robustly Optimized BERT Pretraining Approach" (*https://arxiv.org/abs/1907.11692*), (2019).

4 T. Kudo and J. Richardson, "SentencePiece: A Simple and Language Independent Subword Tokenizer and Detokenizer for Neural Text Processing" (*https://arxiv.org/abs/1808.06226*), (2018).

BERT	[CLS]	Jack	Spa	##rrow	loves	New	York	!	[SEP]	None
XLM-R	<s>	▁Jack	▁Spar	row	▁love	s	▁New	▁York	!	</s>

Here we see that instead of the `[CLS]` and `[SEP]` tokens that BERT uses for sentence classification tasks, XLM-R uses `<s>` and `<\s>` to denote the start and end of a sequence. These tokens are added in the final stage of tokenization, as we'll see next.

The Tokenizer Pipeline

So far we have treated tokenization as a single operation that transforms strings to integers we can pass through the model. This is not entirely accurate, and if we take a closer look we can see that it is actually a full processing pipeline that usually consists of four steps, as shown in Figure 4-1.

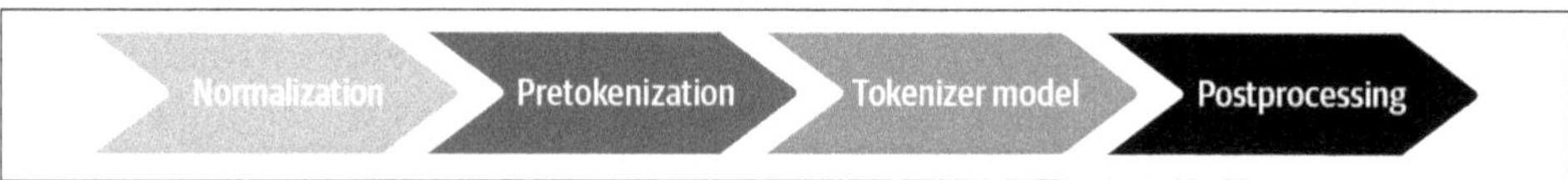

Figure 4-1. The steps in the tokenization pipeline

Let's take a closer look at each processing step and illustrate their effect with the example sentence "Jack Sparrow loves New York!":

Normalization
: This step corresponds to the set of operations you apply to a raw string to make it "cleaner." Common operations include stripping whitespace and removing accented characters. Unicode normalization (*https://oreil.ly/2cp3w*) is another common normalization operation applied by many tokenizers to deal with the fact that there often exist various ways to write the same character. This can make two versions of the "same" string (i.e., with the same sequence of abstract characters) appear different; Unicode normalization schemes like NFC, NFD, NFKC, and NFKD replace the various ways to write the same character with standard forms. Another example of normalization is lowercasing. If the model is expected to only accept and use lowercase characters, this technique can be used to reduce the size of the vocabulary it requires. After normalization, our example string would look like "jack sparrow loves new york!".

Pretokenization
: This step splits a text into smaller objects that give an upper bound to what your tokens will be at the end of training. A good way to think of this is that the pretokenizer will split your text into "words," and your final tokens will be parts of those words. For the languages that allow this (English, German, and many Indo-European languages), strings can typically be split into words on whitespace and punctuation. For example, this step might transform our `["jack", "sparrow",`

`"loves", "new", "york", "!"]`. These words are then simpler to split into subwords with Byte-Pair Encoding (BPE) or Unigram algorithms in the next step of the pipeline. However, splitting into "words" is not always a trivial and deterministic operation, or even an operation that makes sense. For instance, in languages like Chinese, Japanese, or Korean, grouping symbols in semantic units like Indo-European words can be a nondeterministic operation with several equally valid groups. In this case, it might be best to not pretokenize the text and instead use a language-specific library for pretokenization.

Tokenizer model

Once the input texts are normalized and pretokenized, the tokenizer applies a subword splitting model on the words. This is the part of the pipeline that needs to be trained on your corpus (or that has been trained if you are using a pretrained tokenizer). The role of the model is to split the words into subwords to reduce the size of the vocabulary and try to reduce the number of out-of-vocabulary tokens. Several subword tokenization algorithms exist, including BPE, Unigram, and WordPiece. For instance, our running example might look like `[jack, spa, rrow, loves, new, york, !]` after the tokenizer model is applied. Note that at this point we no longer have a list of strings but a list of integers (input IDs); to keep the example illustrative, we've kept the words but dropped the quotes to indicate the transformation.

Postprocessing

This is the last step of the tokenization pipeline, in which some additional transformations can be applied on the list of tokens—for instance, adding special tokens at the beginning or end of the input sequence of token indices. For example, a BERT-style tokenizer would add classifications and separator tokens: `[CLS, jack, spa, rrow, loves, new, york, !, SEP]`. This sequence (recall that this will be a sequence of integers, not the tokens you see here) can then be fed to the model.

Going back to our comparison of XLM-R and BERT, we now understand that SentencePiece adds `<s>` and `<\s>` instead of `[CLS]` and `[SEP]` in the postprocessing step (as a convention, we'll continue to use `[CLS]` and `[SEP]` in the graphical illustrations). Let's go back to the SentencePiece tokenizer to see what makes it special.

The SentencePiece Tokenizer

The SentencePiece tokenizer is based on a type of subword segmentation called Unigram and encodes each input text as a sequence of Unicode characters. This last feature is especially useful for multilingual corpora since it allows SentencePiece to be agnostic about accents, punctuation, and the fact that many languages, like Japanese, do not have whitespace characters. Another special feature of SentencePiece is that whitespace is assigned the Unicode symbol U+2581, or the ▁ character, also called the lower one quarter block character. This enables SentencePiece to detokenize a sequence without ambiguities and without relying on language-specific pretokenizers. In our example from the previous section, for instance, we can see that WordPiece has lost the information that there is no whitespace between "York" and "!". By contrast, SentencePiece preserves the whitespace in the tokenized text so we can convert back to the raw text without ambiguity:

```
"".join(xlmr_tokens).replace(u"\u2581", " ")
```

```
'<s> Jack Sparrow loves New York!</s>'
```

Now that we understand how SentencePiece works, let's see how we can encode our simple example in a form suitable for NER. The first thing to do is load the pretrained model with a token classification head. But instead of loading this head directly from 🤗 Transformers, we will build it ourselves! By diving deeper into the 🤗 Transformers API, we can do this with just a few steps.

Transformers for Named Entity Recognition

In Chapter 2, we saw that for text classification BERT uses the special `[CLS]` token to represent an entire sequence of text. This representation is then fed through a fully connected or dense layer to output the distribution of all the discrete label values, as shown in Figure 4-2.

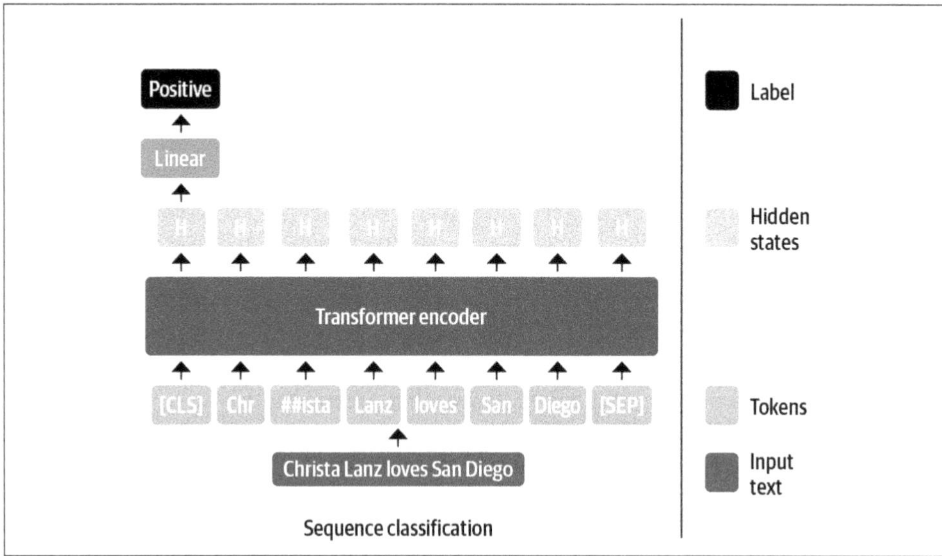

Figure 4-2. Fine-tuning an encoder-based transformer for sequence classification

BERT and other encoder-only transformers take a similar approach for NER, except that the representation of each individual input token is fed into the same fully connected layer to output the entity of the token. For this reason, NER is often framed as a *token classification* task. The process looks something like the diagram in Figure 4-3.

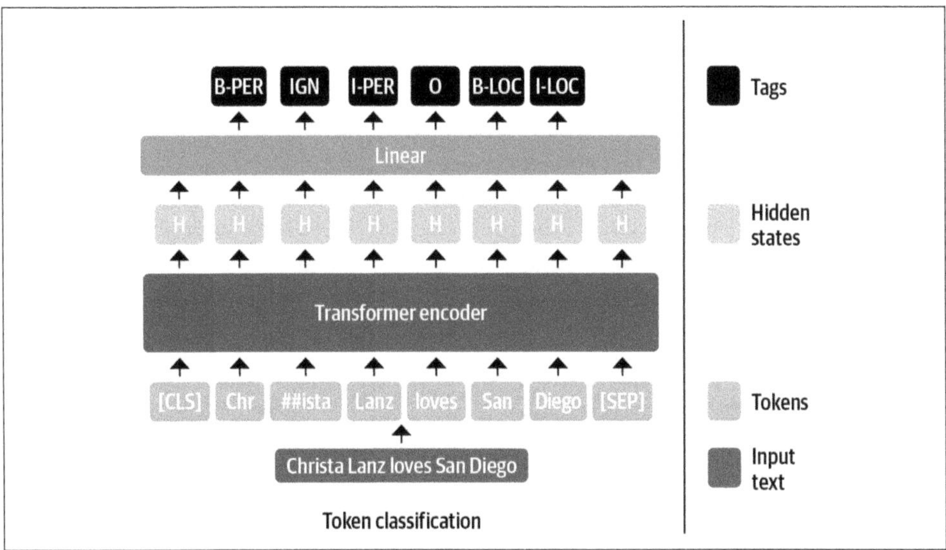

Figure 4-3. Fine-tuning an encoder-based transformer for named entity recognition

So far, so good, but how should we handle subwords in a token classification task? For example, the first name "Christa" in Figure 4-3 is tokenized into the subwords "Chr" and "##ista", so which one(s) should be assigned the `B-PER` label?

In the BERT paper,[5] the authors assigned this label to the first subword ("Chr" in our example) and ignored the following subword ("##ista"). This is the convention we'll adopt here, and we'll indicate the ignored subwords with `IGN`. We can later easily propagate the predicted label of the first subword to the subsequent subwords in the postprocessing step. We could also have chosen to include the representation of the "##ista" subword by assigning it a copy of the `B-LOC` label, but this violates the IOB2 format.

Fortunately, all the architecture aspects we've seen in BERT carry over to XLM-R since its architecture is based on RoBERTa, which is identical to BERT! Next we'll see how 🤗 Transformers supports many other tasks with minor modifications.

---

5 J. Devlin et al., "BERT: Pre-Training of Deep Bidirectional Transformers for Language Understanding" (*https://arxiv.org/abs/1810.04805*), (2018).

The Anatomy of the Transformers Model Class

🤗 Transformers is organized around dedicated classes for each architecture and task. The model classes associated with different tasks are named according to a <ModelName>For<Task> convention, or AutoModelFor<Task> when using the AutoModel classes.

However, this approach has its limitations, and to motivate going deeper into the 🤗 Transformers API, consider the following scenario. Suppose you have a great idea to solve an NLP problem that has been on your mind for a long time with a transformer model. So you set up a meeting with your boss and, with an artfully crafted PowerPoint presentation, you pitch that you could increase the revenue of your department if you can finally solve the problem. Impressed with your colorful presentation and talk of profits, your boss generously agrees to give you one week to build a proof-of-concept. Happy with the outcome, you start working straight away. You fire up your GPU and open a notebook. You execute `from transformers import BertForTaskXY` (note that `TaskXY` is the imaginary task you would like to solve) and color escapes your face as the dreaded red color fills your screen: `ImportError: cannot import name` *`BertForTaskXY`*. Oh no, there is no BERT model for your use case! How can you complete the project in one week if you have to implement the whole model yourself?! Where should you even start?

Don't panic! 🤗 Transformers is designed to enable you to easily extend existing models for your specific use case. You can load the weights from pretrained models, and you have access to task-specific helper functions. This lets you build custom models for specific objectives with very little overhead. In this section, we'll see how we can implement our own custom model.

Bodies and Heads

The main concept that makes 🤗 Transformers so versatile is the split of the architecture into a *body* and *head* (as we saw in Chapter 1). We have already seen that when we switch from the pretraining task to the downstream task, we need to replace the last layer of the model with one that is suitable for the task. This last layer is called the model head; it's the part that is *task-specific*. The rest of the model is called the body; it includes the token embeddings and transformer layers that are *task-agnostic*. This structure is reflected in the 🤗 Transformers code as well: the body of a model is implemented in a class such as `BertModel` or `GPT2Model` that returns the hidden states of the last layer. Task-specific models such as `BertForMaskedLM` or `BertForSequenceClassification` use the base model and add the necessary head on top of the hidden states, as shown in Figure 4-4.

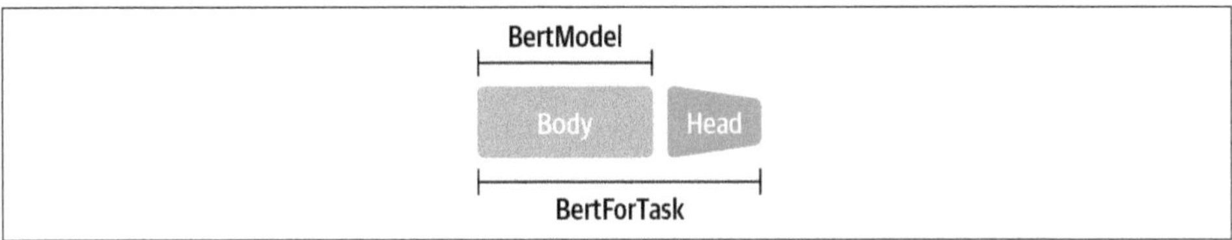

Figure 4-4. The `BertModel` class only contains the body of the model, while the `BertFor<Task>` classes combine the body with a dedicated head for a given task

As we'll see next, this separation of bodies and heads allows us to build a custom head for any task and just mount it on top of a pretrained model.

Creating a Custom Model for Token Classification

Let's go through the exercise of building a custom token classification head for XLM-R. Since XLM-R uses the same model architecture as RoBERTa, we will use RoBERTa as the base model, but augmented with settings specific to XLM-R. Note that this is an educational exercise to show you how to build a custom model for your own task. For token classification, an `XLMRobertaForTokenClassification` class already exists that you can import from 🤗 Transformers. If you want, you can skip to the next section and simply use that one.

To get started, we need a data structure that will represent our XLM-R NER tagger. As a first guess, we'll need a configuration object to initialize the model and a `forward()` function to generate the outputs. Let's go ahead and build our XLM-R class for token classification:

```
import torch.nn as nn
from transformers import XLMRobertaConfig
from transformers.modeling_outputs import TokenClassifierOutput
from transformers.models.roberta.modeling_roberta import RobertaModel
from transformers.models.roberta.modeling_roberta import RobertaPreTrainedModel

class XLMRobertaForTokenClassification(RobertaPreTrainedModel):
    config_class = XLMRobertaConfig

    def __init__(self, config):
        super().__init__(config)
        self.num_labels = config.num_labels
        # Load model body
        self.roberta = RobertaModel(config, add_pooling_layer=False)
        # Set up token classification head
        self.dropout = nn.Dropout(config.hidden_dropout_prob)
        self.classifier = nn.Linear(config.hidden_size, config.num_labels)
        # Load and initialize weights
        self.init_weights()

    def forward(self, input_ids=None, attention_mask=None, token_type_ids=None,
```

```
            labels=None, **kwargs):
    # Use model body to get encoder representations
    outputs = self.roberta(input_ids, attention_mask=attention_mask,
                           token_type_ids=token_type_ids, **kwargs)
    # Apply classifier to encoder representation
    sequence_output = self.dropout(outputs[0])
    logits = self.classifier(sequence_output)
    # Calculate losses
    loss = None
    if labels is not None:
        loss_fct = nn.CrossEntropyLoss()
        loss = loss_fct(logits.view(-1, self.num_labels), labels.view(-1))
    # Return model output object
    return TokenClassifierOutput(loss=loss, logits=logits,
                                 hidden_states=outputs.hidden_states,
                                 attentions=outputs.attentions)
```

The `config_class` ensures that the standard XLM-R settings are used when we initialize a new model. If you want to change the default parameters, you can do this by overwriting the default settings in the configuration. With the `super()` method we call the initialization function of the `RobertaPreTrainedModel` class. This abstract class handles the initialization or loading of pretrained weights. Then we load our model body, which is `RobertaModel`, and extend it with our own classification head consisting of a dropout and a standard feed-forward layer. Note that we set `add_pooling_layer=False` to ensure all hidden states are returned and not only the one associated with the `[CLS]` token. Finally, we initialize all the weights by calling the `init_weights()` method we inherit from `RobertaPreTrainedModel`, which will load the pretrained weights for the model body and randomly initialize the weights of our token classification head.

The only thing left to do is to define what the model should do in a forward pass with a `forward()` method. During the forward pass, the data is first fed through the model body. There are a number of input variables, but the only ones we need for now are `input_ids` and `attention_mask`. The hidden state, which is part of the model body output, is then fed through the dropout and classification layers. If we also provide labels in the forward pass, we can directly calculate the loss. If there is an attention mask we need to do a little bit more work to make sure we only calculate the loss of the unmasked tokens. Finally, we wrap all the outputs in a `TokenClassifierOutput` object that allows us to access elements in a the familiar named tuple from previous chapters.

By just implementing two functions of a simple class, we can build our own custom transformer model. And since we inherit from a `PreTrainedModel`, we instantly get access to all the useful 🤗 Transformer utilities, such as `from_pretrained()`! Let's have a look how we can load pretrained weights into our custom model.

Loading a Custom Model

Now we are ready to load our token classification model. We'll need to provide some additional information beyond the model name, including the tags that we will use to label each entity and the mapping of each tag to an ID and vice versa. All of this information can be derived from our `tags` variable, which as a `ClassLabel` object has a `names` attribute that we can use to derive the mapping:

```
index2tag = {idx: tag for idx, tag in enumerate(tags.names)}
tag2index = {tag: idx for idx, tag in enumerate(tags.names)}
```

We'll store these mappings and the `tags.num_classes` attribute in the `AutoConfig` object that we encountered in Chapter 3. Passing keyword arguments to the `from_pretrained()` method overrides the default values:

```
from transformers import AutoConfig

xlmr_config = AutoConfig.from_pretrained(xlmr_model_name,
                                         num_labels=tags.num_classes,
                                         id2label=index2tag, label2id=tag2index)
```

The `AutoConfig` class contains the blueprint of a model's architecture. When we load a model with `AutoModel.from_pretrained(model_ckpt)`, the configuration file associated with that model is downloaded automatically. However, if we want to modify something like the number of classes or label names, then we can load the configuration first with the parameters we would like to customize.

Now, we can load the model weights as usual with the `from_pretrained()` function with the additional `config` argument. Note that we did not implement loading pretrained weights in our custom model class; we get this for free by inheriting from `RobertaPreTrainedModel`:

```
import torch

device = torch.device("cuda" if torch.cuda.is_available() else "cpu")
xlmr_model = (XLMRobertaForTokenClassification
              .from_pretrained(xlmr_model_name, config=xlmr_config)
              .to(device))
```

As a quick check that we have initialized the tokenizer and model correctly, let's test the predictions on our small sequence of known entities:

```
input_ids = xlmr_tokenizer.encode(text, return_tensors="pt")
pd.DataFrame([xlmr_tokens, input_ids[0].numpy()], index=["Tokens", "Input IDs"])
```

	0	1	2	3	4	5	6	7	8	9
Tokens	<s>	▁Jack	▁Spar	row	▁love	s	▁New	▁York	!	</s>
Input IDs	0	21763	37456	15555	5161	7	2356	5753	38	2

As you can see here, the start <s> and end </s> tokens are given the IDs 0 and 2, respectively.

Finally, we need to pass the inputs to the model and extract the predictions by taking the argmax to get the most likely class per token:

```
outputs = xlmr_model(input_ids.to(device)).logits
predictions = torch.argmax(outputs, dim=-1)
print(f"Number of tokens in sequence: {len(xlmr_tokens)}")
print(f"Shape of outputs: {outputs.shape}")
```

```
Number of tokens in sequence: 10
Shape of outputs: torch.Size([1, 10, 7])
```

Here we see that the logits have the shape `[batch_size, num_tokens, num_tags]`, with each token given a logit among the seven possible NER tags. By enumerating over the sequence, we can quickly see what the pretrained model predicts:

```
preds = [tags.names[p] for p in predictions[0].cpu().numpy()]
pd.DataFrame([xlmr_tokens, preds], index=["Tokens", "Tags"])
```

	0	1	2	3	4	5	6	7	8	9
Tokens	<s>	▁Jack	▁Spar	row	▁love	s	▁New	▁York	!	</s>
Tags	O	I-LOC	B-LOC	B-LOC	O	I-LOC	O	O	I-LOC	B-LOC

Unsurprisingly, our token classification layer with random weights leaves a lot to be desired; let's fine-tune on some labeled data to make it better! Before doing so, let's wrap the preceding steps into a helper function for later use:

```
def tag_text(text, tags, model, tokenizer):
    # Get tokens with special characters
    tokens = tokenizer(text).tokens()
    # Encode the sequence into IDs
    input_ids = xlmr_tokenizer(text, return_tensors="pt").input_ids.to(device)
    # Get predictions as distribution over 7 possible classes
    outputs = model(input_ids)[0]
    # Take argmax to get most likely class per token
    predictions = torch.argmax(outputs, dim=2)
    # Convert to DataFrame
    preds = [tags.names[p] for p in predictions[0].cpu().numpy()]
    return pd.DataFrame([tokens, preds], index=["Tokens", "Tags"])
```

Before we can train the model, we also need to tokenize the inputs and prepare the labels. We'll do that next.

Tokenizing Texts for NER

Now that we've established that the tokenizer and model can encode a single example, our next step is to tokenize the whole dataset so that we can pass it to the XLM-R model for fine-tuning. As we saw in Chapter 2, 🤗 Datasets provides a fast way to tokenize a `Dataset` object with the `map()` operation. To achieve this, recall that we first need to define a function with the minimal signature:

```
function(examples: Dict[str, List]) -> Dict[str, List]
```

where `examples` is equivalent to a slice of a `Dataset`, e.g., `panx_de['train'][:10]`. Since the XLM-R tokenizer returns the input IDs for the model's inputs, we just need to augment this information with the attention mask and the label IDs that encode the information about which token is associated with each NER tag.

Following the approach taken in the 🤗 Transformers documentation (*https://oreil.ly/lGPgh*), let's look at how this works with our single German example by first collecting the words and tags as ordinary lists:

```
words, labels = de_example["tokens"], de_example["ner_tags"]
```

Next, we tokenize each word and use the `is_split_into_words` argument to tell the tokenizer that our input sequence has already been split into words:

```
tokenized_input = xlmr_tokenizer(de_example["tokens"], is_split_into_words=True)
tokens = xlmr_tokenizer.convert_ids_to_tokens(tokenized_input["input_ids"])
pd.DataFrame([tokens], index=["Tokens"])
```

	0	1	2	3	4	5	6	...	18	19	20	21	22	23	24
Tokens	<s>	▁2.000	▁Einwohner	n	▁an	▁der	▁Dan	...	schaft	▁Po	mmer	n	▁	.	</s>

In this example we can see that the tokenizer has split "Einwohnern" into two subwords, "▁Einwohner" and "n". Since we're following the convention that only "▁Einwohner" should be associated with the `B-LOC` label, we need a way to mask the subword representations after the first subword. Fortunately, `tokenized_input` is a class that contains a `word_ids()` function that can help us achieve this:

```
word_ids = tokenized_input.word_ids()
pd.DataFrame([tokens, word_ids], index=["Tokens", "Word IDs"])
```

	0	1	2	3	4	5	6	...	18	19	20	21	22	23	24
Tokens	<s>	▁2.000	▁Einwohner	n	▁an	▁der	▁Dan	...	schaft	▁Po	mmer	n	▁	.	</s>
Word IDs	None	0	1	1	2	3	4	...	9	10	10	10	11	11	None

Here we can see that `word_ids` has mapped each subword to the corresponding index in the `words` sequence, so the first subword, "▁2.000", is assigned the index 0, while "▁Einwohner" and "n" are assigned the index 1 (since "Einwohnern" is the second word in `words`). We can also see that special tokens like `<s>` and `<\s>` are mapped to `None`. Let's set –100 as the label for these special tokens and the subwords we wish to mask during training:

```
previous_word_idx = None
label_ids = []

for word_idx in word_ids:
    if word_idx is None or word_idx == previous_word_idx:
        label_ids.append(-100)
    elif word_idx != previous_word_idx:
        label_ids.append(labels[word_idx])
    previous_word_idx = word_idx

labels = [index2tag[l] if l != -100 else "IGN" for l in label_ids]
index = ["Tokens", "Word IDs", "Label IDs", "Labels"]

pd.DataFrame([tokens, word_ids, label_ids, labels], index=index)
```

	0	1	2	3	4	5	...	19	20	21	22	23	24
Tokens	<s>	▁2.000	▁Einwohner	n	▁an	▁der	...	▁Po	mmer	n	▁	.	</s>
Word IDs	None	0	1	1	2	3	...	10	10	10	11	11	None
Label IDs	-100	0	0	-100	0	0	...	6	-100	-100	0	-100	-100
Labels	IGN	O	O	IGN	O	O	...	I-LOC	IGN	IGN	O	IGN	IGN

Why did we choose –100 as the ID to mask subword representations? The reason is that in PyTorch the cross-entropy loss class `torch.nn.CrossEntropyLoss` has an attribute called `ignore_index` whose value is –100. This index is ignored during training, so we can use it to ignore the tokens associated with consecutive subwords.

And that's it! We can clearly see how the label IDs align with the tokens, so let's scale this out to the whole dataset by defining a single function that wraps all the logic:

```
def tokenize_and_align_labels(examples):
    tokenized_inputs = xlmr_tokenizer(examples["tokens"], truncation=True,
                                      is_split_into_words=True)
    labels = []
    for idx, label in enumerate(examples["ner_tags"]):
        word_ids = tokenized_inputs.word_ids(batch_index=idx)
        previous_word_idx = None
        label_ids = []
        for word_idx in word_ids:
```

```
            if word_idx is None or word_idx == previous_word_idx:
                label_ids.append(-100)
            else:
                label_ids.append(label[word_idx])
            previous_word_idx = word_idx
        labels.append(label_ids)
    tokenized_inputs["labels"] = labels
    return tokenized_inputs
```

We now have all the ingredients we need to encode each split, so let's write a function we can iterate over:

```
def encode_panx_dataset(corpus):
    return corpus.map(tokenize_and_align_labels, batched=True,
                      remove_columns=['langs', 'ner_tags', 'tokens'])
```

By applying this function to a `DatasetDict` object, we get an encoded `Dataset` object per split. Let's use this to encode our German corpus:

```
panx_de_encoded = encode_panx_dataset(panx_ch["de"])
```

Now that we have a model and a dataset, we need to define a performance metric.

Performance Measures

Evaluating a NER model is similar to evaluating a text classification model, and it is common to report results for precision, recall, and F_1-score. The only subtlety is that *all* words of an entity need to be predicted correctly in order for a prediction to be counted as correct. Fortunately, there is a nifty library called *seqeval* (*https://oreil.ly/xbKOp*) that is designed for these kinds of tasks. For example, given some placeholder NER tags and model predictions, we can compute the metrics via seqeval's `classification_report()` function:

```
from seqeval.metrics import classification_report

y_true = [["O", "O", "O", "B-MISC", "I-MISC", "I-MISC", "O"],
          ["B-PER", "I-PER", "O"]]
y_pred = [["O", "O", "B-MISC", "I-MISC", "I-MISC", "I-MISC", "O"],
          ["B-PER", "I-PER", "O"]]
print(classification_report(y_true, y_pred))
```

```
              precision    recall  f1-score   support

        MISC       0.00      0.00      0.00         1
         PER       1.00      1.00      1.00         1

   micro avg       0.50      0.50      0.50         2
   macro avg       0.50      0.50      0.50         2
weighted avg       0.50      0.50      0.50         2
```

As we can see, *seqeval* expects the predictions and labels as lists of lists, with each list corresponding to a single example in our validation or test sets. To integrate these metrics during training, we need a function that can take the outputs of the model and convert them into the lists that *seqeval* expects. The following does the trick by ensuring we ignore the label IDs associated with subsequent subwords:

```
import numpy as np

def align_predictions(predictions, label_ids):
    preds = np.argmax(predictions, axis=2)
    batch_size, seq_len = preds.shape
    labels_list, preds_list = [], []

    for batch_idx in range(batch_size):
        example_labels, example_preds = [], []
        for seq_idx in range(seq_len):
            # Ignore label IDs = -100
            if label_ids[batch_idx, seq_idx] != -100:
                example_labels.append(index2tag[label_ids[batch_idx][seq_idx]])
                example_preds.append(index2tag[preds[batch_idx][seq_idx]])

        labels_list.append(example_labels)
        preds_list.append(example_preds)

    return preds_list, labels_list
```

Equipped with a performance metric, we can move on to actually training the model.

Fine-Tuning XLM-RoBERTa

We now have all the ingredients to fine-tune our model! Our first strategy will be to fine-tune our base model on the German subset of PAN-X and then evaluate its zero-shot cross-lingual performance on French, Italian, and English. As usual, we'll use the 🤗 Transformers `Trainer` to handle our training loop, so first we need to define the training attributes using the `TrainingArguments` class:

```
from transformers import TrainingArguments

num_epochs = 3
batch_size = 24
logging_steps = len(panx_de_encoded["train"]) // batch_size
model_name = f"{xlmr_model_name}-finetuned-panx-de"
training_args = TrainingArguments(
    output_dir=model_name, log_level="error", num_train_epochs=num_epochs,
    per_device_train_batch_size=batch_size,
    per_device_eval_batch_size=batch_size, evaluation_strategy="epoch",
    save_steps=1e6, weight_decay=0.01, disable_tqdm=False,
    logging_steps=logging_steps, push_to_hub=True)
```

Here we evaluate the model's predictions on the validation set at the end of every epoch, tweak the weight decay, and set `save_steps` to a large number to disable checkpointing and thus speed up training.

This is also a good point to make sure we are logged in to the Hugging Face Hub (if you're working in a terminal, you can execute the command `huggingface-cli login` instead):

```
from huggingface_hub import notebook_login

notebook_login()
```

We also need to tell the `Trainer` how to compute metrics on the validation set, so here we can use the `align_predictions()` function that we defined earlier to extract the predictions and labels in the format needed by *seqeval* to calculate the F_1-score:

```
from seqeval.metrics import f1_score

def compute_metrics(eval_pred):
    y_pred, y_true = align_predictions(eval_pred.predictions,
                                       eval_pred.label_ids)
    return {"f1": f1_score(y_true, y_pred)}
```

The final step is to define a *data collator* so we can pad each input sequence to the largest sequence length in a batch. 🤗 Transformers provides a dedicated data collator for token classification that will pad the labels along with the inputs:

```
from transformers import DataCollatorForTokenClassification

data_collator = DataCollatorForTokenClassification(xlmr_tokenizer)
```

Padding the labels is necessary because, unlike in a text classification task, the labels are also sequences. One important detail here is that the label sequences are padded with the value –100, which, as we've seen, is ignored by PyTorch loss functions.

We will train several models in the course of this chapter, so we'll avoid initializing a new model for every `Trainer` by creating a `model_init()` method. This method loads an untrained model and is called at the beginning of the `train()` call:

```
def model_init():
    return (XLMRobertaForTokenClassification
            .from_pretrained(xlmr_model_name, config=xlmr_config)
            .to(device))
```

We can now pass all this information together with the encoded datasets to the `Trainer`:

```
from transformers import Trainer

trainer = Trainer(model_init=model_init, args=training_args,
                  data_collator=data_collator, compute_metrics=compute_metrics,
                  train_dataset=panx_de_encoded["train"],
```

```
                  eval_dataset=panx_de_encoded["validation"],
                  tokenizer=xlmr_tokenizer)
```

and then run the training loop as follows and push the final model to the Hub:

```
trainer.train() trainer.push_to_hub(commit_message="Training completed!")
```

Epoch	Training Loss	Validation Loss	F1
1	0.2652	0.160244	0.822974
2	0.1314	0.137195	0.852747
3	0.0806	0.138774	0.864591

These F1 scores are quite good for a NER model. To confirm that our model works as expected, let's test it on the German translation of our simple example:

```
text_de = "Jeff Dean ist ein Informatiker bei Google in Kalifornien"
tag_text(text_de, tags, trainer.model, xlmr_tokenizer)
```

	0	1	2	3	4	5	...	8	9	10	11	12	13
Tokens	<s>	▁Jeff	▁De	an	▁ist	▁ein	...	▁bei	▁Google	▁in	▁Kaliforni	en	</s>
Tags	O	B-PER	I-PER	I-PER	O	O	...	O	B-ORG	O	B-LOC	I-LOC	O

It works! But we should never get too confident about performance based on a single example. Instead, we should conduct a proper and thorough investigation of the model's errors. In the next section we explore how to do this for the NER task.

Error Analysis

Before we dive deeper into the multilingual aspects of XLM-R, let's take a minute to investigate the errors of our model. As we saw in Chapter 2, a thorough error analysis of your model is one of the most important aspects when training and debugging transformers (and machine learning models in general). There are several failure modes where it might look like the model is performing well, while in practice it has some serious flaws. Examples where training can fail include:

- We might accidentally mask too many tokens and also mask some of our labels to get a really promising loss drop.
- The `compute_metrics()` function might have a bug that overestimates the true performance.
- We might include the zero class or `O` entity in NER as a normal class, which will heavily skew the accuracy and F_1-score since it is the majority class by a large margin.

When the model performs much worse than expected, looking at the errors can yield useful insights and reveal bugs that would be hard to spot by just looking at the code. And even if the model performs well and there are no bugs in the code, error analysis is still a useful tool to understand the model's strengths and weaknesses. These are aspects we always need to keep in mind when we deploy a model in a production environment.

For our analysis we will again use one of the most powerful tools at our disposal, which is to look at the validation examples with the highest loss. We can reuse much of the function we built to analyze the sequence classification model in Chapter 2, but we'll now calculate a loss per token in the sample sequence.

Let's define a method that we can apply to the validation set:

```
from torch.nn.functional import cross_entropy

def forward_pass_with_label(batch):
    # Convert dict of lists to list of dicts suitable for data collator
    features = [dict(zip(batch, t)) for t in zip(*batch.values())]
    # Pad inputs and labels and put all tensors on device
    batch = data_collator(features)
    input_ids = batch["input_ids"].to(device)
    attention_mask = batch["attention_mask"].to(device)
    labels = batch["labels"].to(device)
    with torch.no_grad():
        # Pass data through model
        output = trainer.model(input_ids, attention_mask)
        # logit.size: [batch_size, sequence_length, classes]
        # Predict class with largest logit value on classes axis
        predicted_label = torch.argmax(output.logits, axis=-1).cpu().numpy()
    # Calculate loss per token after flattening batch dimension with view
    loss = cross_entropy(output.logits.view(-1, 7),
                         labels.view(-1), reduction="none")
    # Unflatten batch dimension and convert to numpy array
    loss = loss.view(len(input_ids), -1).cpu().numpy()

    return {"loss":loss, "predicted_label": predicted_label}
```

We can now apply this function to the whole validation set using `map()` and load all the data into a `DataFrame` for further analysis:

```
valid_set = panx_de_encoded["validation"]
valid_set = valid_set.map(forward_pass_with_label, batched=True, batch_size=32)
df = valid_set.to_pandas()
```

The tokens and the labels are still encoded with their IDs, so let's map the tokens and labels back to strings to make it easier to read the results. For the padding tokens with label –100 we assign a special label, `IGN`, so we can filter them later. We also get rid of all the padding in the `loss` and `predicted_label` fields by truncating them to the length of the inputs:

```
index2tag[-100] = "IGN"
df["input_tokens"] = df["input_ids"].apply(
    lambda x: xlmr_tokenizer.convert_ids_to_tokens(x))
df["predicted_label"] = df["predicted_label"].apply(
    lambda x: [index2tag[i] for i in x])
df["labels"] = df["labels"].apply(
    lambda x: [index2tag[i] for i in x])
df['loss'] = df.apply(
    lambda x: x['loss'][:len(x['input_ids'])], axis=1)
df['predicted_label'] = df.apply(
    lambda x: x['predicted_label'][:len(x['input_ids'])], axis=1)
df.head(1)
```

	attention_mask	input_ids	labels	loss	predicted_label	input_tokens
0	[1, 1, 1, 1, 1, 1, 1]	[0, 10699, 11, 15, 16104, 1388, 2]	[IGN, B-ORG, IGN, I-ORG, I-ORG, I-ORG, IGN]	[0.0, 0.014679872, 0.0, 0.009469474, 0.010393422, 0.01293836, 0.0]	[I-ORG, B-ORG, I-ORG, I-ORG, I-ORG, I-ORG, I-ORG]	[<s>, _Ham, a, _(, _Unternehmen, _), </s>]

Each column contains a list of tokens, labels, predicted labels, and so on for each sample. Let's have a look at the tokens individually by unpacking these lists. The `pandas.Series.explode()` function allows us to do exactly that in one line by creating a row for each element in the original rows list. Since all the lists in one row have the same length, we can do this in parallel for all columns. We also drop the padding tokens we named `IGN`, since their loss is zero anyway. Finally, we cast the losses, which are still `numpy.Array` objects, to standard floats:

```
df_tokens = df.apply(pd.Series.explode)
df_tokens = df_tokens.query("labels != 'IGN'")
df_tokens["loss"] = df_tokens["loss"].astype(float).round(2)
df_tokens.head(7)
```

attention_mask	input_ids	labels	loss	predicted_label	input_tokens
1	10699	B-ORG	0.01	B-ORG	_Ham
1	15	I-ORG	0.01	I-ORG	_(
1	16104	I-ORG	0.01	I-ORG	_Unternehmen
1	1388	I-ORG	0.01	I-ORG	_)
1	56530	0	0.00	0	_WE
1	83982	B-ORG	0.34	B-ORG	_Luz
1	10	I-ORG	0.45	I-ORG	_a

With the data in this shape, we can now group it by the input tokens and aggregate the losses for each token with the count, mean, and sum. Finally, we sort the aggregated data by the sum of the losses and see which tokens have accumulated the most loss in the validation set:

```
(
    df_tokens.groupby("input_tokens")[["loss"]]
    .agg(["count", "mean", "sum"])
    .droplevel(level=0, axis=1)  # Get rid of multi-level columns
    .sort_values(by="sum", ascending=False)
    .reset_index()
    .round(2)
    .head(10)
    .T
)
```

	0	1	2	3	4	5	6	7	8	9
input_tokens	▁	▁der	▁in	▁von	▁/	▁und	▁(	▁)	▁''	▁A
count	6066	1388	989	808	163	1171	246	246	2898	125
mean	0.03	0.1	0.14	0.14	0.64	0.08	0.3	0.29	0.02	0.44
sum	200.71	138.05	137.33	114.92	104.28	99.15	74.49	72.35	59.31	54.48

We can observe several patterns in this list:

- The whitespace token has the highest total loss, which is not surprising since it is also the most common token in the list. However, its mean loss is much lower than the other tokens in the list. This means that the model doesn't struggle to classify it.
- Words like "in", "von", "der", and "und" appear relatively frequently. They often appear together with named entities and are sometimes part of them, which explains why the model might mix them up.
- Parentheses, slashes, and capital letters at the beginning of words are rarer but have a relatively high average loss. We will investigate them further.

We can also group the label IDs and look at the losses for each class:

```
(
    df_tokens.groupby("labels")[["loss"]]
    .agg(["count", "mean", "sum"])
    .droplevel(level=0, axis=1)
    .sort_values(by="mean", ascending=False)
    .reset_index()
    .round(2)
    .T
)
```

	0	1	2	3	4	5	6
labels	B-ORG	I-LOC	I-ORG	B-LOC	B-PER	I-PER	O

	0	1	2	3	4	5	6
count	2683	1462	3820	3172	2893	4139	43648
mean	0.66	0.64	0.48	0.35	0.26	0.18	0.03
sum	1769.47	930.94	1850.39	1111.03	760.56	750.91	1354.46

We see that `B-ORG` has the highest average loss, which means that determining the beginning of an organization poses a challenge to our model.

We can break this down further by plotting the confusion matrix of the token classification, where we see that the beginning of an organization is often confused with the subsequent `I-ORG` token:

```
from sklearn.metrics import ConfusionMatrixDisplay, confusion_matrix

def plot_confusion_matrix(y_preds, y_true, labels):
    cm = confusion_matrix(y_true, y_preds, normalize="true")
    fig, ax = plt.subplots(figsize=(6, 6))
    disp = ConfusionMatrixDisplay(confusion_matrix=cm, display_labels=labels)
    disp.plot(cmap="Blues", values_format=".2f", ax=ax, colorbar=False)
    plt.title("Normalized confusion matrix")
    plt.show()

plot_confusion_matrix(df_tokens["labels"], df_tokens["predicted_label"],
                      tags.names)
```

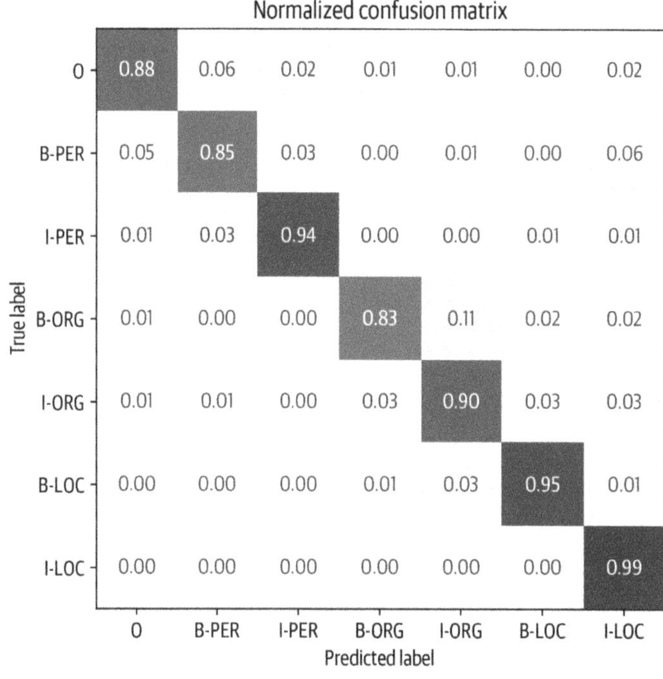

From the plot, we can see that our model tends to confuse the `B-ORG` and `I-ORG` entities the most. Otherwise, it is quite good at classifying the remaining entities, which is clear by the near diagonal nature of the confusion matrix.

Now that we've examined the errors at the token level, let's move on and look at sequences with high losses. For this calculation, we'll revisit our "unexploded" `DataFrame` and calculate the total loss by summing over the loss per token. To do this, let's first write a function that helps us display the token sequences with the labels and the losses:

```
def get_samples(df):
    for _, row in df.iterrows():
        labels, preds, tokens, losses = [], [], [], []
        for i, mask in enumerate(row["attention_mask"]):
            if i not in {0, len(row["attention_mask"])}:
                labels.append(row["labels"][i])
                preds.append(row["predicted_label"][i])
                tokens.append(row["input_tokens"][i])
                losses.append(f"{row['loss'][i]:.2f}")
        df_tmp = pd.DataFrame({"tokens": tokens, "labels": labels,
                               "preds": preds, "losses": losses}).T
        yield df_tmp

df["total_loss"] = df["loss"].apply(sum)
df_tmp = df.sort_values(by="total_loss", ascending=False).head(3)

for sample in get_samples(df_tmp):
    display(sample)
```

	0	1	2	3	4	...	13	14	15	16	17
tokens	▁"	8	.	▁Juli	▁"	...	n	ischen	▁Gar	de	</s>
labels	B-ORG	IGN	IGN	I-ORG	I-ORG	...	IGN	IGN	I-ORG	IGN	IGN
preds	O	O	O	O	O	...	I-ORG	I-ORG	I-ORG	I-ORG	O
losses	7.89	0.00	0.00	6.88	8.05	...	0.00	0.00	0.01	0.00	0.00

	0	1	2	3	4	...	14	15	16	17	18
tokens	▁'	▁"	▁T	K	▁"	...	k	▁"	▁'	ala	</s>
labels	O	O	O	IGN	O	...	IGN	I-LOC	I-LOC	IGN	IGN
preds	O	O	B-ORG	O	O	...	O	O	O	O	O
losses	0.00	0.00	3.59	0.00	0.00	...	0.00	7.66	7.78	0.00	0.00

	0	1	2	3	4	...	10	11	12	13	14
tokens	▁United	▁Nations	▁Multi	dimensional	▁Integra	...	▁the	▁Central	▁African	▁Republic	</s>
labels	B-PER	I-PER	I-PER	IGN	I-PER	...	I-PER	I-PER	I-PER	I-PER	IGN

	0	1	2	3	4	...	10	11	12	13	14
preds	B-ORG	I-ORG	I-ORG	I-ORG	I-ORG	...	I-ORG	I-ORG	I-ORG	I-ORG	I-ORG
losses	6.46	5.59	5.51	0.00	5.11	...	4.77	5.32	5.10	4.87	0.00

It is apparent that something is wrong with the labels of these samples; for example, the United Nations and the Central African Republic are each labeled as a person! At the same time, "8. Juli" in the first example is labeled as an organization. It turns out the annotations for the PAN-X dataset were generated through an automated process. Such annotations are often referred to as "silver standard" (in contrast to the "gold standard" of human-generated annotations), and it is no surprise that there are cases where the automated approach failed to produce sensible labels. In fact, such failure modes are not unique to automatic approaches; even when humans carefully annotate data, mistakes can occur when the concentration of the annotators fades or they simply misunderstand the sentence.

Another thing we noticed earlier was that parentheses and slashes had a relatively high loss. Let's look at a few examples of sequences with an opening parenthesis:

```
df_tmp = df.loc[df["input_tokens"].apply(lambda x: u"\u2581(" in x)].head(2)
for sample in get_samples(df_tmp):
    display(sample)
```

	0	1	2	3	4	5
tokens	▁Ham	a	▁(	▁Unternehmen	▁)	</s>
labels	B-ORG	IGN	I-ORG	I-ORG	I-ORG	IGN
preds	B-ORG	I-ORG	I-ORG	I-ORG	I-ORG	I-ORG
losses	0.01	0.00	0.01	0.01	0.01	0.00

	0	1	2	3	4	5	6	7
tokens	▁Kesk	kül	a	▁(	▁Mart	na	▁)	</s>
labels	B-LOC	IGN	IGN	I-LOC	I-LOC	IGN	I-LOC	IGN
preds	B-LOC	I-LOC	I-LOC	I-LOC	I-LOC	I-LOC	I-LOC	I-LOC
losses	0.02	0.00	0.00	0.01	0.01	0.00	0.01	0.00

In general we would not include the parentheses and their contents as part of the named entity, but this seems to be the way the automatic extraction annotated the documents. In the other examples, the parentheses contain a geographic specification. While this is indeed a location as well, we might want disconnect it from the original location in the annotations. This dataset consists of Wikipedia articles in different languages, and the article titles often contain some sort of explanation in parentheses. For instance, in the first example the text in parentheses indicates that Hama is an

"Unternehmen," or company in English. These are important details to know when we roll out the model, as they might have implications on the downstream performance of the whole pipeline the model is part of.

With a relatively simple analysis, we've identified some weaknesses in both our model and the dataset. In a real use case we would iterate on this step, cleaning up the dataset, retraining the model, and analyzing the new errors until we were satisfied with the performance.

Here we analyzed the errors on a single language, but we are also interested in the performance across languages. In the next section we'll perform some experiments to see how well the cross-lingual transfer in XLM-R works.

Cross-Lingual Transfer

Now that we have fine-tuned XLM-R on German, we can evaluate its ability to transfer to other languages via the `predict()` method of the `Trainer`. Since we plan to evaluate multiple languages, let's create a simple function that does this for us:

```
def get_f1_score(trainer, dataset):
    return trainer.predict(dataset).metrics["test_f1"]
```

We can use this function to examine the performance on the test set and keep track of our scores in a `dict`:

```
f1_scores = defaultdict(dict)
f1_scores["de"]["de"] = get_f1_score(trainer, panx_de_encoded["test"])
print(f"F1-score of [de] model on [de] dataset: {f1_scores['de']['de']:.3f}")
```

```
F1-score of [de] model on [de] dataset: 0.868
```

These are pretty good results for a NER task. Our metrics are in the ballpark of 85%, and we can see that the model seems to struggle the most on the `ORG` entities, probably because these are the least common in the training data and many organization names are rare in XLM-R's vocabulary. How about the other languages? To warm up, let's see how our model fine-tuned on German fares on French:

```
text_fr = "Jeff Dean est informaticien chez Google en Californie"
tag_text(text_fr, tags, trainer.model, xlmr_tokenizer)
```

	0	1	2	3	4	5	6	7	8	9	10	11	12	13
Tokens	<s>	_Jeff	_De	an	_est	_informatic	ien	_chez	_Google	_en	_Cali	for	nie	</s>
Tags	0	B-PER	I-PER	I-PER	0	0	0	0	B-ORG	0	B-LOC	I-LOC	I-LOC	0

Not bad! Although the name and organization are the same in both languages, the model did manage to correctly label the French translation of "Kalifornien". Next, let's quantify how well our German model fares on the whole French test set by writing a simple function that encodes a dataset and generates the classification report on it:

```
def evaluate_lang_performance(lang, trainer):
    panx_ds = encode_panx_dataset(panx_ch[lang])
    return get_f1_score(trainer, panx_ds["test"])
```

```
f1_scores["de"]["fr"] = evaluate_lang_performance("fr", trainer)
print(f"F1-score of [de] model on [fr] dataset: {f1_scores['de']['fr']:.3f}")
```

```
F1-score of [de] model on [fr] dataset: 0.714
```

Although we see a drop of about 15 points in the micro-averaged metrics, remember that our model has not seen a single labeled French example! In general, the size of the performance drop is related to how "far away" the languages are from each other. Although German and French are grouped as Indo-European languages, they technically belong to different language families: Germanic and Romance, respectively.

Next, let's evaluate the performance on Italian. Since Italian is also a Romance language, we expect to get a similar result as we found on French:

```
f1_scores["de"]["it"] = evaluate_lang_performance("it", trainer)
print(f"F1-score of [de] model on [it] dataset: {f1_scores['de']['it']:.3f}")
```

```
F1-score of [de] model on [it] dataset: 0.692
```

Indeed, our expectations are borne out by the F_1-scores. Finally, let's examine the performance on English, which belongs to the Germanic language family:

```
f1_scores["de"]["en"] = evaluate_lang_performance("en", trainer)
print(f"F1-score of [de] model on [en] dataset: {f1_scores['de']['en']:.3f}")
```

```
F1-score of [de] model on [en] dataset: 0.589
```

Surprisingly, our model fares *worst* on English, even though we might intuitively expect German to be more similar to English than French. Having fine-tuned on German and performed zero-shot transfer to French and English, let's next examine when it makes sense to fine-tune directly on the target language.

When Does Zero-Shot Transfer Make Sense?

So far we've seen that fine-tuning XLM-R on the German corpus yields an F_1-score of around 85%, and without *any additional training* the model is able to achieve modest performance on the other languages in our corpus. The question is, how good are these results and how do they compare against an XLM-R model fine-tuned on a monolingual corpus?

In this section we will explore this question for the French corpus by fine-tuning XLM-R on training sets of increasing size. By tracking the performance this way, we can determine at which point zero-shot cross-lingual transfer is superior, which in practice can be useful for guiding decisions about whether to collect more labeled data.

For simplicity, we'll keep the same hyperparameters from the fine-tuning run on the German corpus, except that we'll tweak the `logging_steps` argument of `TrainingArguments` to account for the changing training set sizes. We can wrap this all together in a simple function that takes a `DatasetDict` object corresponding to a monolingual corpus, downsamples it by `num_samples`, and fine-tunes XLM-R on that sample to return the metrics from the best epoch:

```
def train_on_subset(dataset, num_samples):
    train_ds = dataset["train"].shuffle(seed=42).select(range(num_samples))
    valid_ds = dataset["validation"]
    test_ds = dataset["test"]
    training_args.logging_steps = len(train_ds) // batch_size

    trainer = Trainer(model_init=model_init, args=training_args,
        data_collator=data_collator, compute_metrics=compute_metrics,
        train_dataset=train_ds, eval_dataset=valid_ds, tokenizer=xlmr_tokenizer)
    trainer.train()
    if training_args.push_to_hub:
        trainer.push_to_hub(commit_message="Training completed!")

    f1_score = get_f1_score(trainer, test_ds)
    return pd.DataFrame.from_dict(
        {"num_samples": [len(train_ds)], "f1_score": [f1_score]})
```

As we did with fine-tuning on the German corpus, we also need to encode the French corpus into input IDs, attention masks, and label IDs:

```
panx_fr_encoded = encode_panx_dataset(panx_ch["fr"])
```

Next let's check that our function works by running it on a small training set of 250 examples:

```
training_args.push_to_hub = False
metrics_df = train_on_subset(panx_fr_encoded, 250)
metrics_df
```

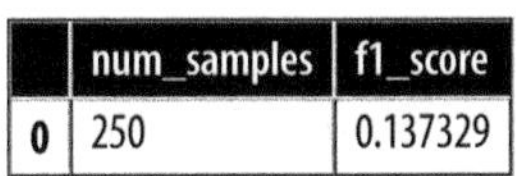

	num_samples	f1_score
0	250	0.137329

We can see that with only 250 examples, fine-tuning on French underperforms the zero-shot transfer from German by a large margin. Let's now increase our training set sizes to 500, 1,000, 2,000, and 4,000 examples to get an idea of how the performance increases:

```
for num_samples in [500, 1000, 2000, 4000]:
    metrics_df = metrics_df.append(
        train_on_subset(panx_fr_encoded, num_samples), ignore_index=True)
```

We can compare how fine-tuning on French samples compares to zero-shot cross-lingual transfer from German by plotting the F_1-scores on the test set as a function of increasing training set size:

```
fig, ax = plt.subplots()
ax.axhline(f1_scores["de"]["fr"], ls="--", color="r")
metrics_df.set_index("num_samples").plot(ax=ax)
plt.legend(["Zero-shot from de", "Fine-tuned on fr"], loc="lower right")
plt.ylim((0, 1))
plt.xlabel("Number of Training Samples")
plt.ylabel("F1 Score")
plt.show()
```

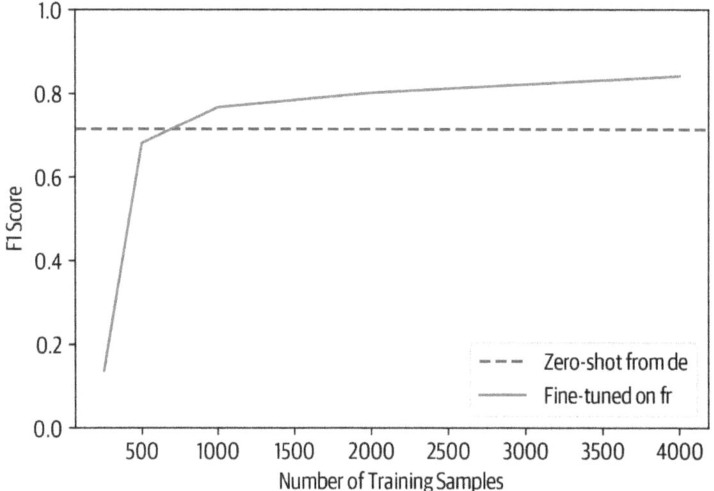

From the plot we can see that zero-shot transfer remains competitive until about 750 training examples, after which fine-tuning on French reaches a similar level of performance to what we obtained when fine-tuning on German. Nevertheless, this result is not to be sniffed at! In our experience, getting domain experts to label even hundreds of documents can be costly, especially for NER, where the labeling process is fine-grained and time-consuming.

There is one final technique we can try to evaluate multilingual learning: fine-tuning on multiple languages at once! Let's see how we can do this.

Fine-Tuning on Multiple Languages at Once

So far we've seen that zero-shot cross-lingual transfer from German to French or Italian produces a drop of around 15 points in performance. One way to mitigate this is by fine-tuning on multiple languages at the same time. To see what type of gains we can get, let's first use the `concatenate_datasets()` function from 🤗 Datasets to concatenate the German and French corpora together:

```
from datasets import concatenate_datasets

def concatenate_splits(corpora):
    multi_corpus = DatasetDict()
    for split in corpora[0].keys():
        multi_corpus[split] = concatenate_datasets(
            [corpus[split] for corpus in corpora]).shuffle(seed=42)
    return multi_corpus

panx_de_fr_encoded = concatenate_splits([panx_de_encoded, panx_fr_encoded])
```

For training, we'll again use the same hyperparameters from the previous sections, so we can simply update the logging steps, model, and datasets in the trainer:

```
training_args.logging_steps = len(panx_de_fr_encoded["train"]) // batch_size
training_args.push_to_hub = True
training_args.output_dir = "xlm-roberta-base-finetuned-panx-de-fr"

trainer = Trainer(model_init=model_init, args=training_args,
    data_collator=data_collator, compute_metrics=compute_metrics,
    tokenizer=xlmr_tokenizer, train_dataset=panx_de_fr_encoded["train"],
    eval_dataset=panx_de_fr_encoded["validation"])

trainer.train()
trainer.push_to_hub(commit_message="Training completed!")
```

Let's have a look at how the model performs on the test set of each language:

```
for lang in langs:
    f1 = evaluate_lang_performance(lang, trainer)
    print(f"F1-score of [de-fr] model on [{lang}] dataset: {f1:.3f}")
```

```
F1-score of [de-fr] model on [de] dataset: 0.866
F1-score of [de-fr] model on [fr] dataset: 0.868
F1-score of [de-fr] model on [it] dataset: 0.815
F1-score of [de-fr] model on [en] dataset: 0.677
```

It performs much better on the French split than before, matching the performance on the German test set. Interestingly, its performance on the Italian and English splits also improves by roughly 10 points! So, even adding training data in another language improves the performance of the model on unseen languages.

Let's round out our analysis by comparing the performance of fine-tuning on each language separately against multilingual learning on all the corpora. Since we have already fine-tuned on the German corpus, we can fine-tune on the remaining languages with our `train_on_subset()` function, with `num_samples` equal to the number of examples in the training set:

```
corpora = [panx_de_encoded]
```

```
# Exclude German from iteration
for lang in langs[1:]:
    training_args.output_dir = f"xlm-roberta-base-finetuned-panx-{lang}"
    # Fine-tune on monolingual corpus
    ds_encoded = encode_panx_dataset(panx_ch[lang])
    metrics = train_on_subset(ds_encoded, ds_encoded["train"].num_rows)
    # Collect F1-scores in common dict
    f1_scores[lang][lang] = metrics["f1_score"][0]
    # Add monolingual corpus to list of corpora to concatenate
    corpora.append(ds_encoded)
```

Now that we've fine-tuned on each language's corpus, the next step is to concatenate all the splits together to create a multilingual corpus of all four languages. As with the previous German and French analysis, we can use the `concatenate_splits()` function to do this step for us on the list of corpora we generated in the previous step:

```
corpora_encoded = concatenate_splits(corpora)
```

Now that we have our multilingual corpus, we run the familiar steps with the trainer:

```
training_args.logging_steps = len(corpora_encoded["train"]) // batch_size
training_args.output_dir = "xlm-roberta-base-finetuned-panx-all"

trainer = Trainer(model_init=model_init, args=training_args,
    data_collator=data_collator, compute_metrics=compute_metrics,
    tokenizer=xlmr_tokenizer, train_dataset=corpora_encoded["train"],
    eval_dataset=corpora_encoded["validation"])

trainer.train()
trainer.push_to_hub(commit_message="Training completed!")
```

The final step is to generate the predictions from the trainer on each language's test set. This will give us an insight into how well multilingual learning is really working. We'll collect the F_1-scores in our `f1_scores` dictionary and then create a `DataFrame` that summarizes the main results from our multilingual experiments:

```
for idx, lang in enumerate(langs):
    f1_scores["all"][lang] = get_f1_score(trainer, corpora[idx]["test"])

scores_data = {"de": f1_scores["de"],
               "each": {lang: f1_scores[lang][lang] for lang in langs},
               "all": f1_scores["all"]}
f1_scores_df = pd.DataFrame(scores_data).T.round(4)
f1_scores_df.rename_axis(index="Fine-tune on", columns="Evaluated on",
                         inplace=True)
f1_scores_df
```

Evaluated on	de	fr	it	en
Fine-tune on				
de	0.8677	0.7141	0.6923	0.5890
each	0.8677	0.8505	0.8192	0.7068

Evaluated on	de	fr	it	en
Fine-tune on				
all	0.8682	0.8647	0.8575	0.7870

From these results we can draw a few general conclusions:

- Multilingual learning can provide significant gains in performance, especially if the low-resource languages for cross-lingual transfer belong to similar language families. In our experiments we can see that German, French, and Italian achieve similar performance in the `all` category, suggesting that these languages are more similar to each other than to English.
- As a general strategy, it is a good idea to focus attention on cross-lingual transfer *within* language families, especially when dealing with different scripts like Japanese.

Interacting with Model Widgets

In this chapter, we've pushed quite a few fine-tuned models to the Hub. Although we could use the `pipeline()` function to interact with them on our local machine, the Hub provides *widgets* that are great for this kind of workflow. An example is shown in Figure 4-5 for our `transformersbook/xlm-roberta-base-finetuned-panx-all` checkpoint, which as you can see has done a good job at identifying all the entities of a German text.

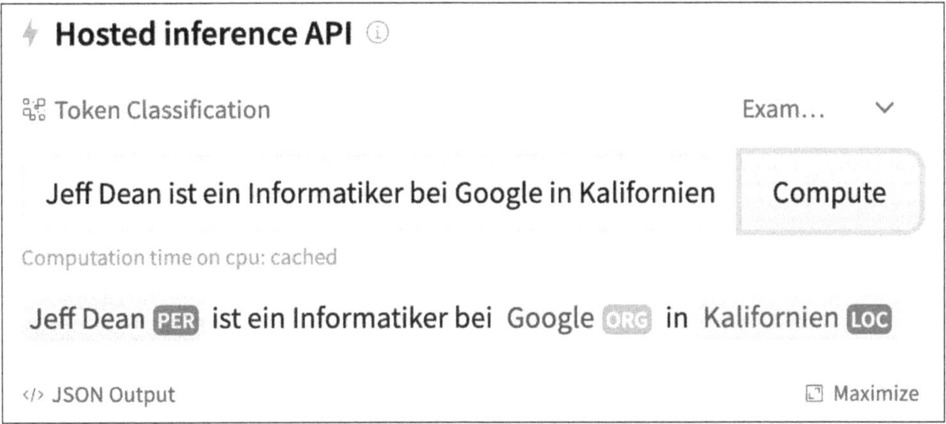

Figure 4-5. Example of a widget on the Hugging Face Hub

Conclusion

In this chapter we saw how to tackle an NLP task on a multilingual corpus using a single transformer pretrained on 100 languages: XLM-R. Although we were able to show that cross-lingual transfer from German to French is competitive when only a small number of labeled examples are available for fine-tuning, this good performance generally does not occur if the target language is significantly different from the one the base model was fine-tuned on or was not one of the 100 languages used during pretraining. Recent proposals like MAD-X are designed precisely for these low-resource scenarios, and since MAD-X is built on top of 🤗 Transformers you can easily adapt the code in this chapter to work with it![6]

So far we have looked at two tasks: sequence classification and token classification. These both fall into the domain of natural language understanding, where text is synthesized into predictions. In the next chapter we have our first look at text generation, where not only the input but also the output of the model is text.

---

6 J. Pfeiffer et al., "MAD-X: An Adapter-Based Framework for Multi-Task Cross-Lingual Transfer" (*https://arxiv.org/abs/2005.00052*), (2020).

CHAPTER 5
Text Generation

One of the most uncanny features of transformer-based language models is their ability to generate text that is almost indistinguishable from text written by humans. A famous example is OpenAI's GPT-2, which when given the prompt:[1]

> In a shocking finding, scientist discovered a herd of unicorns living in a remote, previously unexplored valley, in the Andes Mountains. Even more surprising to the researchers was the fact that the unicorns spoke perfect English.

was able to generate a compelling news article about talking unicorns:

> The scientist named the population, after their distinctive horn, Ovid's Unicorn. These four-horned, silver-white unicorns were previously unknown to science. Now, after almost two centuries, the mystery of what sparked this odd phenomenon is finally solved. Dr. Jorge Pérez, an evolutionary biologist from the University of La Paz, and several companions, were exploring the Andes Mountains when they found a small valley, with no other animals or humans. Pérez noticed that the valley had what appeared to be a natural fountain, surrounded by two peaks of rock and silver snow. Pérez and the others then ventured further into the valley. "By the time we reached the top of one peak, the water looked blue, with some crystals on top," said Pérez. Pérez and his friends were astonished to see the unicorn herd. These creatures could be seen from the air without having to move too much to see them—they were so close they could touch their horns. While examining these bizarre creatures the scientists discovered that the creatures also spoke some fairly regular English ...

1 This example comes from OpenAI's blog post on GPT-2 (*https://openai.com/blog/better-language-models*).

What makes this example so remarkable is that it was generated without any explicit supervision! By simply learning to predict the next word in the text of millions of web pages, GPT-2 and its more powerful descendants like GPT-3 are able to acquire a broad set of skills and pattern recognition abilities that can be activated with different kinds of input prompts. Figure 5-1 shows how language models are sometimes exposed during pretraining to sequences of tasks where they need to predict the following tokens based on the context alone, like addition, unscrambling words, and translation. This allows them to transfer this knowledge effectively during fine-tuning or (if the model is large enough) at inference time. These tasks are not chosen ahead of time, but occur naturally in the huge corpora used to train billion-parameter language models.

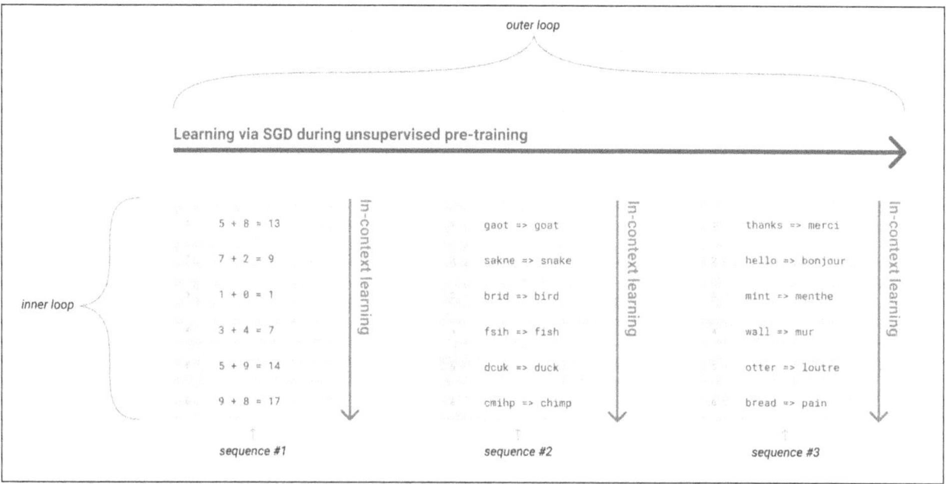

Figure 5-1. During pretraining, language models are exposed to sequences of tasks that can be adapted during inference (courtesy of Tom B. Brown)

The ability of transformers to generate realistic text has led to a diverse range of applications, like InferKit (*https://oreil.ly/I4adh*), Write With Transformer (*https://oreil.ly/ipkap*), AI Dungeon (*https://oreil.ly/8ubC1*), and conversational agents like Google's Meena (*https://oreil.ly/gMegC*) that can even tell corny jokes, as shown in Figure 5-2![2]

2 However, as Delip Rao points out (*https://oreil.ly/mOM3V*), whether Meena *intends* to tell corny jokes is a subtle question.

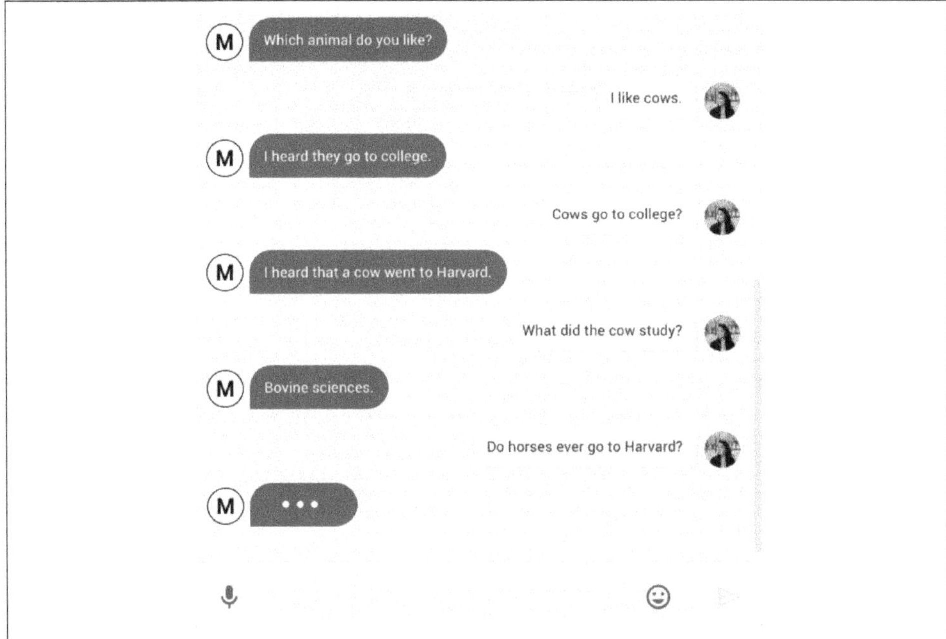

Figure 5-2. Meena on the left telling a corny joke to a human on the right (courtesy of Daniel Adiwardana and Thang Luong)

In this chapter we'll use GPT-2 to illustrate how text generation works for language models and explore how different decoding strategies impact the generated texts.

The Challenge with Generating Coherent Text

So far in this book, we have focused on tackling NLP tasks via a combination of pretraining and supervised fine-tuning. As we've seen, for task-specific heads like sequence or token classification, generating predictions is fairly straightforward; the model produces some logits and we either take the maximum value to get the predicted class, or apply a softmax function to obtain the predicted probabilities per class. By contrast, converting the model's probabilistic output to text requires a *decoding method*, which introduces a few challenges that are unique to text generation:

- The decoding is done *iteratively* and thus involves significantly more compute than simply passing inputs once through the forward pass of a model.
- The *quality* and *diversity* of the generated text depend on the choice of decoding method and associated hyperparameters.

To understand how this decoding process works, let's start by examining how GPT-2 is pretrained and subsequently applied to generate text.

Like other *autoregressive* or *causal language models*, GPT-2 is pretrained to estimate the probability $P(\mathbf{y}|\mathbf{x})$ of a sequence of tokens $\mathbf{y} = y_1, y_2, ...y_t$ occurring in the text, given some initial prompt or context sequence $\mathbf{x} = x_1, x_2, ...x_k$. Since it is impractical to acquire enough training data to estimate $P(\mathbf{y}|\mathbf{x})$ directly, it is common to use the chain rule of probability to factorize it as a product of *conditional* probabilities:

$$P\left(y_1, ..., y_t|\mathbf{x}\right) = \prod_{t=1}^{N} P\left(y_t|y_{<t}, \mathbf{x}\right)$$

where $y_{<t}$ is a shorthand notation for the sequence $y_1, ..., y_{t-1}$. It is from these conditional probabilities that we pick up the intuition that autoregressive language modeling amounts to predicting each word given the preceding words in a sentence; this is exactly what the probability on the righthand side of the preceding equation describes. Notice that this pretraining objective is quite different from BERT's, which utilizes both *past* and *future* contexts to predict a *masked* token.

By now you may have guessed how we can adapt this next token prediction task to generate text sequences of arbitrary length. As shown in Figure 5-3, we start with a prompt like "Transformers are the" and use the model to predict the next token. Once we have determined the next token, we append it to the prompt and then use the new input sequence to generate another token. We do this until we have reached a special end-of-sequence token or a predefined maximum length.

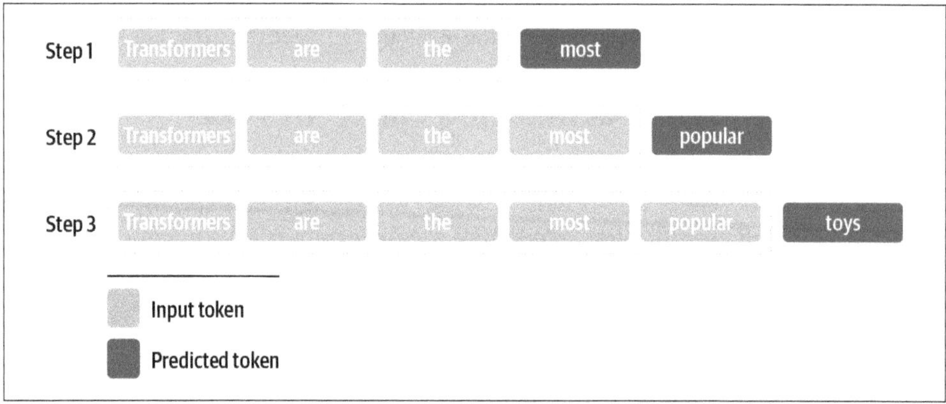

Figure 5-3. Generating text from an input sequence by adding a new word to the input at each step

Since the output sequence is *conditioned* on the choice of input prompt, this type of text generation is often called *conditional text generation*.

At the heart of this process lies a decoding method that determines which token is selected at each timestep. Since the language model head produces a logit $z_{t,i}$ per token in the vocabulary at each step, we can get the probability distribution over the next possible token w_i by taking the softmax:

$$P(y_t = w_i | y_{<t}, \mathbf{x}) = \mathrm{softmax}(z_{t,i})$$

The goal of most decoding methods is to search for the most likely overall sequence by picking a $\hat{\mathbf{y}}$ such that:

$$\hat{\mathbf{y}} = \underset{\mathbf{y}}{\mathrm{argmax}}\, P(\mathbf{y} | \mathbf{x})$$

Finding $\hat{\mathbf{y}}$ directly would involve evaluating every possible sequence with the language model. Since there does not exist an algorithm that can do this in a reasonable amount of time, we rely on approximations instead. In this chapter we'll explore a few of these approximations and gradually build up toward smarter and more complex algorithms that can be used to generate high-quality texts.

Greedy Search Decoding

The simplest decoding method to get discrete tokens from a model's continuous output is to greedily select the token with the highest probability at each timestep:

$$\hat{y}_t = \underset{y_t}{\mathrm{argmax}}\, P(y_t | y_{<t}, \mathbf{x})$$

To see how greedy search works, let's start by loading the 1.5-billion-parameter version of GPT-2 with a language modeling head:[3]

```
import torch
from transformers import AutoTokenizer, AutoModelForCausalLM

device = "cuda" if torch.cuda.is_available() else "cpu"
model_name = "gpt2-xl"
tokenizer = AutoTokenizer.from_pretrained(model_name)
model = AutoModelForCausalLM.from_pretrained(model_name).to(device)
```

Now let's generate some text! Although 🤗 Transformers provides a `generate()` function for autoregressive models like GPT-2, we'll implement this decoding method

3 If you run out of memory on your machine, you can load a smaller GPT-2 version by replacing `model_name = "gpt-xl"` with `model_name = "gpt"`.

ourselves to see what goes on under the hood. To warm up, we'll take the same iterative approach shown in Figure 5-3: we'll use "Transformers are the" as the input prompt and run the decoding for eight timesteps. At each timestep, we pick out the model's logits for the last token in the prompt and wrap them with a softmax to get a probability distribution. We then pick the next token with the highest probability, add it to the input sequence, and run the process again. The following code does the job, and also stores the five most probable tokens at each timestep so we can visualize the alternatives:

```
import        as

input_txt = "Transformers are the"
input_ids = tokenizer(input_txt, return_tensors="pt")["input_ids"].to(device)
iterations = []
n_steps = 8
choices_per_step = 5

with torch.no_grad():
    for _ in range(n_steps):
        iteration = dict()
        iteration["Input"] = tokenizer.decode(input_ids[0])
        output = model(input_ids=input_ids)
        # Select logits of the first batch and the last token and apply softmax
        next_token_logits = output.logits[0, -1, :]
        next_token_probs = torch.softmax(next_token_logits, dim=-1)
        sorted_ids = torch.argsort(next_token_probs, dim=-1, descending=True)
        # Store tokens with highest probabilities
        for choice_idx in range(choices_per_step):
            token_id = sorted_ids[choice_idx]
            token_prob = next_token_probs[token_id].cpu().numpy()
            token_choice = (
                f"{tokenizer.decode(token_id)} ({100 * token_prob:.2f}%)"
            )
            iteration[f"Choice {choice_idx+1}"] = token_choice
        # Append predicted next token to input
        input_ids = torch.cat([input_ids, sorted_ids[None, 0, None]], dim=-1)
        iterations.append(iteration)

pd.DataFrame(iterations)
```

	Input	Choice 1	Choice 2	Choice 3	Choice 4	Choice 5
0	Transformers are the	most (8.53%)	only (4.96%)	best (4.65%)	Transformers (4.37%)	ultimate (2.16%)
1	Transformers are the most	popular (16.78%)	powerful (5.37%)	common (4.96%)	famous (3.72%)	successful (3.20%)
2	Transformers are the most popular	toy (10.63%)	toys (7.23%)	Transformers (6.60%)	of (5.46%)	and (3.76%)
3	Transformers are the most popular toy	line (34.38%)	in (18.20%)	of (11.71%)	brand (6.10%)	line (2.69%)

	Input	Choice 1	Choice 2	Choice 3	Choice 4	Choice 5
4	Transformers are the most popular toy line	in (46.28%)	of (15.09%)	, (4.94%)	on (4.40%)	ever (2.72%)
5	Transformers are the most popular toy line in	the (65.99%)	history (12.42%)	America (6.91%)	Japan (2.44%)	North (1.40%)
6	Transformers are the most popular toy line in the	world (69.26%)	United (4.55%)	history (4.29%)	US (4.23%)	U (2.30%)
7	Transformers are the most popular toy line in the world	, (39.73%)	. (30.64%)	and (9.87%)	with (2.32%)	today (1.74%)

With this simple method we were able to generate the sentence "Transformers are the most popular toy line in the world". Interestingly, this indicates that GPT-2 has internalized some knowledge about the Transformers media franchise, which was created by two toy companies (Hasbro and Takara Tomy). We can also see the other possible continuations at each step, which shows the iterative nature of text generation. Unlike other tasks such as sequence classification where a single forward pass suffices to generate the predictions, with text generation we need to decode the output tokens one at a time.

Implementing greedy search wasn't too hard, but we'll want to use the built-in `generate()` function from 🤗 Transformers to explore more sophisticated decoding methods. To reproduce our simple example, let's make sure sampling is switched off (it's off by default, unless the specific configuration of the model you are loading the checkpoint from states otherwise) and specify the `max_new_tokens` for the number of newly generated tokens:

```
input_ids = tokenizer(input_txt, return_tensors="pt")["input_ids"].to(device)
output = model.generate(input_ids, max_new_tokens=n_steps, do_sample=False)
print(tokenizer.decode(output[0]))
```

```
Transformers are the most popular toy line in the world,
```

Now let's try something a bit more interesting: can we reproduce the unicorn story from OpenAI? As we did previously, we'll encode the prompt with the tokenizer, and we'll specify a larger value for `max_length` to generate a longer sequence of text:

```
max_length = 128
input_txt = """In a shocking finding, scientist discovered \
a herd of unicorns living in a remote, previously unexplored \
valley, in the Andes Mountains. Even more surprising to the \
researchers was the fact that the unicorns spoke perfect English.\n\n
"""
input_ids = tokenizer(input_txt, return_tensors="pt")["input_ids"].to(device)
output_greedy = model.generate(input_ids, max_length=max_length,
                               do_sample=False)
print(tokenizer.decode(output_greedy[0]))
```

```
In a shocking finding, scientist discovered a herd of unicorns living in a
remote, previously unexplored valley, in the Andes Mountains. Even more
surprising to the researchers was the fact that the unicorns spoke perfect
English.


The researchers, from the University of California, Davis, and the University of
Colorado, Boulder, were conducting a study on the Andean cloud forest, which is
home to the rare species of cloud forest trees.


The researchers were surprised to find that the unicorns were able to
communicate with each other, and even with humans.


The researchers were surprised to find that the unicorns were able
```

Well, the first few sentences are quite different from the OpenAI example and amusingly involve different universities being credited with the discovery! We can also see one of the main drawbacks with greedy search decoding: it tends to produce repetitive output sequences, which is certainly undesirable in a news article. This is a common problem with greedy search algorithms, which can fail to give you the optimal solution; in the context of decoding, they can miss word sequences whose overall probability is higher just because high-probability words happen to be preceded by low-probability ones.

Fortunately, we can do better—let's examine a popular method known as *beam search decoding*.

Although greedy search decoding is rarely used for text generation tasks that require diversity, it can be useful for producing short sequences like arithmetic where a deterministic and factually correct output is preferred.[4] For these tasks, you can condition GPT-2 by providing a few line-separated examples in the format `"5 + 8 => 13 \n 7 + 2 => 9 \n 1 + 0 =>"` as the input prompt.

Beam Search Decoding

Instead of decoding the token with the highest probability at each step, beam search keeps track of the top-b most probable next tokens, where b is referred to as the number of *beams* or *partial hypotheses*. The next set of beams are chosen by considering all possible next-token extensions of the existing set and selecting the b most likely extensions. The process is repeated until we reach the maximum length or an EOS

4 N.S. Keskar et al., "CTRL: A Conditional Transformer Language Model for Controllable Generation" (*https://arxiv.org/abs/1909.05858*), (2019).

token, and the most likely sequence is selected by ranking the b beams according to their log probabilities. An example of beam search is shown in Figure 5-4.

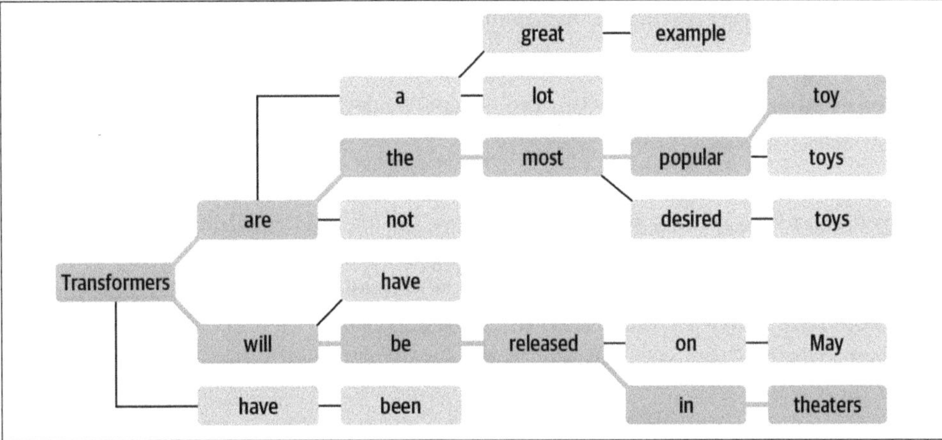

Figure 5-4. Beam search with two beams

Why do we score the sequences using log probabilities instead of the probabilities themselves? That calculating the overall probability of a sequence $P(y_1, y_2, ..., y_t | \mathbf{x})$ involves calculating a *product* of conditional probabilities $P(y_t | y_{<t}, \mathbf{x})$ is one reason. Since each conditional probability is typically a small number in the range $[0, 1]$, taking their product can lead to an overall probability that can easily underflow. This means that the computer can no longer precisely represent the result of the calculation. For example, suppose we have a sequence of $t = 1024$ tokens and generously assume that the probability for each token is 0.5. The overall probability for this sequence is an extremely small number:

```
0.5 ** 1024
```

```
5.562684646268003e-309
```

which leads to numerical instability as we run into underflow. We can avoid this by calculating a related term, the log probability. If we apply the logarithm to the joint and conditional probabilities, then with the help of the product rule for logarithms we get:

$$\log P(y_1, ...y_t | \mathbf{x}) = \sum_{t=1}^{N} \log P(y_t | y_{<t}, \mathbf{x})$$

In other words, the product of probabilities we saw earlier becomes a sum of log probabilities, which is much less likely to run into numerical instabilities. For example, calculating the log probability of the same example as before gives:

```
import numpy as np

sum([np.log(0.5)] * 1024)
```

```
-709.7827128933695
```

This is a number we can easily deal with, and this approach still works for much smaller numbers. Since we only want to compare relative probabilities, we can do this directly with log probabilities.

Let's calculate and compare the log probabilities of the texts generated by greedy and beam search to see if beam search can improve the overall probability. Since 🤗 Transformers models return the unnormalized logits for the next token given the input tokens, we first need to normalize the logits to create a probability distribution over the whole vocabulary for each token in the sequence. We then need to select only the token probabilities that were present in the sequence. The following function implements these steps:

```
import torch.nn.functional as F

def log_probs_from_logits(logits, labels):
    logp = F.log_softmax(logits, dim=-1)
    logp_label = torch.gather(logp, 2, labels.unsqueeze(2)).squeeze(-1)
    return logp_label
```

This gives us the log probability for a single token, so to get the total log probability of a sequence we just need to sum the log probabilities for each token:

```
def sequence_logprob(model, labels, input_len=0):
    with torch.no_grad():
        output = model(labels)
        log_probs = log_probs_from_logits(
            output.logits[:, :-1, :], labels[:, 1:])
        seq_log_prob = torch.sum(log_probs[:, input_len:])
    return seq_log_prob.cpu().numpy()
```

Note that we ignore the log probabilities of the input sequence because they are not generated by the model. We can also see that it is important to align the logits and the labels; since the model predicts the next token, we do not get a logit for the first label, and we don't need the last logit because we don't have a ground truth token for it.

Let's use these functions to first calculate the sequence log probability of the greedy decoder on the OpenAI prompt:

```
logp = sequence_logprob(model, output_greedy, input_len=len(input_ids[0]))
print(tokenizer.decode(output_greedy[0]))
print(f"\nlog-prob: {logp:.2f}")
```

```
In a shocking finding, scientist discovered a herd of unicorns living in a
remote, previously unexplored valley, in the Andes Mountains. Even more
surprising to the researchers was the fact that the unicorns spoke perfect
English.
```

```
The researchers, from the University of California, Davis, and the University of
Colorado, Boulder, were conducting a study on the Andean cloud forest, which is
home to the rare species of cloud forest trees.


The researchers were surprised to find that the unicorns were able to
communicate with each other, and even with humans.


The researchers were surprised to find that the unicorns were able

log-prob: -87.43
```

Now let's compare this to a sequence that is generated with beam search. To activate beam search with the `generate()` function we just need to specify the number of beams with the `num_beams` parameter. The more beams we choose, the better the result potentially gets; however, the generation process becomes much slower since we generate parallel sequences for each beam:

```
output_beam = model.generate(input_ids, max_length=max_length, num_beams=5,
                             do_sample=False)
logp = sequence_logprob(model, output_beam, input_len=len(input_ids[0]))
print(tokenizer.decode(output_beam[0]))
print(f"\nlog-prob: {logp:.2f}")
```

```
In a shocking finding, scientist discovered a herd of unicorns living in a
remote, previously unexplored valley, in the Andes Mountains. Even more
surprising to the researchers was the fact that the unicorns spoke perfect
English.


The discovery of the unicorns was made by a team of scientists from the
University of California, Santa Cruz, and the National Geographic Society.


The scientists were conducting a study of the Andes Mountains when they
discovered a herd of unicorns living in a remote, previously unexplored valley,
in the Andes Mountains. Even more surprising to the researchers was the fact
that the unicorns spoke perfect English

log-prob: -55.23
```

We can see that we get a better log probability (higher is better) with beam search than we did with simple greedy decoding. However, we can see that beam search also suffers from repetitive text. One way to address this is to impose an *n*-gram penalty with the `no_repeat_ngram_size` parameter that tracks which *n*-grams have been seen and sets the next token probability to zero if it would produce a previously seen *n*-gram:

```python
output_beam = model.generate(input_ids, max_length=max_length, num_beams=5,
                             do_sample=False, no_repeat_ngram_size=2)
logp = sequence_logprob(model, output_beam, input_len=len(input_ids[0]))
print(tokenizer.decode(output_beam[0]))
print(f"\nlog-prob: {logp:.2f}")
```

```
In a shocking finding, scientist discovered a herd of unicorns living in a
remote, previously unexplored valley, in the Andes Mountains. Even more
surprising to the researchers was the fact that the unicorns spoke perfect
English.


The discovery was made by a team of scientists from the University of
California, Santa Cruz, and the National Geographic Society.

According to a press release, the scientists were conducting a survey of the
area when they came across the herd. They were surprised to find that they were
able to converse with the animals in English, even though they had never seen a
unicorn in person before. The researchers were

log-prob: -93.12
```

This isn't too bad! We've managed to stop the repetitions, and we can see that despite producing a lower score, the text remains coherent. Beam search with *n*-gram penalty is a good way to find a trade-off between focusing on high-probability tokens (with beam search) while reducing repetitions (with *n*-gram penalty), and it's commonly used in applications such as summarization or machine translation where factual correctness is important. When factual correctness is less important than the diversity of generated output, for instance in open-domain chitchat or story generation, another alternative to reduce repetitions while improving diversity is to use sampling. Let's round out our exploration of text generation by examining a few of the most common sampling methods.

Sampling Methods

The simplest sampling method is to randomly sample from the probability distribution of the model's outputs over the full vocabulary at each timestep:

$$P\left(y_t = w_i \middle| y_{<t}, \mathbf{x}\right) = \operatorname{softmax}\left(z_{t,i}\right) = \frac{\exp\left(z_{t,i}\right)}{\sum_{j=1}^{|V|} \exp\left(z_{t,j}\right)}$$

where $|V|$ denotes the cardinality of the vocabulary. We can easily control the diversity of the output by adding a temperature parameter T that rescales the logits before taking the softmax:

$$P\left(y_t = w_i \middle| y_{<t}, \mathbf{x}\right) = \frac{\exp\left(z_{t,i}/T\right)}{\sum_{j=1}^{|V|} \exp\left(z_{t,j}/T\right)}$$

By tuning T we can control the shape of the probability distribution.[5] When $T \ll 1$, the distribution becomes peaked around the origin and the rare tokens are suppressed. On the other hand, when $T \gg 1$, the distribution flattens out and each token becomes equally likely. The effect of temperature on token probabilities is shown in Figure 5-5.

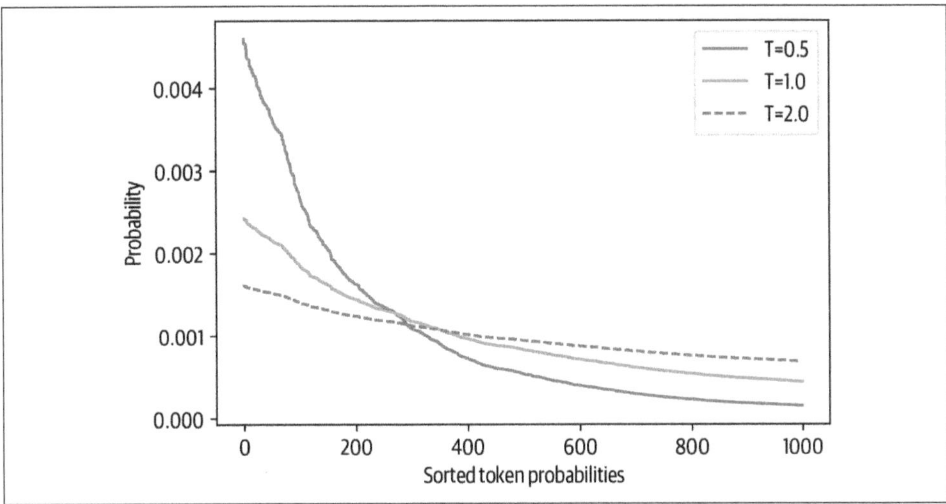

Figure 5-5. Distribution of randomly generated token probabilities for three selected temperatures

To see how we can use temperature to influence the generated text, let's sample with $T = 2$ by setting the `temperature` parameter in the `generate()` function (we'll explain the meaning of the `top_k` parameter in the next section):

```
output_temp = model.generate(input_ids, max_length=max_length, do_sample=True,
                             temperature=2.0, top_k=0)
print(tokenizer.decode(output_temp[0]))
```

```
In a shocking finding, scientist discovered a herd of unicorns living in a
remote, previously unexplored valley, in the Andes Mountains. Even more
surprising to the researchers was the fact that the unicorns spoke perfect
English.
```

5 If you know some physics, you may recognize a striking resemblance to the Boltzmann distribution (*https://oreil.ly/ZsMmx*).

```
While the station aren protagonist receive Pengala nostalgiates tidbitRegarding
Jenny loclonju AgreementCON irrational �rite Continent seaf A jer Turner
Dorbecue WILL Pumpkin mere Thatvernuildagain YoAniamond disse *
Runewitingkusstemprop});b zo coachinginventorymodules deflation press
Vaticanpres Wrestling chargesThingsctureddong Ty physician PET KimBi66 graz Oz
at aff da temporou MD6 radi iter
```

We can clearly see that a high temperature has produced mostly gibberish; by accentuating the rare tokens, we've caused the model to create strange grammar and quite a few made-up words! Let's see what happens if we cool down the temperature:

```
output_temp = model.generate(input_ids, max_length=max_length, do_sample=True,
                             temperature=0.5, top_k=0)
print(tokenizer.decode(output_temp[0]))
```

```
In a shocking finding, scientist discovered a herd of unicorns living in a
remote, previously unexplored valley, in the Andes Mountains. Even more
surprising to the researchers was the fact that the unicorns spoke perfect
English.


The scientists were searching for the source of the mysterious sound, which was
making the animals laugh and cry.


The unicorns were living in a remote valley in the Andes mountains

'When we first heard the noise of the animals, we thought it was a lion or a
tiger,' said Luis Guzman, a researcher from the University of Buenos Aires,
Argentina.


'But when
```

This is significantly more coherent, and even includes a quote from yet another university being credited with the discovery! The main lesson we can draw from temperature is that it allows us to control the quality of the samples, but there's always a trade-off between coherence (low temperature) and diversity (high temperature) that one has to tune to the use case at hand.

Another way to adjust the trade-off between coherence and diversity is to truncate the distribution of the vocabulary. This allows us to adjust the diversity freely with the temperature, but in a more limited range that excludes words that would be too strange in the context (i.e., low-probability words). There are two main ways to do this: top-*k* and nucleus (or top-*p*) sampling. Let's take a look.

Top-k and Nucleus Sampling

Top-*k* and nucleus (top-*p*) sampling are two popular alternatives or extensions to using temperature. In both cases, the basic idea is to restrict the number of possible tokens we can sample from at each timestep. To see how this works, let's first visualize the cumulative probability distribution of the model's outputs at $T = 1$ as seen in Figure 5-6.

Let's tease apart these plots, since they contain a lot of information. In the upper plot we can see a histogram of the token probabilities. It has a peak around 10^{-8} and a second, smaller peak around 10^{-4}, followed by a sharp drop with just a handful of tokens occurring with probability between 10^{-2} and 10^{-1}. Looking at this diagram, we can see that the probability of picking the token with the highest probability (the isolated bar at 10^{-1}) is 1 in 10.

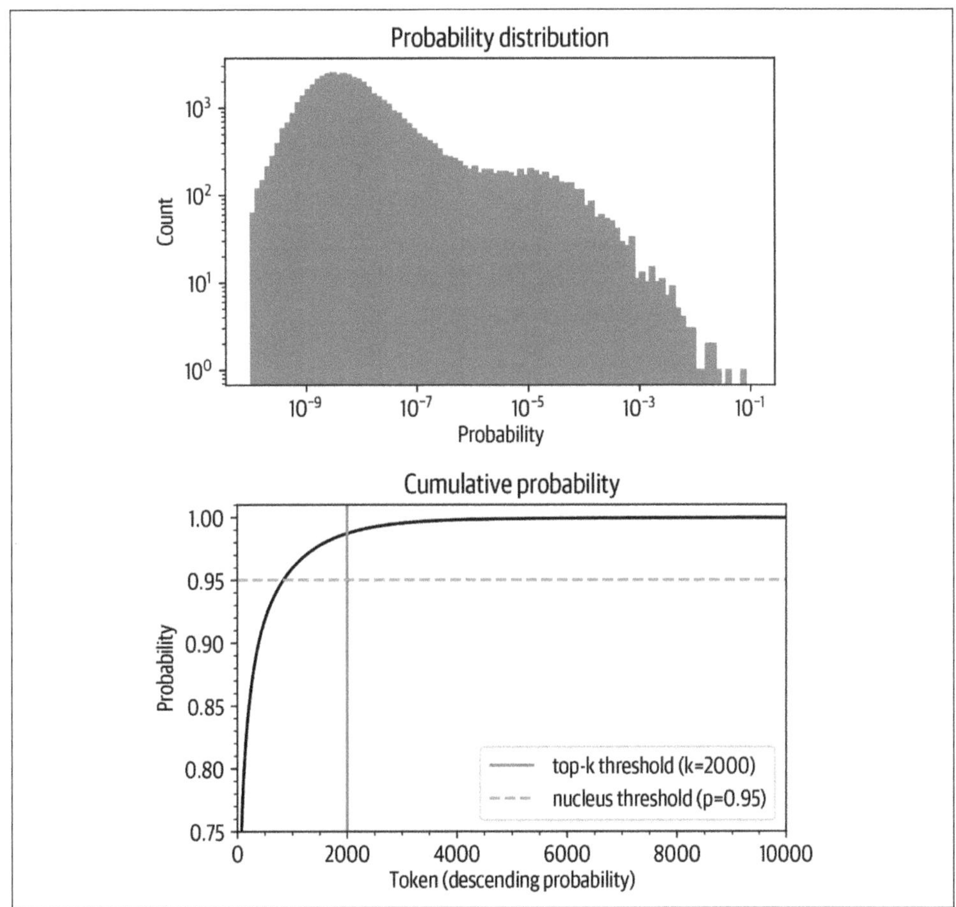

Figure 5-6. Probability distribution of next token prediction (upper) and cumulative distribution of descending token probabilities (lower)

In the lower plot, we've ordered the tokens by descending probability and calculated the cumulative sum of the first 10,000 tokens (in total, there are 50,257 tokens in

GPT-2's vocabulary). The curved line represents the probability of picking any of the preceding tokens. For example, there is roughly a 96% chance of picking any of the 1,000 tokens with the highest probability. We see that the probability rises quickly above 90% but saturates to close to 100% only after several thousand tokens. The plot shows that there is a 1 in 100 chance of not picking any of the tokens that are not even in the top 2,000.

Although these numbers might appear small at first sight, they become important because we sample once per token when generating text. So even if there is only a 1 in 100 or 1,000 chance, if we sample hundreds of times there is a significant chance of picking an unlikely token at some point—and picking such tokens when sampling can badly influence the quality of the generated text. For this reason, we generally want to avoid these very unlikely tokens. This is where top-*k* and top-*p* sampling come into play.

The idea behind top-*k* sampling is to avoid the low-probability choices by only sampling from the *k* tokens with the highest probability. This puts a fixed cut on the long tail of the distribution and ensures that we only sample from likely choices. Going back to Figure 5-6, top-*k* sampling is equivalent to defining a vertical line and sampling from the tokens on the left. Again, the `generate()` function provides an easy method to achieve this with the `top_k` argument:

```
output_topk = model.generate(input_ids, max_length=max_length, do_sample=True,
                             top_k=50)
print(tokenizer.decode(output_topk[0]))
```

```
In a shocking finding, scientist discovered a herd of unicorns living in a
remote, previously unexplored valley, in the Andes Mountains. Even more
surprising to the researchers was the fact that the unicorns spoke perfect
English.


The wild unicorns roam the Andes Mountains in the region of Cajamarca, on the
border with Argentina (Picture: Alamy/Ecole Nationale Supérieure d'Histoire
Naturelle)

The researchers came across about 50 of the animals in the valley. They had
lived in such a remote and isolated area at that location for nearly a thousand
years that
```

This is arguably the most human-looking text we've generated so far. But how do we choose *k*? The value of *k* is chosen manually and is the same for each choice in the sequence, independent of the actual output distribution. We can find a good value for *k* by looking at some text quality metrics, which we will explore in the next chapter—but that fixed cutoff might not be very satisfactory.

An alternative is to use a *dynamic* cutoff. With nucleus or top-*p* sampling, instead of choosing a fixed cutoff value, we set a condition of when to cut off. This condition is when a certain probability mass in the selection is reached. Let's say we set that value to 95%. We then order all tokens in descending order by probability and add one token after another from the top of the list until the sum of the probabilities of the selected tokens is 95%. Returning to Figure 5-6, the value for *p* defines a horizontal line on the cumulative sum of probabilities plot, and we sample only from tokens below the line. Depending on the output distribution, this could be just one (very likely) token or a hundred (more equally likely) tokens. At this point, you are probably not surprised that the `generate()` function also provides an argument to activate top-*p* sampling. Let's try it out:

```
output_topp = model.generate(input_ids, max_length=max_length, do_sample=True,
                             top_p=0.90)
print(tokenizer.decode(output_topp[0]))
```

```
In a shocking finding, scientist discovered a herd of unicorns living in a
remote, previously unexplored valley, in the Andes Mountains. Even more
surprising to the researchers was the fact that the unicorns spoke perfect
English.


The scientists studied the DNA of the animals and came to the conclusion that
the herd are descendants of a prehistoric herd that lived in Argentina about
50,000 years ago.


According to the scientific analysis, the first humans who migrated to South
America migrated into the Andes Mountains from South Africa and Australia, after
the last ice age had ended.


Since their migration, the animals have been adapting to
```

Top-*p* sampling has also produced a coherent story, and this time with a new twist about migrations from Australia to South America. You can even combine the two sampling approaches to get the best of both worlds. Setting `top_k=50` and `top_p=0.9` corresponds to the rule of choosing tokens with a probability mass of 90%, from a pool of at most 50 tokens.

We can also apply beam search when we use sampling. Instead of selecting the next batch of candidate tokens greedily, we can sample them and build up the beams in the same way.

Which Decoding Method Is Best?

Unfortunately, there is no universally "best" decoding method. Which approach is best will depend on the nature of the task you are generating text for. If you want your model to perform a precise task like arithmetic or providing an answer to a specific question, then you should lower the temperature or use deterministic methods like greedy search in combination with beam search to guarantee getting the most likely answer. If you want the model to generate longer texts and even be a bit creative, then you should switch to sampling methods and increase the temperature or use a mix of top-*k* and nucleus sampling.

Conclusion

In this chapter we looked at text generation, which is a very different task from the NLU tasks we encountered previously. Generating text requires at least one forward pass per generated token, and even more if we use beam search. This makes text generation computationally demanding, and one needs the right infrastructure to run a text generation model at scale. In addition, a good decoding strategy that transforms the model's output probabilities into discrete tokens can improve the text quality. Finding the best decoding strategy requires some experimentation and a subjective evaluation of the generated texts.

In practice, however, we don't want to make these decisions based on gut feeling alone! Like with other NLP tasks, we should choose a model performance metric that reflects the problem we want to solve. Unsurprisingly, there are a wide range of choices, and we will encounter the most common ones in the next chapter, where we have a look at how to train and evaluate a model for text summarization. Or, if you can't wait to learn how to train a GPT-type model from scratch, you can skip right to Chapter 10, where we collect a large dataset of code and then train an autoregressive language model on it.

CHAPTER 6

Summarization

At one point or another, you've probably needed to summarize a document, be it a research article, a financial earnings report, or a thread of emails. If you think about it, this requires a range of abilities, such as understanding long passages, reasoning about the contents, and producing fluent text that incorporates the main topics from the original document. Moreover, accurately summarizing a news article is very different from summarizing a legal contract, so being able to do so requires a sophisticated degree of domain generalization. For these reasons, text summarization is a difficult task for neural language models, including transformers. Despite these challenges, text summarization offers the prospect for domain experts to significantly speed up their workflows and is used by enterprises to condense internal knowledge, summarize contracts, automatically generate content for social media releases, and more.

To help you understand the challenges involved, this chapter will explore how we can leverage pretrained transformers to summarize documents. Summarization is a classic sequence-to-sequence (seq2seq) task with an input text and a target text. As we saw in Chapter 1, this is where encoder-decoder transformers excel.

In this chapter we will build our own encoder-decoder model to condense dialogues between several people into a crisp summary. But before we get to that, let's begin by taking a look at one of the canonical datasets for summarization: the CNN/DailyMail corpus.

The CNN/DailyMail Dataset

The CNN/DailyMail dataset consists of around 300,000 pairs of news articles and their corresponding summaries, composed from the bullet points that CNN and the DailyMail attach to their articles. An important aspect of the dataset is that the summaries are *abstractive* and not *extractive*, which means that they consist of new sentences instead of simple excerpts. The dataset is available on the Hub (*https://oreil.ly/jcRmb*); we'll use version 3.0.0, which is a nonanonymized version set up for summarization. We can select versions in a similar manner as splits, we saw in Chapter 4, with a `version` keyword. So let's dive in and have a look at it:

```
from datasets import load_dataset

dataset = load_dataset("cnn_dailymail", version="3.0.0")
print(f"Features: {dataset['train'].column_names}")
```

```
Features: ['article', 'highlights', 'id']
```

The dataset has three columns: `article`, which contains the news articles, `highlights` with the summaries, and `id` to uniquely identify each article. Let's look at an excerpt from an article:

```
sample = dataset["train"][1]
print(f"""
Article (excerpt of 500 characters, total length: {len(sample["article"])}):
""")
print(sample["article"][:500])
print(f'\nSummary (length: {len(sample["highlights"])}):')
print(sample["highlights"])
```

```
Article (excerpt of 500 characters, total length: 3192):

(CNN) -- Usain Bolt rounded off the world championships Sunday by claiming his
third gold in Moscow as he anchored Jamaica to victory in the men's 4x100m
relay. The fastest man in the world charged clear of United States rival Justin
Gatlin as the Jamaican quartet of Nesta Carter, Kemar Bailey-Cole, Nickel
Ashmeade and Bolt won in 37.36 seconds. The U.S finished second in 37.56 seconds
with Canada taking the bronze after Britain were disqualified for a faulty
handover. The 26-year-old Bolt has n

Summary (length: 180):
Usain Bolt wins third gold of world championship .
Anchors Jamaica to 4x100m relay victory .
Eighth gold at the championships for Bolt .
Jamaica double up in women's 4x100m relay .
```

We see that the articles can be very long compared to the target summary; in this particular case the difference is 17-fold. Long articles pose a challenge to most transformer models since the context size is usually limited to 1,000 tokens or so, which is equivalent to a few paragraphs of text. The standard, yet crude way to deal with this for summarization is to simply truncate the texts beyond the model's context size. Obviously there could be important information for the summary toward the end of the text, but for now we need to live with this limitation of the model architectures.

Text Summarization Pipelines

Let's see how a few of the most popular transformer models for summarization perform by first looking qualitatively at the outputs for the preceding example. Although the model architectures we will be exploring have varying maximum input sizes, let's restrict the input text to 2,000 characters to have the same input for all models and thus make the outputs more comparable:

```
sample_text = dataset["train"][1]["article"][:2000]
# We'll collect the generated summaries of each model in a dictionary
summaries = {}
```

A convention in summarization is to separate the summary sentences by a newline. We could add a newline token after each full stop, but this simple heuristic would fail for strings like "U.S." or "U.N." The Natural Language Toolkit (NLTK) package includes a more sophisticated algorithm that can differentiate the end of a sentence from punctuation that occurs in abbreviations:

```
import nltk
from nltk.tokenize import sent_tokenize

nltk.download("punkt")

string = "The U.S. are a country. The U.N. is an organization."
sent_tokenize(string)

['The U.S. are a country.', 'The U.N. is an organization.']
```

In the following sections we will load several large models. If you run out of memory, you can either replace the large models with smaller checkpoints (e.g., "gpt", "t5-small") or skip this section and jump to "Evaluating PEGASUS on the CNN/DailyMail Dataset" on page 154.

Summarization Baseline

A common baseline for summarizing news articles is to simply take the first three sentences of the article. With NLTK's sentence tokenizer, we can easily implement such a baseline:

```
def three_sentence_summary(text):
    return "\n".join(sent_tokenize(text)[:3])

summaries["baseline"] = three_sentence_summary(sample_text)
```

GPT-2

We've already seen in Chapter 5 how GPT-2 can generate text given some prompt. One of the model's surprising features is that we can also use it to generate summaries by simply appending "TL;DR" at the end of the input text. The expression "TL;DR" (too long; didn't read) is often used on platforms like Reddit to indicate a short version of a long post. We will start our summarization experiment by re-creating the procedure of the original paper with the `pipeline()` function from 🤗 Transformers.[1] We create a text generation pipeline and load the large GPT-2 model:

```
from transformers import pipeline, set_seed

set_seed(42)
pipe = pipeline("text-generation", model="gpt2-xl")
gpt2_query = sample_text + "\nTL;DR:\n"
pipe_out = pipe(gpt2_query, max_length=512, clean_up_tokenization_spaces=True)
summaries["gpt2"] = "\n".join(
    sent_tokenize(pipe_out[0]["generated_text"][len(gpt2_query) :]))
```

Here we just store the summaries of the generated text by slicing off the input query and keep the result in a Python dictionary for later comparison.

T5

Next let's try the T5 transformer. As we saw in Chapter 3, the developers of this model performed a comprehensive study of transfer learning in NLP and found they could create a universal transformer architecture by formulating all tasks as text-to-text tasks. The T5 checkpoints are trained on a mixture of unsupervised data (to reconstruct masked words) and supervised data for several tasks, including summarization. These checkpoints can thus be directly used to perform summarization without fine-tuning by using the same prompts used during pretraining. In this framework, the input format for the model to summarize a document is `"summarize: <ARTICLE>"`, and for translation it looks like `"translate English to German: <TEXT>"`. As shown in Figure 6-1, this makes T5 extremely versatile and allows you to solve many tasks with a single model.

We can directly load T5 for summarization with the `pipeline()` function, which also takes care of formatting the inputs in the text-to-text format so we don't need to prepend them with `"summarize"`:

```
pipe = pipeline("summarization", model="t5-large")
pipe_out = pipe(sample_text)
summaries["t5"] = "\n".join(sent_tokenize(pipe_out[0]["summary_text"]))
```

1 A. Radford et al., "Language Models Are Unsupervised Multitask Learners" (*https://openai.com/blog/better-language-models*), OpenAI (2019).

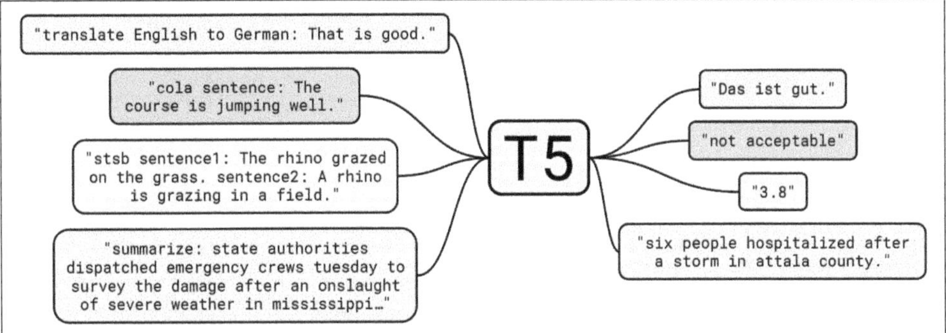

Figure 6-1. Diagram of T5's text-to-text framework (courtesy of Colin Raffel); besides translation and summarization, the CoLA (linguistic acceptability) and STSB (semantic similarity) tasks are shown

BART

BART also uses an encoder-decoder architecture and is trained to reconstruct corrupted inputs. It combines the pretraining schemes of BERT and GPT-2.[2] We'll use the `facebook/bart-large-ccn` checkpoint, which has been specifically fine-tuned on the CNN/DailyMail dataset:

```
pipe = pipeline("summarization", model="facebook/bart-large-cnn")
pipe_out = pipe(sample_text)
summaries["bart"] = "\n".join(sent_tokenize(pipe_out[0]["summary_text"]))
```

PEGASUS

Like BART, PEGASUS is an encoder-decoder transformer.[3] As shown in Figure 6-2, its pretraining objective is to predict masked sentences in multisentence texts. The authors argue that the closer the pretraining objective is to the downstream task, the more effective it is. With the aim of finding a pretraining objective that is closer to summarization than general language modeling, they automatically identified, in a very large corpus, sentences containing most of the content of their surrounding paragraphs (using summarization evaluation metrics as a heuristic for content overlap) and pretrained the PEGASUS model to reconstruct these sentences, thereby obtaining a state-of-the-art model for text summarization.

2 M. Lewis et al., "BART: Denoising Sequence-to-Sequence Pre-training for Natural Language Generation, Translation, and Comprehension" (*https://arxiv.org/abs/1910.13461*), (2019).

3 J. Zhang et al., "PEGASUS: Pre-Training with Extracted Gap-Sentences for Abstractive Summarization" (*https://arxiv.org/abs/1912.08777*), (2019).

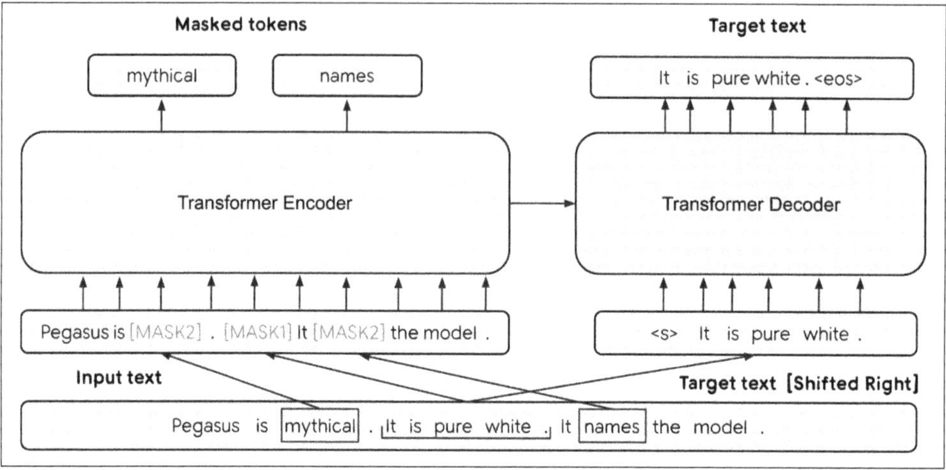

Figure 6-2. Diagram of PEGASUS architecture (courtesy of Jingqing Zhang et al.)

This model has a special token for newlines, which is why we don't need the `sent_tokenize()` function:

```
pipe = pipeline("summarization", model="google/pegasus-cnn_dailymail")
pipe_out = pipe(sample_text)
summaries["pegasus"] = pipe_out[0]["summary_text"].replace(" .<n>", ".\n")
```

Comparing Different Summaries

Now that we have generated summaries with four different models, let's compare the results. Keep in mind that one model has not been trained on the dataset at all (GPT-2), one model has been fine-tuned on this task among others (T5), and two models have exclusively been fine-tuned on this task (BART and PEGASUS). Let's have a look at the summaries these models have generated:

```
print("GROUND TRUTH")
print(dataset["train"][1]["highlights"])
print("")

for model_name in summaries:
    print(model_name.upper())
    print(summaries[model_name])
    print("")
```

```
GROUND TRUTH
Usain Bolt wins third gold of world championship .
Anchors Jamaica to 4x100m relay victory .
Eighth gold at the championships for Bolt .
Jamaica double up in women's 4x100m relay .

BASELINE
```

```
(CNN) -- Usain Bolt rounded off the world championships Sunday by claiming his
third gold in Moscow as he anchored Jamaica to victory in the men's 4x100m
relay.
The fastest man in the world charged clear of United States rival Justin Gatlin
as the Jamaican quartet of Nesta Carter, Kemar Bailey-Cole, Nickel Ashmeade and
Bolt won in 37.36 seconds.
The U.S finished second in 37.56 seconds with Canada taking the bronze after
Britain were disqualified for a faulty handover.

GPT2
Nesta, the fastest man in the world.
Gatlin, the most successful Olympian ever.
Kemar, a Jamaican legend.
Shelly-Ann, the fastest woman ever.
Bolt, the world's greatest athlete.
The team sport of pole vaulting

T5
usain bolt wins his third gold medal of the world championships in the men's
4x100m relay .
the 26-year-old anchored Jamaica to victory in the event in the Russian capital
.
he has now collected eight gold medals at the championships, equaling the record
.

BART
Usain Bolt wins his third gold of the world championships in Moscow.
Bolt anchors Jamaica to victory in the men's 4x100m relay.
The 26-year-old has now won eight gold medals at world championships.
Jamaica's women also win gold in the relay, beating France in the process.

PEGASUS
Usain Bolt wins third gold of world championships.
Anchors Jamaica to victory in men's 4x100m relay.
Eighth gold at the championships for Bolt.
Jamaica also win women's 4x100m relay .
```

The first thing we notice by looking at the model outputs is that the summary generated by GPT-2 is quite different from the others. Instead of giving a summary of the text, it summarizes the characters. Often the GPT-2 model "hallucinates" or invents facts, since it was not explicitly trained to generate truthful summaries. For example, at the time of writing, Nesta is not the fastest man in the world, but sits in ninth place. Comparing the other three model summaries against the ground truth, we see that there is remarkable overlap, with PEGASUS's output bearing the most striking resemblance.

Now that we have inspected a few models, let's try to decide which one we would use in a production setting. All four models seem to provide qualitatively reasonable results, and we could generate a few more examples to help us decide. However, this is not a systematic way of determining the best model! Ideally, we would define a metric, measure it for all models on some benchmark dataset, and choose the one with the best performance. But how do you define a metric for text generation? The standard metrics that we've seen, like accuracy, recall, and precision, are not easy to apply to this task. For each "gold standard" summary written by a human, dozens of other summaries with synonyms, paraphrases, or a slightly different way of formulating the facts could be just as acceptable.

In the next section we will look at some common metrics that have been developed for measuring the quality of generated text.

Measuring the Quality of Generated Text

Good evaluation metrics are important, since we use them to measure the performance of models not only when we train them but also later, in production. If we have bad metrics we might be blind to model degradation, and if they are misaligned with the business goals we might not create any value.

Measuring performance on a text generation task is not as easy as with standard classification tasks such as sentiment analysis or named entity recognition. Take the example of translation; given a sentence like "I love dogs!" in English and translating it to Spanish there can be multiple valid possibilities, like "¡Me encantan los perros!" or "¡Me gustan los perros!" Simply checking for an exact match to a reference translation is not optimal; even humans would fare badly on such a metric because we all write text slightly differently from each other (and even from ourselves, depending on the time of the day or year!). Fortunately, there are alternatives.

Two of the most common metrics used to evaluate generated text are BLEU and ROUGE. Let's take a look at how they're defined.

BLEU

The idea of BLEU is simple:[4] instead of looking at how many of the tokens in the generated texts are perfectly aligned with the reference text tokens, we look at words or *n*-grams. BLEU is a precision-based metric, which means that when we compare the two texts we count the number of words in the generation that occur in the reference and divide it by the length of the generation.

However, there is an issue with this vanilla precision. Assume the generated text just repeats the same word over and over again, and this word also appears in the reference. If it is repeated as many times as the length of the reference text, then we get

4 K. Papineni et al., "BLEU: A Method for Automatic Evaluation of Machine Translation," *Proceedings of the 40th Annual Meeting of the Association for Computational Linguistics* (July 2002): 311–318, *http://dx.doi.org/10.3115/1073083.1073135*.

perfect precision! For this reason, the authors of the BLEU paper introduced a slight modification: a word is only counted as many times as it occurs in the reference. To illustrate this point, suppose we have the reference text "the cat is on the mat" and the generated text "the the the the the the".

From this simple example, we can calculate the precision values as follows:

$$p_{vanilla} = \frac{6}{6}$$

$$p_{mod} = \frac{2}{6}$$

and we can see that the simple correction has produced a much more reasonable value. Now let's extend this by not only looking at single words, but *n*-grams as well. Let's assume we have one generated sentence, *snt*, that we want to compare against a reference sentence, *snt'*. We extract all possible *n*-grams of degree *n* and do the accounting to get the precision p_n:

$$p_n = \frac{\sum_{n\text{-}gram \in snt'} Count_{clip}(n\text{-}gram)}{\sum_{n\text{-}gram \in snt} Count(n\text{-}gram)}$$

In order to avoid rewarding repetitive generations, the count in the numerator is clipped. What this means is that the occurrence count of an *n*-gram is capped at how many times it appears in the reference sentence. Also note that the definition of a sentence is not very strict in this equation, and if you had a generated text spanning multiple sentences you would treat it as one sentence.

In general we have more than one sample in the test set we want to evaluate, so we need to slightly extend the equation by summing over all samples in the corpus *C*:

$$p_n = \frac{\sum_{snt \in C} \sum_{n\text{-}gram \in snt'} Count_{clip}(n\text{-}gram)}{\sum_{snt' \in C} \sum_{n\text{-}gram \in snt} Count(n\text{-}gram)}$$

We're almost there. Since we are not looking at recall, all generated sequences that are short but precise have a benefit compared to sentences that are longer. Therefore, the precision score favors short generations. To compensate for that the authors of BLEU introduced an additional term, the *brevity penalty*:

$$BR = \min\left(1, e^{1 - \ell_{ref}/\ell_{gen}}\right)$$

By taking the minimum, we ensure that this penalty never exceeds 1 and the exponential term becomes exponentially small when the length of the generated text l_{gen} is smaller than the reference text l_{ref}. At this point you might ask, why don't we just use something like an F_1-score to account for recall as well? The answer is that often in translation datasets there are multiple reference sentences instead of just one, so if we also measured recall we would incentivize translations that used all the words from all the references. Therefore, it's preferable to look for high precision in the translation and make sure the translation and reference have a similar length.

Finally, we can put everything together and get the equation for the BLEU score:

$$\text{BLEU-}N = BR \times \left(\prod_{n=1}^{N} p_n \right)^{1/N}$$

The last term is the geometric mean of the modified precision up to n-gram N. In practice, the BLEU-4 score is often reported. However, you can probably already see that this metric has many limitations; for instance, it doesn't take synonyms into account, and many steps in the derivation seem like ad hoc and rather fragile heuristics. You can find a wonderful exposition of BLEU's flaws in Rachel Tatman's blog post "Evaluating Text Output in NLP: BLEU at Your Own Risk" (*https://oreil.ly/nMXRh*).

In general, the field of text generation is still looking for better evaluation metrics, and finding ways to overcome the limits of metrics like BLEU is an active area of research. Another weakness of the BLEU metric is that it expects the text to already be tokenized. This can lead to varying results if the exact same method for text tokenization is not used. The SacreBLEU metric addresses this issue by internalizing the tokenization step; for this reason, it is the preferred metric for benchmarking.

We've now worked through some theory, but what we really want to do is calculate the score for some generated text. Does that mean we need to implement all this logic in Python? Fear not, 🤗 Datasets also provides metrics! Loading a metric works just like loading a dataset:

```
from datasets import load_metric

bleu_metric = load_metric("sacrebleu")
```

The `bleu_metric` object is an instance of the `Metric` class, and works like an aggregator: you can add single instances with `add()` or whole batches via `add_batch()`. Once you have added all the samples you need to evaluate, you then call `compute()` and the metric is calculated. This returns a dictionary with several values, such as the precision for each n-gram, the length penalty, as well as the final BLEU score. Let's look at the example from before:

```
import pandas as pd
import numpy as np

bleu_metric.add(
    prediction="the the the the the the", reference=["the cat is on the mat"])
results = bleu_metric.compute(smooth_method="floor", smooth_value=0)
results["precisions"] = [np.round(p, 2) for p in results["precisions"]]
pd.DataFrame.from_dict(results, orient="index", columns=["Value"])
```

	Value
score	0.0
counts	[2, 0, 0, 0]
totals	[6, 5, 4, 3]
precisions	[33.33, 0.0, 0.0, 0.0]
bp	1.0
sys_len	6
ref_len	6

The BLEU score also works if there are multiple reference translations. This is why `reference` is passed as a list. To make the metric smoother for zero counts in the *n*-grams, BLEU integrates methods to modify the precision calculation. One method is to add a constant to the numerator. That way, a missing *n*-gram does not cause the score to automatically go to zero. For the purpose of explaining the values, we turn it off by setting `smooth_value=0`.

We can see the precision of the 1-gram is indeed 2/6, whereas the precisions for the 2/3/4-grams are all 0. (For more information about the individual metrics, like counts and bp, see the SacreBLEU repository (*https://oreil.ly/kiZPl*).) This means the geometric mean is zero, and thus also the BLEU score. Let's look at another example where the prediction is almost correct:

```
bleu_metric.add(
    prediction="the cat is on mat", reference=["the cat is on the mat"])
results = bleu_metric.compute(smooth_method="floor", smooth_value=0)
results["precisions"] = [np.round(p, 2) for p in results["precisions"]]
pd.DataFrame.from_dict(results, orient="index", columns=["Value"])
```

	Value
score	57.893007
counts	[5, 3, 2, 1]
totals	[5, 4, 3, 2]
precisions	[100.0, 75.0, 66.67, 50.0]

	Value
bp	0.818731
sys_len	5
ref_len	6

We observe that the precision scores are much better. The 1-grams in the prediction all match, and only in the precision scores do we see that something is off. For the 4-gram there are only two candidates, `["the", "cat", "is", "on"]` and `["cat", "is", "on", "mat"]`, where the last one does not match, hence the precision of 0.5.

The BLEU score is widely used for evaluating text, especially in machine translation, since precise translations are usually favored over translations that include all possible and appropriate words.

There are other applications, such as summarization, where the situation is different. There, we want all the important information in the generated text, so we favor high recall. This is where the ROUGE score is usually used.

ROUGE

The ROUGE score was specifically developed for applications like summarization where high recall is more important than just precision.[5] The approach is very similar to the BLEU score in that we look at different *n*-grams and compare their occurrences in the generated text and the reference texts. The difference is that with ROUGE we check how many *n*-grams in the reference text also occur in the generated text. For BLEU we looked at how many *n*-grams in the generated text appear in the reference, so we can reuse the precision formula with the minor modification that we count the (unclipped) occurrence of reference *n*-grams in the generated text in the denominator:

$$\text{ROUGE-}N = \frac{\sum_{\text{snt'} \in C} \sum_{n\text{-}gram \in snt'} Count_{match}(n\text{-}gram)}{\sum_{\text{snt'} \in C} \sum_{n\text{-}gram \in snt'} Count(n\text{-}gram)}$$

This was the original proposal for ROUGE. Subsequently, researchers have found that fully removing precision can have strong negative effects. Going back to the BLEU formula without the clipped counting, we can measure precision as well, and we can then combine both precision and recall ROUGE scores in the harmonic mean to get an F_1-score. This score is the metric that is nowadays commonly reported for ROUGE.

5 C-Y. Lin, "ROUGE: A Package for Automatic Evaluation of Summaries," *Text Summarization Branches Out* (July 2004), *https://aclanthology.org/W04-1013.pdf*.

There is a separate score in ROUGE to measure the longest common substring (LCS), called ROUGE-L. The LCS can be calculated for any pair of strings. For example, the LCS for "abab" and "abc" would be "ab", and its the length would be 2. If we want to compare this value between two samples we need to somehow normalize it because otherwise a longer text would be at an advantage. To achieve this, the inventor of ROUGE came up with an *F*-score-like scheme where the LCS is normalized with the length of the reference and generated text, then the two normalized scores are mixed together:

$$R_{LCS} = \frac{LCS(X, Y)}{m}$$

$$P_{LCS} = \frac{LCS(X, Y)}{n}$$

$$F_{LCS} = \frac{\left(1 + \beta^2\right)R_{LCS}P_{LCS}}{R_{LCS} + \beta P_{LCS}}, \text{where } \beta = P_{LCS}/R_{LCS}$$

That way the LCS score is properly normalized and can be compared across samples. In the 🤗 Datasets implementation, two variations of ROUGE are calculated: one calculates the score per sentence and averages it for the summaries (ROUGE-L), and the other calculates it directly over the whole summary (ROUGE-Lsum).

We can load the metric as follows:

```
rouge_metric = load_metric("rouge")
```

We already generated a set of summaries with GPT-2 and the other models, and now we have a metric to compare the summaries systematically. Let's apply the ROUGE score to all the summaries generated by the models:

```
reference = dataset["train"][1]["highlights"]
records = []
rouge_names = ["rouge1", "rouge2", "rougeL", "rougeLsum"]

for model_name in summaries:
    rouge_metric.add(prediction=summaries[model_name], reference=reference)
    score = rouge_metric.compute()
    rouge_dict = dict((rn, score[rn].mid.fmeasure) for rn in rouge_names)
    records.append(rouge_dict)
pd.DataFrame.from_records(records, index=summaries.keys())
```

	rouge1	rouge2	rougeL	rougeLsum
baseline	0.303571	0.090909	0.214286	0.232143
gpt2	0.187500	0.000000	0.125000	0.187500

	rouge1	rouge2	rougeL	rougeLsum
t5	0.486486	0.222222	0.378378	0.486486
bart	0.582278	0.207792	0.455696	0.506329
pegasus	0.866667	0.655172	0.800000	0.833333

The ROUGE metric in the 🤗 Datasets library also calculates confidence intervals (by default, the 5th and 95th percentiles). The average value is stored in the attribute `mid` and the interval can be retrieved with `low` and `high`.

These results are obviously not very reliable as we only looked at a single sample, but we can compare the quality of the summary for that one example. The table confirms our observation that of the models we considered, GPT-2 performs worst. This is not surprising since it is the only model of the group that was not explicitly trained to summarize. It is striking, however, that the simple first-three-sentence baseline doesn't fare too poorly compared to the transformer models that have on the order of a billion parameters! PEGASUS and BART are the best models overall (higher ROUGE scores are better), but T5 is slightly better on ROUGE-1 and the LCS scores. These results place T5 and PEGASUS as the best models, but again these results should be treated with caution as we only evaluated the models on a single example. Looking at the results in the PEGASUS paper, we would expect the PEGASUS to outperform T5 on the CNN/DailyMail dataset.

Let's see if we can reproduce those results with PEGASUS.

Evaluating PEGASUS on the CNN/DailyMail Dataset

We now have all the pieces in place to evaluate the model properly: we have a dataset with a test set from CNN/DailyMail, we have a metric with ROUGE, and we have a summarization model. We just need to put the pieces together. Let's first evaluate the performance of the three-sentence baseline:

```
def evaluate_summaries_baseline(dataset, metric,
                                column_text="article",
                                column_summary="highlights"):
    summaries = [three_sentence_summary(text) for text in dataset[column_text]]
    metric.add_batch(predictions=summaries,
                     references=dataset[column_summary])
    score = metric.compute()
    return score
```

Now we'll apply the function to a subset of the data. Since the test fraction of the CNN/DailyMail dataset consists of roughly 10,000 samples, generating summaries for all these articles takes a lot of time. Recall from Chapter 5 that every generated token requires a forward pass through the model; generating just 100 tokens for each sample will thus require 1 million forward passes, and if we use beam search this number is multiplied by the number of beams. For the purpose of keeping the calculations relatively fast, we'll subsample the test set and run the evaluation on 1,000 samples instead. This should give us a much more stable score estimation while completing in less than one hour on a single GPU for the PEGASUS model:

```
test_sampled = dataset["test"].shuffle(seed=42).select(range(1000))

score = evaluate_summaries_baseline(test_sampled, rouge_metric)
rouge_dict = dict((rn, score[rn].mid.fmeasure) for rn in rouge_names)
pd.DataFrame.from_dict(rouge_dict, orient="index", columns=["baseline"]).T
```

	rouge1	rouge2	rougeL	rougeLsum
baseline	0.396061	0.173995	0.245815	0.361158

The scores are mostly worse than on the previous example, but still better than those achieved by GPT-2! Now let's implement the same evaluation function for evaluating the PEGASUS model:

```
from tqdm import tqdm
import torch

device = "cuda" if torch.cuda.is_available() else "cpu"

def chunks(list_of_elements, batch_size):
    """Yield successive batch-sized chunks from list_of_elements."""
    for i in range(0, len(list_of_elements), batch_size):
        yield list_of_elements[i : i + batch_size]

def evaluate_summaries_pegasus(dataset, metric, model, tokenizer,
                               batch_size=16, device=device,
                               column_text="article",
                               column_summary="highlights"):
    article_batches = list(chunks(dataset[column_text], batch_size))
    target_batches = list(chunks(dataset[column_summary], batch_size))

    for article_batch, target_batch in tqdm(
        zip(article_batches, target_batches), total=len(article_batches)):

        inputs = tokenizer(article_batch, max_length=1024,  truncation=True,
                        padding="max_length", return_tensors="pt")

        summaries = model.generate(input_ids=inputs["input_ids"].to(device),
                         attention_mask=inputs["attention_mask"].to(device),
                         length_penalty=0.8, num_beams=8, max_length=128)

        decoded_summaries = [tokenizer.decode(s, skip_special_tokens=True,
                                clean_up_tokenization_spaces=True)
               for s in summaries]
```

```
        decoded_summaries = [d.replace("<n>", " ") for d in decoded_summaries]
        metric.add_batch(predictions=decoded_summaries, references=target_batch)

    score = metric.compute()
    return score
```

Let's unpack this evaluation code a bit. First we split the dataset into smaller batches that we can process simultaneously. Then for each batch we tokenize the input articles and feed them to the `generate()` function to produce the summaries using beam search. We use the same generation parameters as proposed in the paper. The new parameter for length penalty ensures that the model does not generate sequences that are too long. Finally, we decode the generated texts, replace the `<n>` token, and add the decoded texts with the references to the metric. At the end, we compute and return the ROUGE scores. Let's now load the model again with the `AutoModelForSeq2SeqLM` class, used for seq2seq generation tasks, and evaluate it:

```
from              import AutoModelForSeq2SeqLM, AutoTokenizer

model_ckpt = "google/pegasus-cnn_dailymail"
tokenizer = AutoTokenizer.from_pretrained(model_ckpt)
model = AutoModelForSeq2SeqLM.from_pretrained(model_ckpt).to(device)
score = evaluate_summaries_pegasus(test_sampled, rouge_metric,
                                   model, tokenizer, batch_size=8)
rouge_dict = dict((rn, score[rn].mid.fmeasure) for rn in rouge_names)
pd.DataFrame(rouge_dict, index=["pegasus"])
```

	rouge1	rouge2	rougeL	rougeLsum
pegasus	0.434381	0.210883	0.307195	0.373231

These numbers are very close to the published results. One thing to note here is that the loss and per-token accuracy are decoupled to some degree from the ROUGE scores. The loss is independent of the decoding strategy, whereas the ROUGE score is strongly coupled.

Since ROUGE and BLEU correlate better with human judgment than loss or accuracy, we should focus on them and carefully explore and choose the decoding strategy when building text generation models. These metrics are far from perfect, however, and one should always consider human judgments as well.

Now that we're equipped with an evaluation function, it's time to train our own model for summarization.

Training a Summarization Model

We've worked through a lot of details on text summarization and evaluation, so let's put this to use to train a custom text summarization model! For our application, we'll use the SAMSum dataset (*https://oreil.ly/n1ggq*) developed by Samsung, which consists of a collection of dialogues along with brief summaries. In an enterprise setting, these dialogues might represent the interactions between a customer and the support center, so generating accurate summaries can help improve customer service and detect common patterns among customer requests. Let's load it and look at an example:

```
dataset_samsum = load_dataset("samsum")
split_lengths = [len(dataset_samsum[split])for split in dataset_samsum]

print(f"Split lengths: {split_lengths}")
print(f"Features: {dataset_samsum['train'].column_names}")
print("\nDialogue:")
print(dataset_samsum["test"][0]["dialogue"])
print("\nSummary:")
print(dataset_samsum["test"][0]["summary"])
```

```
Split lengths: [14732, 819, 818]
Features: ['id', 'dialogue', 'summary']

Dialogue:
Hannah: Hey, do you have Betty's number?
Amanda: Lemme check
Hannah: <file_gif>
Amanda: Sorry, can't find it.
Amanda: Ask Larry
Amanda: He called her last time we were at the park together
Hannah: I don't know him well
Hannah: <file_gif>
Amanda: Don't be shy, he's very nice
Hannah: If you say so..
Hannah: I'd rather you texted him
Amanda: Just text him 🙂
Hannah: Urgh.. Alright
Hannah: Bye
Amanda: Bye bye

Summary:
Hannah needs Betty's number but Amanda doesn't have it. She needs to contact
Larry.
```

The dialogues look like what you would expect from a chat via SMS or WhatsApp, including emojis and placeholders for GIFs. The `dialogue` field contains the full text and the `summary` the summarized dialogue. Could a model that was fine-tuned on the CNN/DailyMail dataset deal with that? Let's find out!

Evaluating PEGASUS on SAMSum

First we'll run the same summarization pipeline with PEGASUS to see what the output looks like. We can reuse the code we used for the CNN/DailyMail summary generation:

```
pipe_out = pipe(dataset_samsum["test"][0]["dialogue"])
print("Summary:")
print(pipe_out[0]["summary_text"].replace(" .<n>", ".\n"))
```

```
Summary:
Amanda: Ask Larry Amanda: He called her last time we were at the park together.
Hannah: I'd rather you texted him.
Amanda: Just text him .
```

We can see that the model mostly tries to summarize by extracting the key sentences from the dialogue. This probably worked relatively well on the CNN/DailyMail dataset, but the summaries in SAMSum are more abstract. Let's confirm this by running the full ROUGE evaluation on the test set:

```
score = evaluate_summaries_pegasus(dataset_samsum["test"], rouge_metric, model,
                                   tokenizer, column_text="dialogue",
                                   column_summary="summary", batch_size=8)

rouge_dict = dict((rn, score[rn].mid.fmeasure) for rn in rouge_names)
pd.DataFrame(rouge_dict, index=["pegasus"])
```

	rouge1	rouge2	rougeL	rougeLsum
pegasus	0.296168	0.087803	0.229604	0.229514

Well, the results aren't great, but this is not unexpected since we've moved quite a bit away from the CNN/DailyMail data distribution. Nevertheless, setting up the evaluation pipeline before training has two advantages: we can directly measure the success of training with the metric and we have a good baseline. Fine-tuning the model on our dataset should result in an immediate improvement in the ROUGE metric, and if that is not the case we'll know something is wrong with our training loop.

Fine-Tuning PEGASUS

Before we process the data for training, let's have a quick look at the length distribution of the input and outputs:

```
d_len = [len(tokenizer.encode(s)) for s in dataset_samsum["train"]["dialogue"]]
s_len = [len(tokenizer.encode(s)) for s in dataset_samsum["train"]["summary"]]

fig, axes = plt.subplots(1, 2, figsize=(10, 3.5), sharey=True)
axes[0].hist(d_len, bins=20, color="C0", edgecolor="C0")
axes[0].set_title("Dialogue Token Length")
axes[0].set_xlabel("Length")
```

```
axes[0].set_ylabel("Count")
axes[1].hist(s_len, bins=20, color="C0", edgecolor="C0")
axes[1].set_title("Summary Token Length")
axes[1].set_xlabel("Length")
plt.tight_layout()
plt.show()
```

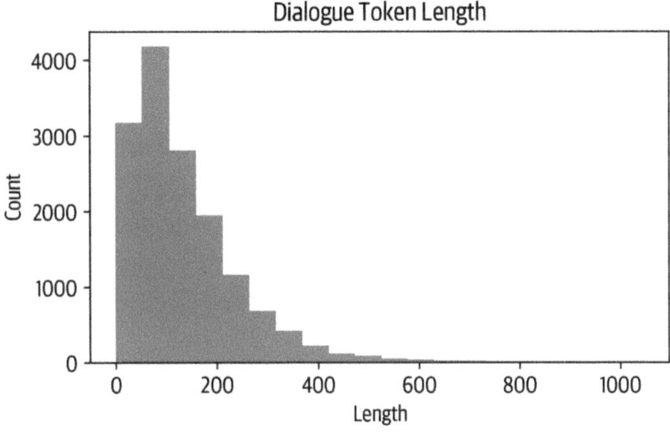

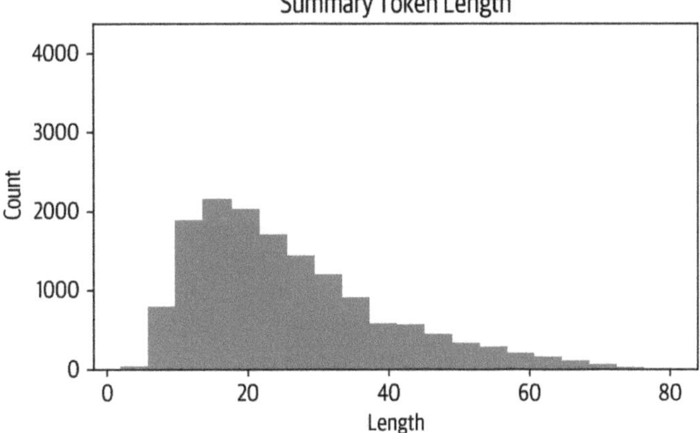

We see that most dialogues are much shorter than the CNN/DailyMail articles, with 100–200 tokens per dialogue. Similarly, the summaries are much shorter, with around 20–40 tokens (the average length of a tweet).

Let's keep those observations in mind as we build the data collator for the `Trainer`. First we need to tokenize the dataset. For now, we'll set the maximum lengths to 1024 and 128 for the dialogues and summaries, respectively:

```
def convert_examples_to_features(example_batch):
    input_encodings = tokenizer(example_batch["dialogue"], max_length=1024,
                                truncation=True)
```

```python
    with tokenizer.as_target_tokenizer():
        target_encodings = tokenizer(example_batch["summary"], max_length=128,
                                     truncation=True)

    return {"input_ids": input_encodings["input_ids"],
            "attention_mask": input_encodings["attention_mask"],
            "labels": target_encodings["input_ids"]}

dataset_samsum_pt = dataset_samsum.map(convert_examples_to_features,
                                       batched=True)
columns = ["input_ids", "labels", "attention_mask"]
dataset_samsum_pt.set_format(type="torch", columns=columns)
```

A new thing in the use of the tokenization step is the `tokenizer.as_target_tokenizer()` context. Some models require special tokens in the decoder inputs, so it's important to differentiate between the tokenization of encoder and decoder inputs. In the `with` statement (called a *context manager*), the tokenizer knows that it is tokenizing for the decoder and can process sequences accordingly.

Now, we need to create the data collator. This function is called in the `Trainer` just before the batch is fed through the model. In most cases we can use the default collator, which collects all the tensors from the batch and simply stacks them. For the summarization task we need to not only stack the inputs but also prepare the targets on the decoder side. PEGASUS is an encoder-decoder transformer and thus has the classic seq2seq architecture. In a seq2seq setup, a common approach is to apply "teacher forcing" in the decoder. With this strategy, the decoder receives input tokens (like in decoder-only models such as GPT-2) that consists of the labels shifted by one in addition to the encoder output; so, when making the prediction for the next token the decoder gets the ground truth shifted by one as an input, as illustrated in the following table:

	decoder_input	label
step		
1	[PAD]	Transformers
2	[PAD, Transformers]	are
3	[PAD, Transformers, are]	awesome
4	[PAD, Transformers, are, awesome]	for
5	[PAD, Transformers, are, awesome, for]	text
6	[PAD, Transformers, are, awesome, for, text]	summarization

We shift it by one so that the decoder only sees the previous ground truth labels and not the current or future ones. Shifting alone suffices since the decoder has masked self-attention that masks all inputs at present and in the future.

So, when we prepare our batch, we set up the decoder inputs by shifting the labels to the right by one. After that, we make sure the padding tokens in the labels are ignored by the loss function by setting them to –100. We actually don't have to do this manually, though, since the `DataCollatorForSeq2Seq` comes to the rescue and takes care of all these steps for us:

```
from transformers import DataCollatorForSeq2Seq

seq2seq_data_collator = DataCollatorForSeq2Seq(tokenizer, model=model)
```

Then, as usual, we set up a the `TrainingArguments` for training:

```
from transformers import TrainingArguments, Trainer

training_args = TrainingArguments(
    output_dir='pegasus-samsum', num_train_epochs=1, warmup_steps=500,
    per_device_train_batch_size=1, per_device_eval_batch_size=1,
    weight_decay=0.01, logging_steps=10, push_to_hub=True,
    evaluation_strategy='steps', eval_steps=500, save_steps=1e6,
    gradient_accumulation_steps=16)
```

One thing that is different from the previous settings is that new argument, `gradient_accumulation_steps`. Since the model is quite big, we had to set the batch size to 1. However, a batch size that is too small can hurt convergence. To resolve that issue, we can use a nifty technique called *gradient accumulation*. As the name suggests, instead of calculating the gradients of the full batch all at once, we make smaller batches and aggregate the gradients. When we have aggregated enough gradients, we run the optimization step. Naturally this is a bit slower than doing it in one pass, but it saves us a lot of GPU memory.

Let's now make sure that we are logged in to Hugging Face so we can push the model to the Hub after training:

```
from huggingface_hub import notebook_login

notebook_login()
```

We have now everything we need to initialize the trainer with the model, tokenizer, training arguments, and data collator, as well as the training and evaluation sets:

```
trainer = Trainer(model=model, args=training_args,
                  tokenizer=tokenizer, data_collator=seq2seq_data_collator,
                  train_dataset=dataset_samsum_pt["train"],
                  eval_dataset=dataset_samsum_pt["validation"])
```

We are ready for training. After training, we can directly run the evaluation function on the test set to see how well the model performs:

```
trainer.train()
score = evaluate_summaries_pegasus(
    dataset_samsum["test"], rouge_metric, trainer.model, tokenizer,
    batch_size=2, column_text="dialogue", column_summary="summary")
```

```
rouge_dict = dict((rn, score[rn].mid.fmeasure) for rn in rouge_names)
pd.DataFrame(rouge_dict, index=[f"pegasus"])
```

	rouge1	rouge2	rougeL	rougeLsum
pegasus	0.427614	0.200571	0.340648	0.340738

We see that the ROUGE scores improved considerably over the model without fine-tuning, so even though the previous model was also trained for summarization, it was not well adapted for the new domain. Let's push our model to the Hub:

```
trainer.push_to_hub("Training complete!")
```

In the next section we'll use the model to generate a few summaries for us.

You can also evaluate the generations as part of the training loop: use the extension of `TrainingArguments` called `Seq2SeqTrainingArguments` and specify `predict_with_generate=True`. Pass it to the dedicated `Trainer` called `Seq2SeqTrainer`, which then uses the `generate()` function instead of the model's forward pass to create predictions for evaluation. Give it a try!

Generating Dialogue Summaries

Looking at the losses and ROUGE scores, it seems the model is showing a significant improvement over the original model trained on CNN/DailyMail only. Let's see what a summary generated on a sample from the test set looks like:

```
gen_kwargs = {"length_penalty": 0.8, "num_beams":8, "max_length": 128}
sample_text = dataset_samsum["test"][0]["dialogue"]
reference = dataset_samsum["test"][0]["summary"]
pipe = pipeline("summarization", model="transformersbook/pegasus-samsum")

print("Dialogue:")
print(sample_text)
print("\nReference Summary:")
print(reference)
print("\nModel Summary:")
print(pipe(sample_text, **gen_kwargs)[0]["summary_text"])
```

```
Dialogue:
Hannah: Hey, do you have Betty's number?
Amanda: Lemme check
Hannah: <file_gif>
Amanda: Sorry, can't find it.
Amanda: Ask Larry
Amanda: He called her last time we were at the park together
Hannah: I don't know him well
Hannah: <file_gif>
```

```
Amanda: Don't be shy, he's very nice
Hannah: If you say so..
Hannah: I'd rather you texted him
Amanda: Just text him 🙂
Hannah: Urgh.. Alright
Hannah: Bye
Amanda: Bye bye

Reference Summary:
Hannah needs Betty's number but Amanda doesn't have it. She needs to contact
Larry.

Model Summary:
Amanda can't find Betty's number. Larry called Betty last time they were at the
park together. Hannah wants Amanda to text Larry instead of calling Betty.
```

That looks much more like the reference summary. It seems the model has learned to synthesize the dialogue into a summary without just extracting passages. Now, the ultimate test: how well does the model work on a custom input?

```
custom_dialogue = """\
Thom: Hi guys, have you heard of transformers?
Lewis: Yes, I used them recently!
Leandro: Indeed, there is a great library by Hugging Face.
Thom: I know, I helped build it ;)
Lewis: Cool, maybe we should write a book about it. What do you think?
Leandro: Great idea, how hard can it be?!
Thom: I am in!
Lewis: Awesome, let's do it together!
"""
print(pipe(custom_dialogue, **gen_kwargs)[0]["summary_text"])
```

```
Thom, Lewis and Leandro are going to write a book about transformers. Thom
helped build a library by Hugging Face. They are going to do it together.
```

The generated summary of the custom dialogue makes sense. It summarizes well that all the people in the discussion want to write the book together and does not simply extract single sentences. For example, it synthesizes the third and fourth lines into a logical combination.

Conclusion

Text summarization poses some unique challenges compared to other tasks that can be framed as classification tasks, like sentiment analysis, named entity recognition, or question answering. Conventional metrics such as accuracy do not reflect the quality of the generated text. As we saw, the BLEU and ROUGE metrics can better evaluate generated texts; however, human judgment remains the best measure.

A common question when working with summarization models is how we can summarize documents where the texts are longer than the model's context length.

Unfortunately, there is no single strategy to solve this problem, and to date this is still an open and active research question. For example, recent work by OpenAI showed how to scale summarization by applying it recursively to long documents and using human feedback in the loop.[6]

In the next chapter we'll look at question answering, which is the task of providing an answer to a question based on a text passage. In contrast to summarization, with this task there exist good strategies to deal with long or many documents, and we'll show you how to scale question answering to thousands of documents.

6 J. Wu et al., "Recursively Summarizing Books with Human Feedback" (*https://arxiv.org/abs/2109.10862*), (2021).

CHAPTER 7

Question Answering

Whether you're a researcher, analyst, or data scientist, chances are that at some point you've needed to wade through oceans of documents to find the information you're looking for. To make matters worse, you're constantly reminded by Google and Bing that there exist better ways to search! For instance, if we search for "When did Marie Curie win her first Nobel Prize?" on Google, we immediately get the correct answer of "1903," as illustrated in Figure 7-1.

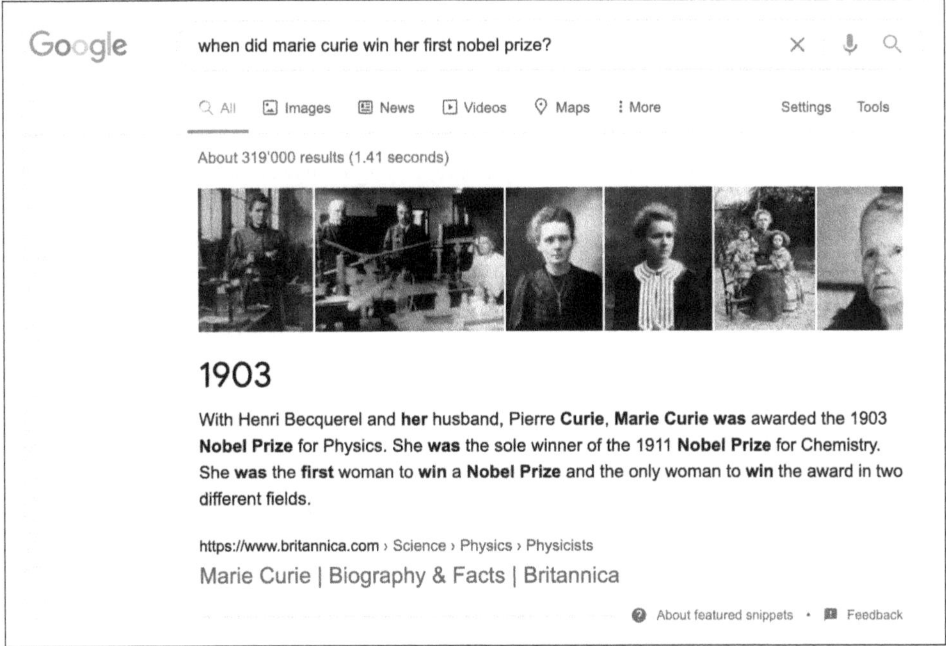

Figure 7-1. A Google search query and corresponding answer snippet

In this example, Google first retrieved around 319,000 documents that were relevant to the query, and then performed an additional processing step to extract the answer snippet with the corresponding passage and web page. It's not hard to see why these answer snippets are useful. For example, if we search for a trickier question like "Which guitar tuning is the best?" Google doesn't provide an answer, and instead we have to click on one of the web pages returned by the search engine to find it ourselves.[1]

The general approach behind this technology is called *question answering* (QA). There are many flavors of QA, but the most common is *extractive QA*, which involves questions whose answer can be identified as a span of text in a document, where the document might be a web page, legal contract, or news article. The two-stage process of first retrieving relevant documents and then extracting answers from them is also the basis for many modern QA systems, including semantic search engines, intelligent assistants, and automated information extractors. In this chapter, we'll apply this process to tackle a common problem facing ecommerce websites: helping consumers answer specific queries to evaluate a product. We'll see that customer reviews can be used as a rich and challenging source of information for QA, and along the way we'll learn how transformers act as powerful *reading comprehension* models that can extract meaning from text. Let's begin by fleshing out the use case.

This chapter focuses on extractive QA, but other forms of QA may be more suitable for your use case. For example, *community QA* involves gathering question-answer pairs that are generated by users on forums like Stack Overflow (*https://stackoverflow.com*), and then using semantic similarity search to find the closest matching answer to a new question. There is also *long-form QA*, which aims to generate complex paragraph-length answers to open-ended questions like "Why is the sky blue?" Remarkably, it is also possible to do QA over tables, and transformer models like TAPAS (*https://oreil.ly/vVPWO*) can even perform aggregations to produce the final answer!

Building a Review-Based QA System

If you've ever purchased a product online, you probably relied on customer reviews to help inform your decision. These reviews can often help answer specific questions like "Does this guitar come with a strap?" or "Can I use this camera at night?" that may be hard to answer from the product description alone. However, popular products can have hundreds to thousands of reviews, so it can be a major drag to find

1 Although, in this particular case, everyone agrees that Drop C is the best guitar tuning.

one that is relevant. One alternative is to post your question on the community QA platforms provided by websites like Amazon, but it usually takes days to get an answer (if you get one at all). Wouldn't it be nice if we could get an immediate answer, like in the Google example from Figure 7-1? Let's see if we can do this using transformers!

The Dataset

To build our QA system we'll use the SubjQA dataset,[2] which consists of more than 10,000 customer reviews in English about products and services in six domains: TripAdvisor, Restaurants, Movies, Books, Electronics, and Grocery. As illustrated in Figure 7-2, each review is associated with a question that can be answered using one or more sentences from the review.[3]

NOKIA
Query: Why is the camera of poor quality?
Review: Item like the picture, fast deliver 3 days well packed, good quality for the price. The camera is decent (as phone cameras go), There is no flash though ...

Figure 7-2. A question about a product and the corresponding review (the answer span is underlined)

2 J. Bjerva et al., "SubjQA: A Dataset for Subjectivity and Review Comprehension" (*https://arxiv.org/abs/2004.14283*), (2020).

3 As we'll soon see, there are also *unanswerable* questions that are designed to produce more robust models.

The interesting aspect of this dataset is that most of the questions and answers are *subjective*; that is, they depend on the personal experience of the users. The example in Figure 7-2 shows why this feature makes the task potentially more difficult than finding answers to factual questions like "What is the currency of the United Kingdom?" First, the query is about "poor quality," which is subjective and depends on the user's definition of quality. Second, important parts of the query do not appear in the review at all, which means it cannot be answered with shortcuts like keyword search or paraphrasing the input question. These features make SubjQA a realistic dataset to benchmark our review-based QA models on, since user-generated content like that shown in Figure 7-2 resembles what we might encounter in the wild.

QA systems are usually categorized by the *domain* of data that they have access to when responding to a query. *Closed-domain* QA deals with questions about a narrow topic (e.g., a single product category), while *open-domain* QA deals with questions about almost anything (e.g., Amazon's whole product catalog). In general, closed-domain QA involves searching through fewer documents than the open-domain case.

To get started, let's download the dataset from the Hugging Face Hub (*https://oreil.ly/iO0s5*). As we did in Chapter 4, we can use the `get_dataset_config_names()` function to find out which subsets are available:

```
from          import get_dataset_config_names

domains = get_dataset_config_names("subjqa")
domains
```

```
['books', 'electronics', 'grocery', 'movies', 'restaurants', 'tripadvisor']
```

For our use case, we'll focus on building a QA system for the Electronics domain. To download the `electronics` subset, we just need to pass this value to the `name` argument of the `load_dataset()` function:

```
from          import load_dataset

subjqa = load_dataset("subjqa", name="electronics")
```

Like other question answering datasets on the Hub, SubjQA stores the answers to each question as a nested dictionary. For example, if we inspect one of the rows in the `answers` column:

```
print(subjqa["train"]["answers"][1])
```

```
{'text': ['Bass is weak as expected', 'Bass is weak as expected, even with EQ
adjusted up'], 'answer_start': [1302, 1302], 'answer_subj_level': [1, 1],
'ans_subj_score': [0.5083333253860474, 0.5083333253860474], 'is_ans_subjective':
[True, True]}
```

we can see that the answers are stored in a `text` field, while the starting character indices are provided in `answer_start`. To explore the dataset more easily, we'll flatten these nested columns with the `flatten()` method and convert each split to a Pandas `DataFrame` as follows:

```
import pandas as pd

dfs = {split: dset.to_pandas() for split, dset in subjqa.flatten().items()}

for split, df in dfs.items():
    print(f"Number of questions in {split}: {df['id'].nunique()}")
```

```
Number of questions in train: 1295
Number of questions in test: 358
Number of questions in validation: 255
```

Notice that the dataset is relatively small, with only 1,908 examples in total. This simulates a real-world scenario, since getting domain experts to label extractive QA datasets is labor-intensive and expensive. For example, the CUAD dataset for extractive QA on legal contracts is estimated to have a value of $2 million to account for the legal expertise needed to annotate its 13,000 examples![4]

There are quite a few columns in the SubjQA dataset, but the most interesting ones for building our QA system are shown in Table 7-1.

Table 7-1. Column names and their descriptions from the SubjQA dataset

Column name	Description
`title`	The Amazon Standard Identification Number (ASIN) associated with each product
`question`	The question
`answers.answer_text`	The span of text in the review labeled by the annotator
`answers.answer_start`	The start character index of the answer span
`context`	The customer review

Let's focus on these columns and take a look at a few of the training examples. We can use the `sample()` method to select a random sample:

```
qa_cols = ["title", "question", "answers.text",
           "answers.answer_start", "context"]
sample_df = dfs["train"][qa_cols].sample(2, random_state=7)
sample_df
```

4 D. Hendrycks et al., "CUAD: An Expert-Annotated NLP Dataset for Legal Contract Review" (*https://arxiv.org/abs/2103.06268*), (2021).

title	question	answers.text	answers.answer_start	context
B005DKZTMG	Does the keyboard lightweight?	[this keyboard is compact]	[215]	I really like this keyboard. I give it 4 stars because it doesn't have a CAPS LOCK key so I never know if my caps are on. But for the price, it really suffices as a wireless keyboard. I have very large hands and this keyboard is compact, but I have no complaints.
B00AAIPT76	How is the battery?	[]	[]	I bought this after the first spare gopro battery I bought wouldn't hold a charge. I have very realistic expectations of this sort of product, I am skeptical of amazing stories of charge time and battery life but I do expect the batteries to hold a charge for a couple of weeks at least and for the charger to work like a charger. In this I was not disappointed. I am a river rafter and found that the gopro burns through power in a hurry so this purchase solved that issue. the batteries held a charge, on shorter trips the extra two batteries were enough and on longer trips I could use my friends JOOS Orange to recharge them.I just bought a newtrent xtreme powerpak and expect to be able to charge these with that so I will not run out of power again.

From these examples we can make a few observations. First, the questions are not grammatically correct, which is quite common in the FAQ sections of ecommerce websites. Second, an empty `answers.text` entry denotes "unanswerable" questions whose answer cannot be found in the review. Finally, we can use the start index and length of the answer span to slice out the span of text in the review that corresponds to the answer:

```
start_idx = sample_df["answers.answer_start"].iloc[0][0]
end_idx = start_idx + len(sample_df["answers.text"].iloc[0][0])
sample_df["context"].iloc[0][start_idx:end_idx]
```

```
'this keyboard is compact'
```

Next, let's get a feel for what types of questions are in the training set by counting the questions that begin with a few common starting words:

```
counts = {}
question_types = ["What", "How", "Is", "Does", "Do", "Was", "Where", "Why"]

for q in question_types:
    counts[q] = dfs["train"]["question"].str.startswith(q).value_counts()[True]

pd.Series(counts).sort_values().plot.barh()
plt.title("Frequency of Question Types")
plt.show()
```

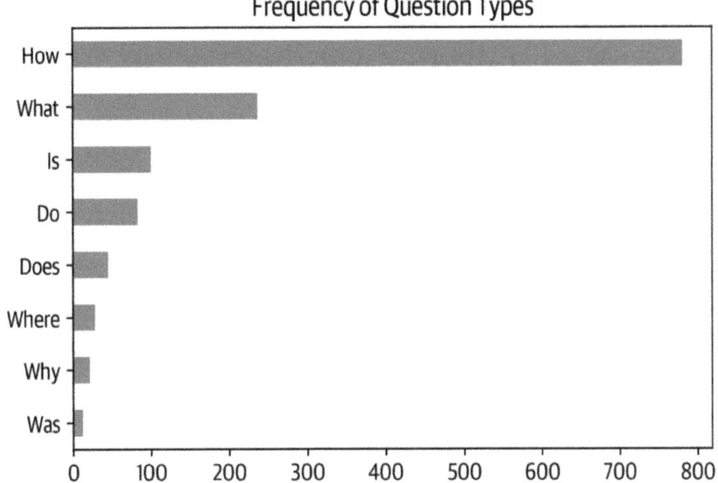

We can see that questions beginning with "How", "What", and "Is" are the most common ones, so let's have a look at some examples:

```
for question_type in ["How", "What", "Is"]:
    for question in (
        dfs["train"][dfs["train"].question.str.startswith(question_type)]
        .sample(n=3, random_state=42)['question']):
        print(question)
```

```
How is the camera?
How do you like the control?
How fast is the charger?
What is direction?
What is the quality of the construction of the bag?
What is your impression of the product?
Is this how zoom works?
Is sound clear?
Is it a wireless keyboard?
```

The Stanford Question Answering Dataset

The *(question, review, [answer sentences])* format of SubjQA is commonly used in extractive QA datasets, and was pioneered in the Stanford Question Answering Dataset (SQuAD).[5] This is a famous dataset that is often used to test the ability of machines to read a passage of text and answer questions about it. The dataset was created by sampling several hundred English articles from Wikipedia, partitioning each

5 P. Rajpurkar et al., "SQuAD: 100,000+ Questions for Machine Comprehension of Text" (*https://arxiv.org/abs/1606.05250*), (2016).

article into paragraphs, and then asking crowdworkers to generate a set of questions and answers for each paragraph. In the first version of SQuAD, each answer to a question was guaranteed to exist in the corresponding passage. But it wasn't long before sequence models started performing better than humans at extracting the correct span of text with the answer. To make the task more difficult, SQuAD 2.0 was created by augmenting SQuAD 1.1 with a set of adversarial questions that are relevant to a given passage but cannot be answered from the text alone.[6] The state of the art as of this book's writing is shown in Figure 7-3, with most models since 2019 surpassing human performance.

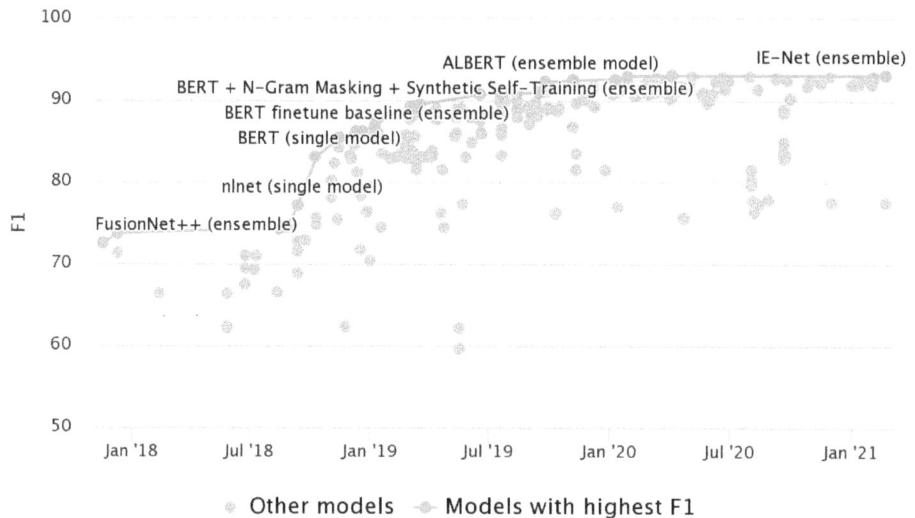

Figure 7-3. Progress on the SQuAD 2.0 benchmark (image from Papers with Code)

However, this superhuman performance does not appear to reflect genuine reading comprehension, since answers to the "unanswerable" questions can usually be identified through patterns in the passages like antonyms. To address these problems Google released the Natural Questions (NQ) dataset,[7] which involves fact-seeking questions obtained from Google Search users. The answers in NQ are much longer than in SQuAD and present a more challenging benchmark.

6 P. Rajpurkar, R. Jia, and P. Liang, "Know What You Don't Know: Unanswerable Questions for SQuAD" (*https://arxiv.org/abs/1806.03822*), (2018).

7 T. Kwiatkowski et al., "Natural Questions: A Benchmark for Question Answering Research," *Transactions of the Association for Computational Linguistics* 7 (March 2019): 452–466, *http://dx.doi.org/10.1162/tacl_a_00276*.

Now that we've explored our dataset a bit, let's dive into understanding how transformers can extract answers from text.

Extracting Answers from Text

The first thing we'll need for our QA system is to find a way to identify a potential answer as a span of text in a customer review. For example, if a we have a question like "Is it waterproof?" and the review passage is "This watch is waterproof at 30m depth", then the model should output "waterproof at 30m". To do this we'll need to understand how to:

- Frame the supervised learning problem.
- Tokenize and encode text for QA tasks.
- Deal with long passages that exceed a model's maximum context size.

Let's start by taking a look at how to frame the problem.

Span classification

The most common way to extract answers from text is by framing the problem as a *span classification* task, where the start and end tokens of an answer span act as the labels that a model needs to predict. This process is illustrated in Figure 7-4.

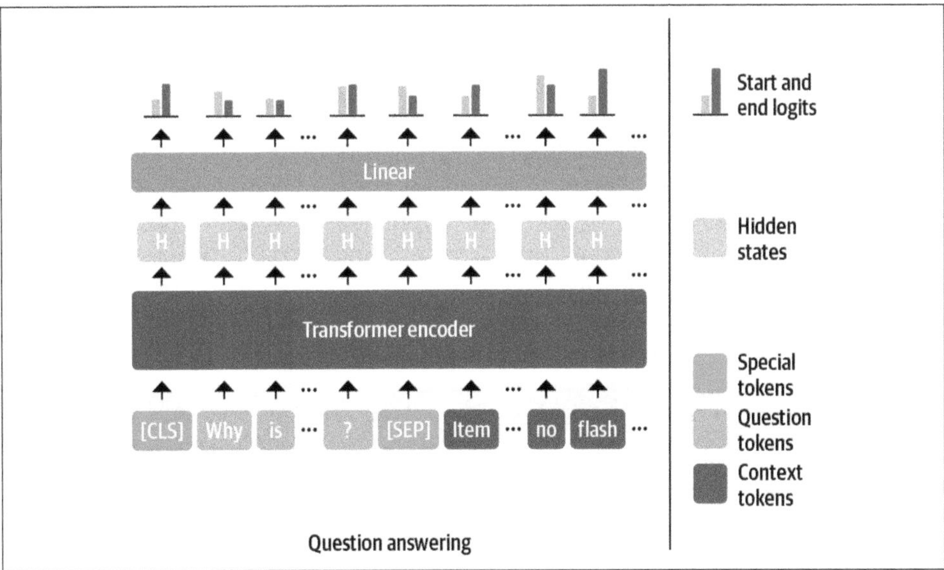

Figure 7-4. The span classification head for QA tasks

Since our training set is relatively small, with only 1,295 examples, a good strategy is to start with a language model that has already been fine-tuned on a large-scale QA dataset like SQuAD. In general, these models have strong reading comprehension capabilities and serve as a good baseline upon which to build a more accurate system. This is a somewhat different approach to that taken in previous chapters, where we typically started with a pretrained model and fine-tuned the task-specific head ourselves. For example, in Chapter 2, we had to fine-tune the classification head because the number of classes was tied to the dataset at hand. For extractive QA, we can actually start with a fine-tuned model since the structure of the labels remains the same across datasets.

You can find a list of extractive QA models by navigating to the Hugging Face Hub (*https://oreil.ly/dzCsC*) and searching for "squad" on the Models tab (Figure 7-5).

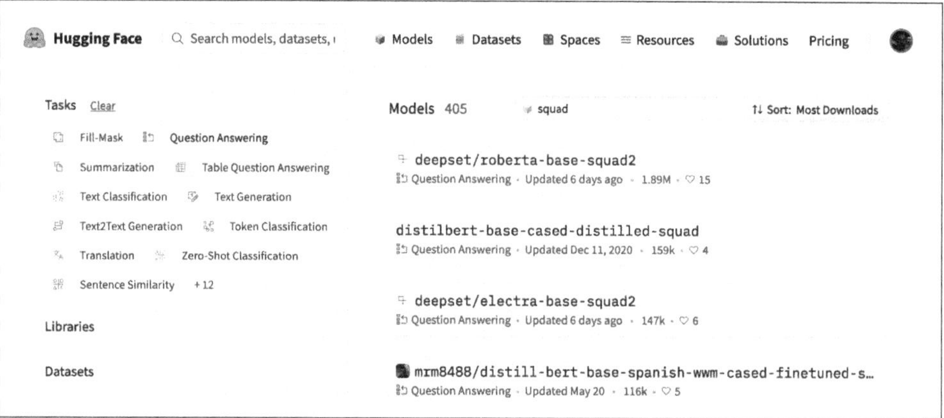

Figure 7-5. A selection of extractive QA models on the Hugging Face Hub

As you can see, at the time of writing, there are more than 350 QA models to choose from—so which one should you pick? In general, the answer depends on various factors like whether your corpus is mono- or multilingual and the constraints of running the model in a production environment. Table 7-2 lists a few models that provide a good foundation to build on.

Table 7-2. Baseline transformer models that are fine-tuned on SQuAD 2.0

Transformer	Description	Number of parameters	F_1-score on SQuAD 2.0
MiniLM	A distilled version of BERT-base that preserves 99% of the performance while being twice as fast	66M	79.5
RoBERTa-base	RoBERTa models have better performance than their BERT counterparts and can be fine-tuned on most QA datasets using a single GPU	125M	83.0
ALBERT-XXL	State-of-the-art performance on SQuAD 2.0, but computationally intensive and difficult to deploy	235M	88.1
XLM-RoBERTa-large	Multilingual model for 100 languages with strong zero-shot performance	570M	83.8

For the purposes of this chapter, we'll use a fine-tuned MiniLM model since it is fast to train and will allow us to quickly iterate on the techniques that we'll be exploring.[8] As usual, the first thing we need is a tokenizer to encode our texts, so let's take a look at how this works for QA tasks.

Tokenizing text for QA

To encode our texts, we'll load the MiniLM model checkpoint from the Hugging Face Hub (*https://oreil.ly/df5Cu*) as usual:

```
from transformers import AutoTokenizer

model_ckpt = "deepset/minilm-uncased-squad2"
tokenizer = AutoTokenizer.from_pretrained(model_ckpt)
```

To see the model in action, let's first try to extract an answer from a short passage of text. In extractive QA tasks, the inputs are provided as (question, context) pairs, so we pass them both to the tokenizer as follows:

```
question = "How much music can this hold?"
context = """An MP3 is about 1 MB/minute, so about 6000 hours depending on \
file size."""
inputs = tokenizer(question, context, return_tensors="pt")
```

Here we've returned PyTorch `Tensor` objects, since we'll need them to run the forward pass through the model. If we view the tokenized inputs as a table:

input_ids	101	2129	2172	2189	2064	2023	...	5834	2006	5371	2946	1012	102
token_type_ids	0	0	0	0	0	0	...	1	1	1	1	1	1
attention_mask	1	1	1	1	1	1	...	1	1	1	1	1	1

we can see the familiar `input_ids` and `attention_mask` tensors, while the `token_type_ids` tensor indicates which part of the inputs corresponds to the question and context (a 0 indicates a question token, a 1 indicates a context token).[9]

To understand how the tokenizer formats the inputs for QA tasks, let's decode the `input_ids` tensor:

```
print(tokenizer.decode(inputs["input_ids"][0]))
```

8 W. Wang et al., "MINILM: Deep Self-Attention Distillation for Task-Agnostic Compression of Pre-Trained Transformers" (*https://arxiv.org/abs/2002.10957*), (2020).

9 Note that the `token_type_ids` are not present in all transformer models. In the case of BERT-like models such as MiniLM, the `token_type_ids` are also used during pretraining to incorporate the next sentence prediction task.

```
[CLS] how much music can this hold? [SEP] an mp3 is about 1 mb / minute, so
about 6000 hours depending on file size. [SEP]
```

We see that for each QA example, the inputs take the format:

```
[CLS] question tokens [SEP] context tokens [SEP]
```

where the location of the first `[SEP]` token is determined by the `token_type_ids`. Now that our text is tokenized, we just need to instantiate the model with a QA head and run the inputs through the forward pass:

```
import
from                import AutoModelForQuestionAnswering

model = AutoModelForQuestionAnswering.from_pretrained(model_ckpt)

with torch.no_grad():
    outputs = model(**inputs)
print(outputs)
```

```
QuestionAnsweringModelOutput(loss=None, start_logits=tensor([[-0.9862, -4.7750,
         -5.4025, -5.2378, -5.2863, -5.5117, -4.9819, -6.1880,
         -0.9862,  0.2596, -0.2144, -1.7136,  3.7806,  4.8561, -1.0546, -3.9097,
         -1.7374, -4.5944, -1.4278,  3.9949,  5.0390, -0.2018, -3.0193, -4.8549,
         -2.3107, -3.5110, -3.5713, -0.9862]]), end_logits=tensor([[-0.9623,
         -5.4733, -5.0326, -5.1639, -5.4278, -5.5151, -5.1749, -4.6233,
         -0.9623, -3.7855, -0.8715, -3.7745, -3.0161, -1.1780,  0.1758, -2.7365,
          4.8934,  0.3046, -3.1761, -3.2762,  0.8937,  5.6606, -0.3623, -4.9554,
         -3.2531, -0.0914,  1.6211, -0.9623]]), hidden_states=None,
attentions=None)
```

Here we can see that we get a `QuestionAnsweringModelOutput` object as the output of the QA head. As illustrated in Figure 7-4, the QA head corresponds to a linear layer that takes the hidden states from the encoder and computes the logits for the start and end spans.[10] This means that we treat QA as a form of token classification, similar to what we encountered for named entity recognition in Chapter 4. To convert the outputs into an answer span, we first need to get the logits for the start and end tokens:

```
start_logits = outputs.start_logits
end_logits = outputs.end_logits
```

If we compare the shapes of these logits to the input IDs:

```
print(f"Input IDs shape: {inputs.input_ids.size()}")
print(f"Start logits shape: {start_logits.size()}")
print(f"End logits shape: {end_logits.size()}")
```

10 See Chapter 2 for details on how these hidden states can be extracted.

```
Input IDs shape: torch.Size([1, 28])
Start logits shape: torch.Size([1, 28])
End logits shape: torch.Size([1, 28])
```

we see that there are two logits (a start and end) associated with each input token. As illustrated in Figure 7-6, larger, positive logits correspond to more likely candidates for the start and end tokens. In this example we can see that the model assigns the highest start token logits to the numbers "1" and "6000", which makes sense since our question is asking about a quantity. Similarly, we see that the end tokens with the highest logits are "minute" and "hours".

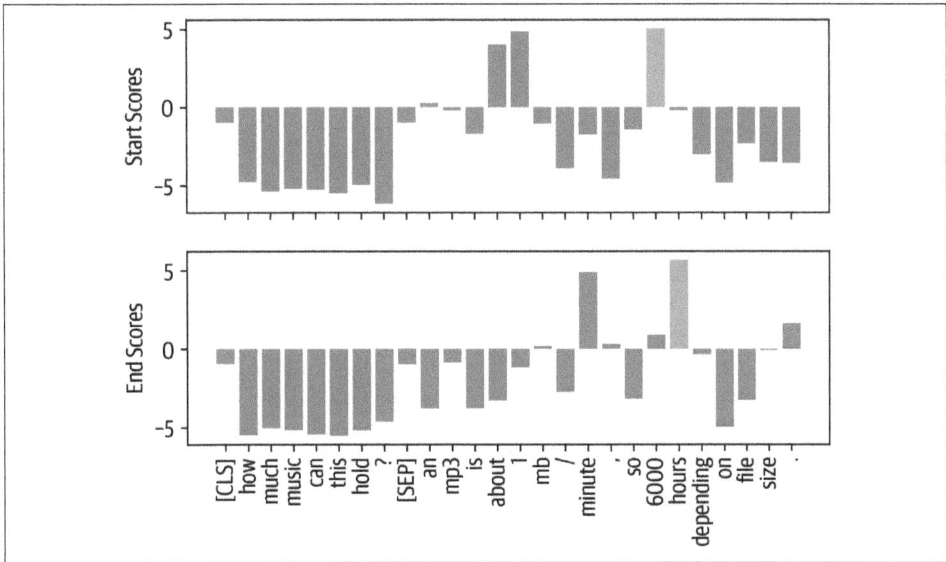

Figure 7-6. Predicted logits for the start and end tokens; the token with the highest score is colored in orange

To get the final answer, we can compute the argmax over the start and end token logits and then slice the span from the inputs. The following code performs these steps and decodes the result so we can print the resulting text:

```
import torch

start_idx = torch.argmax(start_logits)
end_idx = torch.argmax(end_logits) + 1
answer_span = inputs["input_ids"][0][start_idx:end_idx]
answer = tokenizer.decode(answer_span)
print(f"Question: {question}")
print(f"Answer: {answer}")
```

```
Question: How much music can this hold?
Answer: 6000 hours
```

Great, it worked! In 🤗 Transformers, all of these preprocessing and postprocessing steps are conveniently wrapped in a dedicated pipeline. We can instantiate the pipeline by passing our tokenizer and fine-tuned model as follows:

```
from transformers import pipeline

pipe = pipeline("question-answering", model=model, tokenizer=tokenizer)
pipe(question=question, context=context, topk=3)
```

```
[{'score': 0.26516005396842957,
  'start': 38,
  'end': 48,
  'answer': '6000 hours'},
 {'score': 0.2208300083875656,
  'start': 16,
  'end': 48,
  'answer': '1 MB/minute, so about 6000 hours'},
 {'score': 0.10253632068634033,
  'start': 16,
  'end': 27,
  'answer': '1 MB/minute'}]
```

In addition to the answer, the pipeline also returns the model's probability estimate in the `score` field (obtained by taking a softmax over the logits). This is handy when we want to compare multiple answers within a single context. We've also shown that we can have the model predict multiple answers by specifying the `topk` parameter. Sometimes, it is possible to have questions for which no answer is possible, like the empty `answers.answer_start` examples in SubjQA. In these cases the model will assign a high start and end score to the `[CLS]` token, and the pipeline maps this output to an empty string:

```
pipe(question="Why is there no data?", context=context,
     handle_impossible_answer=True)
```

```
{'score': 0.9068416357040405, 'start': 0, 'end': 0, 'answer': ''}
```

In our simple example, we obtained the start and end indices by taking the argmax of the corresponding logits. However, this heuristic can produce out-of-scope answers by selecting tokens that belong to the question instead of the context. In practice, the pipeline computes the best combination of start and end indices subject to various constraints such as being in-scope, requiring the start indices to precede the end indices, and so on.

Dealing with long passages

One subtlety faced by reading comprehension models is that the context often contains more tokens than the maximum sequence length of the model (which is usually a few hundred tokens at most). As illustrated in Figure 7-7, a decent portion of the SubjQA training set contains question-context pairs that won't fit within MiniLM's context size of 512 tokens.

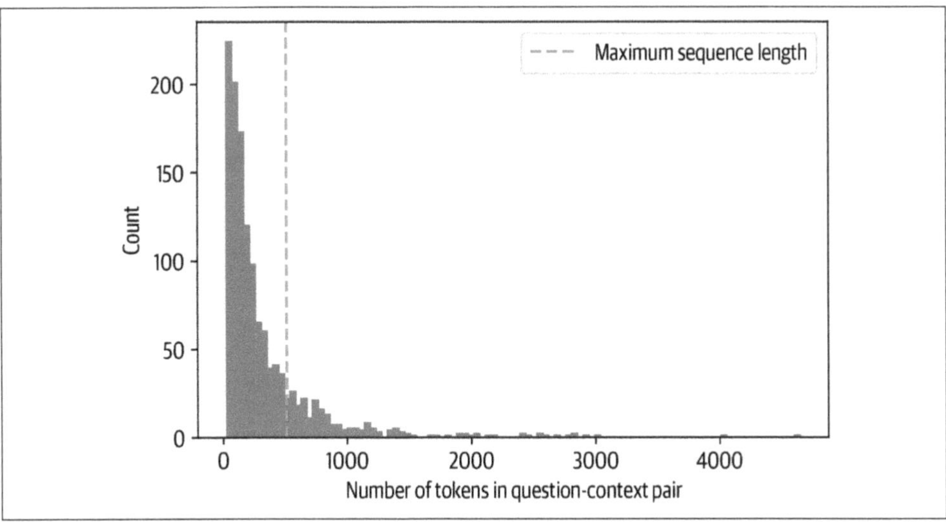

Figure 7-7. Distribution of tokens for each question-context pair in the SubjQA training set

For other tasks, like text classification, we simply truncated long texts under the assumption that enough information was contained in the embedding of the `[CLS]` token to generate accurate predictions. For QA, however, this strategy is problematic because the answer to a question could lie near the end of the context and thus would be removed by truncation. As illustrated in Figure 7-8, the standard way to deal with this is to apply a *sliding window* across the inputs, where each window contains a passage of tokens that fit in the model's context.

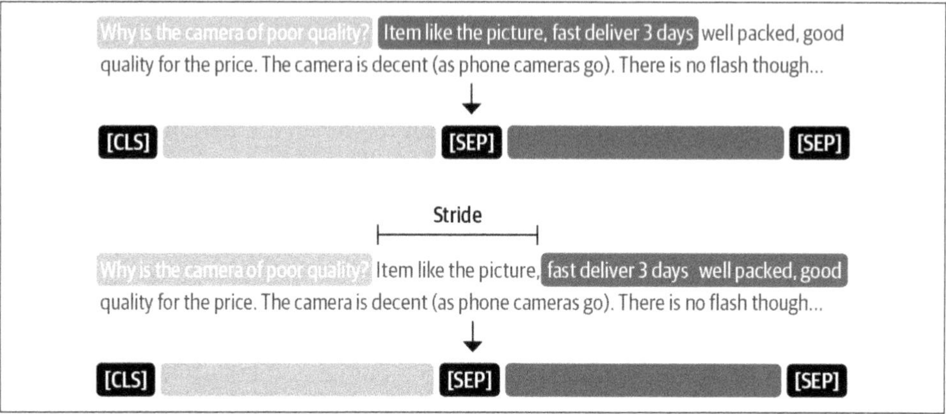
Why is the camera of poor quality?
Item like the picture, fast deliver 3 days well packed, good quality for the price. The camera is decent (as phone cameras go). There is no flash though...
[CLS]
[SEP]
[SEP]
Stride
Why is the camera of poor quality?
Item like the picture, fast deliver 3 days well packed, good quality for the price. The camera is decent (as phone cameras go). There is no flash though...
[CLS]
[SEP]
[SEP]

Figure 7-8. How the sliding window creates multiple question-context pairs for long documents—the first bar corresponds to the question, while the second bar is the context captured in each window

In 🤗 Transformers, we can set `return_overflowing_tokens=True` in the tokenizer to enable the sliding window. The size of the sliding window is controlled by the `max_seq_length` argument, and the size of the stride is controlled by `doc_stride`. Let's grab the first example from our training set and define a small window to illustrate how this works:

```
example = dfs["train"].iloc[0][["question", "context"]]
tokenized_example = tokenizer(example["question"], example["context"],
                              return_overflowing_tokens=True, max_length=100,
                              stride=25)
```

In this case we now get a list of `input_ids`, one for each window. Let's check the number of tokens we have in each window:

```
for idx, window in enumerate(tokenized_example["input_ids"]):
    print(f"Window #{idx} has {len(window)} tokens")
```

```
Window #0 has 100 tokens
Window #1 has 88 tokens
```

Finally, we can see where two windows overlap by decoding the inputs:

```
for window in tokenized_example["input_ids"]:
    print(f"{tokenizer.decode(window)} \n")
```

```
[CLS] how is the bass? [SEP] i have had koss headphones in the past, pro 4aa and
qz - 99. the koss portapro is portable and has great bass response. the work
great with my android phone and can be " rolled up " to be carried in my
motorcycle jacket or computer bag without getting crunched. they are very light
and don't feel heavy or bear down on your ears even after listening to music
with them on all day. the sound is [SEP]

[CLS] how is the bass? [SEP] and don't feel heavy or bear down on your ears even
```

```
after listening to music with them on all day. the sound is night and day better
than any ear - bud could be and are almost as good as the pro 4aa. they are "
open air " headphones so you cannot match the bass to the sealed types, but it
comes close. for $ 32, you cannot go wrong. [SEP]
```

Now that we have some intuition about how QA models can extract answers from text, let's look at the other components we need to build an end-to-end QA pipeline.

Using Haystack to Build a QA Pipeline

In our simple answer extraction example, we provided both the question and the context to the model. However, in reality our system's users will only provide a question about a product, so we need some way of selecting relevant passages from among all the reviews in our corpus. One way to do this would be to concatenate all the reviews of a given product together and feed them to the model as a single, long context. Although simple, the drawback of this approach is that the context can become extremely long and thereby introduce an unacceptable latency for our users' queries. For example, let's suppose that on average, each product has 30 reviews and each review takes 100 milliseconds to process. If we need to process all the reviews to get an answer, this would result in an average latency of 3 seconds per user query—much too long for ecommerce websites!

To handle this, modern QA systems are typically based on the *retriever-reader* architecture, which has two main components:

Retriever
: Responsible for retrieving relevant documents for a given query. Retrievers are usually categorized as *sparse* or *dense*. Sparse retrievers use word frequencies to represent each document and query as a sparse vector.[11] The relevance of a query and a document is then determined by computing an inner product of the vectors. On the other hand, dense retrievers use encoders like transformers to represent the query and document as contextualized embeddings (which are dense vectors). These embeddings encode semantic meaning, and allow dense retrievers to improve search accuracy by understanding the content of the query.

Reader
: Responsible for extracting an answer from the documents provided by the retriever. The reader is usually a reading comprehension model, although at the end of the chapter we'll see examples of models that can generate free-form answers.

11 A vector is sparse if most of its elements are zero.

As illustrated in Figure 7-9, there can also be other components that apply postprocessing to the documents fetched by the retriever or to the answers extracted by the reader. For example, the retrieved documents may need reranking to eliminate noisy or irrelevant ones that can confuse the reader. Similarly, postprocessing of the reader's answers is often needed when the correct answer comes from various passages in a long document.

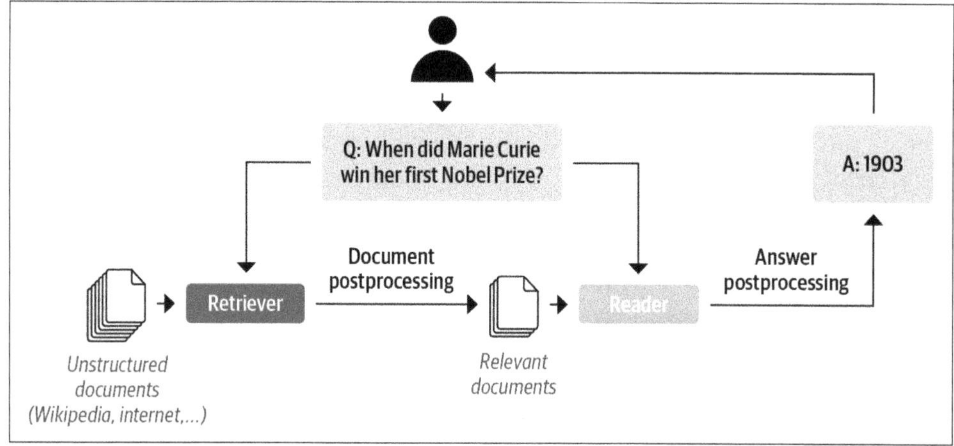

Figure 7-9. The retriever-reader architecture for modern QA systems

To build our QA system, we'll use the *Haystack* library (*https://haystack.deepset.ai*) developed by deepset (*https://deepset.ai*), a German company focused on NLP. Haystack is based on the retriever-reader architecture, abstracts much of the complexity involved in building these systems, and integrates tightly with 🤗 Transformers.

In addition to the retriever and reader, there are two more components involved when building a QA pipeline with Haystack:

Document store
: A document-oriented database that stores documents and metadata which are provided to the retriever at query time

Pipeline
: Combines all the components of a QA system to enable custom query flows, merging documents from multiple retrievers, and more

In this section we'll look at how we can use these components to quickly build a prototype QA pipeline. Later, we'll examine how we can improve its performance.

This chapter was written using version 0.9.0 of the Haystack library. In version 0.10.0 (*https://oreil.ly/qbqgv*), the pipeline and evaluation APIs were redesigned to make it easier to inspect whether the retriever or reader are impacting performance. To see what this chapter's code looks like with the new API, check out the GitHub repository (*https://github.com/nlp-with-transformers/notebooks*).

Initializing a document store

In Haystack, there are various document stores to choose from and each one can be paired with a dedicated set of retrievers. This is illustrated in Table 7-3, where the compatibility of sparse (TF-IDF, BM25) and dense (Embedding, DPR) retrievers is shown for each of the available document stores. We'll explain what all these acronyms mean later in this chapter.

Table 7-3. Compatibility of Haystack retrievers and document stores

	In memory	Elasticsearch	FAISS	Milvus
TF-IDF	Yes	Yes	No	No
BM25	No	Yes	No	No
Embedding	Yes	Yes	Yes	Yes
DPR	Yes	Yes	Yes	Yes

Since we'll be exploring both sparse and dense retrievers in this chapter, we'll use the `ElasticsearchDocumentStore`, which is compatible with both retriever types. Elasticsearch is a search engine that is capable of handling a diverse range of data types, including textual, numerical, geospatial, structured, and unstructured. Its ability to store huge volumes of data and quickly filter it with full-text search features makes it especially well suited for developing QA systems. It also has the advantage of being the industry standard for infrastructure analytics, so there's a good chance your company already has a cluster that you can work with.

To initialize the document store, we first need to download and install Elasticsearch. By following Elasticsearch's guide (*https://oreil.ly/bgmKq*),[12] we can grab the latest release for Linux with `wget` and unpack it with the `tar` shell command:

```
url = """https://artifacts.elastic.co/downloads/elasticsearch/\
elasticsearch-7.9.2-linux-x86_64.tar.gz"""
!wget -nc -q {url}
!tar -xzf elasticsearch-7.9.2-linux-x86_64.tar.gz
```

12 The guide also provides installation instructions for macOS and Windows.

Next we need to start the Elasticsearch server. Since we're running all the code in this book within Jupyter notebooks, we'll need to use Python's `Popen()` function to spawn a new process. While we're at it, let's also run the subprocess in the background using the `chown` shell command:

```
import os
from            import Popen, PIPE, STDOUT

# Run Elasticsearch as a background process
!chown -R daemon:daemon elasticsearch-7.9.2
es_server = Popen(args=['elasticsearch-7.9.2/bin/elasticsearch'],
                  stdout=PIPE, stderr=STDOUT, preexec_fn=lambda: os.setuid(1))
# Wait until Elasticsearch has started
!sleep 30
```

In the `Popen()` function, the `args` specify the program we wish to execute, while `stdout=PIPE` creates a new pipe for the standard output and `stderr=STDOUT` collects the errors in the same pipe. The `preexec_fn` argument specifies the ID of the subprocess we wish to use. By default, Elasticsearch runs locally on port 9200, so we can test the connection by sending an HTTP request to `localhost`:

```
!curl -X GET "localhost:9200/?pretty"
```


```
{
  "name" : "96938eee37cd",
  "cluster_name" : "docker-cluster",
  "cluster_uuid" : "ABGDdvbbRWmMb9Umz79HbA",
  "version" : {
    "number" : "7.9.2",
    "build_flavor" : "default",
    "build_type" : "docker",
    "build_hash" : "d34da0ea4a966c4e49417f2da2f244e3e97b4e6e",
    "build_date" : "2020-09-23T00:45:33.626720Z",
    "build_snapshot" : false,
    "lucene_version" : "8.6.2",
    "minimum_wire_compatibility_version" : "6.8.0",
    "minimum_index_compatibility_version" : "6.0.0-beta1"
  },
  "tagline" : "You Know, for Search"
}
```


Now that our Elasticsearch server is up and running, the next thing to do is instantiate the document store:

```
from                                      import ElasticsearchDocumentStore

# Return the document embedding for later use with dense retriever
document_store = ElasticsearchDocumentStore(return_embedding=True)
```

By default, `ElasticsearchDocumentStore` creates two indices on Elasticsearch: one called `document` for (you guessed it) storing documents, and another called `label` for storing the annotated answer spans. For now, we'll just populate the `document` index with the SubjQA reviews, and Haystack's document stores expect a list of dictionaries with `text` and `meta` keys as follows:

```
{
    "text": "<the-context>",
    "meta": {
        "field_01": "<additional-metadata>",
        "field_02": "<additional-metadata>",
        ...
    }
}
```

The fields in `meta` can be used for applying filters during retrieval. For our purposes we'll include the `item_id` and `q_review_id` columns of SubjQA so we can filter by product and question ID, along with the corresponding training split. We can then loop through the examples in each `DataFrame` and add them to the index with the `write_documents()` method as follows:

```
for split, df in dfs.items():
    # Exclude duplicate reviews
    docs = [{"text": row["context"],
             "meta":{"item_id": row["title"], "question_id": row["id"],
                     "split": split}}
        for _,row in df.drop_duplicates(subset="context").iterrows()]
    document_store.write_documents(docs, index="document")

print(f"Loaded {document_store.get_document_count()} documents")
```

```
Loaded 1615 documents
```

Great, we've loaded all our reviews into an index! To search the index we'll need a retriever, so let's look at how we can initialize one for Elasticsearch.

Initializing a retriever

The Elasticsearch document store can be paired with any of the Haystack retrievers, so let's start by using a sparse retriever based on BM25 (short for "Best Match 25"). BM25 is an improved version of the classic Term Frequency-Inverse Document Frequency (TF-IDF) algorithm and represents the question and context as sparse vectors that can be searched efficiently on Elasticsearch. The BM25 score measures how much matched text is about a search query and improves on TF-IDF by saturating TF values quickly and normalizing the document length so that short documents are favored over long ones.[13]

13 For an in-depth explanation of document scoring with TF-IDF and BM25 see Chapter 23 of *Speech and Language Processing*, 3rd edition, by D. Jurafsky and J.H. Martin (Prentice Hall).

In Haystack, the BM25 retriever is used by default in `ElasticsearchRetriever`, so let's initialize this class by specifying the document store we wish to search over:

```
from haystack.retriever.sparse import ElasticsearchRetriever

es_retriever = ElasticsearchRetriever(document_store=document_store)
```

Next, let's look at a simple query for a single electronics product in the training set. For review-based QA systems like ours, it's important to restrict the queries to a single item because otherwise the retriever would source reviews about products that are not related to a user's query. For example, asking "Is the camera quality any good?" without a product filter could return reviews about phones, when the user might be asking about a specific laptop camera instead. By themselves, the ASIN values in our dataset are a bit cryptic, but we can decipher them with online tools like *amazon ASIN* (*https://amazon-asin.com*) or by simply appending the value of `item_id` to the *www.amazon.com/dp/* URL. The following item ID corresponds to one of Amazon's Fire tablets, so let's use the retriever's `retrieve()` method to ask if it's any good for reading with:

```
item_id = "B0074BW614"
query = "Is it good for reading?"
retrieved_docs = es_retriever.retrieve(
    query=query, top_k=3, filters={"item_id":[item_id], "split":["train"]})
```

Here we've specified how many documents to return with the `top_k` argument and applied a filter on both the `item_id` and `split` keys that were included in the `meta` field of our documents. Each element of `retrieved_docs` is a Haystack `Document` object that is used to represent documents and includes the retriever's query score along with other metadata. Let's have a look at one of the retrieved documents:

```
print(retrieved_docs[0])
```

```
{'text': 'This is a gift to myself.  I have been a kindle user for 4 years and
this is my third one.  I never thought I would want a fire for I mainly use it
for book reading.  I decided to try the fire for when I travel I take my laptop,
my phone and my iPod classic.  I love my iPod but watching movies on the plane
with it can be challenging because it is so small. Laptops battery life is not
as good as the Kindle.  So the Fire combines for me what I needed all three to
do. So far so good.', 'score': 6.243799, 'probability': 0.6857824513476455,
'question': None, 'meta': {'item_id': 'B0074BW614', 'question_id':
'868e311275e26dbafe5af70774a300f3', 'split': 'train'}, 'embedding': None, 'id':
'252e83e25d52df7311d597dc89eef9f6'}
```

In addition to the document's text, we can see the `score` that Elasticsearch computed for its relevance to the query (larger scores imply a better match). Under the hood, Elasticsearch relies on Lucene (*https://lucene.apache.org*) for indexing and search, so by default it uses Lucene's *practical scoring function*. You can find the nitty-gritty details behind the scoring function in the Elasticsearch documentation (*https://oreil.ly/b1Seu*), but in brief terms it first filters the candidate documents by applying a

Boolean test (does the document match the query?), and then applies a similarity metric that's based on representing both the document and the query as vectors.

Now that we have a way to retrieve relevant documents, the next thing we need is a way to extract answers from them. This is where the reader comes in, so let's take a look at how we can load our MiniLM model in Haystack.

Initializing a reader

In Haystack, there are two types of readers one can use to extract answers from a given context:

`FARMReader`
: Based on deepset's *FARM* framework (*https://farm.deepset.ai*) for fine-tuning and deploying transformers. Compatible with models trained using 🤗 Transformers and can load models directly from the Hugging Face Hub.

`TransformersReader`
: Based on the QA pipeline from 🤗 Transformers. Suitable for running inference only.

Although both readers handle a model's weights in the same way, there are some differences in the way the predictions are converted to produce answers:

- In 🤗 Transformers, the QA pipeline normalizes the start and end logits with a softmax in each passage. This means that it is only meaningful to compare answer scores between answers extracted from the same passage, where the probabilities sum to 1. For example, an answer score of 0.9 from one passage is not necessarily better than a score of 0.8 in another. In FARM, the logits are not normalized, so inter-passage answers can be compared more easily.
- The `TransformersReader` sometimes predicts the same answer twice, but with different scores. This can happen in long contexts if the answer lies across two overlapping windows. In FARM, these duplicates are removed.

Since we will be fine-tuning the reader later in the chapter, we'll use the `FARMReader`. As with 🤗 Transformers, to load the model we just need to specify the MiniLM checkpoint on the Hugging Face Hub along with some QA-specific arguments:

```
from haystack.reader.farm import FARMReader

model_ckpt = "deepset/minilm-uncased-squad2"
max_seq_length, doc_stride = 384, 128
reader = FARMReader(model_name_or_path=model_ckpt, progress_bar=False,
                    max_seq_len=max_seq_length, doc_stride=doc_stride,
                    return_no_answer=True)
```

It is also possible to fine-tune a reading comprehension model directly in 🤗 Transformers and then load it in `Transformers Reader` to run inference. For details on how to do the fine-tuning step, see the question answering tutorial in the library's documentation (*https://oreil.ly/VkhIQ*).

In `FARMReader`, the behavior of the sliding window is controlled by the same `max_seq_length` and `doc_stride` arguments that we saw for the tokenizer. Here we've used the values from the MiniLM paper. To confirm, let's now test the reader on our simple example from earlier:

```
print(reader.predict_on_texts(question=question, texts=[context], top_k=1))
```

```
{'query': 'How much music can this hold?', 'no_ans_gap': 12.648084878921509,
'answers': [{'answer': '6000 hours', 'score': 10.69961929321289, 'probability':
0.3988136053085327, 'context': 'An MP3 is about 1 MB/minute, so about 6000 hours
depending on file size.', 'offset_start': 38, 'offset_end': 48,
'offset_start_in_doc': 38, 'offset_end_in_doc': 48, 'document_id':
'e344757014e804eff50faa3ecf1c9c75'}]}
```

Great, the reader appears to be working as expected—so next, let's tie together all our components using one of Haystack's pipelines.

Putting it all together

Haystack provides a `Pipeline` abstraction that allows us to combine retrievers, readers, and other components together as a graph that can be easily customized for each use case. There are also predefined pipelines analogous to those in 🤗 Transformers, but specialized for QA systems. In our case, we're interested in extracting answers, so we'll use the `ExtractiveQAPipeline`, which takes a single retriever-reader pair as its arguments:

```
from                     import ExtractiveQAPipeline

pipe = ExtractiveQAPipeline(reader, es_retriever)
```

Each `Pipeline` has a `run()` method that specifies how the query flow should be executed. For the `ExtractiveQAPipeline` we just need to pass the `query`, the number of documents to retrieve with `top_k_retriever`, and the number of answers to extract from these documents with `top_k_reader`. In our case, we also need to specify a filter over the item ID, which can be done using the `filters` argument as we did with the retriever earlier. Let's run a simple example using our question about the Amazon Fire tablet again, but this time returning the extracted answers:

```
n_answers = 3
preds = pipe.run(query=query, top_k_retriever=3, top_k_reader=n_answers,
                 filters={"item_id": [item_id], "split":["train"]})

print(f"Question: {preds['query']} \n")
```

```
for idx in range(n_answers):
    print(f"Answer {idx+1}: {preds['answers'][idx]['answer']}")
    print(f"Review snippet: ...{preds['answers'][idx]['context']}...")
    print("\n\n")
```

```
Question: Is it good for reading?

Answer 1: I mainly use it for book reading
Review snippet: ... is my third one.  I never thought I would want a fire for I
mainly use it for book reading.  I decided to try the fire for when I travel I
take my la...


Answer 2: the larger screen compared to the Kindle makes for easier reading
Review snippet: ...ght enough that I can hold it to read, but the larger screen
compared to the Kindle makes for easier reading. I love the color, something I
never thou...


Answer 3: it is great for reading books when no light is available
Review snippet: ...ecoming addicted to hers! Our son LOVES it and it is great
for reading books when no light is available. Amazing sound but I suggest good
headphones t...
```

Great, we now have an end-to-end QA system for Amazon product reviews! This is a good start, but notice that the second and third answers are closer to what the question is actually asking. To do better, we'll need some metrics to quantify the performance of the retriever and reader. We'll take a look at that next.

Improving Our QA Pipeline

Although much of the recent research on QA has focused on improving reading comprehension models, in practice it doesn't matter how good your reader is if the retriever can't find the relevant documents in the first place! In particular, the retriever sets an upper bound on the performance of the whole QA system, so it's important to make sure it's doing a good job. With this in mind, let's start by introducing some common metrics to evaluate the retriever so that we can compare the performance of sparse and dense representations.

Evaluating the Retriever

A common metric for evaluating retrievers is *recall*, which measures the fraction of all relevant documents that are retrieved. In this context, "relevant" simply means whether the answer is present in a passage of text or not, so given a set of questions, we can compute recall by counting the number of times an answer appears in the top *k* documents returned by the retriever.

In Haystack, there are two ways to evaluate retrievers:

- Use the retriever's in-built `eval()` method. This can be used for both open- and closed-domain QA, but not for datasets like SubjQA where each document is paired with a single product and we need to filter by product ID for every query.
- Build a custom `Pipeline` that combines a retriever with the `EvalRetriever` class. This enables the implementation of custom metrics and query flows.

A complementary metric to recall is *mean average precision* (mAP), which rewards retrievers that can place the correct answers higher up in the document ranking.

Since we need to evaluate the recall per product and then aggregate across all products, we'll opt for the second approach. Each node in the `Pipeline` graph represents a class that takes some inputs and produces some outputs via a `run()` method:

```
class PipelineNode:
    def __init__(self):
        self.outgoing_edges = 1

    def run(self, **kwargs):
        ...
        return (outputs, "outgoing_edge_name")
```

Here `kwargs` corresponds to the outputs from the previous node in the graph, which is manipulated within the `run()` method to return a tuple of the outputs for the next node, along with a name for the outgoing edge. The only other requirement is to include an `outgoing_edges` attribute that indicates the number of outputs from the node (in most cases `outgoing_edges=1`, unless you have branches in the pipeline that route the inputs according to some criterion).

In our case, we need a node to evaluate the retriever, so we'll use the `EvalRetriever` class whose `run()` method keeps track of which documents have answers that match the ground truth. With this class we can then build up a `Pipeline` graph by adding the evaluation node after a node that represents the retriever itself:

```
from haystack.pipeline import Pipeline
from haystack.eval import EvalDocuments

class EvalRetrieverPipeline:
    def __init__(self, retriever):
        self.retriever = retriever
        self.eval_retriever = EvalDocuments()
        pipe = Pipeline()
        pipe.add_node(component=self.retriever, name="ESRetriever",
```

```
                    inputs=["Query"])
        pipe.add_node(component=self.eval_retriever, name="EvalRetriever",
                    inputs=["ESRetriever"])
        self.pipeline = pipe


pipe = EvalRetrieverPipeline(es_retriever)
```

Notice that each node is given a `name` and a list of `inputs`. In most cases, each node has a single outgoing edge, so we just need to include the name of the previous node in `inputs`.

Now that we have our evaluation pipeline, we need to pass some queries and their corresponding answers. To do this, we'll add the answers to a dedicated `label` index on our document store. Haystack provides a `Label` object that represents the answer spans and their metadata in a standardized fashion. To populate the `label` index, we'll first create a list of `Label` objects by looping over each question in the test set and extracting the matching answers and additional metadata:

```
from haystack import Label

labels = []
for i, row in dfs["test"].iterrows():
    # Metadata used for filtering in the Retriever
    meta = {"item_id": row["title"], "question_id": row["id"]}
    # Populate labels for questions with answers
    if len(row["answers.text"]):
        for answer in row["answers.text"]:
            label = Label(
                question=row["question"], answer=answer, id=i, origin=row["id"],
                meta=meta, is_correct_answer=True, is_correct_document=True,
                no_answer=False)
            labels.append(label)
    # Populate labels for questions without answers
    else:
        label = Label(
            question=row["question"], answer="", id=i, origin=row["id"],
            meta=meta, is_correct_answer=True, is_correct_document=True,
            no_answer=True)
        labels.append(label)
```

If we peek at one of these labels:

```
print(labels[0])
```

```
{'id': 'e28f5e62-85e8-41b2-8a34-fbff63b7a466', 'created_at': None, 'updated_at':
None, 'question': 'What is the tonal balance of these headphones?', 'answer': 'I
have been a headphone fanatic for thirty years', 'is_correct_answer': True,
'is_correct_document': True, 'origin': 'd0781d13200014aa25860e44da9d5ea7',
'document_id': None, 'offset_start_in_doc': None, 'no_answer': False,
'model_id': None, 'meta': {'item_id': 'B00001WRSJ', 'question_id':
'd0781d13200014aa25860e44da9d5ea7'}}
```

we can see the question-answer pair, along with an `origin` field that contains the unique question ID so we can filter the document store per question. We've also added the product ID to the `meta` field so we can filter the labels by product. Now that we have our labels, we can write them to the `label` index on Elasticsearch as follows:

```
document_store.write_labels(labels, index="label")
print(f"""Loaded {document_store.get_label_count(index="label")} \
question-answer pairs""")
```

```
Loaded 358 question-answer pairs
```

Next, we need to build up a mapping between our question IDs and corresponding answers that we can pass to the pipeline. To get all the labels, we can use the `get_all_labels_aggregated()` method from the document store that will aggregate all question-answer pairs associated with a unique ID. This method returns a list of `MultiLabel` objects, but in our case we only get one element since we're filtering by question ID. We can build up a list of aggregated labels as follows:

```
labels_agg = document_store.get_all_labels_aggregated(
    index="label",
    open_domain=True,
    aggregate_by_meta=["item_id"]
)
print(len(labels_agg))
```

```
330
```

By peeking at one of these labels we can see that all the answers associated with a given question are aggregated together in a `multiple_answers` field:

```
print(labels_agg[109])
```

```
{'question': 'How does the fan work?', 'multiple_answers': ['the fan is really
really good', "the fan itself isn't super loud. There is an adjustable dial to
change fan speed"], 'is_correct_answer': True, 'is_correct_document': True,
'origin': '5a9b7616541f700f103d21f8ad41bc4b', 'multiple_document_ids': [None,
None], 'multiple_offset_start_in_docs': [None, None], 'no_answer': False,
'model_id': None, 'meta': {'item_id': 'B002MU1ZRS'}}
```

We now have all the ingredients for evaluating the retriever, so let's define a function that feeds each question-answer pair associated with each product to the evaluation pipeline and tracks the correct retrievals in our `pipe` object:

```
def run_pipeline(pipeline, top_k_retriever=10, top_k_reader=4):
    for l in labels_agg:
        _ = pipeline.pipeline.run(
            query=l.question,
            top_k_retriever=top_k_retriever,
            top_k_reader=top_k_reader,
            top_k_eval_documents=top_k_retriever,
            labels=l,
            filters={"item_id": [l.meta["item_id"]], "split": ["test"]})
```

```
run_pipeline(pipe, top_k_retriever=3)
print(f"Recall@3: {pipe.eval_retriever.recall:.2f}")
```

```
Recall@3: 0.95
```

Great, it works! Notice that we picked a specific value for `top_k_retriever` to specify the number of documents to retrieve. In general, increasing this parameter will improve the recall, but at the expense of providing more documents to the reader and slowing down the end-to-end pipeline. To guide our decision on which value to pick, we'll create a function that loops over several *k* values and compute the recall across the whole test set for each *k*:

```
def evaluate_retriever(retriever, topk_values = [1,3,5,10,20]):
    topk_results = {}

    for topk in topk_values:
        # Create Pipeline
        p = EvalRetrieverPipeline(retriever)
        # Loop over each question-answers pair in test set
        run_pipeline(p, top_k_retriever=topk)
        # Get metrics
        topk_results[topk] = {"recall": p.eval_retriever.recall}

    return pd.DataFrame.from_dict(topk_results, orient="index")


es_topk_df = evaluate_retriever(es_retriever)
```

If we plot the results, we can see how the recall improves as we increase *k*:

```
def plot_retriever_eval(dfs, retriever_names):
    fig, ax = plt.subplots()
    for df, retriever_name in zip(dfs, retriever_names):
        df.plot(y="recall", ax=ax, label=retriever_name)
    plt.xticks(df.index)
    plt.ylabel("Top-k Recall")
    plt.xlabel("k")
    plt.show()

plot_retriever_eval([es_topk_df], ["BM25"])
```

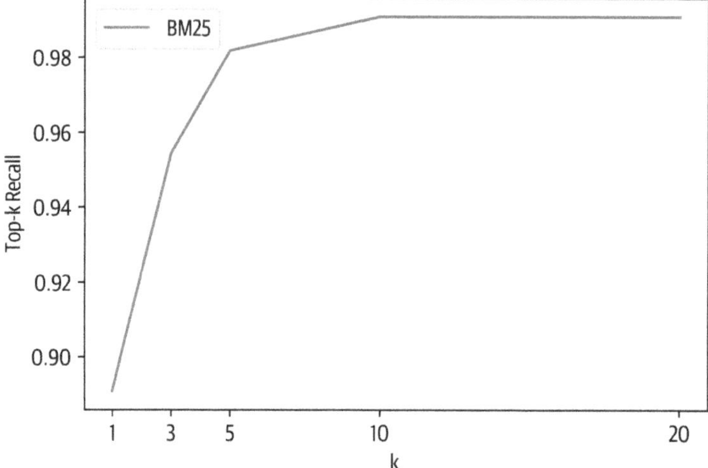

From the plot, we can see that there's an inflection point around $k = 5$ and we get almost perfect recall from $k = 10$ onwards. Let's now take a look at retrieving documents with dense vector techniques.

Dense Passage Retrieval

We've seen that we get almost perfect recall when our sparse retriever returns $k = 10$ documents, but can we do better at smaller values of k? The advantage of doing so is that we can pass fewer documents to the reader and thereby reduce the overall latency of our QA pipeline. A well-known limitation of sparse retrievers like BM25 is that they can fail to capture the relevant documents if the user query contains terms that don't match exactly those of the review. One promising alternative is to use dense embeddings to represent the question and document, and the current state of the art is an architecture known as *Dense Passage Retrieval* (DPR).[14] The main idea behind DPR is to use two BERT models as encoders for the question and the passage. As illustrated in Figure 7-10, these encoders map the input text into a d-dimensional vector representation of the `[CLS]` token.

14 V. Karpukhin et al., "Dense Passage Retrieval for Open-Domain Question Answering" (*https://arxiv.org/abs/2004.04906*), (2020).

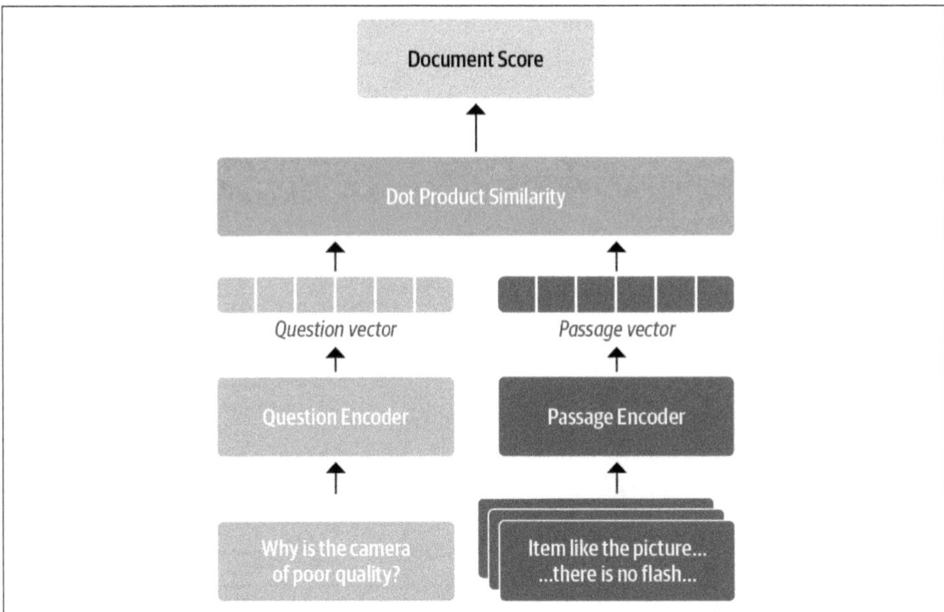

Figure 7-10. DPR's bi-encoder architecture for computing the relevance of a document and query

In Haystack, we can initialize a retriever for DPR in a similar way to what we did for BM25. In addition to specifying the document store, we also need to pick the BERT encoders for the question and passage. These encoders are trained by giving them questions with relevant (positive) passages and irrelevant (negative) passages, where the goal is to learn that relevant question-passage pairs have a higher similarity. For our use case, we'll use encoders that have been fine-tuned on the NQ corpus in this way:

```
from haystack.retriever.dense import DensePassageRetriever

dpr_retriever = DensePassageRetriever(document_store=document_store,
    query_embedding_model="facebook/dpr-question_encoder-single-nq-base",
    passage_embedding_model="facebook/dpr-ctx_encoder-single-nq-base",
    embed_title=False)
```

Here we've also set `embed_title=False` since concatenating the document's title (i.e., `item_id`) doesn't provide any additional information because we filter per product. Once we've initialized the dense retriever, the next step is to iterate over all the indexed documents in our Elasticsearch index and apply the encoders to update the embedding representation. This can be done as follows:

```
document_store.update_embeddings(retriever=dpr_retriever)
```

We're now set to go! We can evaluate the dense retriever in the same way we did for BM25 and compare the top-k recall:

```
dpr_topk_df = evaluate_retriever(dpr_retriever)
plot_retriever_eval([es_topk_df, dpr_topk_df], ["BM25", "DPR"])
```

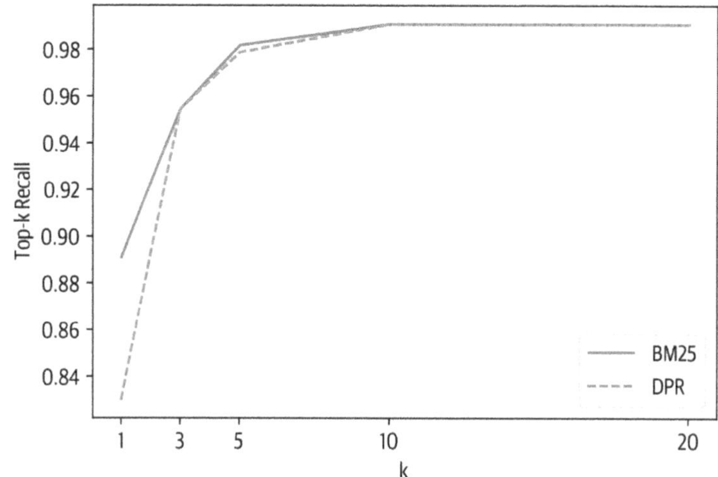

Here we can see that DPR does not provide a boost in recall over BM25 and saturates around $k = 3$.

Performing similarity search of the embeddings can be sped up by using Facebook's FAISS library (*https://oreil.ly/1E8Z0*) as the document store. Similarly, the performance of the DPR retriever can be improved by fine-tuning on the target domain. If you'd like to learn how to fine-tune DPR, check out the Haystack tutorial (*https://oreil.ly/eXyro*).

Now that we've explored the evaluation of the retriever, let's turn to evaluating the reader.

Evaluating the Reader

In extractive QA, there are two main metrics that are used for evaluating readers:

Exact Match (EM)
: A binary metric that gives EM = 1 if the characters in the predicted and ground truth answers match exactly, and EM = 0 otherwise. If no answer is expected, the model gets EM = 0 if it predicts any text at all.

F_1-score
: Measures the harmonic mean of the precision and recall.

Let's see how these metrics work by importing some helper functions from FARM and applying them to a simple example:

```
from farm.evaluation.squad_evaluation import compute_f1, compute_exact

pred = "about 6000 hours"
label = "6000 hours"
print(f"EM: {compute_exact(label, pred)}")
print(f"F1: {compute_f1(label, pred)}")
```

```
EM: 0
F1: 0.8
```

Under the hood, these functions first normalize the prediction and label by removing punctuation, fixing whitespace, and converting to lowercase. The normalized strings are then tokenized as a bag-of-words, before finally computing the metric at the token level. From this simple example we can see that EM is a much stricter metric than the F_1-score: adding a single token to the prediction gives an EM of zero. On the other hand, the F_1-score can fail to catch truly incorrect answers. For example, if our predicted answer span is "about 6000 dollars", then we get:

```
pred = "about 6000 dollars"
print(f"EM: {compute_exact(label, pred)}")
print(f"F1: {compute_f1(label, pred)}")
```

```
EM: 0
F1: 0.4
```

Relying on just the F_1-score is thus misleading, and tracking both metrics is a good strategy to balance the trade-off between underestimating (EM) and overestimating (F_1-score) model performance.

Now in general, there are multiple valid answers per question, so these metrics are calculated for each question-answer pair in the evaluation set, and the best score is selected over all possible answers. The overall EM and F_1 scores for the model are then obtained by averaging over the individual scores of each question-answer pair.

To evaluate the reader we'll create a new pipeline with two nodes: a reader node and a node to evaluate the reader. We'll use the `EvalReader` class that takes the predictions from the reader and computes the corresponding EM and F_1 scores. To compare with the SQuAD evaluation, we'll take the best answers for each query with the `top_1_em` and `top_1_f1` metrics that are stored in `EvalAnswers`:

```python
from haystack.eval import EvalAnswers

def evaluate_reader(reader):
    score_keys = ['top_1_em', 'top_1_f1']
    eval_reader = EvalAnswers(skip_incorrect_retrieval=False)
    pipe = Pipeline()
    pipe.add_node(component=reader, name="QAReader", inputs=["Query"])
    pipe.add_node(component=eval_reader, name="EvalReader", inputs=["QAReader"])

    for l in labels_agg:
        doc = document_store.query(l.question,
                                   filters={"question_id":[l.origin]})
        _ = pipe.run(query=l.question, documents=doc, labels=l)

    return {k:v for k,v in eval_reader.__dict__.items() if k in score_keys}

reader_eval = {}
reader_eval["Fine-tune on SQuAD"] = evaluate_reader(reader)
```

Notice that we specified `skip_incorrect_retrieval=False`. This is to ensure that the retriever always passes the context to the reader (as in the SQuAD evaluation). Now that we've run every question through the reader, let's print the scores:

```python
def plot_reader_eval(reader_eval):
    fig, ax = plt.subplots()
    df = pd.DataFrame.from_dict(reader_eval)
    df.plot(kind="bar", ylabel="Score", rot=0, ax=ax)
    ax.set_xticklabels(["EM", "F1"])
    plt.legend(loc='upper left')
    plt.show()

plot_reader_eval(reader_eval)
```

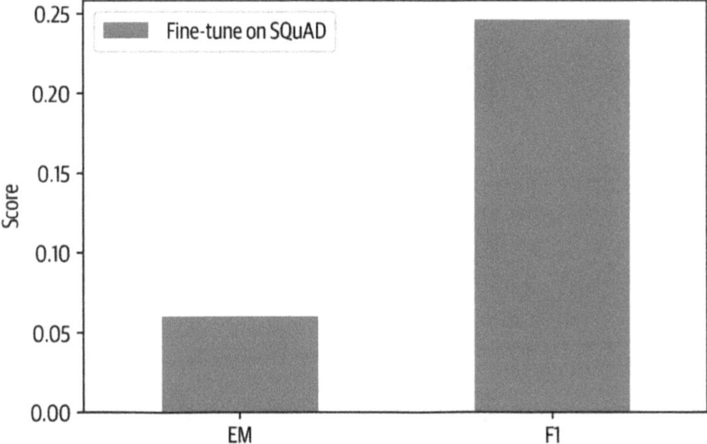

OK, it seems that the fine-tuned model performs significantly worse on SubjQA than on SQuAD 2.0, where MiniLM achieves EM and F_1 scores of 76.1 and 79.5, respectively. One reason for the performance drop is that customer reviews are quite different from the Wikipedia articles the SQuAD 2.0 dataset is generated from, and the language they use is often informal. Another factor is likely the inherent subjectivity of our dataset, where both questions and answers differ from the factual information contained in Wikipedia. Let's look at how to fine-tune a model on a dataset to get better results with domain adaptation.

Domain Adaptation

Although models that are fine-tuned on SQuAD will often generalize well to other domains, we've seen that for SubjQA the EM and F_1 scores of our model were much worse than for SQuAD. This failure to generalize has also been observed in other extractive QA datasets and is understood as evidence that transformer models are particularly adept at overfitting to SQuAD.[15] The most straightforward way to improve the reader is by fine-tuning our MiniLM model further on the SubjQA training set. The `FARMReader` has a `train()` method that is designed for this purpose and expects the data to be in SQuAD JSON format, where all the question-answer pairs are grouped together for each item as illustrated in Figure 7-11.

15 D. Yogatama et al., "Learning and Evaluating General Linguistic Intelligence" (*https://arXiv.org/abs/1901.11373*), (2019).

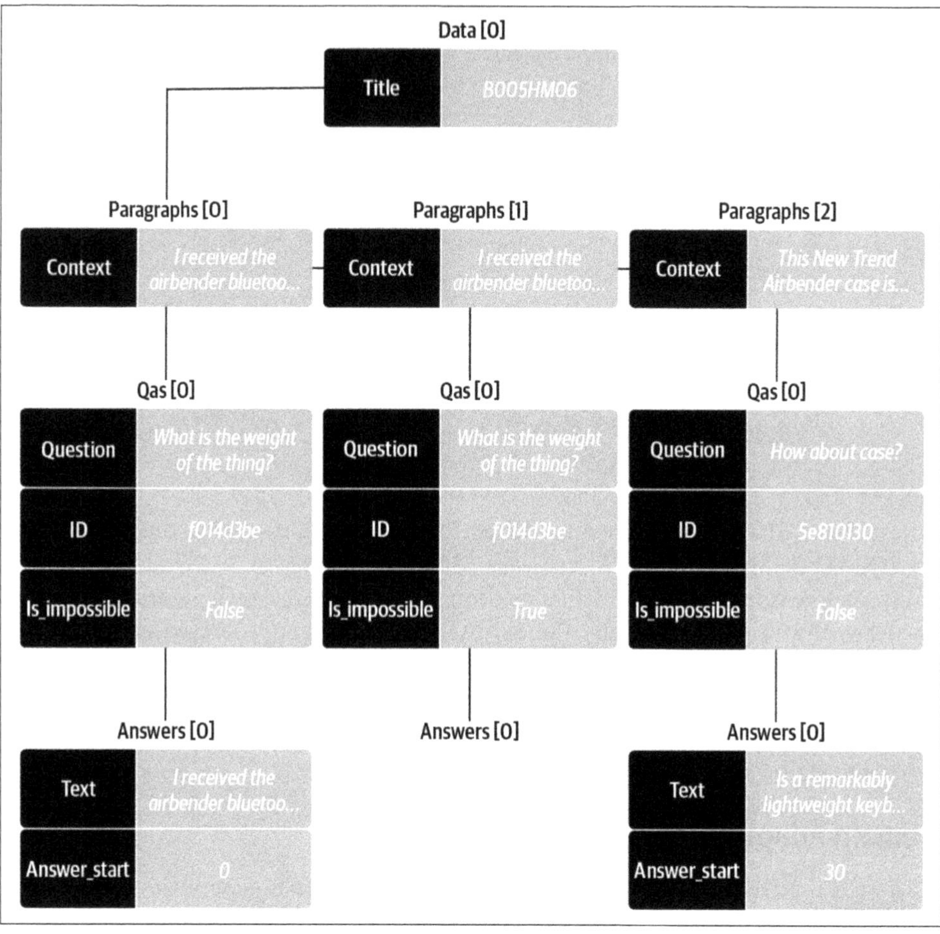

Figure 7-11. Visualization of the SQuAD JSON format

This is quite a complex data format, so we'll need a few functions and some Pandas magic to help us do the conversion. The first thing we need to do is implement a function that can create the `paragraphs` array associated with each product ID. Each element in this array contains a single context (i.e., review) and a `qas` array of question-answer pairs. Here's a function that builds up the `paragraphs` array:

```
def create_paragraphs(df):
    paragraphs = []
    id2context = dict(zip(df["review_id"], df["context"]))
    for review_id, review in id2context.items():
        qas = []
        # Filter for all question-answer pairs about a specific context
        review_df = df.query(f"review_id == '{review_id}'")
        id2question = dict(zip(review_df["id"], review_df["question"]))
        # Build up the qas array
```

```
        for qid, question in id2question.items():
            # Filter for a single question ID
            question_df = df.query(f"id == '{qid}'").to_dict(orient="list")
            ans_start_idxs = question_df["answers.answer_start"][0].tolist()
            ans_text = question_df["answers.text"][0].tolist()
            # Fill answerable questions
            if len(ans_start_idxs):
                answers = [
                    {"text": text, "answer_start": answer_start}
                    for text, answer_start in zip(ans_text, ans_start_idxs)]
                is_impossible = False
            else:
                answers = []
                is_impossible = True
            # Add question-answer pairs to qas
            qas.append({"question": question, "id": qid,
                        "is_impossible": is_impossible, "answers": answers})
        # Add context and question-answer pairs to paragraphs
        paragraphs.append({"qas": qas, "context": review})
    return paragraphs
```

Now, when we apply to the rows of a `DataFrame` associated with a single product ID, we get the SQuAD format:

```
product = dfs["train"].query("title == 'B00001P4ZH'")
create_paragraphs(product)
```

```
[{'qas': [{'question': 'How is the bass?',
    'id': '2543d296da9766d8d17d040ecc781699',
    'is_impossible': True,
    'answers': []}],
  'context': 'I have had Koss headphones ...',
    'id': 'd476830bf9282e2b9033e2bb44bbb995',
    'is_impossible': False,
    'answers': [{'text': 'Bass is weak as expected', 'answer_start': 1302},
     {'text': 'Bass is weak as expected, even with EQ adjusted up',
      'answer_start': 1302}]}],
  'context': 'To anyone who hasn\'t tried all ...'},
 {'qas': [{'question': 'How is the bass?',
    'id': '455575557886d6dfeea5aa19577e5de4',
    'is_impossible': False,
    'answers': [{'text': 'The only fault in the sound is the bass',
      'answer_start': 650}]}],
  'context': "I have had many sub-$100 headphones ..."}]
```

The final step is to then apply this function to each product ID in the `DataFrame` of each split. The following `convert_to_squad()` function does this trick and stores the result in an *electronics-{split}.json* file:

```
import json

def convert_to_squad(dfs):
    for split, df in dfs.items():
```

```
    subjqa_data = {}
    # Create `paragraphs` for each product ID
    groups = (df.groupby("title").apply(create_paragraphs)
        .to_frame(name="paragraphs").reset_index())
    subjqa_data["data"] = groups.to_dict(orient="records")
    # Save the result to disk
    with open(f"electronics-{split}.json", "w+", encoding="utf-8") as f:
        json.dump(subjqa_data, f)

convert_to_squad(dfs)
```

Now that we have the splits in the right format, let's fine-tune our reader by specifying the locations of the train and dev splits, along with where to save the fine-tuned model:

```
train_filename = "electronics-train.json"
dev_filename = "electronics-validation.json"

reader.train(data_dir=".", use_gpu=True, n_epochs=1, batch_size=16,
             train_filename=train_filename, dev_filename=dev_filename)
```

With the reader fine-tuned, let's now compare its performance on the test set against our baseline model:

```
reader_eval["Fine-tune on SQuAD + SubjQA"] = evaluate_reader(reader)
plot_reader_eval(reader_eval)
```

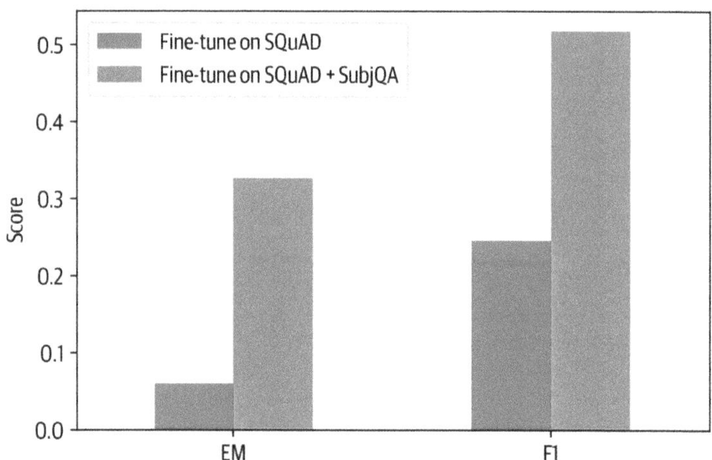

Wow, domain adaptation has increased our EM score by a factor of six and more than doubled the F_1-score! At this point, you might be wondering why we didn't just fine-tune a pretrained language model directly on the SubjQA training set. One reason is that we only have 1,295 training examples in SubjQA while SQuAD has over 100,000, so we might run into challenges with overfitting. Nevertheless, let's take a look at what naive fine-tuning produces. For a fair comparison, we'll use the same language model that was used for fine-tuning our baseline on SQuAD. As before, we'll load up the model with the `FARMReader`:

```
minilm_ckpt = "microsoft/MiniLM-L12-H384-uncased"
minilm_reader = FARMReader(model_name_or_path=minilm_ckpt, progress_bar=False,
                           max_seq_len=max_seq_length, doc_stride=doc_stride,
                           return_no_answer=True)
```

Next, we fine-tune for one epoch:

```
minilm_reader.train(data_dir=".", use_gpu=True, n_epochs=1, batch_size=16,
             train_filename=train_filename, dev_filename=dev_filename)
```

and include the evaluation on the test set:

```
reader_eval["Fine-tune on SubjQA"] = evaluate_reader(minilm_reader)
plot_reader_eval(reader_eval)
```

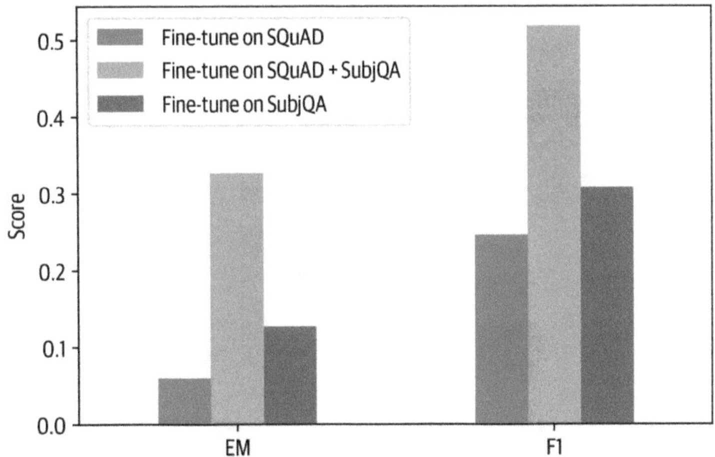

We can see that fine-tuning the language model directly on SubjQA results in considerably worse performance than fine-tuning on SQuAD and SubjQA.

When dealing with small datasets, it is best practice to use cross-validation when evaluating transformers as they can be prone to overfitting. You can find an example of how to perform cross-validation with SQuAD-formatted datasets in the FARM repository (*https://oreil.ly/K3nK8*).

Evaluating the Whole QA Pipeline

Now that we've seen how to evaluate the reader and retriever components individually, let's tie them together to measure the overall performance of our pipeline. To do so, we'll need to augment our retriever pipeline with nodes for the reader and its evaluation. We've seen that we get almost perfect recall at $k = 10$, so we can fix this value and assess the impact this has on the reader's performance (since it will now receive multiple contexts per query compared to the SQuAD-style evaluation):

```
# Initialize retriever pipeline
pipe = EvalRetrieverPipeline(es_retriever)
# Add nodes for reader
eval_reader = EvalAnswers()
pipe.pipeline.add_node(component=reader, name="QAReader",
              inputs=["EvalRetriever"])
pipe.pipeline.add_node(component=eval_reader, name="EvalReader",
              inputs=["QAReader"])
# Evaluate!
run_pipeline(pipe)
# Extract metrics from reader
reader_eval["QA Pipeline (top-1)"] = {
    k:v for k,v in eval_reader.__dict__.items()
    if k in ["top_1_em", "top_1_f1"]}
```

We can then compare the top 1 EM and F_1 scores for the model to predict an answer in the documents returned by the retriever in Figure 7-12.

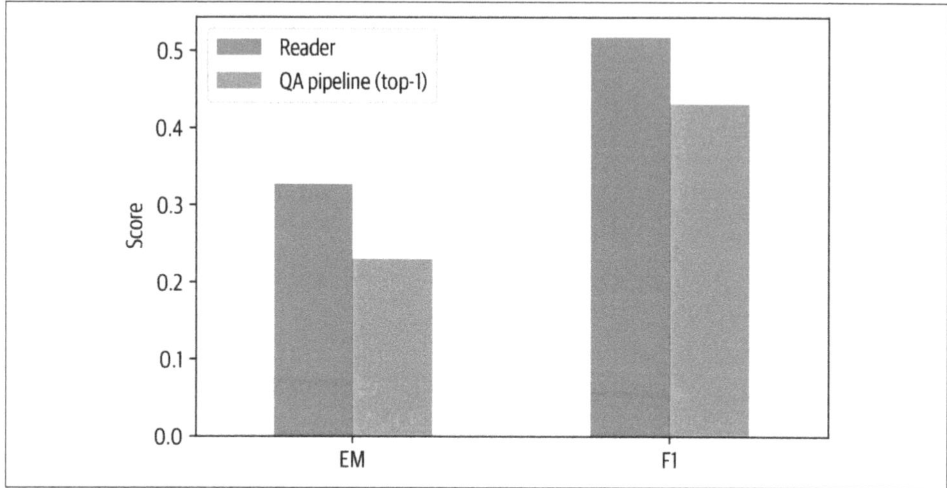

Figure 7-12. Comparison of EM and F_1 scores for the reader against the whole QA pipeline

From this plot we can see the effect that the retriever has on the overall performance. In particular, there is an overall degradation compared to matching the question-context pairs, as is done in the SQuAD-style evaluation. This can be circumvented by increasing the number of possible answers that the reader is allowed to predict.

Until now we have only extracted answer spans from the context, but in general it could be that bits and pieces of the answer are scattered throughout the document and we would like our model to synthesize these fragments into a single coherent answer. Let's have a look at how we can use generative QA to succeed at this task.

Going Beyond Extractive QA

One interesting alternative to extracting answers as spans of text in a document is to generate them with a pretrained language model. This approach is often referred to as *abstractive* or *generative QA* and has the potential to produce better-phrased answers that synthesize evidence across multiple passages. Although less mature than extractive QA, this is a fast-moving field of research, so chances are that these approaches will be widely adopted in industry by the time you are reading this! In this section we'll briefly touch on the current state of the art: *retrieval-augmented generation* (RAG).[16]

RAG extends the classic retriever-reader architecture that we've seen in this chapter by swapping the reader for a *generator* and using DPR as the retriever. The generator is a pretrained sequence-to-sequence transformer like T5 or BART that receives latent vectors of documents from DPR and then iteratively generates an answer based on the query and these documents. Since DPR and the generator are differentiable, the whole process can be fine-tuned end-to-end as illustrated in Figure 7-13.

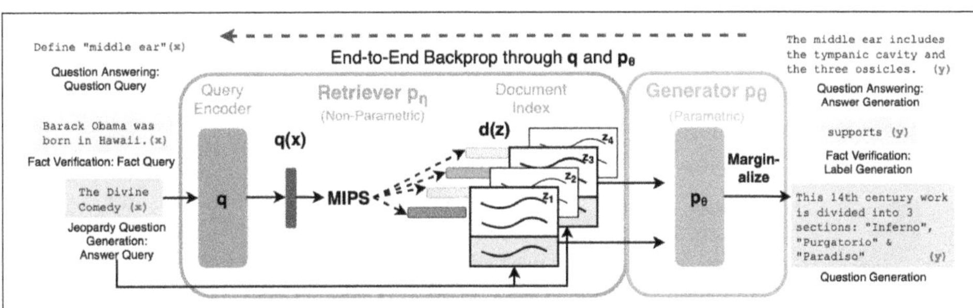

Figure 7-13. The RAG architecture for fine-tuning a retriever and generator end-to-end (courtesy of Ethan Perez)

To show RAG in action we'll use the `DPRetriever` from earlier, so we just need to instantiate a generator. There are two types of RAG models to choose from:

RAG-Sequence
: Uses the same retrieved document to generate the complete answer. In particular, the top k documents from the retriever are fed to the generator, which produces

16 P. Lewis et al., "Retrieval-Augmented Generation for Knowledge-Intensive NLP Tasks" (*https://arxiv.org/abs/2005.11401*), (2020).

an output sequence for each document, and the result is marginalized to obtain the best answer.

RAG-Token
: Can use a different document to generate each token in the answer. This allows the generator to synthesize evidence from multiple documents.

Since RAG-Token models tend to perform better than RAG-Sequence ones, we'll use the token model that was fine-tuned on NQ as our generator. Instantiating a generator in Haystack is similar to instantiating the reader, but instead of specifying the `max_seq_length` and `doc_stride` parameters for a sliding window over the contexts, we specify hyperparameters that control the text generation:

```
from haystack.generator.transformers import RAGenerator

generator = RAGenerator(model_name_or_path="facebook/rag-token-nq",
                        embed_title=False, num_beams=5)
```

Here `num_beams` specifies the number of beams to use in beam search (text generation is covered at length in Chapter 5). As we did with the DPR retriever, we don't embed the document titles since our corpus is always filtered per product ID.

The next thing to do is tie together the retriever and generator using Haystack's `GenerativeQAPipeline`:

```
from haystack.pipeline import GenerativeQAPipeline

pipe = GenerativeQAPipeline(generator=generator, retriever=dpr_retriever)
```

In RAG, both the query encoder and the generator are trained end-to-end, while the context encoder is frozen. In Haystack, the `GenerativeQAPipeline` uses the query encoder from `RAGenerator` and the context encoder from `DensePassageRetriever`.

Let's now give RAG a spin by feeding in some queries about the Amazon Fire tablet from before. To simplify the querying, we'll write a simple function that takes the query and prints out the top answers:

```
def generate_answers(query, top_k_generator=3):
    preds = pipe.run(query=query, top_k_generator=top_k_generator,
                     top_k_retriever=5, filters={"item_id":["B0074BW614"]})
    print(f"Question: {preds['query']} \n")
    for idx in range(top_k_generator):
        print(f"Answer {idx+1}: {preds['answers'][idx]['answer']}")
```

OK, now we're ready to give it a test:

```
generate_answers(query)
```

```
Question: Is it good for reading?

Answer 1:  the screen is absolutely beautiful
Answer 2:  the Screen is absolutely beautiful
Answer 3:  Kindle fire
```

This result isn't too bad for an answer, but it does suggest that the subjective nature of the question is confusing the generator. Let's try with something a bit more factual:

```
generate_answers("What is the main drawback?")
```

```
Question: What is the main drawback?

Answer 1:  the price
Answer 2:  no flash support
Answer 3:  the cost
```

This is more sensible! To get better results we could fine-tune RAG end-to-end on SubjQA; we'll leave this as an exercise, but if you're interested in exploring it there are scripts in the 🤗 Transformers repository (*https://oreil.ly/oZz4S*) to help you get started.

Conclusion

Well, that was a whirlwind tour of QA, and you probably have many more questions that you'd like answered (pun intended!). In this chapter, we discussed two approaches to QA (extractive and generative) and examined two different retrieval algorithms (BM25 and DPR). Along the way, we saw that domain adaptation can be a simple technique to boost the performance of our QA system by a significant margin, and we looked at a few of the most common metrics that are used for evaluating such systems. Although we focused on closed-domain QA (i.e., a single domain of electronic products), the techniques in this chapter can easily be generalized to the open-domain case; we recommend reading Cloudera's excellent Fast Forward QA series (*https://oreil.ly/Fd6lc*) to see what's involved.

Deploying QA systems in the wild can be a tricky business to get right, and our experience is that a significant part of the value comes from first providing end users with useful search capabilities, followed by an extractive component. In this respect, the reader can be used in novel ways beyond answering on-demand user queries. For example, researchers at Grid Dynamics (*https://oreil.ly/CGLh1*) were able to use their reader to automatically extract a set of pros and cons for each product in a client's catalog. They also showed that a reader can be used to extract named entities in a zero-shot fashion by creating queries like "What kind of camera?" Given its infancy and subtle failure modes, we recommend exploring generative QA only once the other two approaches have been exhausted. This "hierarchy of needs" for tackling QA problems is illustrated in Figure 7-14.

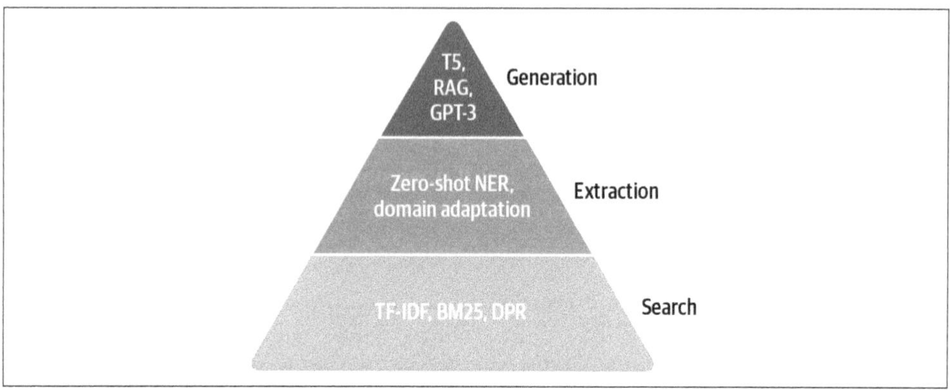

Figure 7-14. The QA hierarchy of needs

Looking ahead, one exciting research area is *multimodal QA*, which involves QA over multiple modalities like text, tables, and images. As described in the MultiModalQA benchmark,[17] such systems could enable users to answer complex questions that integrate information across different modalities, like "When was the famous painting with two touching fingers completed?" Another area with practical business applications is QA over a *knowledge graph*, where the nodes of the graph correspond to real-world entities and their relations are defined by the edges. By encoding factoids as (*subject*, *predicate*, *object*) triples, one can use the graph to answer questions about a missing element. For an example that combines transformers with knowledge graphs, see the Haystack tutorials (*https://oreil.ly/n7lZb*). One more promising direction is *automatic question generation* as a way to do some form of unsupervised/weakly supervised training using unlabeled data or data augmentation. Two recent examples include the papers on the Probably Answered Questions (PAQ) benchmark and synthetic data augmentation for cross-lingual settings.[18]

In this chapter we've seen that in order to successfully use QA models for real-world use cases we need to apply a few tricks, such as implementing a fast retrieval pipeline to make predictions in near real time. Still, applying a QA model to a handful of preselected documents can take a couple of seconds on production hardware. Although this may not sound like much, imagine how different your experience would be if you had to wait a few seconds to get the results of a Google search—a few seconds of wait time can decide the fate of your transformer-powered application. In the next chapter we'll have a look at a few methods to accelerate model predictions further.

17 A. Talmor et al., "MultiModalQA: Complex Question Answering over Text, Tables and Images" (*https://arxiv.org/abs/2104.06039*), (2021).

18 P. Lewis et al., "PAQ: 65 Million Probably-Asked Questions and What You Can Do with Them" (*https://arxiv.org/abs/2102.07033*), (2021); A. Riabi et al., "Synthetic Data Augmentation for Zero-Shot Cross-Lingual Question Answering" (*https://arxiv.org/abs/2010.12643*), (2020).

CHAPTER 8

Making Transformers Efficient in Production

In the previous chapters, you've seen how transformers can be fine-tuned to produce great results on a wide range of tasks. However, in many situations accuracy (or whatever metric you're optimizing for) is not enough; your state-of-the-art model is not very useful if it's too slow or large to meet the business requirements of your application. An obvious alternative is to train a faster and more compact model, but the reduction in model capacity is often accompanied by a degradation in performance. So what can you do when you need a fast, compact, yet highly accurate model?

In this chapter we will explore four complementary techniques that can be used to speed up the predictions and reduce the memory footprint of your transformer models: *knowledge distillation*, *quantization*, *pruning*, and *graph optimization* with the Open Neural Network Exchange (ONNX) format and ONNX Runtime (ORT). We'll also see how some of these techniques can be combined to produce significant performance gains. For example, this was the approach taken by the Roblox engineering team in their article "How We Scaled Bert to Serve 1+ Billion Daily Requests on CPUs" (*https://oreil.ly/QdNIk*), who as shown in Figure 8-1 found that combining knowledge distillation and quantization enabled them to improve the latency and throughput of their BERT classifier by over a factor of 30!

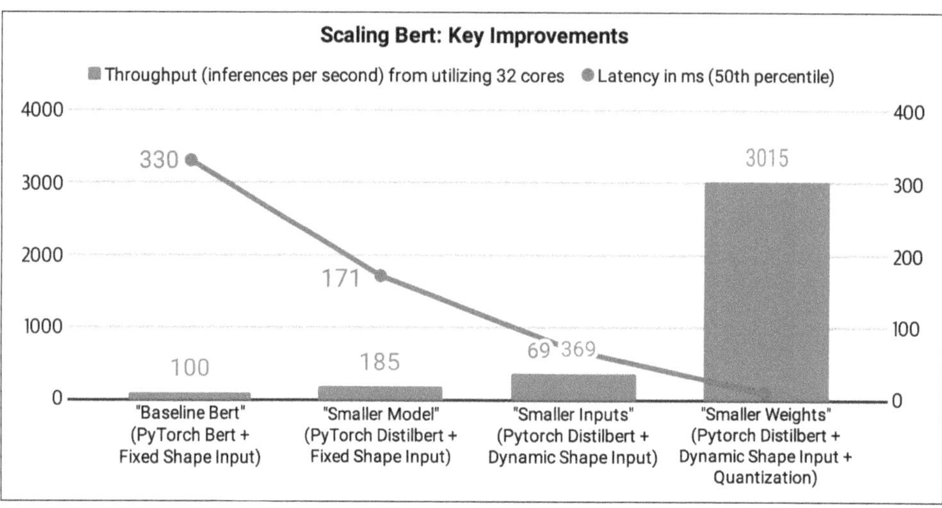

Figure 8-1. How Roblox scaled BERT with knowledge distillation, dynamic padding, and weight quantization (photo courtesy of Roblox employees Quoc N. Le and Kip Kaehler)

To illustrate the benefits and trade-offs associated with each technique, we'll use intent detection as a case study; this is an important component of text-based assistants, where low latencies are critical for maintaining a conversation in real time. Along the way you'll learn how to create custom trainers, perform efficient hyperparameter search, and gain a sense of what it takes to implement cutting-edge research with 🤗 Transformers. Let's dive in!

Intent Detection as a Case Study

Let's suppose that we're trying to build a text-based assistant for our company's call center so that customers can request their account balance or make bookings without needing to speak with a human agent. In order to understand the goals of a customer, our assistant will need to be able to classify a wide variety of natural language text into a set of predefined actions or *intents*. For example, a customer might send a message like the following about an upcoming trip:

> Hey, I'd like to rent a vehicle from Nov 1st to Nov 15th in Paris and I need a 15 passenger van

and our intent classifier could automatically categorize this as a *Car Rental* intent, which then triggers an action and response. To be robust in a production environment, our classifier will also need to be able to handle *out-of-scope* queries, where a customer makes a query that doesn't belong to any of the predefined intents and the system should yield a fallback response. For example, in the second case shown in Figure 8-2, a customer asks a question about sports (which is out of scope), and the text assistant mistakenly classifies it as one of the known in-scope intents and returns the payday response. In the third case, the text assistant has been trained to detect out-of-scope queries (usually labeled as a separate class) and informs the customer about which topics it can answer questions about.

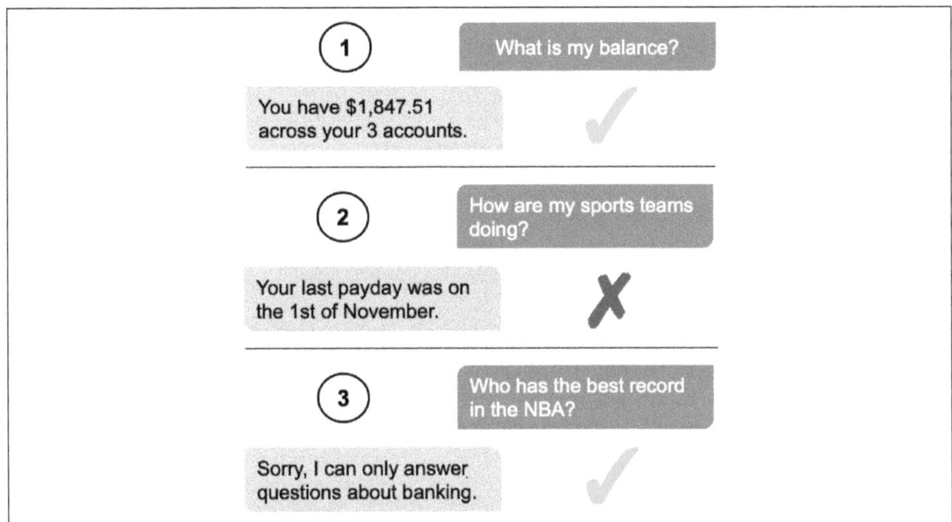

Figure 8-2. Three exchanges between a human (right) and a text-based assistant (left) for personal finance (courtesy of Stefan Larson et al.)

As a baseline, we've fine-tuned a BERT-base model that achieves around 94% accuracy on the CLINC150 dataset.[1] This dataset includes 22,500 in-scope queries across 150 intents and 10 domains like banking and travel, and also includes 1,200 out-of-scope queries that belong to an `oos` intent class. In practice we would also gather our own in-house dataset, but using public data is a great way to iterate quickly and generate preliminary results.

To get started, let's download our fine-tuned model from the Hugging Face Hub and wrap it in a pipeline for text classification:

```
from transformers import pipeline

bert_ckpt = "transformersbook/bert-base-uncased-finetuned-clinc"
pipe = pipeline("text-classification", model=bert_ckpt)
```

Now that we have a pipeline, we can pass a query to get the predicted intent and confidence score from the model:

1 S. Larson et al., "An Evaluation Dataset for Intent Classification and Out-of-Scope Prediction" (*https://arxiv.org/abs/1909.02027*), (2019).

```
query = """Hey, I'd like to rent a vehicle from Nov 1st to Nov 15th in
Paris and I need a 15 passenger van"""
pipe(query)
```

```
[{'label': 'car_rental', 'score': 0.549003541469574}]
```

Great, the `car_rental` intent makes sense. Let's now look at creating a benchmark that we can use to evaluate the performance of our baseline model.

Creating a Performance Benchmark

Like other machine learning models, deploying transformers in production environments involves a trade-off among several constraints, the most common being:[2]

Model performance
: How well does our model perform on a well-crafted test set that reflects production data? This is especially important when the cost of making errors is large (and best mitigated with a human in the loop), or when we need to run inference on millions of examples and small improvements to the model metrics can translate into large gains in aggregate.

Latency
: How fast can our model deliver predictions? We usually care about latency in real-time environments that deal with a lot of traffic, like how Stack Overflow needed a classifier to quickly detect unwelcome comments on the website (*https://oreil.ly/cf7QX*).

Memory
: How can we deploy billion-parameter models like GPT-2 or T5 that require gigabytes of disk storage and RAM? Memory plays an especially important role in mobile or edge devices, where a model has to generate predictions without access to a powerful cloud server.

Failing to address these constraints can have a negative impact on the user experience of your application. More commonly, it can lead to ballooning costs from running expensive cloud servers that may only need to handle a few requests. To explore how each of these constraints can be optimized with various compression techniques, let's begin by creating a simple benchmark that measures each quantity for a given pipeline and test set. A skeleton of what we'll need is given by the following class:

---

2 As described by Emmanuel Ameisen in *Building Machine Learning Powered Applications* (O'Reilly), business or product metrics are the *most* important ones to consider. After all, it doesn't matter how accurate your model is if it doesn't solve a problem your business cares about. In this chapter we'll assume that you have already defined the metrics that matter for your application and focus on optimizing the model metrics.

```python
class PerformanceBenchmark:
    def __init__(self, pipeline, dataset, optim_type="BERT baseline"):
        self.pipeline = pipeline
        self.dataset = dataset
        self.optim_type = optim_type

    def compute_accuracy(self):
        # We'll define this later
        pass

    def compute_size(self):
        # We'll define this later
        pass

    def time_pipeline(self):
        # We'll define this later
        pass

    def run_benchmark(self):
        metrics = {}
        metrics[self.optim_type] = self.compute_size()
        metrics[self.optim_type].update(self.time_pipeline())
        metrics[self.optim_type].update(self.compute_accuracy())
        return metrics
```

We've defined an `optim_type` parameter to keep track of the different optimization techniques that we'll cover in this chapter. We'll use the `run_benchmark()` method to collect all the metrics in a dictionary, with keys given by `optim_type`.

Let's now put some flesh on the bones of this class by computing the model accuracy on the test set. First we need some data to test on, so let's download the CLINC150 dataset that was used to fine-tune our baseline model. We can get the dataset from the Hub with 🤗 Datasets as follows:

```python
from datasets import load_dataset

clinc = load_dataset("clinc_oos", "plus")
```

Here, the `plus` configuration refers to the subset that contains the out-of-scope training examples. Each example in the CLINC150 dataset consists of a query in the `text` column and its corresponding intent. We'll use the test set to benchmark our models, so let's take a look at one of the dataset's examples:

```python
sample = clinc["test"][42]
sample
```

```
{'intent': 133, 'text': 'transfer $100 from my checking to saving account'}
```

The intents are provided as IDs, but we can easily get the mapping to strings (and vice versa) by accessing the `features` attribute of the dataset:

```
intents = clinc["test"].features["intent"]
intents.int2str(sample["intent"])
```

```
'transfer'
```

Now that we have a basic understanding of the contents in the CLINC150 dataset, let's implement the `compute_accuracy()` method of `PerformanceBenchmark`. Since the dataset is balanced across the intent classes, we'll use accuracy as our metric. We can load this metric with 🤗 Datasets as follows:

```
from datasets import load_metric

accuracy_score = load_metric("accuracy")
```

The accuracy metric expects the predictions and references (i.e., the ground truth labels) to be integers. We can use the pipeline to extract the predictions from the `text` field and then use the `str2int()` method of our `intents` object to map each prediction to its corresponding ID. The following code collects all the predictions and labels in lists before returning the accuracy on the dataset. Let's also add it to our `PerformanceBenchmark` class:

```
def compute_accuracy(self):
    """This overrides the PerformanceBenchmark.compute_accuracy() method"""
    preds, labels = [], []
    for example in self.dataset:
        pred = self.pipeline(example["text"])[0]["label"]
        label = example["intent"]
        preds.append(intents.str2int(pred))
        labels.append(label)
    accuracy = accuracy_score.compute(predictions=preds, references=labels)
    print(f"Accuracy on test set - {accuracy['accuracy']:.3f}")
    return accuracy

PerformanceBenchmark.compute_accuracy = compute_accuracy
```

Next, let's compute the size of our model by using the `torch.save()` function from PyTorch to serialize the model to disk. Under the hood, `torch.save()` uses Python's `pickle` module and can be used to save anything from models to tensors to ordinary Python objects. In PyTorch, the recommended way to save a model is by using its `state_dict`, which is a Python dictionary that maps each layer in a model to its learnable parameters (i.e., weights and biases). Let's see what is stored in the `state_dict` of our baseline model:

```
list(pipe.model.state_dict().items())[42]
```

```
('bert.encoder.layer.2.attention.self.value.weight',
 tensor([[-1.0526e-02, -3.2215e-02,  2.2097e-02,  ..., -6.0953e-03,
           4.6521e-03,  2.9844e-02],
         [-1.4964e-02, -1.0915e-02,  5.2396e-04,  ...,  3.2047e-05,
          -2.6890e-02, -2.1943e-02],
         [-2.9640e-02, -3.7842e-03, -1.2582e-02,  ..., -1.0917e-02,
```

```
        3.1152e-02, -9.7786e-03],
      ...,
      [-1.5116e-02, -3.3226e-02,  4.2063e-02,  ..., -5.2652e-03,
        1.1093e-02,  2.9703e-03],
      [-3.6809e-02,  5.6848e-02, -2.6544e-02,  ..., -4.0114e-02,
        6.7487e-03,  1.0511e-03],
      [-2.4961e-02,  1.4747e-03, -5.4271e-02,  ...,  2.0004e-02,
        2.3981e-02, -4.2880e-02]]))
```

We can clearly see that each key/value pair corresponds to a specific layer and tensor in BERT. So if we save our model with:

```
torch.save(pipe.model.state_dict(), "model.pt")
```

we can then use the `Path.stat()` function from Python's `pathlib` module to get information about the underlying files. In particular, `Path("model.pt").stat().st_size` will give us the model size in bytes. Let's put this all together in the `compute_size()` function and add it to `PerformanceBenchmark`:

```
import torch
from pathlib import Path

def compute_size(self):
    """This overrides the PerformanceBenchmark.compute_size() method"""
    state_dict = self.pipeline.model.state_dict()
    tmp_path = Path("model.pt")
    torch.save(state_dict, tmp_path)
    # Calculate size in megabytes
    size_mb = Path(tmp_path).stat().st_size / (1024 * 1024)
    # Delete temporary file
    tmp_path.unlink()
    print(f"Model size (MB) - {size_mb:.2f}")
    return {"size_mb": size_mb}

PerformanceBenchmark.compute_size = compute_size
```

Finally let's implement the `time_pipeline()` function so that we can time the average latency per query. For this application, latency refers to the time it takes to feed a text query to the pipeline and return the predicted intent from the model. Under the hood the pipeline also tokenizes the text, but this is around one thousand times faster than generating the predictions and thus adds a negligible contribution to the overall latency. A simple way to measure the execution time of a code snippet is to use the `perf_counter()` function from Python's `time` module. This function has a better time resolution than the `time.time()` function and is well suited for getting precise results.

We can use `perf_counter()` to time our pipeline by passing our test query and calculating the time difference in milliseconds between the start and end:

```
from time import perf_counter
```

```
for _ in range(3):
    start_time = perf_counter()
    _ = pipe(query)
    latency = perf_counter() - start_time
    print(f"Latency (ms) - {1000 * latency:.3f}")
```

```
Latency (ms) - 85.367
Latency (ms) - 85.241
Latency (ms) - 87.275
```

These results exhibit quite some spread in the latencies and suggest that timing a single pass through the pipeline can give wildly different results each time we run the code. So instead, we'll collect the latencies over many runs and then use the resulting distribution to calculate the mean and standard deviation, which will give us an idea about the spread in values. The following code does what we need and includes a phase to warm up the CPU before performing the actual timed run:

```
import         as

def time_pipeline(self, query="What is the pin number for my account?"):
    """This overrides the PerformanceBenchmark.time_pipeline() method"""
    latencies = []
    # Warmup
    for _ in range(10):
        _ = self.pipeline(query)
    # Timed run
    for _ in range(100):
        start_time = perf_counter()
        _ = self.pipeline(query)
        latency = perf_counter() - start_time
        latencies.append(latency)
    # Compute run statistics
    time_avg_ms = 1000 * np.mean(latencies)
    time_std_ms = 1000 * np.std(latencies)
    print(f"Average latency (ms) - {time_avg_ms:.2f} +\- {time_std_ms:.2f}")
    return {"time_avg_ms": time_avg_ms, "time_std_ms": time_std_ms}

PerformanceBenchmark.time_pipeline = time_pipeline
```

To keeps things simple, we'll use the same `query` value to benchmark all our models. In general, the latency will depend on the query length, and a good practice is to benchmark your models with queries that they're likely to encounter in production environments.

Now that our `PerformanceBenchmark` class is complete, let's give it a spin! Let's start by benchmarking our BERT baseline. For the baseline model, we just need to pass the pipeline and the dataset we wish to perform the benchmark on. We'll collect the results in the `perf_metrics` dictionary to keep track of each model's performance:

```
pb = PerformanceBenchmark(pipe, clinc["test"])
perf_metrics = pb.run_benchmark()
```

```
Model size (MB) - 418.16
Average latency (ms) - 54.20 +\- 1.91
Accuracy on test set - 0.867
```

Now that we have a reference point, let's look at our first compression technique: knowledge distillation.

The average latency values will differ depending on what type of hardware you are running on. For example, you can usually get better performance by running inference on a GPU since it enables batch processing. For the purposes of this chapter, what's important is the relative difference in latencies between models. Once we have determined the best-performing model, we can then explore different backends to reduce the absolute latency if needed.

Making Models Smaller via Knowledge Distillation

Knowledge distillation is a general-purpose method for training a smaller *student* model to mimic the behavior of a slower, larger, but better-performing *teacher*. Originally introduced in 2006 in the context of ensemble models,[3] it was later popularized in a famous 2015 paper that generalized the method to deep neural networks and applied it to image classification and automatic speech recognition.[4]

Given the trend toward pretraining language models with ever-increasing parameter counts (the largest at the time of writing having over one trillion parameters),[5] knowledge distillation has also become a popular strategy to compress these huge models and make them more suitable for building practical applications.

Knowledge Distillation for Fine-Tuning

So how is knowledge actually "distilled" or transferred from the teacher to the student during training? For supervised tasks like fine-tuning, the main idea is to augment the ground truth labels with a distribution of "soft probabilities" from the teacher which provide complementary information for the student to learn from. For example, if our BERT-base classifier assigns high probabilities to multiple intents, then this could be a sign that these intents lie close to each other in the feature space. By training the student to mimic these probabilities, the goal is to distill some of this "dark

3 C. Buciluă et al., "Model Compression," *Proceedings of the 12th ACM SIGKDD International Conference on Knowledge Discovery and Data Mining* (August 2006): 535–541, *https://doi.org/10.1145/1150402.1150464*.

4 G. Hinton, O. Vinyals, and J. Dean, "Distilling the Knowledge in a Neural Network" (*https://arxiv.org/abs/1503.02531*), (2015).

5 W. Fedus, B. Zoph, and N. Shazeer, "Switch Transformers: Scaling to Trillion Parameter Models with Simple and Efficient Sparsity" (*https://arxiv.org/abs/2101.03961*), (2021).

knowledge"[6] that the teacher has learned—that is, knowledge that is not available from the labels alone.

Mathematically, the way this works is as follows. Suppose we feed an input sequence x to the teacher to generate a vector of logits $\mathbf{z}(x) = [z_1(x), ..., z_N(x)]$. We can convert these logits into probabilities by applying a softmax function:

$$\frac{\exp\left(z_i(x)\right)}{\sum_j \exp\left(z_i(x)\right)}$$

This isn't quite what we want, though, because in many cases the teacher will assign a high probability to one class, with all other class probabilities close to zero. When that happens, the teacher doesn't provide much additional information beyond the ground truth labels, so instead we "soften" the probabilities by scaling the logits with a temperature hyperparameter T before applying the softmax:[7]

$$p_i(x) = \frac{\exp\left(z_i(x)/T\right)}{\sum_j \exp\left(z_i(x)/T\right)}$$

As shown in Figure 8-3, higher values of T produce a softer probability distribution over the classes and reveal much more information about the decision boundary that the teacher has learned for each training example. When $T = 1$ we recover the original softmax distribution.

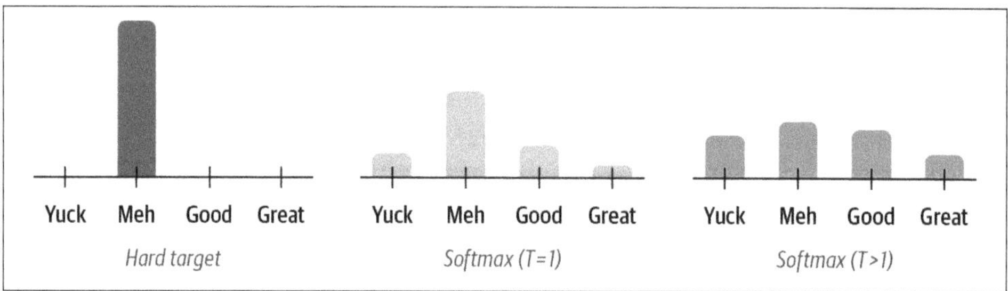

Figure 8-3. Comparison of a hard label that is one-hot encoded (left), softmax probabilities (middle), and softened class probabilities (right)

6 Geoff Hinton coined this term in a talk (*https://oreil.ly/OkHGp*) to refer to the observation that softened probabilities reveal the hidden knowledge of the teacher.

7 We also encountered temperature in the context of text generation in Chapter 5.

Since the student also produces softened probabilities $q_i(x)$ of its own, we can use the Kullback–Leibler (KL) (*https://oreil.ly/8nKQG*) divergence to measure the difference between the two probability distributions:

$$D_{KL}(p, q) = \sum_i p_i(x) \log \frac{p_i(x)}{q_i(x)}$$

With the KL divergence we can calculate how much is lost when we approximate the probability distribution of the teacher with the student. This allows us to define a knowledge distillation loss:

$$L_{KD} = T^2 D_{KL}$$

where T^2 is a normalization factor to account for the fact that the magnitude of the gradients produced by soft labels scales as $1/T^2$. For classification tasks, the student loss is then a weighted average of the distillation loss with the usual cross-entropy loss L_{CE} of the ground truth labels:

$$L_{\text{student}} = \alpha L_{CE} + (1 - \alpha) L_{KD}$$

where α is a hyperparameter that controls the relative strength of each loss. A diagram of the whole process is shown in Figure 8-4; the temperature is set to 1 at inference time to recover the standard softmax probabilities.

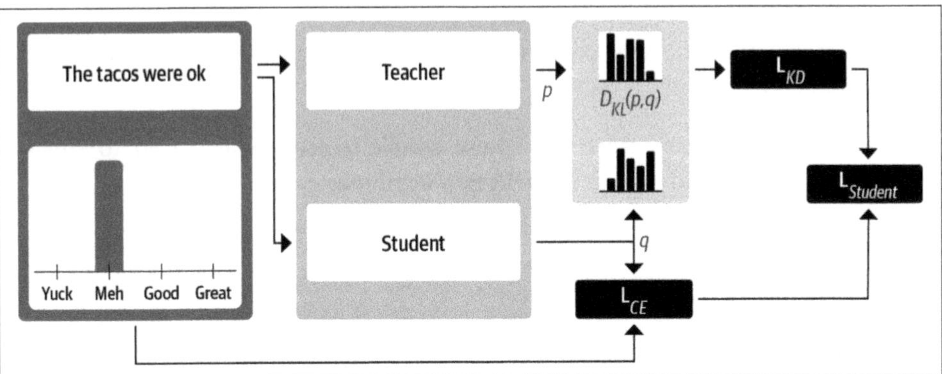

Figure 8-4. The knowledge distillation process

Knowledge Distillation for Pretraining

Knowledge distillation can also be used during pretraining to create a general-purpose student that can be subsequently fine-tuned on downstream tasks. In this case, the teacher is a pretrained language model like BERT, which transfers its knowledge about masked language modeling to the student. For example, in the DistilBERT paper,[8] the masked language modeling loss L_{mlm} is augmented with a term from knowledge distillation and a cosine embedding loss $L_{cos} = 1 - \cos\left(h_s, h_t\right)$ to align the directions of the hidden state vectors between the teacher and student:

$$L_{\text{DistilBERT}} = \alpha L_{mlm} + \beta L_{KD} + \gamma L_{cos}$$

Since we already have a fine-tuned BERT-base model, let's see how we can use knowledge distillation to fine-tune a smaller and faster model. To do that we'll need a way to augment the cross-entropy loss with an L_{KD} term. Fortunately we can do this by creating our own trainer!

Creating a Knowledge Distillation Trainer

To implement knowledge distillation we need to add a few things to the `Trainer` base class:

- The new hyperparameters α and T, which control the relative weight of the distillation loss and how much the probability distribution of the labels should be smoothed
- The fine-tuned teacher model, which in our case is BERT-base
- A new loss function that combines the cross-entropy loss with the knowledge distillation loss

Adding the new hyperparameters is quite simple, since we just need to subclass `TrainingArguments` and include them as new attributes:

```
from              import TrainingArguments

class DistillationTrainingArguments(TrainingArguments):
    def __init__(self, *args, alpha=0.5, temperature=2.0, **kwargs):
        super().__init__(*args, **kwargs)
        self.alpha = alpha
        self.temperature = temperature
```

8 V. Sanh et al., "DistilBERT, a Distilled Version of BERT: Smaller, Faster, Cheaper and Lighter" (*https://arxiv.org/abs/1910.01108*), (2019).

For the trainer itself, we need a new loss function. The way to implement this is by subclassing `Trainer` and overriding the `compute_loss()` method to include the knowledge distillation loss term L_{KD}:

```
import torch.nn as nn
import torch.nn.functional as F
from transformers import Trainer

class DistillationTrainer(Trainer):
    def __init__(self, *args, teacher_model=None, **kwargs):
        super().__init__(*args, **kwargs)
        self.teacher_model = teacher_model

    def compute_loss(self, model, inputs, return_outputs=False):
        outputs_stu = model(**inputs)
        # Extract cross-entropy loss and logits from student
        loss_ce = outputs_stu.loss
        logits_stu = outputs_stu.logits
        # Extract logits from teacher
        with torch.no_grad():
            outputs_tea = self.teacher_model(**inputs)
            logits_tea = outputs_tea.logits
        # Soften probabilities and compute distillation loss
        loss_fct = nn.KLDivLoss(reduction="batchmean")
        loss_kd = self.args.temperature ** 2 * loss_fct(
            F.log_softmax(logits_stu / self.args.temperature, dim=-1),
            F.softmax(logits_tea / self.args.temperature, dim=-1))
        # Return weighted student loss
        loss = self.args.alpha * loss_ce + (1. - self.args.alpha) * loss_kd
        return (loss, outputs_stu) if return_outputs else loss
```

Let's unpack this code a bit. When we instantiate `DistillationTrainer` we pass a `teacher_model` argument with a teacher that has already been fine-tuned on our task. Next, in the `compute_loss()` method we extract the logits from the student and teacher, scale them by the temperature, and then normalize them with a softmax before passing them to PyTorch's `nn.KLDivLoss()` function for computing the KL divergence. One quirk with `nn.KLDivLoss()` is that it expects the inputs in the form of log probabilities and the labels as normal probabilities. That's why we've used the `F.log_softmax()` function to normalize the student's logits, while the teacher's logits are converted to probabilities with a standard softmax. The `reduction=batchmean` argument in `nn.KLDivLoss()` specifies that we average the losses over the batch dimension.

You can also perform knowledge distillation with the Keras API of the 🤗 Transformers library. To do this, you'll need to implement a custom `Distiller` class that overrides the `train_step()`, `test_step()`, and `compile()` methods of `tf.keras.Model()`. See the Keras documentation (*https://oreil.ly/6qp0F*) for an example of how to do this.

Choosing a Good Student Initialization

Now that we have our custom trainer, the first question you might have is which pretrained language model should we pick for the student? In general we should pick a smaller model for the student to reduce the latency and memory footprint. A good rule of thumb from the literature is that knowledge distillation works best when the teacher and student are of the same *model type*.[9] One possible reason for this is that different model types, say BERT and RoBERTa, can have different output embedding spaces, which hinders the ability of the student to mimic the teacher. In our case study the teacher is BERT, so DistilBERT is a natural candidate to initialize the student with since it has 40% fewer parameters and has been shown to achieve strong results on downstream tasks.

First we'll need to tokenize and encode our queries, so let's instantiate the tokenizer from DistilBERT and create a simple `tokenize_text()` function to take care of the preprocessing:

```
from transformers import AutoTokenizer

student_ckpt = "distilbert-base-uncased"
student_tokenizer = AutoTokenizer.from_pretrained(student_ckpt)

def tokenize_text(batch):
    return student_tokenizer(batch["text"], truncation=True)

clinc_enc = clinc.map(tokenize_text, batched=True, remove_columns=["text"])
clinc_enc = clinc_enc.rename_column("intent", "labels")
```

Here we've removed the `text` column since we no longer need it, and we've also renamed the `intent` column to `labels` so it can be automatically detected by the trainer.[10]

Now that we've processed our texts, the next thing we need to do is define the hyperparameters and `compute_metrics()` function for our `DistillationTrainer`. We'll

9 Y. Kim and H. Awadalla, "FastFormers: Highly Efficient Transformer Models for Natural Language Understanding" (*https://arxiv.org/abs/2010.13382*), (2020).

10 By default, the `Trainer` looks for a column called `labels` when fine-tuning on classification tasks. You can also override this behavior by specifying the `label_names` argument of `TrainingArguments`.

also push all of our models to the Hugging Face Hub, so let's start by logging in to our account:

```
from huggingface_hub import notebook_login

notebook_login()
```

Next, we'll define the metrics to track during training. As we did in the performance benchmark, we'll use accuracy as the main metric. This means we can reuse our `accuracy_score()` function in the `compute_metrics()` function that we'll include in `DistillationTrainer`:

```
def compute_metrics(pred):
    predictions, labels = pred
    predictions = np.argmax(predictions, axis=1)
    return accuracy_score.compute(predictions=predictions, references=labels)
```

In this function, the predictions from the sequence modeling head come in the form of logits, so we use the `np.argmax()` function to find the most confident class prediction and compare that against the ground truth label.

Next we need to define the training arguments. To warm up, we'll set $\alpha = 1$ to see how well DistilBERT performs without any signal from the teacher.[11] Then we will push our fine-tuned model to a new repository called `distilbert-base-uncased-finetuned-clinc`, so we just need to specify that in the `output_dir` argument of `DistillationTrainingArguments`:

```
batch_size = 48

finetuned_ckpt = "distilbert-base-uncased-finetuned-clinc"
student_training_args = DistillationTrainingArguments(
    output_dir=finetuned_ckpt, evaluation_strategy = "epoch",
    num_train_epochs=5, learning_rate=2e-5,
    per_device_train_batch_size=batch_size,
    per_device_eval_batch_size=batch_size, alpha=1, weight_decay=0.01,
    push_to_hub=True)
```

We've also tweaked a few of the default hyperparameter values, like the number of epochs, the weight decay, and the learning rate. The next thing to do is initialize a student model. Since we will be doing multiple runs with the trainer, we'll create a `student_init()` function to initialize the model with each new run. When we pass this function to the `DistillationTrainer`, this will ensure we initialize a new model each time we call the `train()` method.

11 This approach of fine-tuning a general-purpose, distilled language model is sometimes referred to as "task-agnostic" distillation.

One other thing we need to do is provide the student model with the mappings between each intent and label ID. These mappings can be obtained from our BERT-base model that we downloaded in the pipeline:

```
id2label = pipe.model.config.id2label
label2id = pipe.model.config.label2id
```

With these mappings, we can now create a custom model configuration with the `AutoConfig` class hat we encountered in Chapters 3 and 4. Let's use this to create a configuration for our student with the information about the label mappings:

```
from                 import AutoConfig

num_labels = intents.num_classes
student_config = (AutoConfig
                  .from_pretrained(student_ckpt, num_labels=num_labels,
                                   id2label=id2label, label2id=label2id))
```

Here we've also specified the number of classes our model should expect. We can then provide this configuration to the `from_pretrained()` function of the `AutoModelForSequenceClassification` class as follows:

```
import
from                 import AutoModelForSequenceClassification

device = torch.device("cuda" if torch.cuda.is_available() else "cpu")

def student_init():
    return (AutoModelForSequenceClassification
            .from_pretrained(student_ckpt, config=student_config).to(device))
```

We now have all the ingredients needed for our distillation trainer, so let's load the teacher and fine-tune:

```
teacher_ckpt = "transformersbook/bert-base-uncased-finetuned-clinc"
teacher_model = (AutoModelForSequenceClassification
                 .from_pretrained(teacher_ckpt, num_labels=num_labels)
                 .to(device))

distilbert_trainer = DistillationTrainer(model_init=student_init,
    teacher_model=teacher_model, args=student_training_args,
    train_dataset=clinc_enc['train'], eval_dataset=clinc_enc['validation'],
    compute_metrics=compute_metrics, tokenizer=student_tokenizer)

distilbert_trainer.train()
```

Epoch	Training Loss	Validation Loss	Accuracy
1	4.2923	3.289337	0.742258
2	2.6307	1.883680	0.828065
3	1.5483	1.158315	0.896774
4	1.0153	0.861815	0.909355

Epoch	Training Loss	Validation Loss	Accuracy
5	0.7958	0.777289	0.917419

The 92% accuracy on the validation set looks quite good compared to the 94% that the BERT-base teacher achieves. Now that we've fine-tuned DistilBERT, let's push the model to the Hub so we can reuse it later:

```
distilbert_trainer.push_to_hub("Training completed!")
```

With our model now safely stored on the Hub, we can immediately use it in a pipeline for our performance benchmark:

```
finetuned_ckpt = "transformersbook/distilbert-base-uncased-finetuned-clinc"
pipe = pipeline("text-classification", model=finetuned_ckpt)
```

We can then pass this pipeline to our `PerformanceBenchmark` class to compute the metrics associated with this model:

```
optim_type = "DistilBERT"
pb = PerformanceBenchmark(pipe, clinc["test"], optim_type=optim_type)
perf_metrics.update(pb.run_benchmark())
```

```
Model size (MB) - 255.89
Average latency (ms) - 27.53 +\- 0.60
Accuracy on test set - 0.858
```

To compare these results against our baseline, let's create a scatter plot of the accuracy against the latency, with the radius of each point corresponding to the size of the model on disk. The following function does what we need and marks the current optimization type as a dashed circle to aid the comparison to previous results:

```
import pandas as pd

def plot_metrics(perf_metrics, current_optim_type):
    df = pd.DataFrame.from_dict(perf_metrics, orient='index')

    for idx in df.index:
        df_opt = df.loc[idx]
        # Add a dashed circle around the current optimization type
        if idx == current_optim_type:
            plt.scatter(df_opt["time_avg_ms"], df_opt["accuracy"] * 100,
                        alpha=0.5, s=df_opt["size_mb"], label=idx,
                        marker='$\u25CC$')
        else:
            plt.scatter(df_opt["time_avg_ms"], df_opt["accuracy"] * 100,
                        s=df_opt["size_mb"], label=idx, alpha=0.5)

    legend = plt.legend(bbox_to_anchor=(1,1))
    for handle in legend.legendHandles:
        handle.set_sizes([20])

    plt.ylim(80,90)
```

```
    # Use the slowest model to define the x-axis range
    xlim = int(perf_metrics["BERT baseline"]["time_avg_ms"] + 3)
    plt.xlim(1, xlim)
    plt.ylabel("Accuracy (%)")
    plt.xlabel("Average latency (ms)")
    plt.show()

plot_metrics(perf_metrics, optim_type)
```

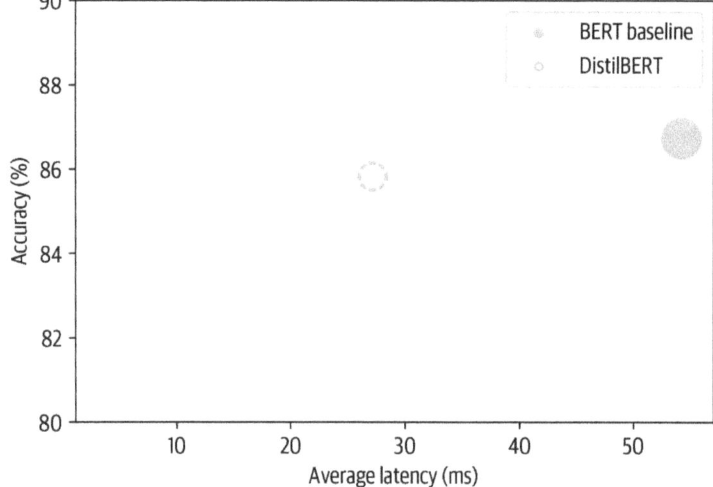

From the plot we can see that by using a smaller model we've managed to significantly decrease the average latency. And all this at the price of just over a 1% reduction in accuracy! Let's see if we can close that last gap by including the distillation loss of the teacher and finding good values for α and T.

Finding Good Hyperparameters with Optuna

To find good values for α and T, we could do a grid search over the 2D parameter space. But a much better alternative is to use *Optuna*,[12] which is an optimization framework designed for just this type of task. Optuna formulates the search problem in terms of an objective function that is optimized through multiple *trials*. For example, suppose we wished to minimize Rosenbrock's "banana function" (*https://oreil.ly/hPk8h*):

$$f(x, y) = (1 - x)^2 + 100\left(y - x^2\right)^2$$

12 T. Akiba et al., "Optuna: A Next-Generation Hyperparameter Optimization Framework" (*https://arxiv.org/abs/1907.10902*), (2019).

which is a famous test case for optimization frameworks. As shown in Figure 8-5, the function gets its name from the curved contours and has a global minimum at $(x, y) = (1, 1)$. Finding the valley is an easy optimization problem, but converging to the global minimum is not.

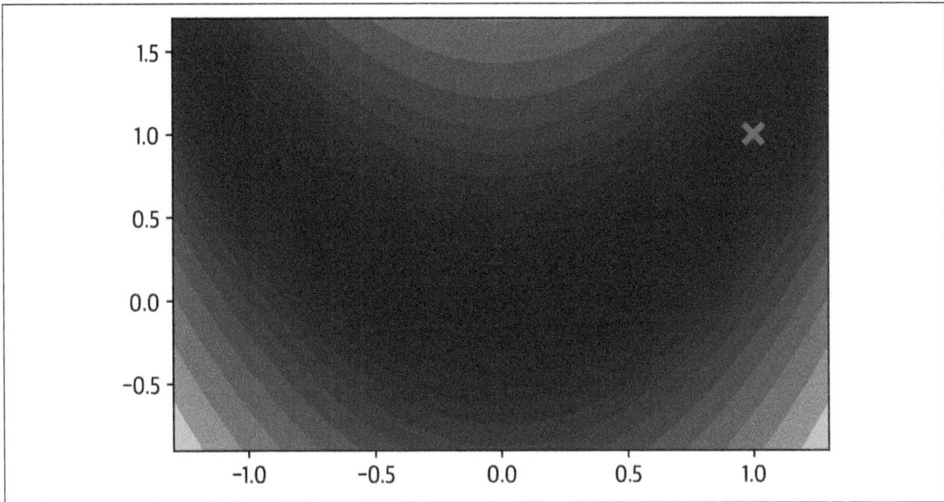

Figure 8-5. Plot of the Rosenbrock function of two variables

In Optuna, we can find the minimum of $f(x, y)$ by defining an `objective()` function that returns the value of $f(x, y)$:

```
def objective(trial):
    x = trial.suggest_float("x", -2, 2)
    y = trial.suggest_float("y", -2, 2)
    return (1 - x) ** 2 + 100 * (y - x ** 2) ** 2
```

The `trial.suggest_float` object specifies the parameter ranges to sample uniformly from; Optuna also provides `suggest_int` and `suggest_categorical` for integer and categorical parameters, respectively. Optuna collects multiple trials as a *study*, so to create one we just pass the `objective()` function to `study.optimize()` as follows:

```
import optuna

study = optuna.create_study()
study.optimize(objective, n_trials=1000)
```

Once the study is completed, we can then find the best parameters as follows:

```
study.best_params
```

```
{'x': 1.003024865971437, 'y': 1.00315167589307}
```

We see that with one thousand trials, Optuna has managed to find values for x and y that are reasonably close to the global minimum. To use Optuna in 🤗 Transformers, we use similar logic by first defining the hyperparameter space that we wish to optimize over. In addition to α and T, we'll include the number of training epochs as follows:

```
def hp_space(trial):
    return {"num_train_epochs": trial.suggest_int("num_train_epochs", 5, 10),
        "alpha": trial.suggest_float("alpha", 0, 1),
        "temperature": trial.suggest_int("temperature", 2, 20)}
```

Running the hyperparameter search with the `Trainer` is then quite simple; we just need to specify the number of trials to run and a direction to optimize for. Because we want the best possible accuracy, we specify `direction="maximize"` in the `hyper parameter_ search()` method of the trainer and pass the hyperparameter search space as follows:

```
best_run = distilbert_trainer.hyperparameter_search(
    n_trials=20, direction="maximize", hp_space=hp_space)
```

The `hyperparameter_search()` method returns a `BestRun` object, which contains the value of the objective that was maximized (by default, the sum of all metrics) and the hyperparameters it used for that run:

```
print(best_run)
```

```
BestRun(run_id='1', objective=0.927741935483871,
hyperparameters={'num_train_epochs': 10, 'alpha': 0.12468168730193585,
'temperature': 7})
```

This value of α tells us that most of the training signal is coming from the knowledge distillation term. Let's update our training arguments with these values and run the final training run:

```
for k,v in best_run.hyperparameters.items():
    setattr(student_training_args, k, v)

# Define a new repository to store our distilled model
distilled_ckpt = "distilbert-base-uncased-distilled-clinc"
student_training_args.output_dir = distilled_ckpt

# Create a new Trainer with optimal parameters
distil_trainer = DistillationTrainer(model_init=student_init,
    teacher_model=teacher_model, args=student_training_args,
    train_dataset=clinc_enc['train'], eval_dataset=clinc_enc['validation'],
    compute_metrics=compute_metrics, tokenizer=student_tokenizer)

distil_trainer.train();
```

Epoch	Training Loss	Validation Loss	Accuracy
1	0.9031	0.574540	0.736452
2	0.4481	0.285621	0.874839
3	0.2528	0.179766	0.918710
4	0.1760	0.139828	0.929355
5	0.1416	0.121053	0.934839
6	0.1243	0.111640	0.934839
7	0.1133	0.106174	0.937742
8	0.1075	0.103526	0.938710
9	0.1039	0.101432	0.938065
10	0.1018	0.100493	0.939355

Remarkably, we've been able to train the student to match the accuracy of the teacher, despite it having almost half the number of parameters! Let's push the model to the Hub for future use:

```
distil_trainer.push_to_hub("Training complete")
```

Benchmarking Our Distilled Model

Now that we have an accurate student, let's create a pipeline and redo our benchmark to see how we perform on the test set:

```
distilled_ckpt = "transformersbook/distilbert-base-uncased-distilled-clinc"
pipe = pipeline("text-classification", model=distilled_ckpt)
optim_type = "Distillation"
pb = PerformanceBenchmark(pipe, clinc["test"], optim_type=optim_type)
perf_metrics.update(pb.run_benchmark())
```

```
Model size (MB) - 255.89
Average latency (ms) - 25.96 +\- 1.63
Accuracy on test set - 0.868
```

To put these results in context, let's also visualize them with our `plot_metrics()` function:

```
plot_metrics(perf_metrics, optim_type)
```

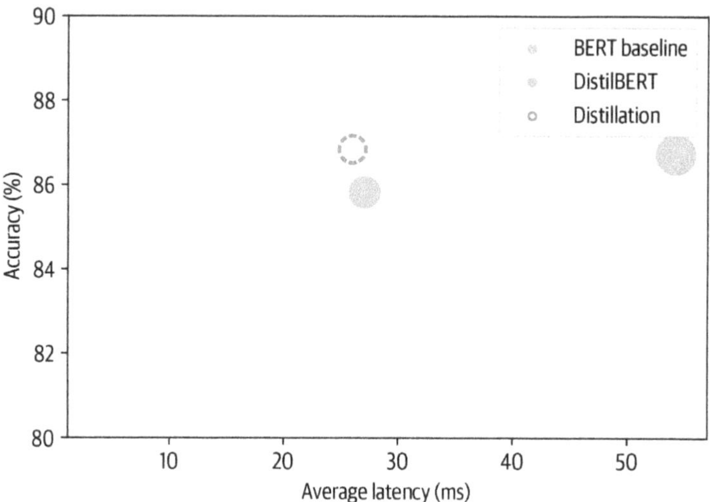

As expected, the model size and latency remain essentially unchanged compared to the DistilBERT benchmark, but the accuracy has improved and even surpassed the performance of the teacher! One way to interpret this surprising result is that the teacher has likely not been fine-tuned as systematically as the student. This is great, but we can actually compress our distilled model even further using a technique known as quantization. That's the topic of the next section.

Making Models Faster with Quantization

We've now seen that with knowledge distillation we can reduce the computational and memory cost of running inference by transferring the information from a teacher into a smaller student. Quantization takes a different approach; instead of reducing the number of computations, it makes them much more efficient by representing the weights and activations with low-precision data types like 8-bit integer (INT8) instead of the usual 32-bit floating point (FP32). Reducing the number of bits means the resulting model requires less memory storage, and operations like matrix multiplication can be performed much faster with integer arithmetic. Remarkably, these performance gains can be realized with little to no loss in accuracy!

A Primer on Floating-Point and Fixed-Point Numbers

Most transformers today are pretrained and fine-tuned with floating-point numbers (usually FP32 or a mix of FP16 and FP32), since they provide the precision needed to accommodate the very different ranges of weights, activations, and gradients. A floating-point number like FP32 represents a sequence of 32 bits that are grouped in terms of a *sign*, *exponent*, and *significand*. The sign determines whether the number is positive or negative, while the significand corresponds to the number of significant digits, which are scaled using the exponent in some fixed base (usually 2 for binary or 10 for decimal).

For example, the number 137.035 can be expressed as a decimal floating-point number through the following arithmetic:

$$137.035 = (-1)^0 \times 1.37035 \times 10^2$$

where the 1.37035 is the significand and 2 is the exponent of the base 10. Through the exponent we can represent a wide range of real numbers, and the decimal or binary point can be placed anywhere relative to the significant digits (hence the name "floating-point").

However, once a model is trained, we only need the forward pass to run inference, so we can reduce the precision of the data types without impacting the accuracy too much. For neural networks it is common to use a *fixed-point format* for the low-precision data types, where real numbers are represented as B-bit integers that are scaled by a common factor for all variables of the same type. For example, 137.035 can be represented as the integer 137,035 that is scaled by 1/1,000. We can control the range and precision of a fixed-point number by adjusting the scaling factor.

The basic idea behind quantization is that we can "discretize" the floating-point values f in each tensor by mapping their range $[f_{\max}, f_{\min}]$ into a smaller one $[q_{\max}, q_{\min}]$ of fixed-point numbers q, and linearly distributing all values in between. Mathematically, this mapping is described by the following equation:

$$f = \left(\frac{f_{\max} - f_{\min}}{q_{\max} - q_{\min}}\right)(q - Z) = S(q - Z)$$

where the scale factor S is a positive floating-point number and the constant Z has the same type as q and is called the *zero point* because it corresponds to the quantized value of the floating-point value $f = 0$. Note that the map needs to be *affine* so that we get back floating-point numbers when we dequantize the fixed-point ones.[13] An illustration of the conversion is shown in Figure 8-6.

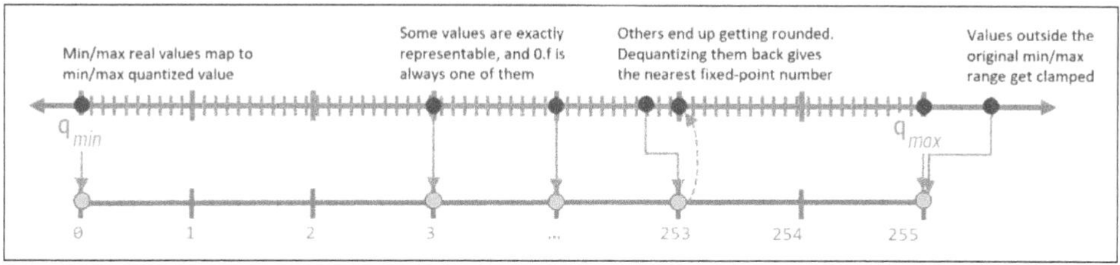

Figure 8-6. Quantizing floating-point numbers as unsigned 8-bit integers (courtesy of Manas Sahni)

Now, one of the main reasons why transformers (and deep neural networks more generally) are prime candidates for quantization is that the weights and activations tend to take values in relatively small ranges. This means we don't have to squeeze the whole range of possible FP32 numbers into, say, the $2^8 = 256$ numbers represented by INT8. To see this, let's pick out one of the attention weight matrices from our distilled model and plot the frequency distribution of the values:

```
import                    as

state_dict = pipe.model.state_dict()
weights = state_dict["distilbert.transformer.layer.0.attention.out_lin.weight"]
plt.hist(weights.flatten().numpy(), bins=250, range=(-0.3,0.3), edgecolor="C0")
plt.show()
```

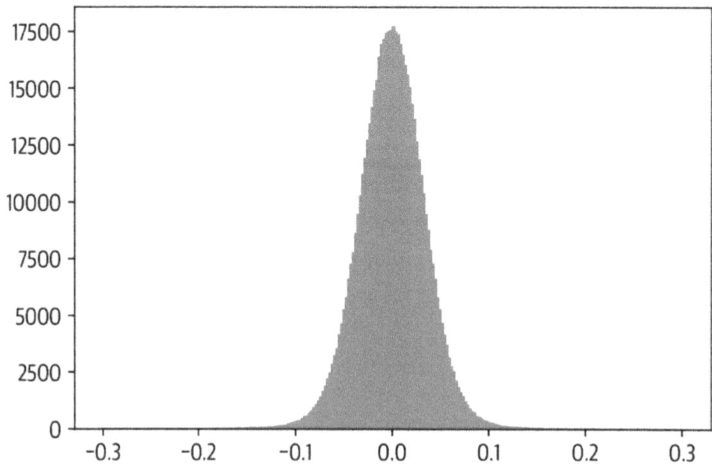

13 An affine map is just a fancy name for the $y = Ax + b$ map that you're familiar with in the linear layers of a neural network.

As we can see, the values of the weights are distributed in the small range $[-0.1, 0.1]$ around zero. Now, suppose we want to quantize this tensor as a signed 8-bit integer. In that case, the range of possible values for our integers is $[q_{max}, q_{min}] = [-128, 127]$. The zero point coincides with the zero of FP32 and the scale factor is calculated according to the previous equation:

```
zero_point = 0
scale = (weights.max() - weights.min()) / (127 - (-128))
```

To obtain the quantized tensor, we just need to invert the mapping $q = f / S + Z$, clamp the values, round them to the nearest integer, and represent the result in the `torch.int8` data type using the `Tensor.char()` function:

```
(weights / scale + zero_point).clamp(-128, 127).round().char()
```

```
tensor([[ -5,  -8,   0,  ...,  -6,  -4,   8],
        [  8,   3,   1,  ...,  -4,   7,   0],
        [ -9,  -6,   5,  ...,   1,   5,  -3],
        ...,
        [  6,   0,  12,  ...,   0,   6,  -1],
        [  0,  -2, -12,  ...,  12,  -7, -13],
        [-13,  -1, -10,  ...,   8,   2,  -2]], dtype=torch.int8)
```

Great, we've just quantized our first tensor! In PyTorch we can simplify the conversion by using the `quantize_per_tensor()` function together with a quantized data type, `torch.qint`, that is optimized for integer arithmetic operations:

```
from torch import quantize_per_tensor

dtype = torch.qint8
quantized_weights = quantize_per_tensor(weights, scale, zero_point, dtype)
quantized_weights.int_repr()
```

```
tensor([[ -5,  -8,   0,  ...,  -6,  -4,   8],
        [  8,   3,   1,  ...,  -4,   7,   0],
        [ -9,  -6,   5,  ...,   1,   5,  -3],
        ...,
        [  6,   0,  12,  ...,   0,   6,  -1],
        [  0,  -2, -12,  ...,  12,  -7, -13],
        [-13,  -1, -10,  ...,   8,   2,  -2]], dtype=torch.int8)
```

The plot in Figure 8-7 shows very clearly the discretization that's induced by only mapping some of the weight values precisely and rounding the rest.

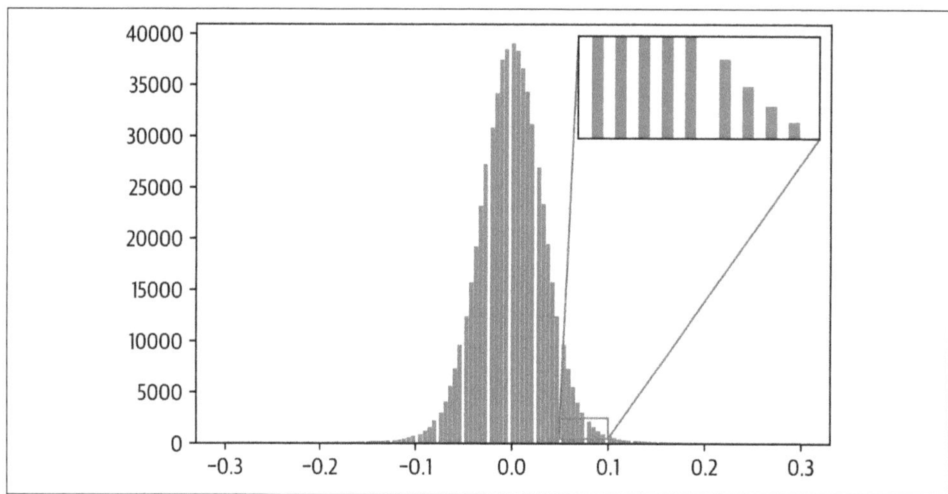

Figure 8-7. Effect of quantization on a transformer's weights

To round out our little analysis, let's compare how long it takes to compute the multiplication of two weight tensors with FP32 and INT8 values. For the FP32 tensors, we can multiply them using PyTorch's nifty `@` operator:

```
%%timeit
weights @ weights
```

```
393 µs ± 3.84 µs per loop (mean ± std. dev. of 7 runs, 1000 loops each)
```

For the quantized tensors we need the `QFunctional` wrapper class so that we can perform operations with the special `torch.qint8` data type:

```
from                    import QFunctional

q_fn = QFunctional()
```

This class supports various elementary operations, like addition, and in our case we can time the multiplication of our quantized tensors as follows:

```
%%timeit
q_fn.mul(quantized_weights, quantized_weights)
```

```
23.3 µs ± 298 ns per loop (mean ± std. dev. of 7 runs, 10000 loops each)
```

Compared to our FP32 computation, using the INT8 tensors is almost 100 times faster! Even larger gains can be obtained by using dedicated backends for running quantized operators efficiently. As of this book's writing, PyTorch supports:

- x86 CPUs with AVX2 support or higher
- ARM CPUs (typically found in mobile/embedded devices)

Since INT8 numbers have four times fewer bits than FP32 numbers, quantization also reduces the memory storage requirements by up to a factor of four. In our simple example we can verify this by comparing the underlying storage size of our weight tensor and its quantized cousin by using the `Tensor.storage()` function and the `getsizeof()` function from Python's `sys` module:

```
import sys

sys.getsizeof(weights.storage()) / sys.getsizeof(quantized_weights.storage())
```

```
3.999633833760527
```

For a full-scale transformer, the actual compression rate depends on which layers are quantized (as we'll see in the next section it is only the linear layers that typically get quantized).

So what's the catch with quantization? Changing the precision for all computations in our model introduces small disturbances at each point in the model's computational graph, which can compound and affect the model's performance. There are several ways to quantize a model, which all have pros and cons. For deep neural networks, there are typically three main approaches to quantization:

Dynamic quantization
: When using dynamic quantization nothing is changed during training and the adaptations are only performed during inference. Like with all the quantization methods we will discuss, the weights of the model are converted to INT8 ahead of inference time. In addition to the weights, the model's activations are also quantized. This approach is dynamic because the quantization happens on the fly. This means that all the matrix multiplications can be calculated with highly optimized INT8 functions. Of all the quantization methods discussed here, dynamic quantization is the simplest one. However, with dynamic quantization the activations are written and read to memory in floating-point format. This conversion between integer and floating point can be a performance bottleneck.

Static quantization
: Instead of computing the quantization of the activations on the fly, we can avoid the conversion to floating point by precomputing the quantization scheme. Static quantization achieves this by observing the activation patterns on a representative sample of the data ahead of inference time. The ideal quantization scheme is calculated and then saved. This enables us to skip the conversion between INT8 and FP32 values and speeds up the computations. However, it requires access to a good data sample and introduces an additional step in the pipeline, since we now need to train and determine the quantization scheme before we can perform inference. There is also one aspect that static quantization does not address: the discrepancy between the precision during training and inference, which leads to a performance drop in the model's metrics (e.g., accuracy).

Quantization-aware training

The effect of quantization can be effectively simulated during training by "fake" quantization of the FP32 values. Instead of using INT8 values during training, the FP32 values are rounded to mimic the effect of quantization. This is done during both the forward and the backward pass and improves performance in terms of model metrics over static and dynamic quantization.

The main bottleneck for running inference with transformers is the compute and memory bandwidth associated with the enormous numbers of weights in these models. For this reason, dynamic quantization is currently the best approach for transformer-based models in NLP. In smaller computer vision models the limiting factor is the memory bandwidth of the activations, which is why static quantization is generally used (or quantization-aware training in cases where the performance drops are too significant).

Implementing dynamic quantization in PyTorch is quite simple and can be done with a single line of code:

```
from [illegible] import quantize_dynamic

model_ckpt = "transformersbook/distilbert-base-uncased-distilled-clinc"
tokenizer = AutoTokenizer.from_pretrained(model_ckpt)
model = (AutoModelForSequenceClassification
         .from_pretrained(model_ckpt).to("cpu"))

model_quantized = quantize_dynamic(model, {nn.Linear}, dtype=torch.qint8)
```

Here we pass to `quantize_dynamic()` the full-precision model and specify the set of PyTorch layer classes in that model that we want to quantize. The `dtype` argument specifies the target precision and can be `fp16` or `qint8`. A good practice is to pick the lowest precision that you can tolerate with respect to your evaluation metrics. In this chapter we'll use INT8, which as we'll soon see has little impact on our model's accuracy.

Benchmarking Our Quantized Model

With our model now quantized, let's pass it through the benchmark and visualize the results:

```
pipe = pipeline("text-classification", model=model_quantized,
                tokenizer=tokenizer)
optim_type = "Distillation + quantization"
pb = PerformanceBenchmark(pipe, clinc["test"], optim_type=optim_type)
perf_metrics.update(pb.run_benchmark())
```

```
Model size (MB) - 132.40
Average latency (ms) - 12.54 +\- 0.73
Accuracy on test set - 0.876
```

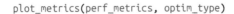

```
plot_metrics(perf_metrics, optim_type)
```

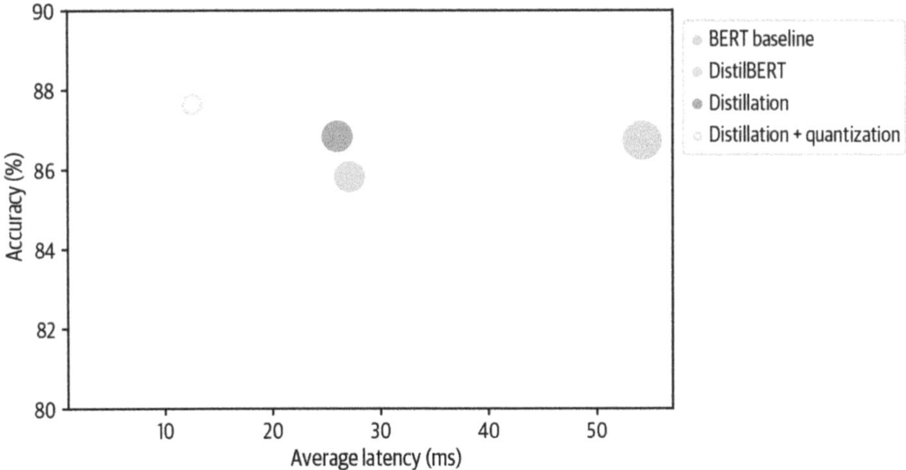

Nice, the quantized model is almost half the size of our distilled one and has even gained a slight accuracy boost! Let's see if we can push our optimization to the limit with a powerful framework called the ONNX Runtime.

Optimizing Inference with ONNX and the ONNX Runtime

ONNX (*https://onnx.ai*) is an open standard that defines a common set of operators and a common file format to represent deep learning models in a wide variety of frameworks, including PyTorch and TensorFlow.[14] When a model is exported to the ONNX format, these operators are used to construct a computational graph (often called an *intermediate representation*) that represents the flow of data through the neural network. An example of such a graph for BERT-base is shown in Figure 8-8, where each node receives some input, applies an operation like `Add` or `Squeeze`, and then feeds the output to the next set of nodes.

14 There is a separate standard called ONNX-ML that is designed for traditional machine learning models like random forests and frameworks like Scikit-learn.

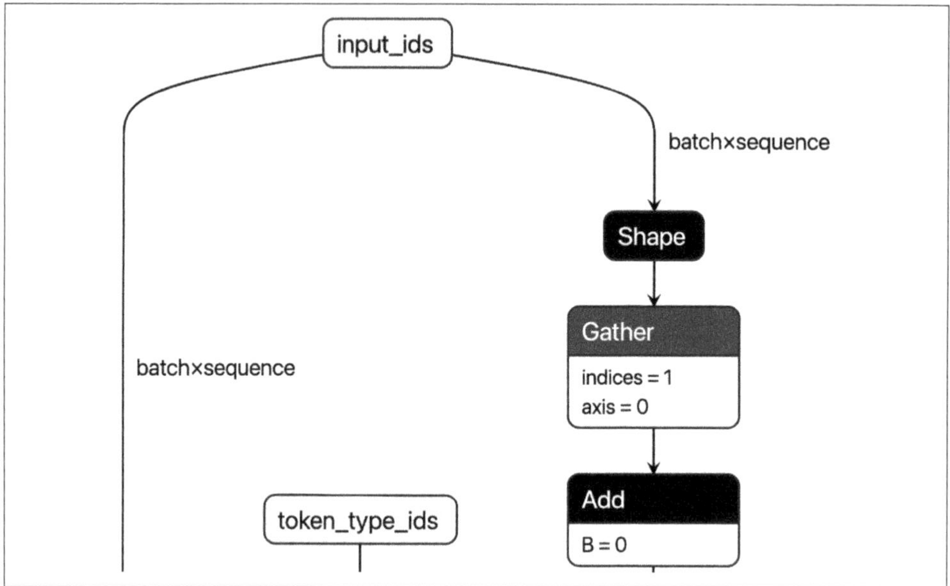

Figure 8-8. A section of the ONNX graph for BERT-base, visualized in Netron

By exposing a graph with standardized operators and data types, ONNX makes it easy to switch between frameworks. For example, a model trained in PyTorch can be exported to ONNX format and then imported in TensorFlow (and vice versa).

Where ONNX really shines is when it is coupled with a dedicated accelerator like ONNX Runtime (*https://onnxruntime.ai*), or ORT for short.[15] ORT provides tools to optimize the ONNX graph through techniques like operator fusion and constant folding,[16] and defines an interface to *execution providers* that allow you to run the model on different types of hardware. This is a powerful abstraction. Figure 8-9 shows the high-level architecture of the ONNX and ORT ecosystem.

---

15 Other popular accelerators include NVIDIA's TensorRT (*https://oreil.ly/HnNZx*) and Apache TVM (*https://oreil.ly/7KUyt*).

16 A fused operation involves merging one operator (usually an activation function) into another so that they can be executed together. For example, suppose we want to apply an activation f to a matrix product $A \times B$. Normally the result of the product needs to be written back to the GPU memory before the activation is computed. Operator fusion allows as to compute $f(A \times B)$ in a single step. Constant folding refers to the process of evaluating constant expressions at compile time instead of runtime.

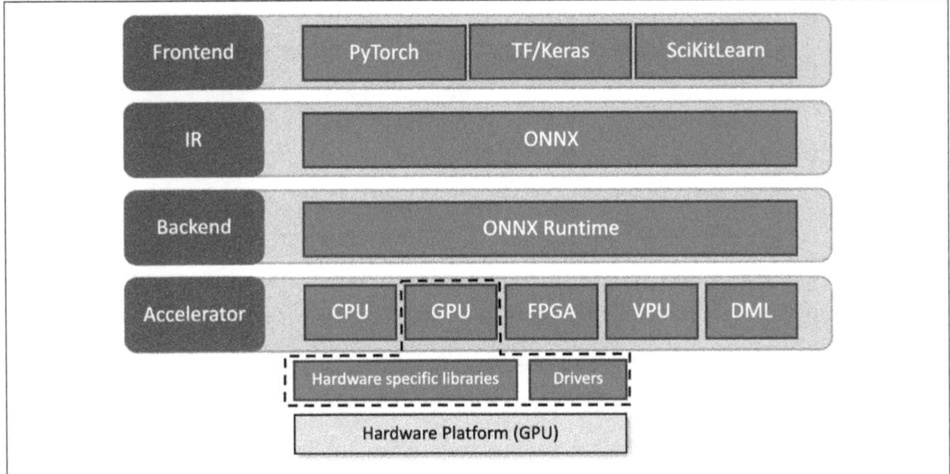

Figure 8-9. Architecture of the ONNX and ONNX Runtime ecosystem (courtesy of the ONNX Runtime team)

To see ORT in action, the first thing we need to do is convert our distilled model into the ONNX format. The 🤗 Transformers library has a built-in function called `convert_graph_to_onnx.convert()` that simplifies the process by taking the following steps:

1. Initialize the model as a `Pipeline`.
2. Run placeholder inputs through the pipeline so that ONNX can record the computational graph.
3. Define dynamic axes to handle dynamic sequence lengths.
4. Save the graph with network parameters.

To use this function, we first need to set some OpenMP (*https://openmp.org*) environment variables for ONNX:

```
import os
from psutil import cpu_count

os.environ["OMP_NUM_THREADS"] = f"{cpu_count()}"
os.environ["OMP_WAIT_POLICY"] = "ACTIVE"
```

OpenMP is an API designed for developing highly parallelized applications. The `OMP_NUM_THREADS` environment variable sets the number of threads to use for parallel computations in the ONNX Runtime, while `OMP_WAIT_POLICY=ACTIVE` specifies that waiting threads should be active (i.e., using CPU processor cycles).

Next, let's convert our distilled model to the ONNX format. Here we need to specify the argument `pipeline_name="text-classification"` since `convert()` wraps the model in a 🤗 Transformers `pipeline()` function during the conversion. In addition to the `model_ckpt`, we also pass the tokenizer to initialize the pipeline:

```
from transformers.convert_graph_to_onnx import convert

model_ckpt = "transformersbook/distilbert-base-uncased-distilled-clinc"
onnx_model_path = Path("onnx/model.onnx")
convert(framework="pt", model=model_ckpt, tokenizer=tokenizer,
        output=onnx_model_path, opset=12, pipeline_name="text-classification")
```

ONNX uses *operator sets* to group together immutable operator specifications, so `opset=12` corresponds to a specific version of the ONNX library.

Now that we have our model saved, we need to create an `InferenceSession` instance to feed inputs to the model:

```
from                import (GraphOptimizationLevel, InferenceSession,
                            SessionOptions)

def create_model_for_provider(model_path, provider="CPUExecutionProvider"):
    options = SessionOptions()
    options.intra_op_num_threads = 1
    options.graph_optimization_level = GraphOptimizationLevel.ORT_ENABLE_ALL
    session = InferenceSession(str(model_path), options, providers=[provider])
    session.disable_fallback()
    return session

onnx_model = create_model_for_provider(onnx_model_path)
```

Now when we call `onnx_model.run()`, we can get the class logits from the ONNX model. Let's test this out with an example from the test set. Since the output from `convert()` tells us that ONNX expects just the `input_ids` and `attention_mask` as inputs, we need to drop the `label` column from our sample:

```
inputs = clinc_enc["test"][:1]
del inputs["labels"]
logits_onnx = onnx_model.run(None, inputs)[0]
logits_onnx.shape
```

```
(1, 151)
```

Once we have the logits, we can easily get the predicted label by taking the argmax:

```
np.argmax(logits_onnx)
```

```
61
```

which indeed agrees with the ground truth label:

```
clinc_enc["test"][0]["labels"]
```

```
61
```

The ONNX model is not compatible with the `text-classification` pipeline, so we'll create our own class that mimics the core behavior:

```
from scipy.special import softmax

class OnnxPipeline:
    def __init__(self, model, tokenizer):
        self.model = model
        self.tokenizer = tokenizer

    def __call__(self, query):
        model_inputs = self.tokenizer(query, return_tensors="pt")
        inputs_onnx = {k: v.cpu().detach().numpy()
                       for k, v in model_inputs.items()}
        logits = self.model.run(None, inputs_onnx)[0][0, :]
        probs = softmax(logits)
        pred_idx = np.argmax(probs).item()
        return [{"label": intents.int2str(pred_idx), "score": probs[pred_idx]}]
```

We can then test this on our simple query to see if we recover the `car_rental` intent:

```
pipe = OnnxPipeline(onnx_model, tokenizer)
pipe(query)
```

```
[{'label': 'car_rental', 'score': 0.7848334}]
```

Great, our pipeline works as expected. The next step is to create a performance benchmark for ONNX models. Here we can build on the work we did with the `PerformanceBenchmark` class by simply overriding the `compute_size()` method and leaving the `compute_accuracy()` and `time_pipeline()` methods intact. The reason we need to override the `compute_size()` method is that we cannot rely on the `state_dict` and `torch.save()` to measure a model's size, since `onnx_model` is technically an ONNX `InferenceSession` object that doesn't have access to the attributes of PyTorch's `nn.Module`. In any case, the resulting logic is simple and can be implemented as follows:

```
class OnnxPerformanceBenchmark(PerformanceBenchmark):
    def __init__(self, *args, model_path, **kwargs):
        super().__init__(*args, **kwargs)
        self.model_path = model_path

    def compute_size(self):
        size_mb = Path(self.model_path).stat().st_size / (1024 * 1024)
        print(f"Model size (MB) - {size_mb:.2f}")
        return {"size_mb": size_mb}
```

With our new benchmark, let's see how our distilled model performs when converted to ONNX format:

```
optim_type = "Distillation + ORT"
pb = OnnxPerformanceBenchmark(pipe, clinc["test"], optim_type,
                              model_path="onnx/model.onnx")
perf_metrics.update(pb.run_benchmark())
```

```
Model size (MB) - 255.88
Average latency (ms) - 21.02 +\- 0.55
Accuracy on test set - 0.868
```

```
plot_metrics(perf_metrics, optim_type)
```

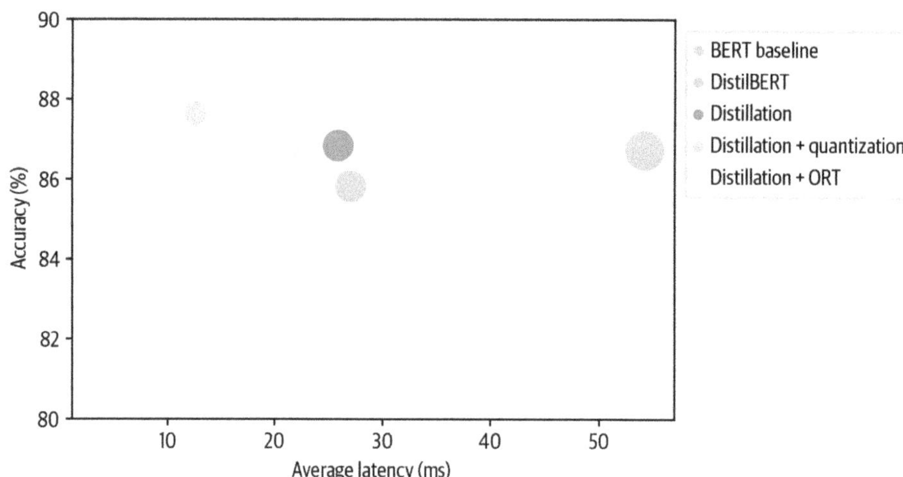

Remarkably, converting to the ONNX format and using the ONNX Runtime has given our distilled model (i.e. the "Distillation" circle in the plot) a boost in latency! Let's see if we can squeeze out a bit more performance by adding quantization to the mix.

Similar to PyTorch, ORT offers three ways to quantize a model: dynamic, static, and quantization-aware training. As we did with PyTorch, we'll apply dynamic quantization to our distilled model. In ORT, the quantization is applied through the `quantize_dynamic()` function, which requires a path to the ONNX model to quantize, a target path to save the quantized model to, and the data type to reduce the weights to:

```
from onnxruntime.quantization import quantize_dynamic, QuantType

model_input = "onnx/model.onnx"
model_output = "onnx/model.quant.onnx"
quantize_dynamic(model_input, model_output, weight_type=QuantType.QInt8)
```

Now that the model is quantized, let's run it through our benchmark:

```
onnx_quantized_model = create_model_for_provider(model_output)
pipe = OnnxPipeline(onnx_quantized_model, tokenizer)
optim_type = "Distillation + ORT (quantized)"
pb = OnnxPerformanceBenchmark(pipe, clinc["test"], optim_type,
                              model_path=model_output)
perf_metrics.update(pb.run_benchmark())
```

```
Model size (MB) - 64.20
Average latency (ms) - 9.24 +\- 0.29
Accuracy on test set - 0.877
```

```
plot_metrics(perf_metrics, optim_type)
```

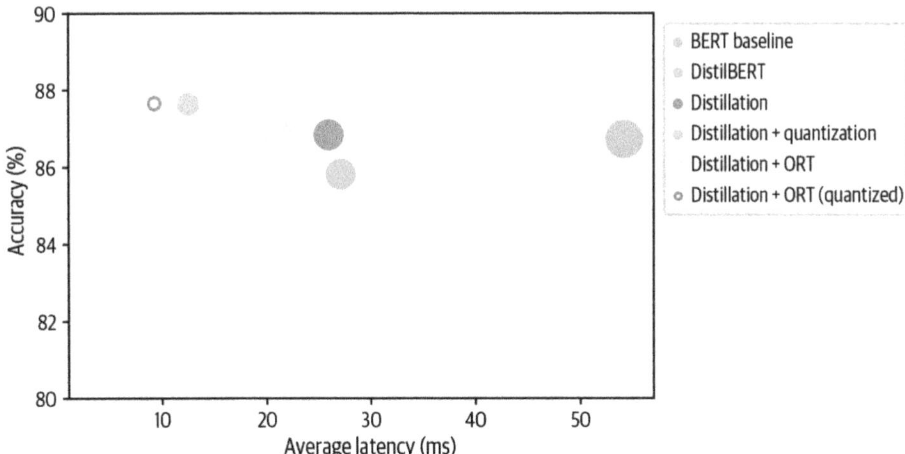

ORT quantization has reduced the model size and latency by around 30% compared to the model obtained from PyTorch quantization (the distillation + quantization blob). One reason for this is that PyTorch only optimizes the `nn.Linear` modules, while ONNX quantizes the embedding layer as well. From the plot we can also see that applying ORT quantization to our distilled model has provided an almost three-fold gain compared to our BERT baseline!

This concludes our analysis of techniques to speed up transformers for inference. We have seen that methods such as quantization reduce the model size by reducing the precision of the representation. Another strategy to reduce the size is to remove some weights altogether. This technique is called *weight pruning*, and it's the focus of the next section.

Making Models Sparser with Weight Pruning

So far we've seen that knowledge distillation and weight quantization are quite effective at producing faster models for inference, but in some cases you might also have strong constraints on the memory footprint of your model. For example, if our product manager suddenly decides that our text assistant needs to be deployed on a mobile device, then we'll need our intent classifier to take up as little storage space as possible. To round out our survey of compression methods, let's take a look at how we can shrink the number of parameters in our model by identifying and removing the least important weights in the network.

Sparsity in Deep Neural Networks

As shown in Figure 8-10, the main idea behind pruning is to gradually remove weight connections (and potentially neurons) during training such that the model becomes progressively sparser. The resulting pruned model has a smaller number of nonzero parameters, which can then be stored in a compact sparse matrix format. Pruning can be also combined with quantization to obtain further compression.

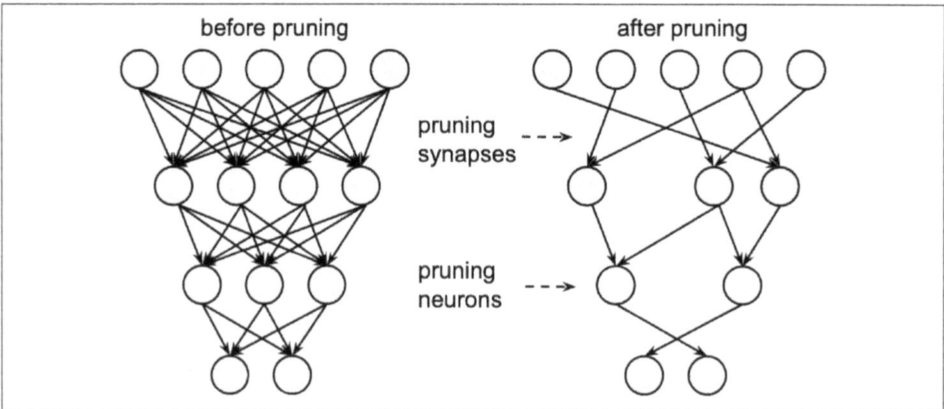

Figure 8-10. Weights and neurons before and after pruning (courtesy of Song Han)

Weight Pruning Methods

Mathematically, the way most weight pruning methods work is to calculate a matrix **S** of *importance scores* and then select the top k percent of weights by importance:

$$\mathrm{Top}_k(\mathbf{S})_{ij} = \begin{cases} 1 & \text{if } S_{ij} \text{ in top } k\,\% \\ 0 & \text{otherwise} \end{cases}$$

In effect, k acts as a new hyperparameter to control the amount of sparsity in the model—that is, the proportion of weights that are zero-valued. Lower values of k correspond to sparser matrices. From these scores we can then define a *mask matrix* **M** that masks the weights W_{ij} during the forward pass with some input x_i and effectively creates a sparse network of activations a_i:

$$a_i = \sum_k W_{ik} M_{ik} x_k$$

As discussed in the tongue-in-cheek "Optimal Brain Surgeon" paper,[17] at the heart of each pruning method are a set of questions that need to be considered:

- Which weights should be eliminated?
- How should the remaining weights be adjusted for best performance?
- How can such network pruning be done in a computationally efficient way?

The answers to these questions inform how the score matrix **S** is computed, so let's begin by looking at one of the earliest and most popular pruning methods: magnitude pruning.

Magnitude pruning

As the name suggests, magnitude pruning calculates the scores according to the magnitude of the weights $\mathbf{S} = \left(\mid W_{ij} \mid \right)_{1 \le j, j \le n}$ and then derives the masks from $\mathbf{M} = \mathrm{Top}_k(\mathbf{S})$. In the literature it is common to apply magnitude pruning in an iterative fashion by first training the model to learn which connections are important and pruning the weights of least importance.[18] The sparse model is then retrained and the process repeated until the desired sparsity is reached.

One drawback with this approach is that it is computationally demanding: at every step of pruning we need to train the model to convergence. For this reason it is generally better to gradually increase the initial sparsity s_i (which is usually zero) to a final value s_f after some number of steps N:[19]

$$s_t = s_f + \left(s_i - s_f\right)\left(1 - \frac{t - t_0}{N\Delta t}\right)^3 \qquad \text{for } t \in \left\{t_0, t_0 + \Delta t, \ldots, t_0 + N\Delta t\right\}$$

Here the idea is to update the binary masks **M** every Δt steps to allow masked weights to reactivate during training and recover from any potential loss in accuracy that is induced by the pruning process. As shown in Figure 8-11, the cubic factor implies that the rate of weight pruning is highest in the early phases (when the number of redundant weights is large) and gradually tapers off.

17 B. Hassibi and D. Stork, "Second Order Derivatives for Network Pruning: Optimal Brain Surgeon," *Proceedings of the 5th International Conference on Neural Information Processing Systems* (November 1992): 164–171, *https://papers.nips.cc/paper/1992/hash/303ed4c69846ab36c2904d3ba8573050-Abstract.html.*

18 S. Han et al., "Learning Both Weights and Connections for Efficient Neural Networks" (*https://arxiv.org/abs/1506.02626*), (2015).

19 M. Zhu and S. Gupta, "To Prune, or Not to Prune: Exploring the Efficacy of Pruning for Model Compression" (*https://arxiv.org/abs/1710.01878*), (2017).

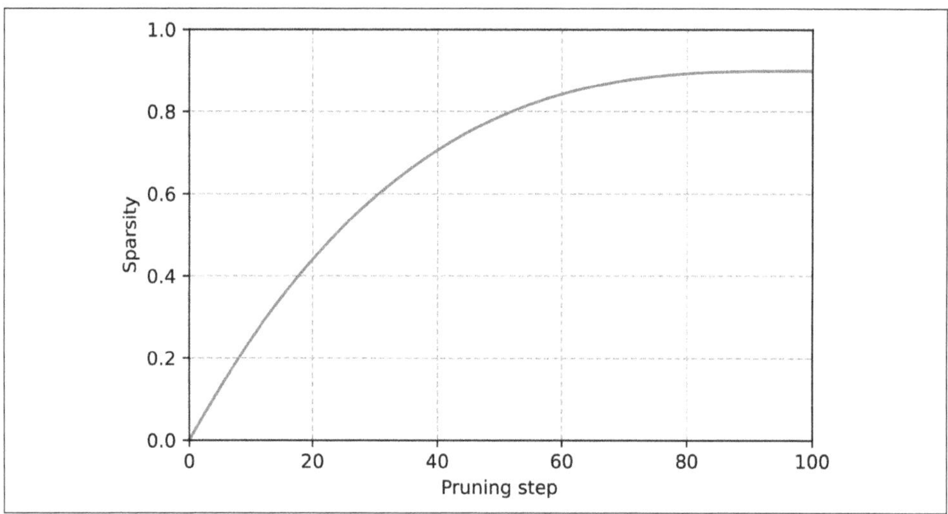

Figure 8-11. The cubic sparsity scheduler used for pruning

One problem with magnitude pruning is that it is really designed for pure supervised learning, where the importance of each weight is directly related to the task at hand. By contrast, in transfer learning the importance of the weights is primarily determined by the pretraining phase, so magnitude pruning can remove connections that are important for the fine-tuning task. Recently, an adaptive approach called movement pruning has been proposed by Hugging Face researchers—let's take a look.[20]

Movement pruning

The basic idea behind movement pruning is to *gradually* remove weights during fine-tuning such that the model becomes progressively *sparser*. The key novelty is that both the weights and the scores are learned during fine-tuning. So, instead of being derived directly from the weights (like with magnitude pruning), the scores in movement pruning are arbitrary and are learned through gradient descent like any other neural network parameter. This implies that in the backward pass, we also track the gradient of the loss L with respect to the scores S_{ij}.

Once the scores are learned, it is then straightforward to generate the binary mask using $\mathbf{M} = \text{Top}_k(\mathbf{S})$.[21]

20 V. Sanh, T. Wolf, and A.M. Rush, "Movement Pruning: Adaptive Sparsity by Fine-Tuning" (*https://arxiv.org/abs/2005.07683*), (2020).

21 There is also a "soft" version of movement pruning where instead of picking the top k% of weights, one uses a global threshold τ to define the binary mask: $\mathbf{M} = (\mathbf{S} > \tau)$.

The intuition behind movement pruning is that the weights that are "moving" the most from zero are the most important ones to keep. In other words, the positive weights increase during fine-tuning (and vice versa for the negative weights), which is equivalent to saying that the scores increase as the weights move away from zero. As shown in Figure 8-12, this behavior differs from magnitude pruning, which selects as the most important weights those that are *furthest* from zero.

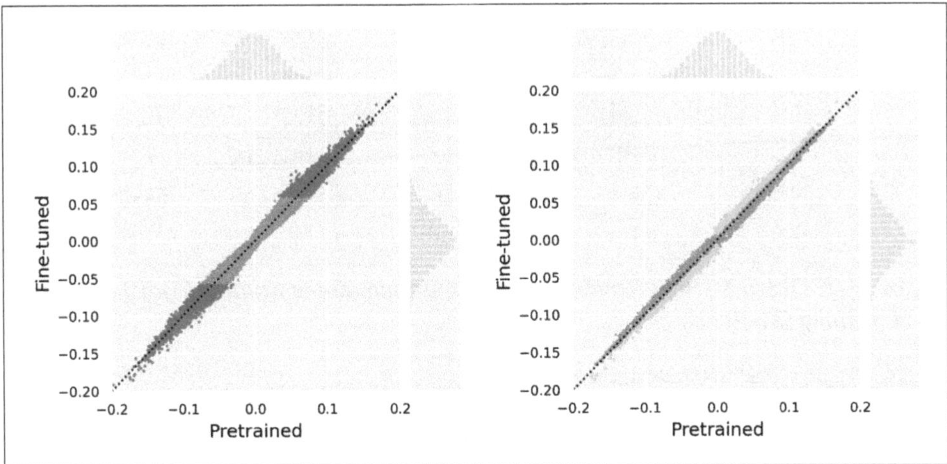

Figure 8-12. Comparison of weights removed during magnitude pruning (left) and movement pruning (right)

These differences between the two pruning methods are also evident in the distribution of the remaining weights. As shown in Figure 8-13, magnitude pruning produces two clusters of weights, while movement pruning produces a smoother distribution.

As of this book's writing, 🤗 Transformers does not support pruning methods out of the box. Fortunately, there is a nifty library called *Neural Networks Block Movement Pruning* (*https://oreil.ly/aHEvD*) that implements many of these ideas, and we recommend checking it out if memory constraints are a concern.

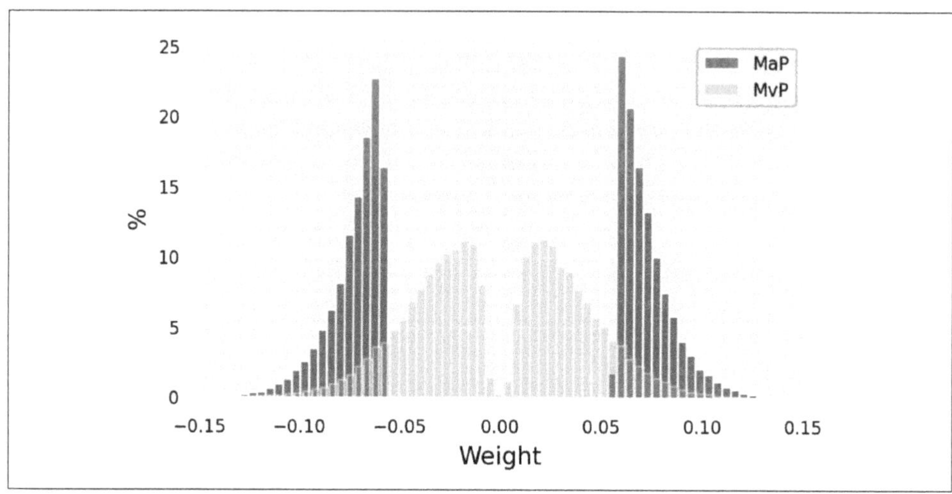

Figure 8-13. Distribution of remaining weights for magnitude pruning (MaP) and movement pruning (MvP)

Conclusion

We've seen that optimizing transformers for deployment in production environments involves compression along two dimensions: latency and memory footprint. Starting from a fine-tuned model, we applied distillation, quantization, and optimizations through ORT to significantly reduce both of these. In particular, we found that quantization and conversion in ORT gave the largest gains with minimal effort.

Although pruning is an effective strategy for reducing the storage size of transformer models, current hardware is not optimized for sparse matrix operations, which limits the usefulness of this technique. However, this is an active area of research, and by the time this book hits the shelves many of these limitations may have been resolved.

So where to from here? All of the techniques in this chapter can be adapted to other tasks, such as question answering, named entity recognition, or language modeling. If you find yourself struggling to meet the latency requirements or your model is eating up all your compute budget, we suggest giving one of them a try.

In the next chapter, we'll switch gears away from performance optimization and explore every data scientist's worst nightmare: dealing with few to no labels.

CHAPTER 9

Dealing with Few to No Labels

There is one question so deeply ingrained into every data scientist's mind that it's usually the first thing they ask at the start of a new project: is there any labeled data? More often than not, the answer is "no" or "a little bit," followed by an expectation from the client that your team's fancy machine learning models should still perform well. Since training models on very small datasets does not typically yield good results, one obvious solution is to annotate more data. However, this takes time and can be very expensive, especially if each annotation requires domain expertise to validate.

Fortunately, there are several methods that are well suited for dealing with few to no labels! You may already be familiar with some of them, such as *zero-shot* or *few-shot learning*, as witnessed by GPT-3's impressive ability to perform a diverse range of tasks with just a few dozen examples.

In general, the best-performing method will depend on the task, the amount of available data, and what fraction of that data is labeled. The decision tree shown in Figure 9-1 can help guide us through the process of picking the most appropriate method.

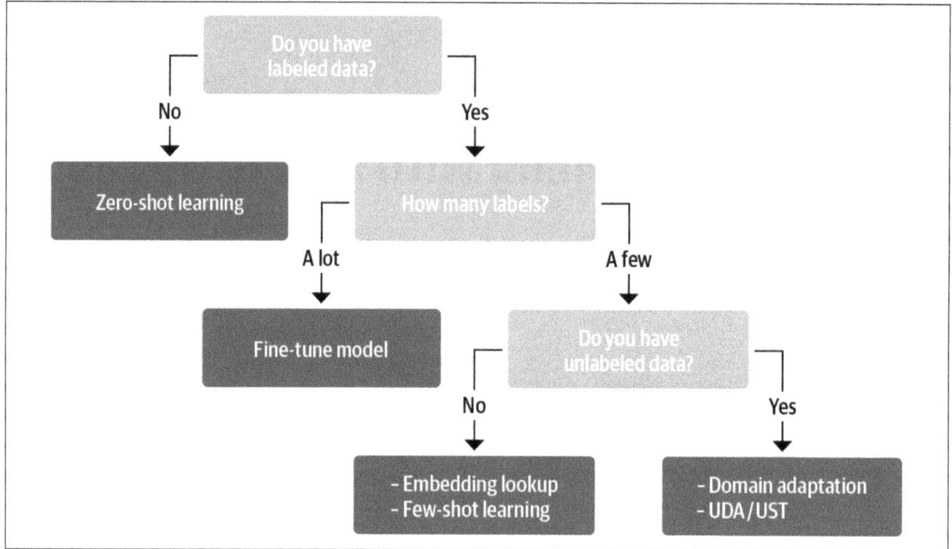

Figure 9-1. Several techniques that can be used to improve model performance in the absence of large amounts of labeled data

Let's walk through this decision tree step-by-step:

1. *Do you have labeled data?*
   Even a handful of labeled samples can make a difference with regard to which method works best. If you have no labeled data at all, you can start with the zero-shot learning approach, which often sets a strong baseline to work from.

2. *How many labels?*
   If labeled data is available, the deciding factor is how much. If you have a lot of training data available you can use the standard fine-tuning approach discussed in Chapter 2.

3. *Do you have unlabeled data?*
   If you only have a handful of labeled samples it can help immensely if you have access to large amounts of unlabeled data. If you have access to unlabeled data you can either use it to fine-tune the language model on the domain before training a classifier, or you can use more sophisticated methods such as unsupervised data augmentation (UDA) or uncertainty-aware self-training (UST).[1] If you don't have any unlabeled data available, you don't have the option of annotating more

1 Q. Xie et al., "Unsupervised Data Augmentation for Consistency Training" (*https://arxiv.org/abs/1904.12848*), (2019); S. Mukherjee and A.H. Awadallah, "Uncertainty-Aware Self-Training for Few-Shot Text Classification" (*https://arxiv.org/abs/2006.15315*), (2020).

data. In this case you can use few-shot learning or use the embeddings from a pretrained language model to perform lookups with a nearest neighbor search.

In this chapter we'll work our way through this decision tree by tackling a common problem facing many support teams that use issue trackers like Jira (*https://oreil.ly/TVqZQ*) or GitHub (*https://oreil.ly/e0Bd1*) to assist their users: tagging issues with metadata based on the issue's description. These tags might define the issue type, the product causing the problem, or which team is responsible for handling the reported issue. Automating this process can have a big impact on productivity and enables the support teams to focus on helping their users. As a running example, we'll use the GitHub issues associated with a popular open source project: 🤗 Transformers! Let's now take a look at what information is contained in these issues, how to frame the task, and how to get the data.

The methods presented in this chapter work well for text classification, but other techniques such as data augmentation may be necessary for tackling more complex tasks like named entity recognition, question answering, or summarization.

Building a GitHub Issues Tagger

If you navigate to the Issues tab (*https://oreil.ly/StdH3*) of the 🤗 Transformers repository, you'll find issues like the one shown in Figure 9-2, which contains a title, a description, and a set of tags or labels that characterize the issue. This suggests a natural way to frame the supervised learning task: given a title and description of an issue, predict one or more labels. Since each issue can be assigned a variable number of labels, this means we are dealing with a *multilabel text classification* problem. This is usually more challenging than the multiclass problem that we encountered in Chapter 2, where each tweet was assigned to only one emotion.

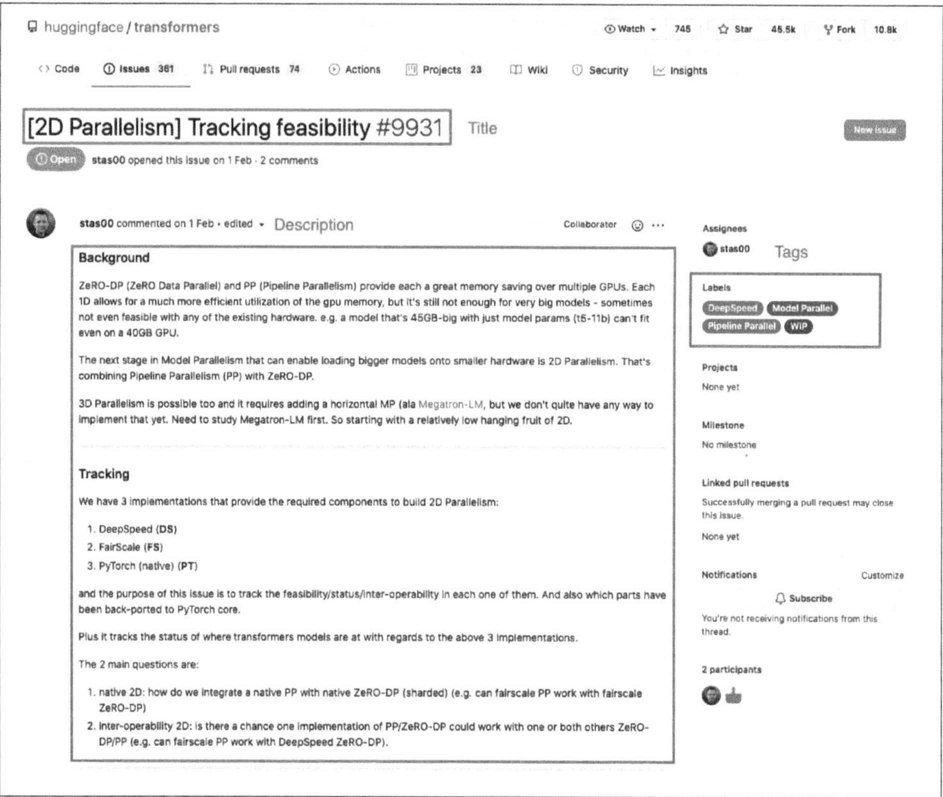

Figure 9-2. A typical GitHub issue on the 🤗 Transformers repository

Now that we've seen what the GitHub issues look like, let's see how we can download them to create our dataset.

Getting the Data

To grab all the repository's issues, we'll use the GitHub REST API (*https://oreil.ly/q605k*) to poll the `Issues` endpoint (*https://oreil.ly/qXdWV*). This endpoint returns a list of JSON objects, with each containing a large number of fields about the issue at hand, including its state (open or closed), who opened the issue, as well as the title, body, and labels we saw in Figure 9-2.

Since it takes a while to fetch all the issues, we've included a *github-issues-transformers.jsonl* file in this book's GitHub repository (*https://oreil.ly/if2dm*), along with a `fetch_issues()` function that you can use to download them yourself.

The GitHub REST API treats pull requests as issues, so our dataset contains a mix of both. To keep things simple, we'll develop our classifier for both types of issue, although in practice you might consider building two separate classifiers to have more fine-grained control over the model's performance.

Now that we know how to grab the data, let's take a look at cleaning it up.

Preparing the Data

Once we've downloaded all the issues, we can load them using Pandas:

```
import pandas as pd

dataset_url = "https://git.io/nlp-with-transformers"
df_issues = pd.read_json(dataset_url, lines=True)
print(f"DataFrame shape: {df_issues.shape}")
```

```
DataFrame shape: (9930, 26)
```

There are almost 10,000 issues in our dataset, and by looking at a single row we can see that the information retrieved from the GitHub API contains many fields such as URLs, IDs, dates, users, title, body, as well as labels:

```
cols = ["url", "id", "title", "user", "labels", "state", "created_at", "body"]
df_issues.loc[2, cols].to_frame()
```

	2
url	https://api.github.com/repos/huggingface/trans...
id	849529761
title	[DeepSpeed] ZeRO stage 3 integration: getting ...
user	{'login': 'stas00', 'id': 10676103, 'node_id':...
labels	[{'id': 2659267025, 'node_id': 'MDU6TGFiZWwyNj...
state	open
created_at	2021-04-02 23:40:42
body	**[This is not yet alive, preparing for the re...

The `labels` column is the thing that we're interested in, and each row contains a list of JSON objects with metadata about each label:

```
[
   {
      "id":2659267025,
      "node_id":"MDU6TGFiZWwyNjU5MjY3MDI1",
      "url":"https://api.github.com/repos/huggingface...",
      "name":"DeepSpeed",
      "color":"4D34F7",
```

```
        "default":false,
        "description":""
    }
]
```

For our purposes, we're only interested in the name field of each label object, so let's overwrite the labels column with just the label names:

```
df_issues["labels"] = (df_issues["labels"]
                       .apply(lambda x: [meta["name"] for meta in x]))
df_issues[["labels"]].head()
```

	labels
0	[]
1	[]
2	[DeepSpeed]
3	[]
4	[]

Now each row in the labels column is a list of GitHub labels, so we can compute the length of each row to find the number of labels per issue:

```
df_issues["labels"].apply(lambda x : len(x)).value_counts().to_frame().T
```

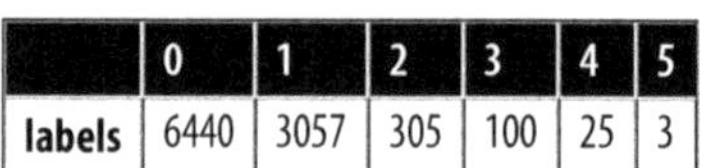

	0	1	2	3	4	5
labels	6440	3057	305	100	25	3

This shows that the majority of issues have zero or one label, and much fewer have more than one. Next let's take a look at the top 10 most frequent labels in the dataset. In Pandas we can do this by "exploding" the labels column so that each label in the list becomes a row, and then simply counting the occurrences of each label:

```
df_counts = df_issues["labels"].explode().value_counts()
print(f"Number of labels: {len(df_counts)}")
# Display the top-8 label categories
df_counts.to_frame().head(8).T
```

```
Number of labels: 65
```

	wontfix	model card	Core: Tokenization	New model	Core: Modeling	Help wanted	Good First Issue	Usage
labels	2284	649	106	98	64	52	50	46

We can see that there are 65 unique labels in the dataset and that the classes are very imbalanced, with wontfix and model card being the most common labels. To make the classification problem more tractable, we'll focus on building a tagger for a subset of the labels. For example, some labels, such as `Good First Issue` or `Help Wanted`, are potentially very difficult to predict from the issue's description, while others, such as `model card`, could be classified with a simple rule that detects when a model card is added on the Hugging Face Hub.

The following code filters the dataset for the subset of labels that we'll work with, along with a standardization of the names to make them easier to read:

```
label_map = {"Core: Tokenization": "tokenization",
             "New model": "new model",
             "Core: Modeling": "model training",
             "Usage": "usage",
             "Core: Pipeline": "pipeline",
             "TensorFlow": "tensorflow or tf",
             "PyTorch": "pytorch",
             "Examples": "examples",
             "Documentation": "documentation"}

def filter_labels(x):
    return [label_map[label] for label in x if label in label_map]

df_issues["labels"] = df_issues["labels"].apply(filter_labels)
all_labels = list(label_map.values())
```

Now let's look at the distribution of the new labels:

```
df_counts = df_issues["labels"].explode().value_counts()
df_counts.to_frame().T
```

	tokenization	new model	model training	usage	pipeline	tensorflow or tf	pytorch	documentation	examples
labels	106	98	64	46	42	41	37	28	24

Later in this chapter we'll find it useful to treat the unlabeled issues as a separate training split, so let's create a new column that indicates whether the issue is unlabeled or not:

```
df_issues["split"] = "unlabeled"
mask = df_issues["labels"].apply(lambda x: len(x)) > 0
df_issues.loc[mask, "split"] = "labeled"
df_issues["split"].value_counts().to_frame()
```

	split
unlabeled	9489
labeled	441

Let's now take a look at an example:

```
for column in ["title", "body", "labels"]:
    print(f"{column}: {df_issues[column].iloc[26][:500]}\n")
```

```
title: Add new CANINE model

body: # 🌟 New model addition

## Model description

Google recently proposed a new **C**haracter **A**rchitecture with **N**o
 tokenization **I**n **N**eural **E**ncoders architecture (CANINE). Not only
 the title is exciting:

Pipelined NLP systems have largely been superseded by end-to-end neural
 modeling, yet nearly all commonly-used models still require an explicit
 tokenization step. While recent tokenization approaches based on data-derived
 subword lexicons are less brittle than manually en

labels: ['new model']
```

In this example a new model architecture is proposed, so the `new model` tag makes sense. We can also see that the `title` contains information that will be useful for our classifier, so let's concatenate it with the issue's description in the `body` field:

```
df_issues["text"] = (df_issues
                     .apply(lambda x: x["title"] + "\n\n" + x["body"], axis=1))
```

Before we look at the rest of the data, let's check for any duplicates in the data and drop them with the `drop_duplicates()` method:

```
len_before = len(df_issues)
df_issues = df_issues.drop_duplicates(subset="text")
print(f"Removed {(len_before-len(df_issues))/len_before:.2%} duplicates.")
```

```
Removed 1.88% duplicates.
```

We can see that there were a few duplicate issues in our dataset, but they only represented a small percentage. As we've done in other chapters, it's also a good idea to have a quick look at the number of words in our texts to see if we'll lose much information when we truncate to each model's context size:

```
import numpy as np
import matplotlib.pyplot as plt

(df_issues["text"].str.split().apply(len)
 .hist(bins=np.linspace(0, 500, 50), grid=False, edgecolor="C0"))
plt.title("Words per issue")
plt.xlabel("Number of words")
plt.ylabel("Number of issues")
plt.show()
```

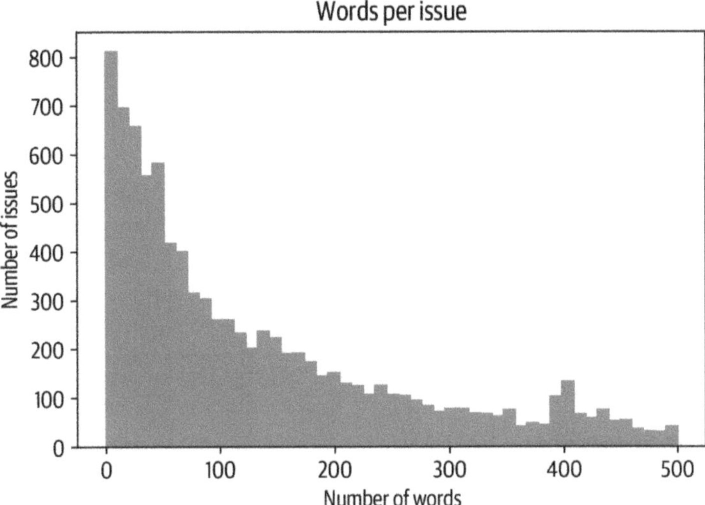

The distribution has the long tail characteristic of many text datasets. Most of the texts are fairly short, but there are also issues with more than 500 words. It is common to have some very long issues, especially when error messages and code snippets are posted along with them. Given that most transformer models have a context size of 512 tokens or larger, truncating a handful of long issues is not likely to affect the overall performance. Now that we've explored and cleaned up our dataset, the final thing to do is define our training and validation sets to benchmark our classifiers. Let's take a look at how to do this.

Creating Training Sets

Creating training and validation sets is a bit trickier for multlilabel problems because there is no guaranteed balance for all labels. However, it can be approximated, and we can use the Scikit-multilearn library (*http://scikit.ml*), which is specifically set up for this purpose. The first thing we need to do is transform our set of labels, like `pytorch` and `tokenization`, into a format that the model can process. Here we can use Scikit-learn's `MultiLabelBinarizer` class, which takes a list of label names and creates a vector with zeros for absent labels and ones for present labels. We can test this by fitting `MultiLabelBinarizer` on `all_labels` to learn the mapping from label name to ID as follows:

```
from sklearn.preprocessing import MultiLabelBinarizer

mlb = MultiLabelBinarizer()
mlb.fit([all_labels])
mlb.transform([["tokenization", "new model"], ["pytorch"]])
```

```
array([[0, 0, 0, 1, 0, 0, 0, 1, 0],
       [0, 0, 0, 0, 0, 1, 0, 0, 0]])
```

In this simple example we can see the first row has two ones corresponding to the `tokenization` and `new model` labels, while the second row has just one hit with `pytorch`.

To create the splits we can use the `iterative_train_test_split()` function from Scikit-multilearn, which creates the train/test splits iteratively to achieve balanced labels. We wrap it in a function that we can apply to `DataFrames`. Since the function expects a two-dimensional feature matrix, we need to add a dimension to the possible indices before making the split:

```
from skmultilearn.model_selection import iterative_train_test_split

def balanced_split(df, test_size=0.5):
    ind = np.expand_dims(np.arange(len(df)), axis=1)
    labels = mlb.transform(df["labels"])
    ind_train, _, ind_test, _ = iterative_train_test_split(ind, labels,
                                                           test_size)
    return df.iloc[ind_train[:, 0]], df.iloc[ind_test[:,0]]
```

Armed with the `balanced_split()` function, we can split the data into supervised and unsupervised datasets, and then create balanced training, validation, and test sets for the supervised part:

```
from sklearn.model_selection import train_test_split

df_clean = df_issues[["text", "labels", "split"]].reset_index(drop=True).copy()
df_unsup = df_clean.loc[df_clean["split"] == "unlabeled", ["text", "labels"]]
df_sup = df_clean.loc[df_clean["split"] == "labeled", ["text", "labels"]]

np.random.seed(0)
df_train, df_tmp = balanced_split(df_sup, test_size=0.5)
df_valid, df_test = balanced_split(df_tmp, test_size=0.5)
```

Finally, let's create a `DatasetDict` with all the splits so that we can easily tokenize the dataset and integrate with the `Trainer`. Here we'll use the nifty `from_pandas()` method to load each split directly from the corresponding Pandas `DataFrame`:

```
from datasets import Dataset, DatasetDict

ds = DatasetDict({
    "train": Dataset.from_pandas(df_train.reset_index(drop=True)),
    "valid": Dataset.from_pandas(df_valid.reset_index(drop=True)),
    "test": Dataset.from_pandas(df_test.reset_index(drop=True)),
    "unsup": Dataset.from_pandas(df_unsup.reset_index(drop=True))})
```

This looks good, so the last thing to do is to create some training slices so that we can evaluate the performance of each classifier as a function of the training set size.

Creating Training Slices

The dataset has the two characteristics that we'd like to investigate in this chapter: sparse labeled data and multilabel classification. The training set consists of only 220 examples to train with, which is certainly a challenge even with transfer learning. To drill down into how each method in this chapter performs with little labeled data, we'll also create slices of the training data with even fewer samples. We can then plot the number of samples against the performance and investigate various regimes. We'll start with only eight samples per label and build up until the slice covers the full training set using the `iterative_train_test_split()` function:

```
np.random.seed(0)
all_indices = np.expand_dims(list(range(len(ds["train"]))), axis=1)
indices_pool = all_indices
labels = mlb.transform(ds["train"]["labels"])
train_samples = [8, 16, 32, 64, 128]
train_slices, last_k = [], 0

for i, k in enumerate(train_samples):
    # Split off samples necessary to fill the gap to the next split size
    indices_pool, labels, new_slice, _ = iterative_train_test_split(
        indices_pool, labels, (k-last_k)/len(labels))
    last_k = k
    if i==0: train_slices.append(new_slice)
    else: train_slices.append(np.concatenate((train_slices[-1], new_slice)))

# Add full dataset as last slice
train_slices.append(all_indices), train_samples.append(len(ds["train"]))
train_slices = [np.squeeze(train_slice) for train_slice in train_slices]
```

Note that this iterative approach only approximately splits the samples to the desired size, since it is not always possible to find a balanced split at a given split size:

```
print("Target split sizes:")
print(train_samples)
print("Actual split sizes:")
print([len(x) for x in train_slices])
```

```
Target split sizes:
[8, 16, 32, 64, 128, 223]
Actual split sizes:
[10, 19, 36, 68, 134, 223]
```

We'll use the specified split sizes as the labels for the following plots. Great, we've finally prepared our dataset into training splits—let's next take a look at training a strong baseline model!

Implementing a Naive Bayesline

Whenever you start a new NLP project, it's always a good idea to implement a set of strong baselines. There are two main reasons for this:

1. A baseline based on regular expressions, handcrafted rules, or a very simple model might already work really well to solve the problem. In these cases, there is no reason to bring out big guns like transformers, which are generally more complex to deploy and maintain in production environments.
2. The baselines provide quick checks as you explore more complex models. For example, suppose you train BERT-large and get an accuracy of 80% on your validation set. You might write it off as a hard dataset and call it a day. But what if you knew that a simple classifier like logistic regression gets 95% accuracy? That would raise your suspicions and prompt you to debug your model.

So let's start our analysis by training a baseline model. For text classification, a great baseline is a *Naive Bayes classifier* as it is very simple, quick to train, and fairly robust to perturbations in the inputs. The Scikit-learn implementation of Naive Bayes does not support multilabel classification out of the box, but fortunately we can again use the Scikit-multilearn library to cast the problem as a one-versus-rest classification task where we train L binary classifiers for L labels. First, let's use a multilabel binarizer to create a new `label_ids` column in our training sets. We can use the `map()` function to take care of all the processing in one go:

```
def prepare_labels(batch):
    batch["label_ids"] = mlb.transform(batch["labels"])
    return batch

ds = ds.map(prepare_labels, batched=True)
```

To measure the performance of our classifiers, we'll use the micro and macro F_1-scores, where the former tracks performance on the frequent labels and the latter on all labels disregarding the frequency. Since we'll be evaluating each model across different-sized training splits, let's create a `defaultdict` with a list to store the scores per split:

```
from collections import defaultdict

macro_scores, micro_scores = defaultdict(list), defaultdict(list)
```

Now we're finally ready to train our baseline! Here's the code to train the model and evaluate our classifier across increasing training set sizes:

```
from sklearn.naive_bayes import MultinomialNB
from sklearn.metrics import classification_report
from skmultilearn.problem_transform import BinaryRelevance
from sklearn.feature_extraction.text import CountVectorizer
```

```python
for train_slice in train_slices:
    # Get training slice and test data
    ds_train_sample = ds["train"].select(train_slice)
    y_train = np.array(ds_train_sample["label_ids"])
    y_test = np.array(ds["test"]["label_ids"])
    # Use a simple count vectorizer to encode our texts as token counts
    count_vect = CountVectorizer()
    X_train_counts = count_vect.fit_transform(ds_train_sample["text"])
    X_test_counts = count_vect.transform(ds["test"]["text"])
    # Create and train our model!
    classifier = BinaryRelevance(classifier=MultinomialNB())
    classifier.fit(X_train_counts, y_train)
    # Generate predictions and evaluate
    y_pred_test = classifier.predict(X_test_counts)
    clf_report = classification_report(
        y_test, y_pred_test, target_names=mlb.classes_, zero_division=0,
        output_dict=True)
    # Store metrics
    macro_scores["Naive Bayes"].append(clf_report["macro avg"]["f1-score"])
    micro_scores["Naive Bayes"].append(clf_report["micro avg"]["f1-score"])
```

There's quite a lot going on in this block of code, so let's unpack it. First, we get the training slice and encode the labels. Then we use a count vectorizer to encode the texts by simply creating a vector of the size of the vocabulary where each entry corresponds to the frequency with which a token appeared in the text. This is called a *bag-of-words* approach, since all information on the order of the words is lost. Then we train the classifier and use the predictions on the test set to get the micro and macro F_1-scores via the classification report.

With the following helper function we can plot the results of this experiment:

```python
import matplotlib.pyplot as plt

def plot_metrics(micro_scores, macro_scores, sample_sizes, current_model):
    fig, (ax0, ax1) = plt.subplots(1, 2, figsize=(10, 4), sharey=True)

    for run in micro_scores.keys():
        if run == current_model:
            ax0.plot(sample_sizes, micro_scores[run], label=run, linewidth=2)
            ax1.plot(sample_sizes, macro_scores[run], label=run, linewidth=2)
        else:
            ax0.plot(sample_sizes, micro_scores[run], label=run,
                     linestyle="dashed")
            ax1.plot(sample_sizes, macro_scores[run], label=run,
                     linestyle="dashed")

    ax0.set_title("Micro F1 scores")
    ax1.set_title("Macro F1 scores")
    ax0.set_ylabel("Test set F1 score")
    ax0.legend(loc="lower right")
    for ax in [ax0, ax1]:
```

```
        ax.set_xlabel("Number of training samples")
        ax.set_xscale("log")
        ax.set_xticks(sample_sizes)
        ax.set_xticklabels(sample_sizes)
        ax.minorticks_off()
    plt.tight_layout()
    plt.show()

plot_metrics(micro_scores, macro_scores, train_samples, "Naive Bayes")
```

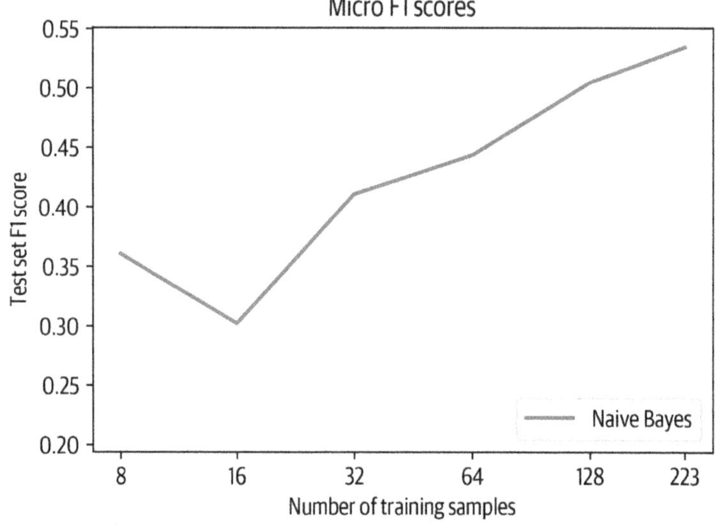

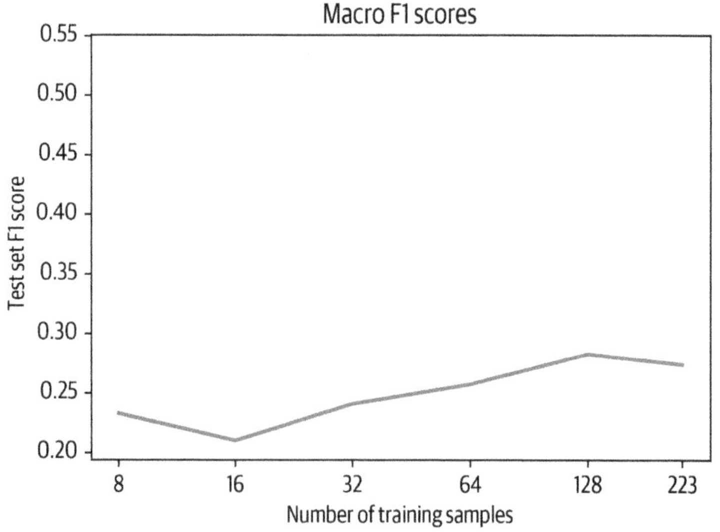

Note that we plot the number of samples on a logarithmic scale. From the figure we can see that the micro and macro F_1-scores both improve as we increase the number of training samples. With so few samples to train on, the results are also slightly noisy since each slice can have a different class distribution. Nevertheless, what's important here is the trend, so let's now see how these results fare against transformer-based approaches!

Working with No Labeled Data

The first technique that we'll consider is *zero-shot classification*, which is suitable in settings where you have no labeled data at all. This is surprisingly common in industry, and might occur because there is no historic data with labels or because acquiring the labels for the data is difficult. We will cheat a bit in this section since we will still use the test data to measure the performance, but we will not use any data to train the model (otherwise the comparison to the following approaches would be difficult).

The goal of zero-shot classification is to make use of a pretrained model without any additional fine-tuning on your task-specific corpus. To get a better idea of how this could work, recall that language models like BERT are pretrained to predict masked tokens in text on thousands of books and large Wikipedia dumps. To successfully predict a missing token, the model needs to be aware of the topic in the context. We can try to trick the model into classifying a document for us by providing a sentence like:

> "This section was about the topic [MASK]."

The model should then give a reasonable suggestion for the document's topic, since this is a natural text to occur in the dataset.[2]

Let's illustrate this further with the following toy problem: suppose you have two children, and one of them likes movies with cars while the other enjoys movies with animals better. Unfortunately, they have already seen all the ones you know, so you want to build a function that tells you what topic a new movie is about. Naturally, you turn to transformers for this task. The first thing to try is to load BERT-base in the `fill-mask` pipeline, which uses the masked language model to predict the content of the masked tokens:

```
from transformers import pipeline

pipe = pipeline("fill-mask", model="bert-base-uncased")
```

2 We thank Joe Davison (*https://joeddav.github.io*) for suggesting this approach to us.

Next, let's construct a little movie description and add a prompt to it with a masked word. The goal of the prompt is to guide the model to help us make a classification. The `fill-mask` pipeline returns the most likely tokens to fill in the masked spot:

```
movie_desc = "The main characters of the movie madacascar \
are a lion, a zebra, a giraffe, and a hippo. "
prompt = "The movie is about [MASK]."

output = pipe(movie_desc + prompt)
for element in output:
    print(f"Token {element['token_str']}:\t{element['score']:.3f}%")
```

```
Token animals:  0.103%
Token lions:    0.066%
Token birds:    0.025%
Token love:     0.015%
Token hunting:  0.013%
```

Clearly, the model predicts only tokens that are related to animals. We can also turn this around, and instead of getting the most likely tokens we can query the pipeline for the probability of a few given tokens. For this task we might choose `cars` and `animals`, so we can pass them to the pipeline as targets:

```
output = pipe(movie_desc + prompt, targets=["animals", "cars"])
for element in output:
    print(f"Token {element['token_str']}:\t{element['score']:.3f}%")
```

```
Token animals:  0.103%
Token cars:     0.001%
```

Unsurprisingly, the predicted probability for the token `cars` is much smaller than for `animals`. Let's see if this also works for a description that is closer to cars:

```
movie_desc = "In the movie transformers aliens \
can morph into a wide range of vehicles."

output = pipe(movie_desc + prompt, targets=["animals", "cars"])
for element in output:
    print(f"Token {element['token_str']}:\t{element['score']:.3f}%")
```

```
Token cars:     0.139%
Token animals:  0.006%
```

It does! This is only a simple example, and if we want to make sure it works well we should test it thoroughly, but it illustrates the key idea of many approaches discussed in this chapter: find a way to adapt a pretrained model for another task without training it. In this case we set up a prompt with a mask in such a way that we can use a masked language model directly for classification. Let's see if we can do better by adapting a model that has been fine-tuned on a task that's closer to text classification: *natural language inference* (NLI).

Using the masked language model for classification is a nice trick, but we can do better still by using a model that has been trained on a task that is closer to classification. There is a neat proxy task called *text entailment* that fits the bill. In text entailment, the model needs to determine whether two text passages are likely to follow or contradict each other. Models are typically trained to detect entailments and contradictions with datasets such as Multi-Genre NLI Corpus (MNLI) or Cross-Lingual NLI Corpus (XNLI).[3]

Each sample in these datasets is composed of three parts: a premise, a hypothesis, and a label, which can be one of `entailment`, `neutral`, or `contradiction`. The `entailment` label is assigned when the hypothesis text is necessarily true under the premise. The `contradiction` label is used when the hypothesis is necessarily false or inappropriate under the premise. If neither of these cases applies, then the `neutral` label is assigned. See Table 9-1 for examples of each.

Table 9-1. The three classes in the MLNI dataset

Premise	Hypothesis	Label
His favourite color is blue.	He is into heavy metal music.	`neutral`
She finds the joke hilarious.	She thinks the joke is not funny at all.	`contradiction`
The house was recently built.	The house is new.	`entailment`

Now, it turns out that we can hijack a model trained on the MNLI dataset to build a classifier without needing any labels at all! The key idea is to treat the text we wish to classify as the premise, and then formulate the hypothesis as:

> "This example is about {label}."

where we insert the class name for the label. The entailment score then tells us how likely that premise is to be about that topic, and we can run this for any number of classes sequentially. The downside of this approach is that we need to execute a forward pass for each class, which makes it less efficient than a standard classifier. Another slightly tricky aspect is that the choice of label names can have a large impact on the accuracy, and choosing labels with semantic meaning is generally the best approach. For example, if the label is simply `Class 1`, the model has no hint what this might mean and whether this constitutes a contradiction or entailment.

🤗 Transformers has an MNLI model for zero-shot classification built in. We can initialize it via a pipeline as follows:

3 A. Williams, N. Nangia, and S.R. Bowman, "A Broad-Coverage Challenge Corpus for Sentence Understanding Through Inference" (*https://arxiv.org/abs/1704.05426*), (2018); A. Conneau et al., "XNLI: Evaluating Cross-Lingual Sentence Representations" (*https://arxiv.org/abs/1809.05053*), (2018).

```
from transformers import pipeline

pipe = pipeline("zero-shot-classification", device=0)
```

The setting `device=0` makes sure that the model runs on the GPU instead of the default CPU to speed up inference. To classify a text, we simply need to pass it to the pipeline along with the label names. In addition, we can set `multi_label=True` to ensure that all the scores are returned and not only the maximum for single-label classification:

```
sample = ds["train"][0]
print(f"Labels: {sample['labels']}")
output = pipe(sample["text"], all_labels, multi_label=True)
print(output["sequence"][:400])
print("\nPredictions:")

for label, score in zip(output["labels"], output["scores"]):
    print(f"{label}, {score:.2f}")
```

```
Labels: ['new model']
Add new CANINE model

# ★ New model addition

## Model description

Google recently proposed a new **C**haracter **A**rchitecture with **N**o
tokenization **I**n **N**eural **E**ncoders architecture (CANINE). Not only the
title is exciting:

> Pipelined NLP systems have largely been superseded by end-to-end neural
modeling, yet nearly all commonly-used models still require an explicit tokeni

Predictions:
new model, 0.98
tensorflow or tf, 0.37
examples, 0.34
usage, 0.30
pytorch, 0.25
documentation, 0.25
model training, 0.24
tokenization, 0.17
pipeline, 0.16
```

Since we are using a subword tokenizer, we can even pass code to the model! The tokenization might not be very efficient because only a small fraction of the pretraining dataset for the zero-shot pipeline consists of code snippets, but since code is also made up of a lot of natural words this is not a big issue. Also, the code block might contain important information, such as the framework (PyTorch or TensorFlow).

We can see that the model is very confident that this text is about a new model, but it also produces relatively high scores for the other labels. An important aspect for zero-shot classification is the domain we're operating in. The texts we are dealing with here are very technical and mostly about coding, which makes them quite different from the original text distribution in the MNLI dataset. Thus, it is not surprising that this is a challenging task for the model; it might work much better for some domains than others, depending on how close they are to the training data.

Let's write a function that feeds a single example through the zero-shot pipeline, and then scale it out to the whole validation set by running `map()`:

```
def zero_shot_pipeline(example):
    output = pipe(example["text"], all_labels, multi_label=True)
    example["predicted_labels"] = output["labels"]
    example["scores"] = output["scores"]
    return example

ds_zero_shot = ds["valid"].map(zero_shot_pipeline)
```

Now that we have our scores, the next step is to determine which set of labels should be assigned to each example. There are a few options we can experiment with:

- Define a threshold and select all labels above the threshold.
- Pick the top *k* labels with the *k* highest scores.

To help us determine which method is best, let's write a `get_preds()` function that applies one of the approaches to retrieve the predictions:

```
def get_preds(example, threshold=None, topk=None):
    preds = []
    if threshold:
        for label, score in zip(example["predicted_labels"], example["scores"]):
            if score >= threshold:
                preds.append(label)
    elif topk:
        for i in range(topk):
            preds.append(example["predicted_labels"][i])
    else:
        raise ValueError("Set either `threshold` or `topk`.")
    return {"pred_label_ids": list(np.squeeze(mlb.transform([preds])))}
```

Next, let's write a second function, `get_clf_report()`, that returns the Scikit-learn classification report from a dataset with the predicted labels:

```
def get_clf_report(ds):
    y_true = np.array(ds["label_ids"])
    y_pred = np.array(ds["pred_label_ids"])
    return classification_report(
        y_true, y_pred, target_names=mlb.classes_, zero_division=0,
        output_dict=True)
```

Armed with these two functions, let's start with the top-*k* method by increasing *k* for several values and then plotting the micro and macro F_1-scores across the validation set:

```
macros, micros = [], []
topks = [1, 2, 3, 4]
for topk in topks:
    ds_zero_shot = ds_zero_shot.map(get_preds, batched=False,
                                    fn_kwargs={'topk': topk})
    clf_report = get_clf_report(ds_zero_shot)
    micros.append(clf_report['micro avg']['f1-score'])
    macros.append(clf_report['macro avg']['f1-score'])

plt.plot(topks, micros, label='Micro F1')
plt.plot(topks, macros, label='Macro F1')
plt.xlabel("Top-k")
plt.ylabel("F1-score")
plt.legend(loc='best')
plt.show()
```

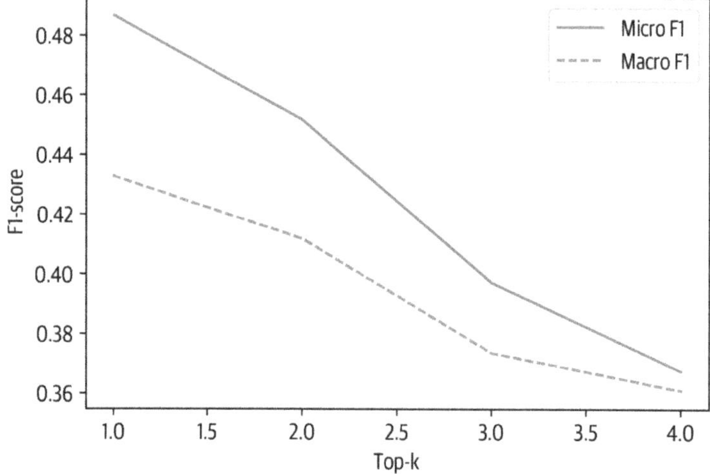

From the plot we can see that the best results are obtained by selecting the label with the highest score per example (top 1). This is perhaps not so surprising, given that most of the examples in our datasets have only one label. Let's now compare this against setting a threshold, so we can potentially predict more than one label per example:

```
macros, micros = [], []
thresholds = np.linspace(0.01, 1, 100)
for threshold in thresholds:
    ds_zero_shot = ds_zero_shot.map(get_preds,
                                    fn_kwargs={"threshold": threshold})
    clf_report = get_clf_report(ds_zero_shot)
```

```
    micros.append(clf_report["micro avg"]["f1-score"])
    macros.append(clf_report["macro avg"]["f1-score"])

plt.plot(thresholds, micros, label="Micro F1")
plt.plot(thresholds, macros, label="Macro F1")
plt.xlabel("Threshold")
plt.ylabel("F1-score")
plt.legend(loc="best")
plt.show()
```

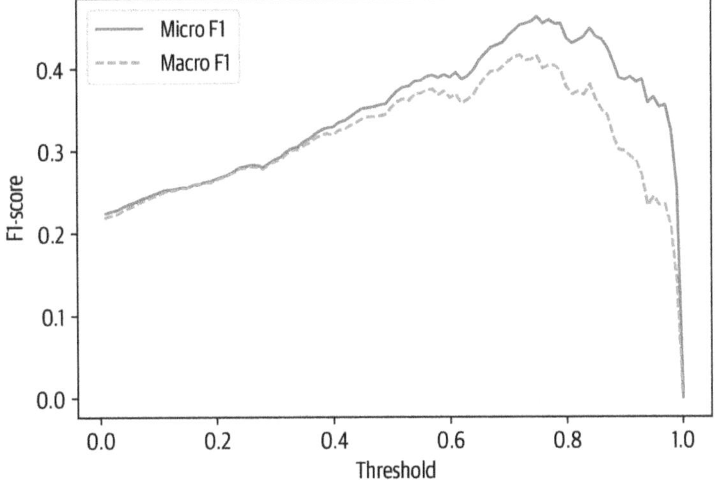


```
best_t, best_micro = thresholds[np.argmax(micros)], np.max(micros)
print(f'Best threshold (micro): {best_t} with F1-score {best_micro:.2f}.')
best_t, best_macro = thresholds[np.argmax(macros)], np.max(macros)
print(f'Best threshold (micro): {best_t} with F1-score {best_macro:.2f}.')
```

```
Best threshold (micro): 0.75 with F1-score 0.46.
Best threshold (micro): 0.72 with F1-score 0.42.
```

This approach fares somewhat worse than the top-1 results, but we can see the precision/recall trade-off clearly in this graph. If we set the threshold too low, then there are too many predictions, which leads to a low precision. If we set the threshold too high, then we will make hardly any predictions, which produces a low recall. From the plot we can see that a threshold value of around 0.8 is the sweet spot between the two.

Since the top-1 method performs best, let's use this to compare zero-shot classification against Naive Bayes on the test set:

```
ds_zero_shot = ds['test'].map(zero_shot_pipeline)
ds_zero_shot = ds_zero_shot.map(get_preds, fn_kwargs={'topk': 1})
clf_report = get_clf_report(ds_zero_shot)
for train_slice in train_slices:
```

```
    macro_scores['Zero Shot'].append(clf_report['macro avg']['f1-score'])
    micro_scores['Zero Shot'].append(clf_report['micro avg']['f1-score'])

plot_metrics(micro_scores, macro_scores, train_samples, "Zero Shot")
```

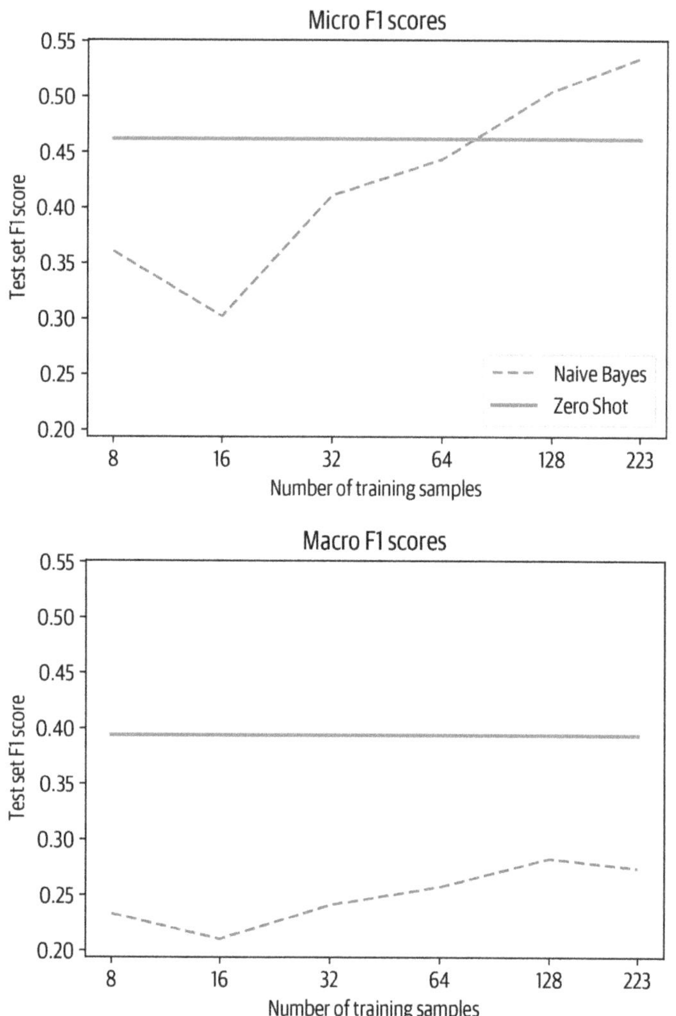

Comparing the zero-shot pipeline to the baseline, we observe two things:

1. If we have less than 50 labeled samples, the zero-shot pipeline handily outperforms the baseline.
2. Even above 50 samples, the performance of the zero-shot pipeline is superior when considering both the micro and macro F_1-scores. The results for the micro F_1-score tell us that the baseline performs well on the frequent classes, while the

zero-shot pipeline excels at those since it does not require any examples to learn from.

You might notice a slight paradox in this section: although we talk about dealing with no labels, we still use the validation and test sets. We use them to showcase different techniques and to make the results comparable between them. Even in a real use case, it makes sense to gather a handful of labeled examples to run some quick evaluations. The important point is that we did not adapt the parameters of the model with the data; instead, we just adapted some hyperparameters.

If you find it difficult to get good results on your own dataset, here are a few things you can do to improve the zero-shot pipeline:

- The way the pipeline works makes it very sensitive to the names of the labels. If the names don't make much sense or are not easily connected to the texts, the pipeline will likely perform poorly. Either try using different names or use several names in parallel and aggregate them in an extra step.
- Another thing you can improve is the form of the hypothesis. By default it is `hypothesis="This is example is about {}"`, but you can pass any other text to the pipeline. Depending on the use case, this might improve the performance.

Let's now turn to the regime where we have a few labeled examples we can use to train a model.

Working with a Few Labels

In most NLP projects, you'll have access to at least a few labeled examples. The labels might come directly from a client or cross-company team, or you might decide to just sit down and annotate a few examples yourself. Even for the previous approach, we needed a few labeled examples to evaluate how well the zero-shot approach worked. In this section, we'll have a look at how we can best leverage the few, precious labeled examples that we have. Let's start by looking at a technique known as data augmentation that can help us multiply the little labeled data that we have.

Data Augmentation

One simple but effective way to boost the performance of text classifiers on small datasets is to apply *data augmentation* techniques to generate new training examples from the existing ones. This is a common strategy in computer vision, where images are randomly perturbed without changing the meaning of the data (e.g., a slightly rotated cat is still a cat). For text, data augmentation is somewhat trickier because perturbing the words or characters can completely change the meaning. For example, the two questions "Are elephants heavier than mice?" and "Are mice heavier than elephants?" differ by a single word swap, but have opposite answers. However, if the text consists of more than a few sentences (like our GitHub issues do), then the noise introduced by these types of transformations will generally not affect the label. In practice, there are two types of data augmentation techniques that are commonly used:

Back translation
: Take a text in the source language, translate it into one or more target languages using machine translation, and then translate it back to the source language. Back translation tends to works best for high-resource languages or corpora that don't contain too many domain-specific words.

Token perturbations
: Given a text from the training set, randomly choose and perform simple transformations like random synonym replacement, word insertion, swap, or deletion.[4]

Examples of these transformations are shown in Table 9-2. For a detailed list of other data augmentation techniques for NLP, we recommend reading Amit Chaudhary's blog post "A Visual Survey of Data Augmentation in NLP" (*https://oreil.ly/j6euX*).

Table 9-2. Different types of data augmentation techniques for text

Augmentation	Sentence
None	Even if you defeat me Megatron, others will rise to defeat your tyranny
Synonym replace	Even if you kill me Megatron, others will prove to defeat your tyranny
Random insert	Even if you defeat me Megatron, others humanity will rise to defeat your tyranny
Random swap	You even if defeat me Megatron, others will rise defeat to tyranny your
Random delete	Even if you me Megatron, others to defeat tyranny
Back translate (German)	Even if you defeat me, others will rise up to defeat your tyranny

You can implement back translation using machine translation models like M2M100 (*https://oreil.ly/gfJCq*), while libraries like *NlpAug* (*https://oreil.ly/UVRci*) and *TextAttack* (*https://oreil.ly/NMtYi*) provide various recipes for token perturbations. In this section, we'll focus on using synonym replacement as it's simple to implement and gets across the main idea behind data augmentation.

4 J. Wei and K. Zou, "EDA: Easy Data Augmentation Techniques for Boosting Performance on Text Classification Tasks" (*https://arxiv.org/abs/1901.11196*), (2019).

We'll use the `ContextualWordEmbsAug` augmenter from NlpAug to leverage the contextual word embeddings of DistilBERT for our synonym replacements. Let's start with a simple example:

```
from transformers import set_seed
import nlpaug.augmenter.word as naw

set_seed(3)
aug = naw.ContextualWordEmbsAug(model_path="distilbert-base-uncased",
                                device="cpu", action="substitute")

text = "Transformers are the most popular toys"
print(f"Original text: {text}")
print(f"Augmented text: {aug.augment(text)}")
```

```
Original text: Transformers are the most popular toys
Augmented text: transformers'the most popular toys
```

Here we can see how the word "are" has been replaced with an apostrophe to generate a new synthetic training example. We can wrap this augmentation in a simple function as follows:

```
def augment_text(batch, transformations_per_example=1):
    text_aug, label_ids = [], []
    for text, labels in zip(batch["text"], batch["label_ids"]):
        text_aug += [text]
        label_ids += [labels]
        for _ in range(transformations_per_example):
            text_aug += [aug.augment(text)]
            label_ids += [labels]
    return {"text": text_aug, "label_ids": label_ids}
```

Now when we pass this function to the `map()` method, we can generate any number of new examples with the `transformations_per_example` argument. We can use this function in our code to train the Naive Bayes classifier by simply adding one line after we select the slice:

```
ds_train_sample = ds_train_sample.map(augment_text, batched=True,
    remove_columns=ds_train_sample.column_names).shuffle(seed=42)
```

Including this and rerunning the analysis produces the plot shown here:

```
plot_metrics(micro_scores, macro_scores, train_samples, "Naive Bayes + Aug")
```

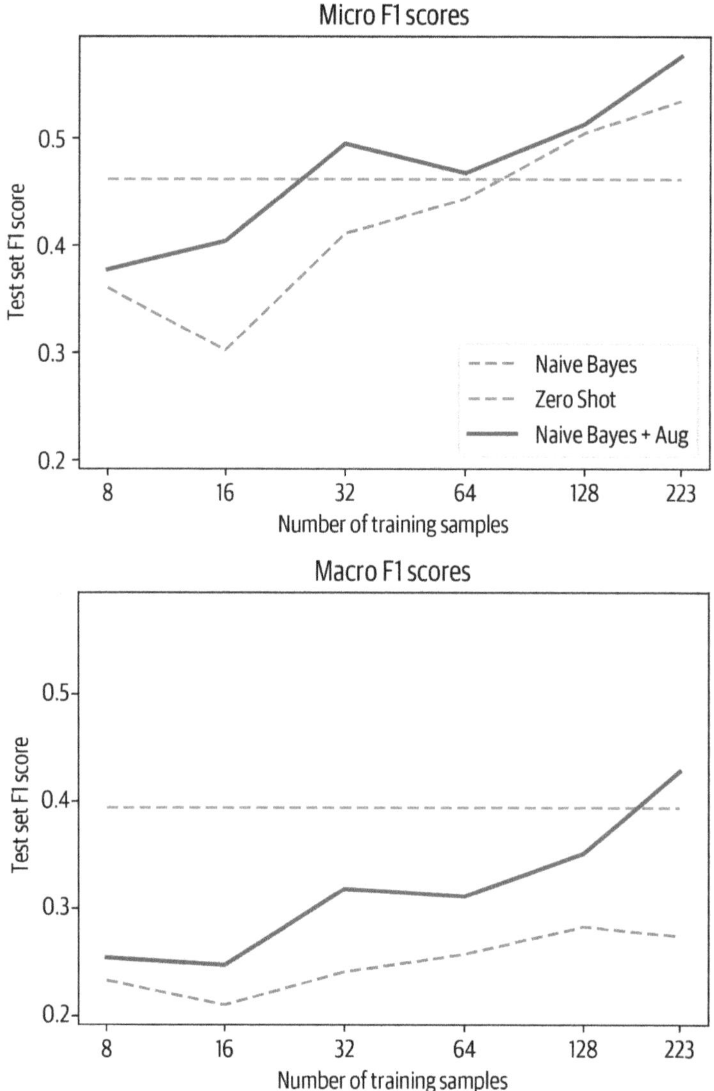

From the figure, we can see that a small amount of data augmentation improves the F_1-score of the Naive Bayes classifier by around 5 points, and it overtakes the zero-shot pipeline for the macro scores once we have around 170 training samples. Let's now take a look at a method based on using the embeddings of large language models.

Using Embeddings as a Lookup Table

Large language models such as GPT-3 have been shown to be excellent at solving tasks with limited data. The reason is that these models learn useful representations of text that encode information across many dimensions, such as sentiment, topic, text structure, and more. For this reason, the embeddings of large language models can be used to develop a semantic search engine, find similar documents or comments, or even classify text.

In this section we'll create a text classifier that's modeled after the OpenAI API classification endpoint (*https://oreil.ly/aMgIr*). The idea follows a three-step process:

1. Use the language model to embed all labeled texts.
2. Perform a nearest neighbor search over the stored embeddings.
3. Aggregate the labels of the nearest neighbors to get a prediction.

The process is illustrated in Figure 9-3, which shows how labeled data is embedded with a model and stored with the labels. When a new text needs to be classified it is embedded as well, and the label is given based on the labels of the nearest neighbors. It is important to calibrate the number of neighbors to be searched for, as too few might be noisy and too many might mix in neighboring groups.

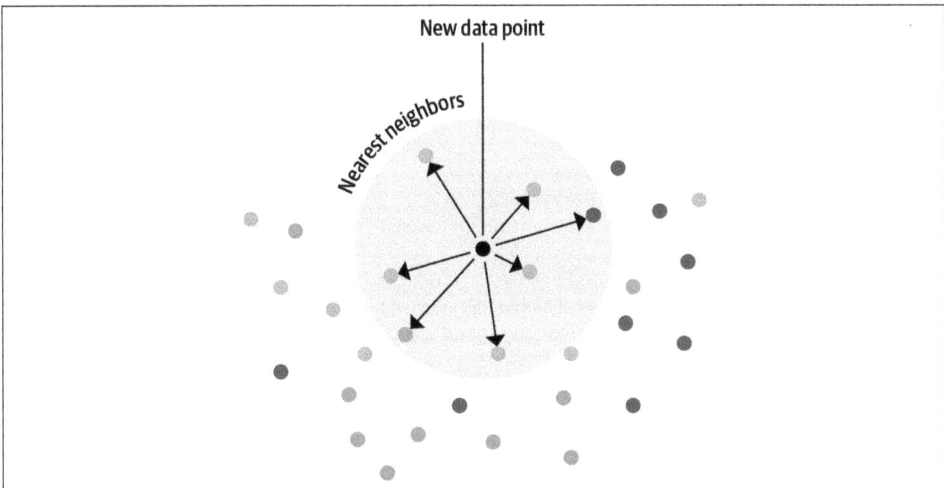

Figure 9-3. An illustration of nearest neighbor embedding lookup

The beauty of this approach is that no model fine-tuning is necessary to leverage the few available labeled data points. Instead, the main decision to make this approach work is to select an appropriate model that is ideally pretrained on a similar domain to your dataset.

Since GPT-3 is only available through the OpenAI API, we'll use GPT-2 to test the technique. Specifically, we'll use a variant of GPT-2 that was trained on Python code, which will hopefully capture some of the context contained in our GitHub issues.

Let's write a helper function that takes a list of texts and uses the model to create a single-vector representation for each text. One problem we have to deal with is that transformer models like GPT-2 will actually return one embedding vector per token. For example, given the sentence "I took my dog for a walk", we can expect several embedding vectors, one for each token. But what we really want is a single embedding vector for the whole sentence (or GitHub issue in our application). To deal with this, we can use a technique called *pooling*. One of the simplest pooling methods is to average the token embeddings, which is called *mean pooling*. With mean pooling, the only thing we need to watch out for is that we don't include padding tokens in the average, so we can use the attention mask to handle that.

To see how this works, let's load a GPT-2 tokenizer and model, define the mean pooling operation, and wrap the whole process in a simple `embed_text()` function:

```
import
from              import AutoTokenizer, AutoModel

model_ckpt = "miguelvictor/python-gpt2-large"
tokenizer = AutoTokenizer.from_pretrained(model_ckpt)
model = AutoModel.from_pretrained(model_ckpt)

def mean_pooling(model_output, attention_mask):
    # Extract the token embeddings
    token_embeddings = model_output[0]
    # Compute the attention mask
    input_mask_expanded = (attention_mask
                           .unsqueeze(-1)
                           .expand(token_embeddings.size())
                           .float())
    # Sum the embeddings, but ignore masked tokens
    sum_embeddings = torch.sum(token_embeddings * input_mask_expanded, 1)
    sum_mask = torch.clamp(input_mask_expanded.sum(1), min=1e-9)
    # Return the average as a single vector
    return sum_embeddings / sum_mask

def embed_text(examples):
    inputs = tokenizer(examples["text"], padding=True, truncation=True,
                       max_length=128, return_tensors="pt")
    with torch.no_grad():
        model_output = model(**inputs)
    pooled_embeds = mean_pooling(model_output, inputs["attention_mask"])
    return {"embedding": pooled_embeds.cpu().numpy()}
```

Now we can get the embeddings for each split. Note that GPT-style models don't have a padding token, and therefore we need to add one before we can get the embeddings in a batched fashion as implemented in the preceding code. We'll just recycle the end-of-string token for this purpose:

```
tokenizer.pad_token = tokenizer.eos_token
embs_train = ds["train"].map(embed_text, batched=True, batch_size=16)
embs_valid = ds["valid"].map(embed_text, batched=True, batch_size=16)
embs_test = ds["test"].map(embed_text, batched=True, batch_size=16)
```

Now that we have all the embeddings, we need to set up a system to search them. We could write a function that calculates, say, the cosine similarity between a new text embedding that we'll query and the existing embeddings in the training set. Alternatively, we can use a built-in structure of 🤗 Datasets called a *FAISS index*.[5] We already encountered FAISS in Chapter 7. You can think of this as a search engine for embeddings, and we'll have a closer look at how it works in a minute. We can use an existing field of the dataset to create a FAISS index with `add_faiss_index()`, or we can load new embeddings into the dataset with `add_faiss_index_from_external_arrays()`. Let's use the former function to add our training embeddings to the dataset as follows:

```
embs_train.add_faiss_index("embedding")
```

This created a new FAISS index called `embedding`. We can now perform a nearest neighbor lookup by calling the function `get_nearest_examples()`. It returns the closest neighbors as well as the matching score for each neighbor. We need to specify the query embedding as well as the number of nearest neighbors to retrieve. Let's give it a spin and have a look at the documents that are closest to an example:

```
i, k = 0, 3 # Select the first query and 3 nearest neighbors
rn, nl = "\r\n\r\n", "\n" # Used to remove newlines in text for compact display

query =  np.array(embs_valid[i]["embedding"], dtype=np.float32)
scores, samples = embs_train.get_nearest_examples("embedding", query, k=k)

print(f"QUERY LABELS: {embs_valid[i]['labels']}")
print(f"QUERY TEXT:\n{embs_valid[i]['text'][:200].replace(rn, nl)} [...]\n")
print("="*50)
print(f"Retrieved documents:")
for score, label, text in zip(scores, samples["labels"], samples["text"]):
    print("="*50)
    print(f"TEXT:\n{text[:200].replace(rn, nl)} [...]")
    print(f"SCORE: {score:.2f}")
    print(f"LABELS: {label}")
```

```
QUERY LABELS: ['new model']
QUERY TEXT:
Implementing efficient self attention in T5
```

5 J. Johnson, M. Douze, and H. Jégou, "Billion-Scale Similarity Search with GPUs" (*https://arxiv.org/abs/1702.08734*), (2017).

```
# ⭐ New model addition
My teammates and I (including @ice-americano) would like to use efficient self
attention methods such as Linformer, Performer and [...]

==================================================
Retrieved documents:
==================================================
TEXT:
Add Linformer model

# ⭐ New model addition
## Model description
### Linformer: Self-Attention with Linear Complexity
Paper published June 9th on ArXiv: https://arxiv.org/abs/2006.04768
La [...]
SCORE: 54.92
LABELS: ['new model']
==================================================
TEXT:
Add FAVOR+ / Performer attention

# ⭐ FAVOR+ / Performer attention addition
Are there any plans to add this new attention approximation block to
Transformers library?
## Model description
The n [...]
SCORE: 57.90
LABELS: ['new model']
==================================================
TEXT:
Implement DeLighT: Very Deep and Light-weight Transformers

# ⭐ New model addition
## Model description
DeLight, that delivers similar or better performance than transformer-based
models with sign [...]
SCORE: 60.12
LABELS: ['new model']
```

Nice! This is exactly what we hoped for: the three retrieved documents that we got via embedding lookup all have the same labels and we can already see from the titles that they are all very similar. The query as well as the retrieved documents revolve around adding new and efficient transformer models. The question remains, however, what is the best value for *k*? Similarly, how we should then aggregate the labels of the retrieved documents? Should we, for example, retrieve three documents and assign all labels that occurred at least twice? Or should we go for 20 and use all labels that appeared at least 5 times? Let's investigate this systematically: we'll try several values for *k* and then vary the threshold $m < k$ for label assignment with a helper function. We'll record the macro and micro performance for each setting so we can decide later which run performed best. Instead of looping over each sample in the validation set we can make use of the function `get_nearest_examples_batch()`, which accepts a batch of queries:

```
def get_sample_preds(sample, m):
    return (np.sum(sample["label_ids"], axis=0) >= m).astype(int)

def find_best_k_m(ds_train, valid_queries, valid_labels, max_k=17):
    max_k = min(len(ds_train), max_k)
    perf_micro = np.zeros((max_k, max_k))
    perf_macro = np.zeros((max_k, max_k))
    for k in range(1, max_k):
        for m in range(1, k + 1):
            _, samples = ds_train.get_nearest_examples_batch("embedding",
                                                             valid_queries, k=k)
            y_pred = np.array([get_sample_preds(s, m) for s in samples])
            clf_report = classification_report(valid_labels, y_pred,
                target_names=mlb.classes_, zero_division=0, output_dict=True)
            perf_micro[k, m] = clf_report["micro avg"]["f1-score"]
            perf_macro[k, m] = clf_report["macro avg"]["f1-score"]
    return perf_micro, perf_macro
```

Let's check what the best values would be with all the training samples and visualize the scores for all *k* and *m* configurations:

```
valid_labels = np.array(embs_valid["label_ids"])
valid_queries = np.array(embs_valid["embedding"], dtype=np.float32)
perf_micro, perf_macro = find_best_k_m(embs_train, valid_queries, valid_labels)

fig, (ax0, ax1) = plt.subplots(1, 2, figsize=(10, 3.5), sharey=True)
ax0.imshow(perf_micro)
ax1.imshow(perf_macro)

ax0.set_title("micro scores")
ax0.set_ylabel("k")
ax1.set_title("macro scores")
for ax in [ax0, ax1]:
    ax.set_xlim([0.5, 17 - 0.5])
    ax.set_ylim([17 - 0.5, 0.5])
    ax.set_xlabel("m")
plt.show()
```

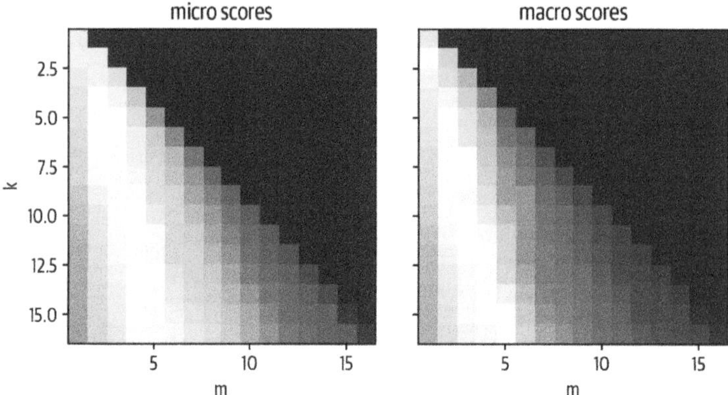

From the plots we can see that there is a pattern: choosing m too large or small for a given k yields suboptimal results. The best performance is achieved when choosing a ratio of approximately $m/k = 1/3$. Let's see which k and m give the best result overall:

```
k, m = np.unravel_index(perf_micro.argmax(), perf_micro.shape)
print(f"Best k: {k}, best m: {m}")
```

```
Best k: 15, best m: 5
```

The perfomance is best when we choose $k = 15$ and $m = 5$, or in other words when we retrieve the 15 nearest neighbors and then assign the labels that occurred at least 5 times. Now that we have a good method for finding the best values for the embedding lookup, we can play the same game as with the Naive Bayes classifier where we go through the slices of the training set and evaluate the performance. Before we can slice the dataset, we need to remove the index since we cannot slice a FAISS index like the dataset. The rest of the loops stay exactly the same, with the addition of using the validation set to get the best k and m values:

```
embs_train.drop_index("embedding")
test_labels = np.array(embs_test["label_ids"])
test_queries = np.array(embs_test["embedding"], dtype=np.float32)

for train_slice in train_slices:
    # Create a Faiss index from training slice
    embs_train_tmp = embs_train.select(train_slice)
    embs_train_tmp.add_faiss_index("embedding")
    # Get best k, m values with validation set
    perf_micro, _ = find_best_k_m(embs_train_tmp, valid_queries, valid_labels)
    k, m = np.unravel_index(perf_micro.argmax(), perf_micro.shape)
    # Get predictions on test set
    _, samples = embs_train_tmp.get_nearest_examples_batch("embedding",
                                                            test_queries,
                                                            k=int(k))
    y_pred = np.array([get_sample_preds(s, m) for s in samples])
    # Evaluate predictions
```

```
    clf_report = classification_report(test_labels, y_pred,
        target_names=mlb.classes_, zero_division=0, output_dict=True,)
    macro_scores["Embedding"].append(clf_report["macro avg"]["f1-score"])
    micro_scores["Embedding"].append(clf_report["micro avg"]["f1-score"])

plot_metrics(micro_scores, macro_scores, train_samples, "Embedding")
```

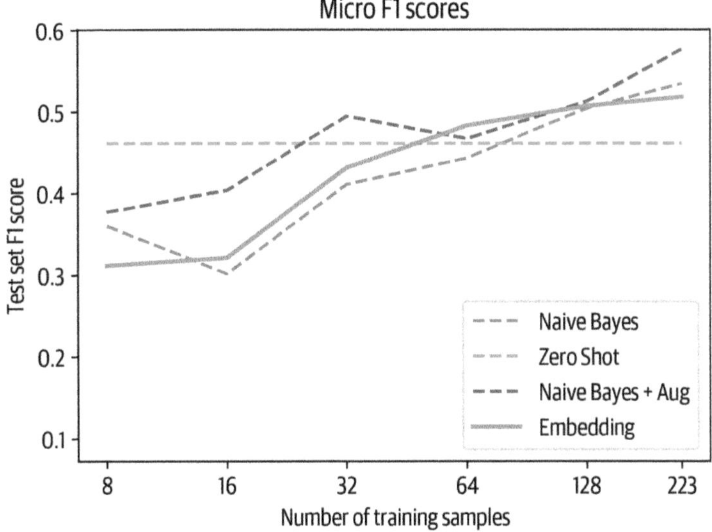

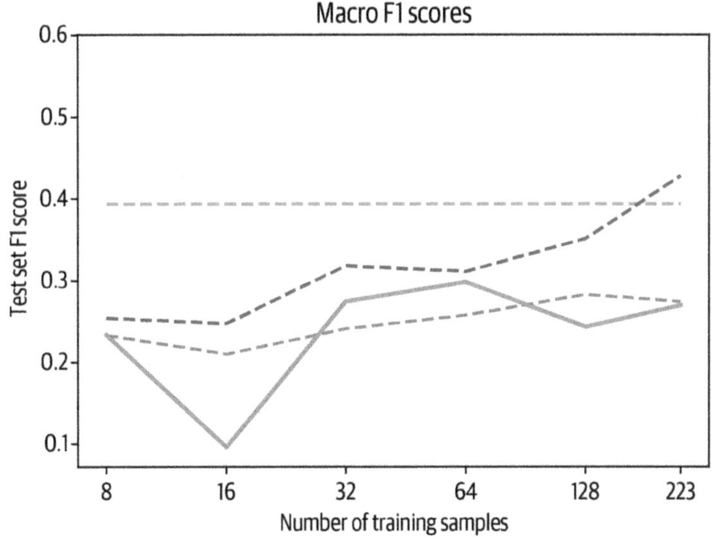

The embedding lookup is competitive on the micro scores with the previous approaches while just having two "learnable" parameters, k and m, but performs slightly worse on the macro scores.

Take these results with a grain of salt; which method works best strongly depends on the domain. The zero-shot pipeline's training data is quite different from the GitHub issues dataset we're using it on, which contains a lot of code that the model likely has not encountered much before. For a more common task such as sentiment analysis of reviews, the pipeline might work much better. Similarly, the embeddings' quality depends on the model and the data it was trained on. We tried half a dozen models, such as `sentence-transformers/stsb-roberta-large`, which was trained to give high-quality embeddings of sentences, and `microsoft/codebert-base` and `dbernsohn/roberta-python`, which were trained on code and documentation. For this specific use case, GPT-2 trained on Python code worked best.

Since you don't actually need to change anything in your code besides replacing the model checkpoint name to test another model, you can quickly try out a few models once you have the evaluation pipeline set up.

Let's now compare this simple embedding trick against simply fine-tuning a transformer on the limited data we have.

Efficient Similarity Search with FAISS

We first encountered FAISS in Chapter 7, where we used it to retrieve documents via the DPR embeddings. Here we'll explain briefly how the FAISS library works and why it is a powerful tool in the ML toolbox.

We are used to performing fast text queries on huge datasets such as Wikipedia or the web with search engines such as Google. When we move from text to embeddings, we would like to maintain that performance; however, the methods used to speed up text queries don't apply to embeddings.

To speed up text search we usually create an inverted index that maps terms to documents. An inverted index works like an index at the end of a book: each word is mapped to the pages (or in our case, document) it occurs in. When we later run a query we can quickly look up in which documents the search terms appear. This works well with discrete objects such as words, but does not work with continuous objects such as vectors. Each document likely has a unique vector, and therefore the index will never match with a new vector. Instead of looking for exact matches, we need to look for close or similar matches.

When we want to find the most similar vectors in a database to a query vector, in theory we need to compare the query vector to each of the n vectors in the database. For a small database such as we have in this chapter this is no problem, but if we scaled this up to thousands or even million of entries we would need to wait a while for each query to be processed.

FAISS addresses this issue with several tricks. The main idea is to partition the dataset. If we only need to compare the query vector to a subset of the database, we can speed up the process significantly. But if we just randomly partition the dataset, how can we decide which partition to search, and what guarantees do we get for finding the most similar entries? Evidently, there must be a better solution: apply k-means clustering to the dataset! This clusters the embeddings into groups by similarity. Furthermore, for each group we get a centroid vector, which is the average of all members of the group (Figure 9-4).

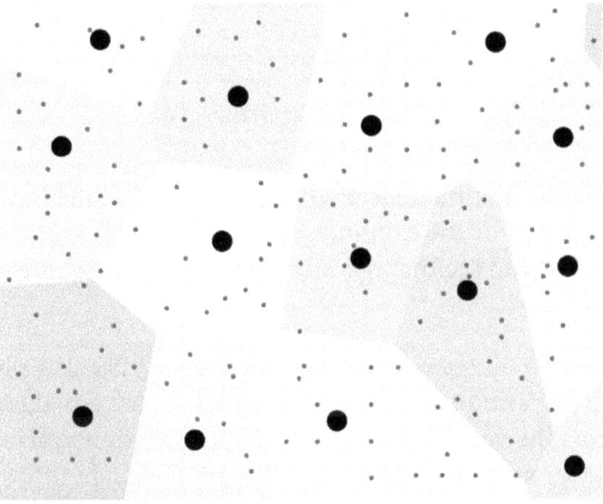

Figure 9-4. The structure of a FAISS index: the gray points represent data points added to the index, the bold black points are the cluster centers found via k-means clustering, and the colored areas represent the regions belonging to a cluster center

Given such a grouping, searching among n vectors is much easier: we first search across the k centroids for the one that is most similar to our query (k comparisons), and then we search within the group ($\frac{k}{n}$ elements to compare). This reduces the number of comparisons from n to $k + \frac{n}{k}$. So the question is, what is the best option for k? If it is too small, each group still contains many samples we need to compare against in the second step, and if k is too large there are many centroids we need to search through. Looking for the minimum of the function $f(k) = k + \frac{n}{k}$ with respect to k, we find $k = \sqrt{n}$. In fact, we can visualize this with the following graphic with $n = 2^{20}$.

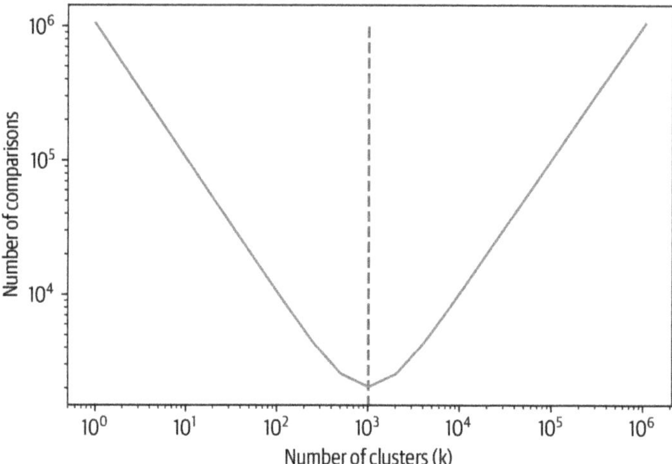

In the plot you can see the number of comparisons as a function of the number of clusters. We are looking for the minimum of this function, where we need to do the least comparisons. We can see that the minimum is exactly where we expected to see it, at $\sqrt{2^{20}} = 2^{10} = 1,024$.

In addition to speeding up queries with partitioning, FAISS also allows you to utilize GPUs for a further speedup. If memory becomes a concern there are also several options to compress the vectors with advanced quantization schemes. If you want to use FAISS for your project, the repository has a simple guide (*https://oreil.ly/QmvzR*) for you to choose the right methods for your use case.

One of the largest projects to use FAISS was the creation of the CCMatrix corpus by Facebook (*https://oreil.ly/ennlr*). The authors used multilingual embeddings to find parallel sentences in different languages. This enormous corpus was subsequently used to train M2M100 (*https://oreil.ly/XzSH9*), a large machine translation model that is able to directly translate between any of 100 languages.

Fine-Tuning a Vanilla Transformer

If we have access to labeled data, we can also try to do the obvious thing: simply fine-tune a pretrained transformer model. In this section, we'll use the standard BERT checkpoint as a starting point. Later, we'll see the effect that fine-tuning the language model has on performance.

For many applications, starting with a pretrained BERT-like model is a good idea. However, if the domain of your corpus differs significantly from the pretraining corpus (which is usually Wikipedia), you should explore the many models that are available on the Hugging Face Hub. Chances are someone has already pretrained a model on your domain!

Let's start by loading the pretrained tokenizer, tokenizing our dataset, and getting rid of the columns we don't need for training and evaluation:

```
import torch
from transformers import (AutoTokenizer, AutoConfig,
                          AutoModelForSequenceClassification)

model_ckpt = "bert-base-uncased"
tokenizer = AutoTokenizer.from_pretrained(model_ckpt)

def tokenize(batch):
    return tokenizer(batch["text"], truncation=True, max_length=128)
ds_enc = ds.map(tokenize, batched=True)
ds_enc = ds_enc.remove_columns(['labels', 'text'])
```

The multilabel loss function expects the labels to be of type float, since it also allows for class probabilities instead of discrete labels. Therefore, we need to change the type of the column `label_ids`. Since changing the format of the column element-wise does not play well with Arrow's typed format, we'll do a little workaround. First, we create a new column with the labels. The format of that column is inferred from the first element. Then we delete the original column and rename the new one to take the place of the original one:

```
ds_enc.set_format("torch")
ds_enc = ds_enc.map(lambda x: {"label_ids_f": x["label_ids"].to(torch.float)},
                    remove_columns=["label_ids"])
ds_enc = ds_enc.rename_column("label_ids_f", "label_ids")
```

Since we are likely to quickly overfit the training data due to its limited size, we set `load_best_model_at_end=True` and choose the best model based on the micro F_1-score:

```
from transformers import Trainer, TrainingArguments

training_args_fine_tune = TrainingArguments(
    output_dir="./results", num_train_epochs=20, learning_rate=3e-5,
    lr_scheduler_type='constant', per_device_train_batch_size=4,
    per_device_eval_batch_size=32, weight_decay=0.0,
    evaluation_strategy="epoch", save_strategy="epoch",logging_strategy="epoch",
    load_best_model_at_end=True, metric_for_best_model='micro f1',
    save_total_limit=1, log_level='error')
```

We need the F_1-score to choose the best model, so we need to make sure it is calculated during the evaluation. Because the model returns the logits, we first need to normalize the predictions with a sigmoid function and can then binarize them with a simple threshold. Then we return the scores we are interested in from the classification report:

```
from scipy.special import expit as sigmoid

def compute_metrics(pred):
    y_true = pred.label_ids
    y_pred = sigmoid(pred.predictions)
    y_pred = (y_pred>0.5).astype(float)

    clf_dict = classification_report(y_true, y_pred, target_names=all_labels,
                                     zero_division=0, output_dict=True)
    return {"micro f1": clf_dict["micro avg"]["f1-score"],
            "macro f1": clf_dict["macro avg"]["f1-score"]}
```

Now we are ready to rumble! For each training set slice we train a classifier from scratch, load the best model at the end of the training loop, and store the results on the test set:

```
config = AutoConfig.from_pretrained(model_ckpt)
config.num_labels = len(all_labels)
config.problem_type = "multi_label_classification"

for train_slice in train_slices:
    model = AutoModelForSequenceClassification.from_pretrained(model_ckpt,
                                                               config=config)
    trainer = Trainer(
        model=model, tokenizer=tokenizer,
        args=training_args_fine_tune,
        compute_metrics=compute_metrics,
        train_dataset=ds_enc["train"].select(train_slice),
        eval_dataset=ds_enc["valid"],)

    trainer.train()
    pred = trainer.predict(ds_enc["test"])
    metrics = compute_metrics(pred)
    macro_scores["Fine-tune (vanilla)"].append(metrics["macro f1"])
    micro_scores["Fine-tune (vanilla)"].append(metrics["micro f1"])

plot_metrics(micro_scores, macro_scores, train_samples, "Fine-tune (vanilla)")
```

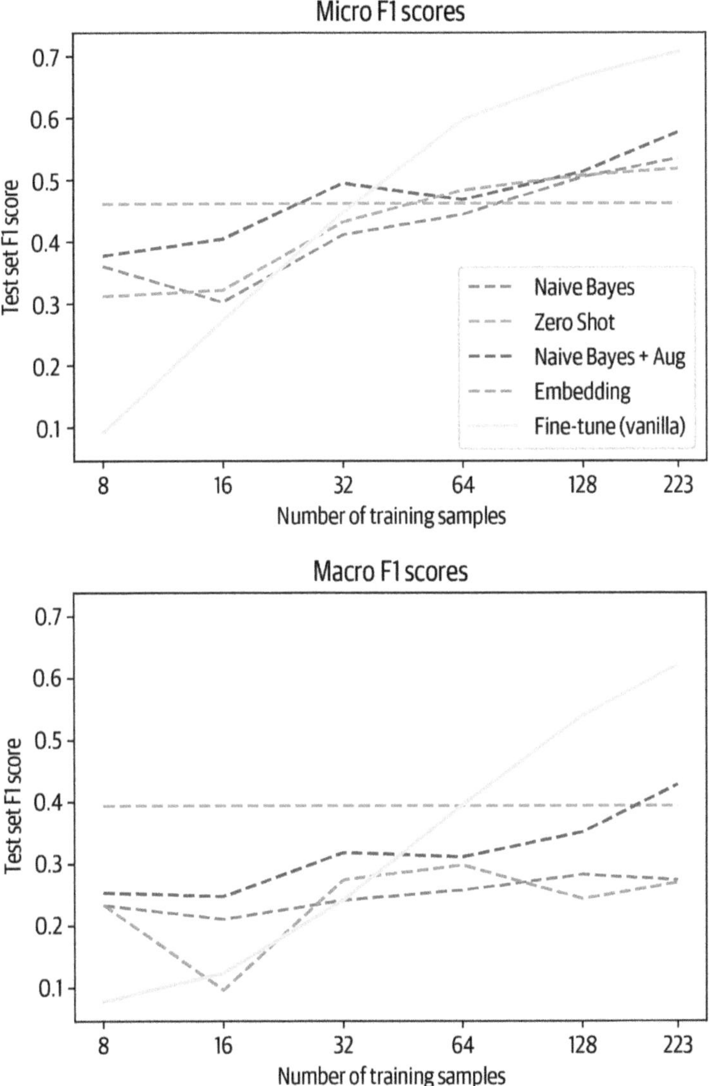

First of all we see that simply fine-tuning a vanilla BERT model on the dataset leads to competitive results when we have access to around 64 examples. We also see that before this the behavior is a bit erratic, which is again due to training a model on a small sample where some labels can be unfavorably unbalanced. Before we make use of the unlabeled part of our dataset, let's take a quick look at another promising approach for using language models in the few-shot domain.

In-Context and Few-Shot Learning with Prompts

We saw earlier in this chapter that we can use a language model like BERT or GPT-2 and adapt it to a supervised task by using prompts and parsing the model's token predictions. This is different from the classic approach of adding a task-specific head and tuning the model parameters for the task. On the plus side, this approach does not require any training data, but on the negative side it seems we can't leverage labeled data if we have access to it. There is a middle ground that we can sometimes take advantage of called *in-context* or *few-shot learning*.

To illustrate the concept, consider an English to French translation task. In the zero-shot paradigm, we would construct a prompt that might look as follows:

```
prompt = """\
Translate English to French:
thanks =>
"""
```

This hopefully prompts the model to predict the tokens of the word "merci". We already saw when using GPT-2 for summarization in Chapter 6 that adding "TL;DR" to a text prompted the model to generate a summary without explicitly being trained to do this. An interesting finding of the GPT-3 paper was the ability of large language models to effectively learn from examples presented in the prompt—so, the previous translation example could be augmented with several English to German examples, which would make the model perform much better on this task.[6]

Furthermore, the authors found that the larger the models are scaled, the better they are at using the in-context examples, leading to significant performance boosts. Although GPT-3-sized models are challenging to use in production, this is an exciting emerging research field and people have built cool applications, such as a natural language shell where commands are entered in natural language and parsed by GPT-3 to shell commands.

An alternative approach to using labeled data is to create examples of the prompts and desired predictions and continue training the language model on these examples. A novel method called ADAPET uses such an approach and beats GPT-3 on a wide variety of tasks,[7] tuning the model with generated prompts. Recent work by Hugging Face researchers suggests that such an approach can be more data-efficient than fine-tuning a custom head.[8]

---

6 T. Brown et al., "Language Models Are Few-Shot Learners" (*https://arxiv.org/abs/2005.14165*), (2020).

7 D. Tam et al., "Improving and Simplifying Pattern Exploiting Training" (*https://arxiv.org/abs/2103.11955*), (2021).

8 T. Le Scao and A.M. Rush, "How Many Data Points Is a Prompt Worth?" (*https://arxiv.org/abs/2103.08493*), (2021).

In this section we briefly looked at various ways to make good use of the few labeled examples that we have. Very often we also have access to a lot of unlabeled data in addition to the labeled examples; in the next section we'll discuss how to make good use of that.

Leveraging Unlabeled Data

Although having access to large volumes of high-quality labeled data is the best-case scenario to train a classifier, this does not mean that unlabeled data is worthless. Just think about the pretraining of most models we have used: even though they are trained on mostly unrelated data from the internet, we can leverage the pretrained weights for other tasks on a wide variety of texts. This is the core idea of transfer learning in NLP. Naturally, if the downstream task has similar textual structure as the pretraining texts the transfer works better, so if we can bring the pretraining task closer to the downstream objective we could potentially improve the transfer.

Let's think about this in terms of our concrete use case: BERT is pretrained on the BookCorpus and English Wikipedia, and texts containing code and GitHub issues are definitely a small niche in these datasets. If we pretrained BERT from scratch we could do it on a crawl of all of the issues on GitHub, for example. However, this would be expensive, and a lot of aspects about language that BERT has learned are still valid for GitHub issues. So is there a middle ground between retraining from scratch and just using the model as is for classification? There is, and it is called domain adaptation (which we also saw for question answering in Chapter 7). Instead of retraining the language model from scratch, we can continue training it on data from our domain. In this step we use the classic language model objective of predicting masked words, which means we don't need any labeled data. After that we can load the adapted model as a classifier and fine-tune it, thus leveraging the unlabeled data.

The beauty of domain adaptation is that compared to labeled data, unlabeled data is often abundantly available. Furthermore, the adapted model can be reused for many use cases. Imagine you want to build an email classifier and apply domain adaptation on all your historic emails. You can later use the same model for named entity recognition or another classification task like sentiment analysis, since the approach is agnostic to the downstream task.

Let's now see the steps we need to take to fine-tune a pretrained language model.

Fine-Tuning a Language Model

In this section we'll fine-tune the pretrained BERT model with masked language modeling on the unlabeled portion of our dataset. To do this we only need two new concepts: an extra step when tokenizing the data and a special data collator. Let's start with the tokenization.

In addition to the ordinary tokens from the text the tokenizer also adds special tokens to the sequence, such as the `[CLS]` and `[SEP]` tokens that are used for classification and next sentence prediction. When we do masked language modeling, we want to make sure we don't train the model to also predict these tokens. For this reason we mask them from the loss, and we can get a mask when tokenizing by setting `return_special_tokens_mask=True`. Let's retokenize the text with that setting:

```
def tokenize(batch):
    return tokenizer(batch["text"], truncation=True,
                     max_length=128, return_special_tokens_mask=True)

ds_mlm = ds.map(tokenize, batched=True)
ds_mlm = ds_mlm.remove_columns(["labels", "text", "label_ids"])
```

What's missing to start with masked language modeling is the mechanism to mask tokens in the input sequence and have the target tokens in the outputs. One way we could approach this is by setting up a function that masks random tokens and creates labels for these sequences. But this would double the size of the dataset, since we would also store the target sequence in the dataset, and it would mean we would use the same masking of a sequence every epoch.

A much more elegant solution is to use a data collator. Remember that the data collator is the function that builds the bridge between the dataset and the model calls. A batch is sampled from the dataset, and the data collator prepares the elements in the batch to feed them to the model. In the simplest case we have encountered, it simply concatenates the tensors of each element into a single tensor. In our case we can use it to do the masking and label generation on the fly. That way we don't need to store the labels and we get new masks every time we sample. The data collator for this task is called `DataCollatorForLanguageModeling`. We initialize it with the model's tokenizer and the fraction of tokens we want to mask via the `mlm_probability` argument. We'll use this collator to mask 15% of the tokens, which follows the procedure in the BERT paper:

```
from              import DataCollatorForLanguageModeling, set_seed

data_collator = DataCollatorForLanguageModeling(tokenizer=tokenizer,
                                                mlm_probability=0.15)
```

Let's have a quick look at the data collator in action to see what it actually does. To quickly show the results in a `DataFrame`, we switch the return formats of the tokenizer and the data collator to NumPy:

```
set_seed(3)
data_collator.return_tensors = "np"
inputs = tokenizer("Transformers are awesome!", return_tensors="np")
```

```
outputs = data_collator([{"input_ids": inputs["input_ids"][0]}])

pd.DataFrame({
    "Original tokens": tokenizer.convert_ids_to_tokens(inputs["input_ids"][0]),
    "Masked tokens": tokenizer.convert_ids_to_tokens(outputs["input_ids"][0]),
    "Original input_ids": original_input_ids,
    "Masked input_ids": masked_input_ids,
    "Labels": outputs["labels"][0]}).T
```

	0	1	2	3	4	5
Original tokens	[CLS]	transformers	are	awesome	!	[SEP]
Masked tokens	[CLS]	transformers	are	awesome	[MASK]	[SEP]
Original input_ids	101	19081	2024	12476	999	102
Masked input_ids	101	19081	2024	12476	103	102
Labels	-100	-100	-100	-100	999	-100

We see that the token corresponding to the exclamation mark has been replaced with a mask token. In addition, the data collator returned a label array, which is –100 for the original tokens and the token ID for the masked tokens. As we have seen previously, the entries containing –100 are ignored when calculating the loss. Let's switch the format of the data collator back to PyTorch:

```
data_collator.return_tensors = "pt"
```

With the tokenizer and data collator in place, we are ready to fine-tune the masked language model. We set up the `TrainingArguments` and `Trainer` as usual:

```
from transformers import AutoModelForMaskedLM

training_args = TrainingArguments(
    output_dir = f"{model_ckpt}-issues-128", per_device_train_batch_size=32,
    logging_strategy="epoch", evaluation_strategy="epoch", save_strategy="no",
    num_train_epochs=16, push_to_hub=True, log_level="error", report_to="none")

trainer = Trainer(
        model=AutoModelForMaskedLM.from_pretrained("bert-base-uncased"),
        tokenizer=tokenizer, args=training_args, data_collator=data_collator,
        train_dataset=ds_mlm["unsup"], eval_dataset=ds_mlm["train"])

trainer.train()

trainer.push_to_hub("Training complete!")
```

We can access the trainer's log history to look at the training and validation losses of the model. All logs are stored in `trainer.state.log_history` as a list of dictionaries that we can easily load into a Pandas `DataFrame`. Since the training and validation loss are recorded at different steps, there are missing values in the dataframe. For this reason we drop the missing values before plotting the metrics:

```
df_log = pd.DataFrame(trainer.state.log_history)

(df_log.dropna(subset=["eval_loss"]).reset_index()["eval_loss"]
 .plot(label="Validation"))
df_log.dropna(subset=["loss"]).reset_index()["loss"].plot(label="Train")

plt.xlabel("Epochs")
plt.ylabel("Loss")
plt.legend(loc="upper right")
plt.show()
```

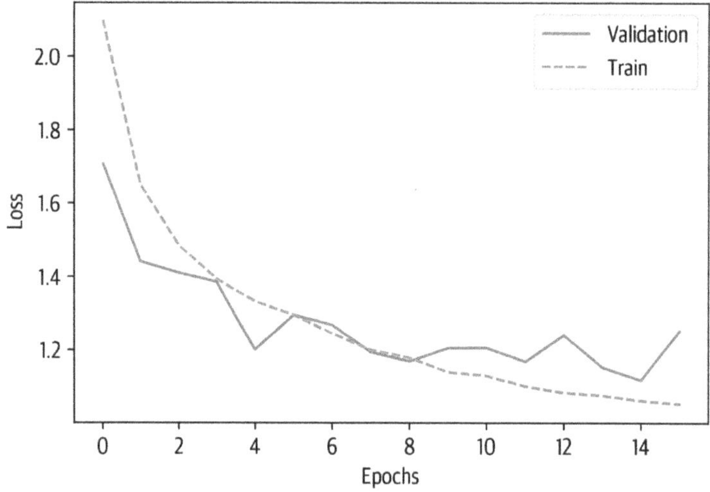

It seems that both the training and validation loss went down considerably. So let's check if we can also see an improvement when we fine-tune a classifier based on this model.

Fine-Tuning a Classifier

Now we'll repeat the fine-tuning procedure, but with the slight difference that we load our own custom checkpoint:

```
model_ckpt = f'{model_ckpt}-issues-128'
config = AutoConfig.from_pretrained(model_ckpt)
config.num_labels = len(all_labels)
config.problem_type = "multi_label_classification"

for train_slice in train_slices:
    model = AutoModelForSequenceClassification.from_pretrained(model_ckpt,
                                                               config=config)
    trainer = Trainer(
        model=model,
        tokenizer=tokenizer,
        args=training_args_fine_tune,
        compute_metrics=compute_metrics,
        train_dataset=ds_enc["train"].select(train_slice),
        eval_dataset=ds_enc["valid"],
    )

    trainer.train()
    pred = trainer.predict(ds_enc['test'])
    metrics = compute_metrics(pred)
    # DA refers to domain adaptation
    macro_scores['Fine-tune (DA)'].append(metrics['macro f1'])
    micro_scores['Fine-tune (DA)'].append(metrics['micro f1'])
```

Comparing the results to the fine-tuning based on vanilla BERT, we see that we get an advantage especially in the low-data domain. We also gain a few percentage points in the regime where more labeled data is available:

```
plot_metrics(micro_scores, macro_scores, train_samples, "Fine-tune (DA)")
```

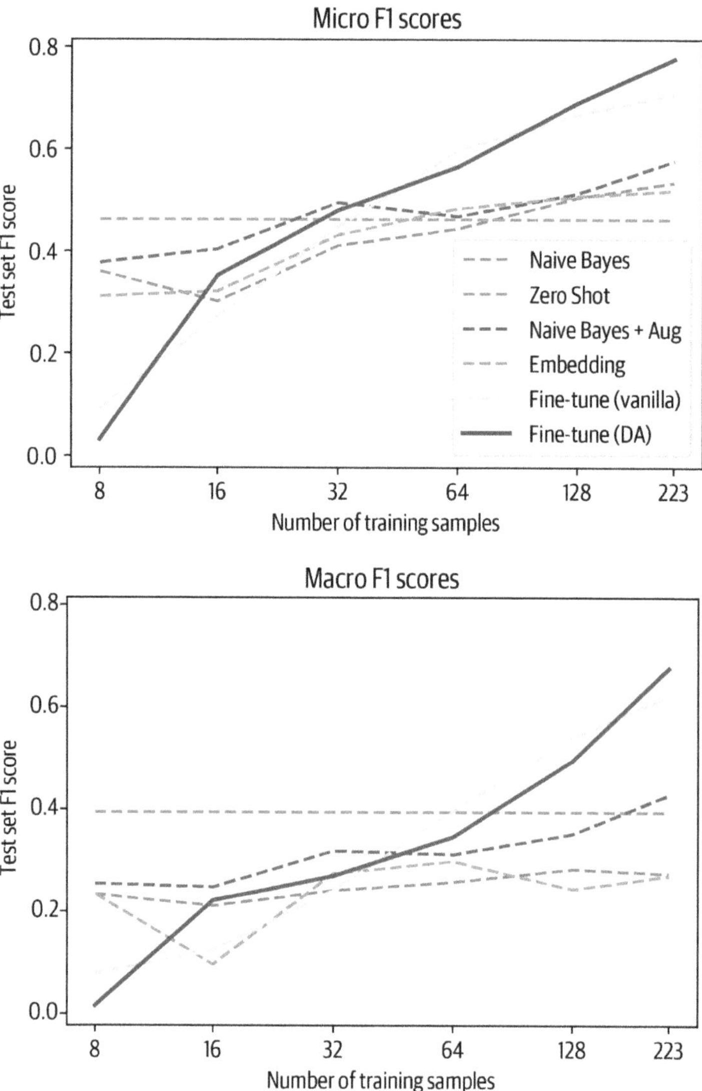

This highlights that domain adaptation can provide a slight boost to the model's performance with unlabeled data and little effort. Naturally, the more unlabeled data and the less labeled data you have, the more impact you will get with this method. Before we conclude this chapter, we'll show you a few more tricks for taking advantage of unlabeled data.

Advanced Methods

Fine-tuning the language model before tuning the classification head is a simple yet reliable method to boost performance. However, there are sophisticated methods than can leverage unlabeled data even further. We summarize a few of these methods here, which should provide a good starting point if you need more performance.

Unsupervised data augmentation

The key idea behind unsupervised data augmentation (UDA) is that a model's predictions should be consistent for an unlabeled example and a slightly distorted one. Such distortions are introduced with standard data augmentation strategies such as token replacement and back translation. Consistency is then enforced by minimizing the KL divergence between the predictions of the original and distorted examples. This process is illustrated in Figure 9-5, where the consistency requirement is incorporated by augmenting the cross-entropy loss with an additional term from the unlabeled examples. This means that one trains a model on the labeled data with the standard supervised approach, but constrains the model to make consistent predictions on the unlabeled data.

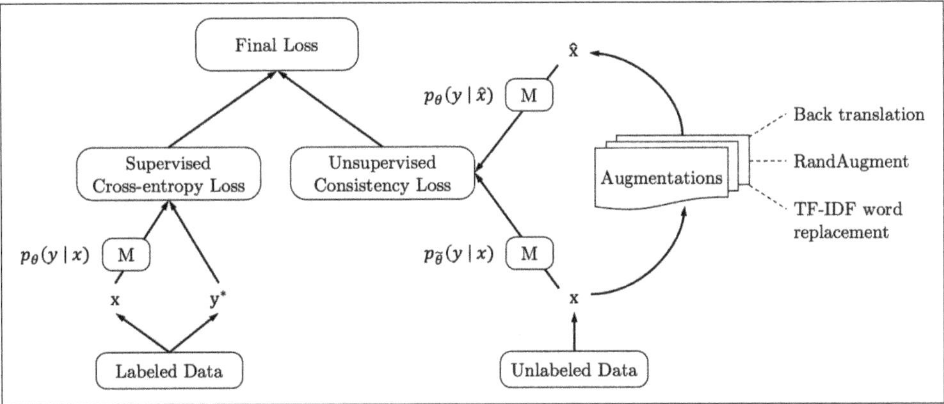

Figure 9-5. Training a model M with UDA (courtesy of Qizhe Xie)

The performance of this approach is quite impressive: with a handful of labeled examples, BERT models trained with UDA get similar performance to models trained on thousands of examples. The downside is that you need a data augmentation pipeline, and training takes much longer since you need multiple forward passes to generate the predicted distributions on the unlabeled and augmented examples.

Uncertainty-aware self-training

Another promising method to leverage unlabeled data is uncertainty-aware self-training (UST). The idea here is to train a teacher model on the labeled data and then use that model to create pseudo-labels on the unlabeled data. Then a student is trained on the pseudo-labeled data, and after training it becomes the teacher for the next iteration.

One interesting aspect of this method is how the pseudo-labels are generated: to get an uncertainty measure of the model's predictions the same input is fed several times through the model with dropout turned on. Then the variance in the predictions gives a proxy for the certainty of the model on a specific sample. With that uncertainty measure the pseudo-labels are then sampled using a method called Bayesian Active Learning by Disagreement (BALD). The full training pipeline is illustrated in Figure 9-6.

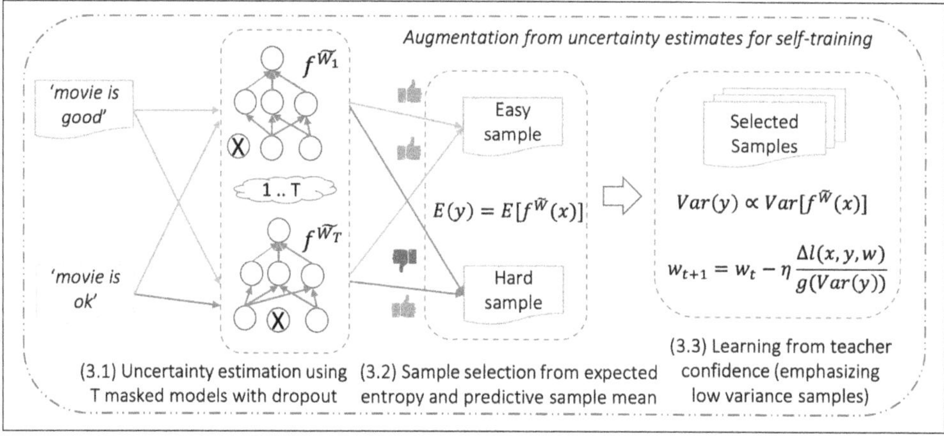

Figure 9-6. The UST method consists of a teacher that generates pseudo-labels and a student that is subsequently trained on those labels; after the student is trained it becomes the teacher and the step is repeated (courtesy of Subhabrata Mukherjee)[9]

With this iteration scheme the teacher continuously gets better at creating pseudo-labels, and thus the model's performance improves. In the end this approach gets within a few percent of models trained on the full training data with thousands of samples and even beats UDA on several datasets.

Now that we've seen a few advanced methods, let's take a step back and summarize what we've learned in this chapter.

9 S. Mukherjee and A.H. Awadallah, "Uncertainty-Aware Self-Training for Few-Shot Text Classification" (*https://arxiv.org/abs/2006.15315*), (2020).

Conclusion

In this chapter we've seen that even if we have only a few or even no labels, not all hope is lost. We can utilize models that have been pretrained on other tasks, such as the BERT language model or GPT-2 trained on Python code, to make predictions on the new task of GitHub issue classification. Furthermore, we can use domain adaptation to get an additional boost when training the model with a normal classification head.

Which of the presented approaches will work best on a specific use case depends on a variety of aspects: how much labeled data you have, how noisy is it, how close the data is to the pretraining corpus, and so on. To find out what works best, it is a good idea to set up an evaluation pipeline and then iterate quickly. The flexible API of 🤗 Transformers allows you to quickly load a handful of models and compare them without the need for any code changes. There are over 10,000 models on the Hugging Face Hub, and chances are somebody has worked on a similar problem in the past and you can build on top of this.

One aspect that is beyond the scope of this book is the trade-off between a more complex approach like UDA or UST and getting more data. To evaluate your approach, it makes sense to at least build a validation and test set early on. At every step of the way you can also gather more labeled data. Usually annotating a few hundred examples is a matter of a couple of hours' or a few days' work, and there are many tools that can assist you in doing so. Depending on what you are trying to achieve, it can make sense to invest some time in creating a small, high-quality dataset rather than engineering a very complex method to compensate for the lack thereof. With the methods we've presented in this chapter you can ensure that you get the most value out of your precious labeled data.

Here, we have ventured into the low-data regime and seen that transformer models are still powerful even with just a hundred examples. In the next chapter we'll look at the complete opposite case: we'll see what we can do when we have hundreds of gigabytes of data and a lot of compute. We'll train a large transformer model from scratch to autocomplete code for us.

CHAPTER 10

Training Transformers from Scratch

In the opening paragraph of this book, we mentioned a sophisticated application called GitHub Copilot that uses GPT-like transformers to perform code autocompletion, a feature that is particularly useful when programming in a new language or framework or learning to code, or for automatically producing boilerplate code. Other products that use AI models for this purpose include TabNine (*https://tabnine.com*) and Kite (*https://kite.com*). Later, in Chapter 5, we had a closer look at how we can use GPT models to generate high-quality text. In this chapter, we'll close the circle and build our very own GPT-like model for generating Python source code! We call the resulting model *CodeParrot*.

So far we've mostly worked on data-constrained applications where the amount of labeled training data is limited. In these cases, transfer learning helped us build performant models. We took transfer learning to the limit in Chapter 9, where we barely used any training data at all.

In this chapter we'll move to the other extreme and look at what we can do when we are drowning in all the data we could possibly want. We'll explore the pretraining step itself and learn how to train a transformer from scratch. In working through this problem, we'll look at some aspects of training that we have not considered yet, such as the following:

- Gathering and processing a very large dataset
- Creating a custom tokenizer for our dataset
- Training a model on multiple GPUs at scale

To efficiently train large models with billions of parameters, we'll need special tools for distributed training. Although the `Trainer` from 🤗 Transformers supports distributed training, we'll take the opportunity to showcase a powerful PyTorch library called 🤗 Accelerate. We'll end up touching on some of the largest NLP models in use today—but first, we need to find a sufficiently large dataset.

Unlike the code in the others in this book (which can be run with a Jupyter notebook on a single GPU), the training code in this chapter is designed to be run as a script with multiple GPUs. If you want to train your own version of CodeParrot, we recommend running the script provided in the 🤗 Transformers repository (*https://oreil.ly/ZyPPR*).

Large Datasets and Where to Find Them

There are many domains where you may actually have a large amount of data at hand, ranging from legal documents to biomedical datasets to programming codebases. In most cases, these datasets are unlabeled, and their large size means that they can usually only be labeled through the use of heuristics, or by using accompanying metadata that is stored during the gathering process.

Nevertheless, a very large corpus can be useful even when it is unlabeled or only heuristically labeled. We saw an example of this in Chapter 9, where we used the unlabeled part of a dataset to fine-tune a language model for domain adaptation. This approach typically yields a performance gain when limited data is available. The decision to train from scratch rather than fine-tune an existing model is mostly dictated by the size of your fine-tuning corpus and the domain differences between the available pretrained models and the corpus.

Using a pretrained model forces you to use the model's corresponding tokenizer, but using a tokenizer that is trained on a corpus from another domain is typically suboptimal. For example, using GPT's pretrained tokenizer on legal documents, other languages, or even completely different sequences such as musical notes or DNA sequences will result in poor tokenization (as we will see shortly).

As the amount of training data you have access to gets closer to the amount of data used for pretraining, it thus becomes interesting to consider training the model and the tokenizer from scratch, provided the necessary computational resources are available. Before we discuss the different pretraining objectives further, we first need to build a large corpus suitable for pretraining. Building such a corpus comes with its own set of challenges, which we'll explore in the next section.

Challenges of Building a Large-Scale Corpus

The quality of a model after pretraining largely reflects the quality of the pretraining corpus. In particular, the model will inherit any defects in the pretraining corpus. Thus, before we attempt to create one of our own it's good to be aware of some of the common issues and challenges that are associated with building large corpora for pretraining.

As the dataset gets larger and larger, the chances that you can fully control—or at least have a precise idea of—what is inside it diminish. A very large dataset will most likely not have been assembled by dedicated creators that craft one example at a time, while being aware and knowledgeable of the full pipeline and the task that the machine learning model will be applied to. Instead, it is much more likely that a very large dataset will have been created in an automatic or semiautomatic way by collecting data that is generated as a side effect of other activities. For instance, it may consist of all the documents (e.g., contracts, purchase orders, etc.) that a company stores, logs from user activities, or data gathered from the internet.

There are several important consequences that follow from the fact that large-scale datasets are mostly created with a high degree of automation. An important consideration is that there is limited control over both their content and the way they are created, and thus the risk of training a model on biased and lower-quality data increases. Recent investigations of famous large-scale datasets like BookCorpus and C4, which were used to train BERT and T5, respectively, have uncovered (among other things) that:[1]

- A significant proportion of the C4 corpus is machine-translated rather than translated by humans.
- Disparate erasure of African-American English as a result of stopword filtering in C4 has resulted in an underrepresentation of such content.
- It is typically difficult in a large text corpus to find a middle ground between including (often too much) sexually or other explicit content and totally erasing all mention of sexuality or gender. As a surprising consequence of this, a rather common word like "sex" (which can have both neutral and explicit meanings) is completely unknown to a tokenizer that is trained on C4, since this word is fully absent from the corpus.
- There are many occurrences of copyright violation in BookCorpus, and probably in other large-scale datasets as well.[2]
- There is genre skew toward "romance" novels in BookCorpus.

---

1 Y. Zhu et al., "Aligning Books and Movies: Towards Story-Like Visual Explanations by Watching Movies and Reading Books" (*https://arxiv.org/abs/1506.06724*), (2015); J. Dodge et al., "Documenting the English Colossal Clean Crawled Corpus" (*https://arxiv.org/abs/2104.08758*), (2021).

2 J. Bandy and N. Vincent, "Addressing *Documentation Debt* in Machine Learning Research: A Retrospective Datasheet for BookCorpus" (*https://arxiv.org/abs/2105.05241*), (2021).

These discoveries might not be incompatible with downstream usage of the models trained on these corpora. For instance, the strong overrepresentation of romance novels in BookCorpus is probably acceptable if the model is intended to be used as a romance novel writing tool or for a building a game.

Let's illustrate the notion of a model being skewed by the data by comparing text generations from GPT and GPT-2. GPT was mostly trained on BookCorpus, while GPT-2 was trained on web pages, blogs, and news articles linked from Reddit. We'll compare similar-sized versions of both models on the same prompt, so that the main difference is the pretraining dataset, and we'll use the `text-generation` pipeline to investigate the model outputs:

```
from transformers import pipeline, set_seed

generation_gpt = pipeline("text-generation", model="openai-gpt")
generation_gpt2 = pipeline("text-generation", model="gpt2")
```

Next, let's create a simple function to count the number of parameters in each model:

```
def model_size(model):
    return sum(t.numel() for t in model.parameters())

print(f"GPT  size: {model_size(generation_gpt.model)/1000**2:.1f}M parameters")
print(f"GPT2 size: {model_size(generation_gpt2.model)/1000**2:.1f}M parameters")
```

```
GPT  size: 116.5M parameters
GPT2 size: 124.4M parameters
```

The original GPT model is about the same size as the smallest GPT-2 model. Now we can generate three different completions from each model, each with the same input prompt:

```
def enum_pipeline_ouputs(pipe, prompt, num_return_sequences):
    out = pipe(prompt, num_return_sequences=num_return_sequences,
               clean_up_tokenization_spaces=True)
    return "\n".join(f"{i+1}." + s["generated_text"] for i, s in enumerate(out))

prompt = "\nWhen they came back"
print("GPT completions:\n" + enum_pipeline_ouputs(generation_gpt, prompt, 3))
print("")
print("GPT-2 completions:\n" + enum_pipeline_ouputs(generation_gpt2, prompt, 3))
```

```
GPT completions:
1.
When they came back.
 " we need all we can get, " jason said once they had settled into the back of
the truck without anyone stopping them. " after getting out here, it 'll be up
to us what to find. for now
2.
When they came back.
 his gaze swept over her body. he 'd dressed her, too, in the borrowed clothes
that she 'd worn for the journey.
```

```
 " i thought it would be easier to just leave you there. " a woman like
3.
When they came back to the house and she was sitting there with the little boy.
 " don't be afraid, " he told her. she nodded slowly, her eyes wide. she was so
lost in whatever she discovered that tom knew her mistake

GPT-2 completions:
1.
When they came back we had a big dinner and the other guys went to see what
their opinion was on her. I did an hour and they were happy with it.
2.
When they came back to this island there had been another massacre, but he could
not help but feel pity for the helpless victim who had been left to die, and
that they had failed that day. And so was very, very grateful indeed.
3.
When they came back to our house after the morning, I asked if she was sure. She
said, "Nope." The two kids were gone that morning. I thought they were back to
being a good friend.

When Dost
```

By just sampling a handful of outputs from both models we can already see the distinctive "romance" skew in GPT generation, which will typically imagine a dialogue with a romantic interaction between a woman and a man. On the other hand, GPT-2 was trained on webtext linked to and from Reddit articles and mostly adopts a neutral "they" in its generations, which contain "blog-like" or adventure-related elements.

In general, any model trained on a dataset will reflect the language bias and over- or underrepresentation of populations and events in its training data. These biases in the behavior of the model are important to take into consideration with regard to the target audience interacting with the model; for some useful guidelines, we refer you to a paper by Google that provides a framework for dataset development.[3]

This brief introduction should give you an idea of the difficult challenges you face when creating large text corpora. With these in mind, let's now take a look at creating our own dataset!

Building a Custom Code Dataset

To simplify the task a bit, we'll focus on building a code generation model for the Python programming language only.[4] The first thing we'll need is a large pretraining corpus consisting of Python source code. Fortunately, there is a natural resource that every software engineer knows: GitHub! The famous code-sharing website hosts

3 B. Hutchinson et al., "Towards Accountability for Machine Learning Datasets: Practices from Software Engineering and Infrastructure" (*https://arxiv.org/abs/2010.13561*), (2020).

4 By comparison, GitHub Copilot supports over a dozen programming languages.

terabytes of code repositories that are openly accessible and can be downloaded and used according to their respective licenses. At the time of this book's writing, GitHub hosts more than 20 million code repositories. Many of them are small or test repositories created by users for learning, future side projects, or testing purposes.

GitHub repositories can be accessed in two main ways:

- Via the GitHub REST API (*https://oreil.ly/brhxw*), like we saw in Chapter 9 when we downloaded all the GitHub issues of the 🤗 Transformers repository
- Via public dataset inventories like Google BigQuery (*https://oreil.ly/dYsVT*)

Since the REST API is rate limited and we need a lot data for our pretraining corpus, we'll use Google BigQuery to extract all the Python repositories. The `bigquery-public-data.github_repos.contents` table contains copies of all ASCII files that are less than 10 MB in size. Projects also need to be open source to be included, as determined by GitHub's License API (*https://oreil.ly/N9zHb*).

The Google BigQuery dataset doesn't contain star or downstream usage information. For those attributes, we can use the GitHub REST API or a service like Libraries.io (*https://libraries.io*) that monitors open source packages. Indeed, a team from GitHub recently released a dataset called CodeSearchNet (*https://oreil.ly/daE43*) that filtered repositories used in at least one downstream task using information from Libraries.io.

Let's have a look at what it takes to create our code dataset with Google BigQuery.

Creating a dataset with Google BigQuery

We'll begin by extracting all the Python files in GitHub public repositories from the snapshot on Google BigQuery. For the sake of reproducibility and in case the policy around free usage of BigQuery changes in the future, we will also share this dataset on the Hugging Face Hub. The steps to export these files are adapted from the TransCoder implementation (*https://oreil.ly/vih2m*) and are as follows:[5]

1. Create a Google Cloud account (a free trial should be sufficient).
2. Create a Google BigQuery project under your account.
3. In this project, create a dataset.
4. In this dataset, create a table where the results of the SQL request will be stored.

5 M.-A. Lachaux et al., "Unsupervised Translation of Programming Languages" (*https://arxiv.org/abs/2006.03511*), (2020).

5. Prepare and run the following SQL query on the `github_repos` (to save the query results, select More > Query Options, check the "Set a destination table for query results" box, and specify the table name):

```
SELECT
  f.repo_name, f.path, c.copies, c.size, c.content, l.license
FROM
  `bigquery-public-data.github_repos.files` AS f
JOIN
  `bigquery-public-data.github_repos.contents` AS c
ON
  f.id = c.id
JOIN
  `bigquery-public-data.github_repos.licenses` AS l
ON
  f.repo_name = l.repo_name
WHERE
  NOT c.binary
  AND ((f.path LIKE '%.py')
    AND (c.size BETWEEN 1024
      AND 1048575))
```

This command processes about 2.6 TB of data to extract 26.8 million files. The result is a dataset of about 50 GB of compressed JSON files, each containing the source code of Python files. We filtered to remove empty files and small files such as *__init__.py* that don't contain much useful information. We also filtered out files larger than 1 MB, and we downloaded the licenses for all the files so we can filter the training data based on licenses if we want later on.

Next, we'll download the results to our local machine. If you try this at home, make sure you have good bandwidth available and at least 50 GB of free disk space. The easiest way to get the resulting table to your local machine is to follow this two-step process:

1. Export your results to Google Cloud:
   a. Create a bucket and a folder in Google Cloud Storage (GCS).
   b. Export your table to this bucket by selecting Export > Export to GCS, with an export format of JSON and gzip compression.
2. To download the bucket to your machine, use the `gsutil` library (*https://oreil.ly/JzgRk*):
   a. Install `gsutil` with `pip install gsutil`.
   b. Configure `gsutil` with your Google account: `gsutil config`.
   c. Copy your bucket on your machine:

```
$ gsutil -m -o
"GSUtil:parallel_process_count=1" cp -r gs://<name_of_bucket>
```

Alternatively, you can directly download the dataset from the Hugging Face Hub with the following command:

```
$ git clone https://huggingface.co/datasets/transformersbook/codeparrot
```

To Filter the Noise or Not?

Anybody can create a GitHub repository, so the quality of the projects varies. There are some conscious choices to be made regarding how we want the system to perform in a real-world setting. Having some noise in the training dataset will make our system more robust to noisy inputs at inference time, but will also make its predictions more random. Depending on the intended use and whole system integration, you may choose more or less noisy data and add pre- and postfiltering operations.

For the educational purposes of the present chapter and to keep the data preparation code concise, we will not filter according to stars or usage and will just grab all the Python files in the GitHub BigQuery dataset. Data preparation, however, is a crucial step, and you should make sure you clean up your dataset as much as possible. In our case a few things to consider are whether to balance the programming languages in the dataset; filter low-quality data (e.g., via GitHub stars or references from other repos); remove duplicated code samples; take copyright information into account; investigate the language used in documentation, comments, or docstrings; and remove personal identifying information such as passwords or keys.

Working with a 50 GB dataset can be challenging; it requires sufficient disk space, and one must be careful not to run out of RAM. In the following section, we'll have a look how 🤗 Datasets helps deal with these constraints of working with large datasets on small machines.

Working with Large Datasets

Loading a very large dataset is often a challenging task, in particular when the data is larger than your machine's RAM. For a large-scale pretraining dataset, this is a very common situation. In our example, we have 50 GB of compressed data and about 200 GB of uncompressed data, which is difficult to extract and load into the RAM memory of a standard-sized laptop or desktop computer.

Thankfully, 🤗 Datasets has been designed from the ground up to overcome this problem with two specific features that allow you to set yourself free from RAM and hard drive space limitations: memory mapping and streaming.

Memory mapping

To overcome RAM limitations, 🤗 Datasets uses a mechanism for zero-copy and zero-overhead memory mapping that is activated by default. Basically, each dataset is cached on the drive in a file that is a direct reflection of the content in RAM memory. Instead of loading the dataset in RAM, 🤗 Datasets opens a read-only pointer to this file and uses it as a substitute for RAM, basically using the hard drive as a direct extension of the RAM memory.

Up to now we have mostly used 🤗 Datasets to access remote datasets on the Hugging Face Hub. Here, we will directly load our 50 GB of compressed JSON files that we have stored locally in the `codeparrot` repository. Since the JSON files are compressed, we first need to decompress them, which 🤗 Datasets takes care of for us. Be careful, because this requires about 180 GB of free disk space! However, it will use almost no RAM. By setting `delete_extracted=True` in the dataset's downloading configuration, we can make sure that we delete all the files we don't need anymore as soon as possible:

```
from datasets import load_dataset, DownloadConfig

download_config = DownloadConfig(delete_extracted=True)
dataset = load_dataset("./codeparrot", split="train",
                       download_config=download_config)
```

Under the hood, 🤗 Datasets extracted and read all the compressed JSON files by loading them in a single optimized cache file. Let's see how big this dataset is once loaded:

```
import psutil

print(f"Number of python files code in dataset : {len(dataset)}")
ds_size = sum(os.stat(f["filename"]).st_size for f in dataset.cache_files)
# os.stat.st_size is expressed in bytes, so we convert to GB
print(f"Dataset size (cache file) : {ds_size / 2**30:.2f} GB")
# Process.memory_info is expressed in bytes, so we convert to MB
print(f"RAM used: {psutil.Process(os.getpid()).memory_info().rss >> 20} MB")
```

```
Number of python files code in dataset : 18695559
Dataset size (cache file) : 183.68 GB
RAM memory used: 4924 MB
```

As we can see, the dataset is much larger than our typical RAM memory, but we can still load and access it, and we're actually using a very limited amount of memory.

You may wonder if this will make our training I/O-bound. In practice, NLP data is usually very lightweight to load in comparison to the model processing computations, so this is rarely an issue. In addition, the zero-copy/zero-overhead format uses Apache Arrow under the hood, which makes it very efficient to access any element. Depending on the speed of your hard drive and the batch size, iterating over the dataset can typically be done at a rate of a few tenths of a GB/s to several GB/s. This is great, but what if you can't free enough disk space to store the full dataset locally? Everybody knows the feeling of helplessness when you get a full disk warning and need to painfully try to reclaim a few GB by looking for hidden files to delete. Luckily, you don't need to store the full dataset locally if you use the streaming feature of 🤗 Datasets!

Streaming

Some datasets (reaching up to 1 TB or more) will be difficult to fit even on a standard hard drive. In this case, an alternative to scaling up the server you are using is to *stream* the dataset. This is also possible with 🤗 Datasets for a number of compressed or uncompressed file formats that can be read line by line, like JSON Lines, CSV, or text (either raw or zip, gzip, or zstandard compressed). Let's load our dataset directly from the compressed JSON files instead of creating a cache file from them:

```
streamed_dataset = load_dataset('./codeparrot', split="train", streaming=True)
```

As you'll see, loading the dataset is instantaneous! In streaming mode, the compressed JSON files will be opened and read on the fly. Our dataset is now an `IterableDataset` object. This means that we cannot access random elements of it, like `streamed_dataset[1264]`, but we need to read it in order, for instance with `next(iter(streamed_dataset))`. It's still possible to use methods like `shuffle()`, but these will operate by fetching a buffer of examples and shuffling within this buffer (the size of the buffer is adjustable). When several files are provided as raw files (like our 184 files here), `shuffle()` will also randomize the order of files for the iteration.

The samples of a streamed dataset are identical to the samples of a nonstreamed dataset, as we can see:

```
iterator = iter(streamed_dataset)

print(dataset[0] == next(iterator))
print(dataset[1] == next(iterator))

True
True
```

The main interest of using a streaming dataset is that loading this dataset will not create a cache file on the drive or require any (significant) RAM memory. The original raw files are extracted and read on the fly when a new batch of examples is requested, and only that batch is loaded in memory. This reduces the memory footprint of our dataset from 180 GB to 50 GB. But we can take this one step further—instead of pointing to the local dataset we can reference the dataset on the Hub, and then directly download samples without downloading the raw files locally:

```
remote_dataset = load_dataset('transformersbook/codeparrot', split="train",
                              streaming=True)
```

This dataset behaves exactly like the previous one, but behind the scenes downloads the examples on the fly. With such a setup, we can then use arbitrarily large datasets on an (almost) arbitrarily small server. Let's push our dataset with a train and validation split to the Hugging Face Hub and access it with streaming.

Adding Datasets to the Hugging Face Hub

Pushing our dataset to the Hugging Face Hub will allow us to:

- Easily access it from our training server.
- See how streaming datasets work seamlessly with datasets from the Hub.
- Share it with the community, including you, dear reader!

To upload the dataset, we first need to log in to our Hugging Face account by running the following command in the terminal and providing the relevant credentials:

```
$ huggingface-cli login
```

This is equivalent to the `notebook_login()` helper function we used in previous chapters. Once this is done, we can directly create a new dataset on the Hub and upload the compressed JSON files. To simplify things, we will create two repositories: one for the train split and one for the validation split. We can do this by running the `repo create` command of the CLI as follows:

```
$ huggingface-cli repo create --type dataset --organization transformersbook \
codeparrot-train
$ huggingface-cli repo create --type dataset --organization transformersbook \
codeparrot-valid
```

Here we've specified that the repository should be a dataset (in contrast to the model repositories used to store weights), along with the organization we'd like to store the repositories under. If you're running this code under your personal account, you can omit the `--organization` flag. Next, we need to clone these empty repositories to our local machine, copy the JSON files to them, and push the changes to the Hub. We will take the last compressed JSON file out of the 184 we have as the validation file (i.e., roughly 0.5 percent of our dataset). Execute these commands to clone the repository from the Hub to your local machine:

```
$ git clone https://huggingface.co/datasets/transformersbook/codeparrot-train
$ git clone https://huggingface.co/datasets/transformersbook/codeparrot-valid
```

Next, copy all but the last GitHub file as the training set:

```
$ cd codeparrot-train
$ cp ../codeparrot/*.json.gz .
$ rm ./file-000000000183.json.gz
```

Then commit the files and push them to the Hub:

```
$ git add .
$ git commit -m "Adding dataset files"
$ git push
```

Now, repeat the process for the validation set:

```
$ cd ../codeparrot-valid
$ cp ../codeparrot/file-000000000183.json.gz .
$ mv ./file-000000000183.json.gz ./file-000000000183_validation.json.gz
$ git add .
$ git commit -m "Adding dataset files"
$ git push
```

The `git add .` step can take a couple of minutes since a hash of all the files is computed. Uploading all the files will also take a little while. Since this will enable us to use streaming later in the chapter, however, this is not lost time, and this step will allow us to go significantly faster in the rest of our experiments. Note that we added a `_validation` suffix to the validation filename. This will enable us to load it later as a validation split.

And that's it! Our two splits of the dataset as well as the full dataset are now live on the Hugging Face Hub at the following URLs:

- *https://huggingface.co/datasets/transformersbook/codeparrot*
- *https://huggingface.co/datasets/transformersbook/codeparrot-train*
- *https://huggingface.co/datasets/transformersbook/codeparrot-valid*

It's good practice to add README cards that explain how the datasets were created and provide as much useful information about them as possible. A well-documented dataset is more likely to be useful to other people, as well as your future self. You can read the 🤗 Datasets README guide (*https://oreil.ly/Tv9bq*) for a detailed description of how to write good dataset documentation. You can also use the web editor to modify your README cards directly on the Hub later.

Building a Tokenizer

Now that we have gathered and loaded our large dataset, let's see how we can efficiently process the data to feed to our model. In the previous chapters we've used tokenizers that accompanied the models we used. This made sense since these models were pretrained using data passed through a specific preprocessing pipeline defined in the tokenizer. When using a pretrained model, it's important to stick with the same preprocessing design choices selected for pretraining. Otherwise the model may be fed out-of-distribution patterns or unknown tokens.

However, when we train a new model, using a tokenizer prepared for another dataset can be suboptimal. Here are a few examples of the kinds of problems we might run into when using an existing tokenizer:

- The T5 tokenizer was trained on the C4 (*https://oreil.ly/wsYIC*) corpus that we encountered earlier, but an extensive step of stopword filtering was used to create it. As a result, the T5 tokenizer has never seen common English words such as "sex."
- The CamemBERT tokenizer was also trained on a very large corpus of text, but only comprising French text (the French subset of the OSCAR (*https://oreil.ly/hgO5J*) corpus). As such, it is unaware of common English words such "being."

We can easily test these features of each tokenizer in practice:

```
from transformers import AutoTokenizer

def tok_list(tokenizer, string):
    input_ids = tokenizer(string, add_special_tokens=False)["input_ids"]
    return [tokenizer.decode(tok) for tok in input_ids]

tokenizer_T5 = AutoTokenizer.from_pretrained("t5-base")
tokenizer_camembert = AutoTokenizer.from_pretrained("camembert-base")

print(f'T5 tokens for "sex": {tok_list(tokenizer_T5,"sex")}')
print(f'CamemBERT tokens for "being": {tok_list(tokenizer_camembert,"being")}')
```

```
T5 tokens for "sex": ['', 's', 'ex']
CamemBERT tokens for "being": ['be', 'ing']
```

In many cases, splitting such short and common words into subparts will be inefficient, since this will increase the input sequence length of the model (which has limited context). Therefore, it's important to be aware of the domain and preprocessing of the dataset that was used to train the tokenizer. The tokenizer and model can encode bias from the dataset that has an impact on the downstream behavior of the model. To create an optimal tokenizer for our dataset, we thus need to train one ourselves. Let's see how this can be done.

Training a model involves starting from a given set of weights and using backpropagation from an error signal on a designed objective to minimize the loss of the model and find an optimal set of weights for the model to perform the task defined by the training objective. Training a tokenizer, on the other hand, does *not* involve backpropagation or weights. It is a way to create an optimal mapping from a string of text to a list of integers that can be ingested by the model. In today's tokenizers, the optimal string-to-integer conversion involves a vocabulary consisting of a list of atomic strings and an associated method to convert, normalize, cut, or map a text string into a list of indices with this vocabulary. This list of indices is then the input for our neural network.

The Tokenizer Model

As you saw in Chapter 4, the tokenizer is a processing pipeline consisting of four steps: normalization, pretokenization, the tokenizer model, and postprocessing. The part of the tokenizer pipeline that can be trained on data is the tokenizer model. As we discussed in Chapter 2, there are several subword tokenization algorithms that can be used, such as BPE, WordPiece, and Unigram.

BPE starts from a list of basic units (single characters) and creates a vocabulary by a process of progressively creating new tokens formed by merging the most frequently co-occurring basic units and adding them to the vocabulary. This process is reiterated until a predefined vocabulary size is reached.

Unigram starts from the other end, by initializing its base vocabulary with all the words in the corpus, and potential subwords. Then it progressively removes or splits the less useful tokens to obtain a smaller and smaller vocabulary, until the target vocabulary size is reached. WordPiece is a predecessor of Unigram, and its official implementation was never open-sourced by Google.

The impact of these various algorithms on downstream performance varies depending on the task, and overall it's quite difficult to identify if one algorithm is clearly superior to the others. Both BPE and Unigram have reasonable performance in most cases, but let's have a look at some aspects to consider when evaluating.

Measuring Tokenizer Performance

The optimality and performance of a tokenizer are challenging to measure in practice. Some possible metrics include:

- *Subword fertility*, which calculates the average number of subwords produced per tokenized word

- *Proportion of continued words*, which refers to the proportion of tokenized words in a corpus that are split into at least two subtokens
- *Coverage metrics* like the proportion of unknown words or rarely used tokens in a tokenized corpus

In addition, robustness to misspelling or noise is often estimated, as well as model performance on such out-of-domain examples, as this strongly depends on the tokenization process.

These measures give a set of different views on the tokenizer's performance, but they tend to ignore the interaction of the tokenizer with the model. For example, subword fertility can be minimized by including all the possible words in the vocabulary, but this will produce a very large vocabulary for the model.

In the end, the performance of the various tokenization approaches is thus generally best estimated by using the downstream performance of the model as the ultimate metric. For instance, the good performance of early BPE approaches was demonstrated by showing improved performance on machine translation tasks by models trained using these tokenizers and vocabularies instead of character- or word-based tokenization.

Let's see how we can build our own tokenizer optimized for Python code.

A Tokenizer for Python

We need a custom tokenizer for our use case: tokenizing Python code. The question of pretokenization merits some discussion for programming languages. If we split on whitespaces and remove them, we will lose all the indentation information, which in Python is important for the semantics of the program (just think about `while` loops, or `if-then-else` statements). On the other hand, line breaks are not meaningful and can be added or removed without impact on the semantics. Similarly, splitting on punctuation, like an underscore, which is used to compose a single variable name from several subparts, might not make as much sense as it would in natural language. Using a natural language pretokenizer for tokenizing code thus seems potentially suboptimal.

Let's see if there are any tokenizers in the collection provided on the Hub that might be useful to us. We want a tokenizer that preserves spaces, so a good candidate could be a byte-level tokenizer like the one from GPT-2. Let's load this tokenizer and explore its tokenization properties:

```
from transformers import AutoTokenizer

python_code = r"""def say_hello():
    print("Hello, World!")
```

```
# Print it
say_hello()
"""
tokenizer = AutoTokenizer.from_pretrained("gpt2")
print(tokenizer(python_code).tokens())
```

```
['def', 'Ġsay', '_', 'hello', '():', 'Ċ', 'Ġ', 'Ġ', 'Ġ', 'Ġprint', '("',
'Hello', ',', 'ĠWorld', '!"', ')', 'Ġ#', 'ĠPrint', 'Ġit', 'Ċ', 'Ċ', 'say', '_',
'hello', '()', 'Ċ']
```

Python has a built-in `tokenize` module that splits Python code strings into meaningful units (code operation, comments, indent and dedent, etc.). One issue with using this approach is that this pretokenizer is Python-based and as such is typically rather slow and limited by the Python global interpreter lock (GIL). On the other hand, most of the tokenizers in the 🤗 Transformers library are provided by the 🤗 Tokenizers library and are coded in Rust. The Rust tokenizers are many orders of magnitude faster to train and to use, and we will thus likely want to use them given the size of our corpus.

This is quite a strange output, so let's try to understand what is happening here by running the various submodules of the tokenizer's pipeline. First let's see what normalization is applied in this tokenizer:

```
print(tokenizer.backend_tokenizer.normalizer)
```

```
None
```

As we can see, the GPT-2 tokenizer uses no normalization. It works directly on the raw Unicode inputs without any normalization steps. Let's now take a look at the pretokenization:

```
print(tokenizer.backend_tokenizer.pre_tokenizer.pre_tokenize_str(python_code))
```

```
[('def', (0, 3)), ('Ġsay', (3, 7)), ('_', (7, 8)), ('hello', (8, 13)), ('():',
(13, 16)), ('ĊĠĠĠ', (16, 20)), ('Ġprint', (20, 26)), ('("', (26, 28)), ('Hello',
(28, 33)), (',', (33, 34)), ('ĠWorld', (34, 40)), ('!")', (40, 43)), ('Ġ#', (43,
45)), ('ĠPrint', (45, 51)), ('Ġit', (51, 54)), ('Ċ', (54, 55)), ('Ċ', (55, 56)),
('say', (56, 59)), ('_', (59, 60)), ('hello', (60, 65)), ('()', (65, 67)), ('Ċ',
(67, 68))]
```

What are all these `Ġ` symbols, and what are the numbers accompanying the tokens? Let's explain both and see if we can understand better how this tokenizer works.

Let's start with the numbers. 🤗 Tokenizers has a very useful feature for switching between strings and tokens, called *offset tracking*. All the operations on the input string are tracked so that it's possible to know exactly what part of the input string a token after tokenization corresponds to. These numbers simply indicate where in the original string each token comes from; for instance, the word `'hello'` in the first line corresponds to the characters 8 to 13 in the original string. If some characters are removed in a normalization step, we are thus still able to associate each token with the respective part in the original string.

The other curious feature of the tokenized text is the odd-looking characters, such as Ċ and Ġ. *Byte-level* means that this tokenizer works on bytes instead of Unicode characters. Each Unicode character is composed of between 1 and 4 bytes, depending on the character. The nice thing about bytes is that while there are 143,859 Unicode characters in the Unicode alphabet, there are only 256 elements in the byte alphabet, and you can express each Unicode character as a sequence of these bytes. If we work on bytes we can thus express all the strings composed from the UTF-8 world as longer strings in this alphabet of 256 values. That is, we can have a model using an alphabet of only 256 words and be able to process any Unicode string. Let's have a look at what the byte representations of some characters look like:

```
a, e = u"a", u"€"
byte = ord(a.encode("utf-8"))
print(f'`{a}` is encoded as `{a.encode("utf-8")}` with a single byte: {byte}')
byte = [ord(chr(i)) for i in e.encode("utf-8")]
print(f'`{e}` is encoded as `{e.encode("utf-8")}` with three bytes: {byte}')
```

```
`a` is encoded as `b'a'` with a single byte: 97
`€` is encoded as `b'\xe2\x82\xac'` with three bytes: [226, 130, 172]
```

At this point you might wonder: why work on a byte level? Think back to our discussion in Chapter 2 about the trade-offs between character and word tokens. We could decide to build our vocabulary from the 143,859 Unicode characters, but we would also like to include words—i.e., combinations of Unicode characters—in our vocabulary, so this (already very large) size is only a lower bound for the total size of the vocabulary. This will make our model's embedding layer very large because it comprises one vector for each vocabulary token.

On the other extreme, if we only use the 256 byte values as our vocabulary, the input sequences will be segmented in many small pieces (each byte constituting the Unicode characters), and as such our model will have to work on long inputs and spend significant compute power on reconstructing Unicode characters from their separate bytes, and then words from these characters. See the paper accompanying the ByT5 model release for a detailed study of this overhead.[6]

A middle-ground solution is to construct a medium-sized vocabulary by extending the 256-word vocabulary with the most common combinations of bytes. This is the approach taken by the BPE algorithm. The idea is to progressively construct a vocabulary of a predefined size by creating new vocabulary tokens through iteratively

6 L. Xue et al., "ByT5: Towards a Token-Free Future with Pre-Trained Byte-to-Byte Models" (*https://arxiv.org/abs/2105.13626*), (2021).

merging the most frequently co-occurring pair of tokens in the vocabulary. For instance, if t and h occur very frequently together, like in English, we'll add a token th to the vocabulary to model this pair of tokens instead of keeping them separated. The t and h tokens are kept in the vocabulary to tokenize instances where they do not occur together. Starting from a basic vocabulary of elementary units, we can then model any string efficiently.

Be careful not to confuse the "byte" in "Byte-Pair Encoding" with the "byte" in "byte-level." The name Byte-Pair Encoding comes from a data compression technique proposed by Philip Gage in 1994, originally operating on bytes.[7] Unlike what this name might indicate, standard BPE algorithms in NLP typically operate on Unicode strings rather than bytes (although there is a new type of BPE that specifically works on bytes, called *byte-level BPE*). If we read our Unicode strings in bytes we can thus reuse a simple BPE subword splitting algorithm.

There is just one issue when using a typical BPE algorithm in NLP. These algorithms are designed to work with clean Unicode string as inputs, not bytes, and expect regular ASCII characters in the inputs, without spaces or control characters. But in the Unicode characters corresponding to the 256 first bytes, there are many control characters (newline, tab, escape, line feed, and other nonprintable characters). To overcome this problem, the GPT-2 tokenizer first maps all the 256 input bytes to Unicode strings that can easily be digested by the standard BPE algorithms—that is, we will map our 256 elementary values to Unicode strings that all correspond to standard printable Unicode characters.

It's not very important that these Unicode characters are each encoded with 1 byte or more; what is important is that we have 256 single values at the end, forming our base vocabulary, and that these 256 values are correctly handled by our BPE algorithm. Let's see some examples of this mapping with the GPT-2 tokenizer. We can access the entire mapping as follows:

```
from                                              import bytes_to_unicode

byte_to_unicode_map = bytes_to_unicode()
unicode_to_byte_map = dict((v, k) for k, v in byte_to_unicode_map.items())
base_vocab = list(unicode_to_byte_map.keys())

print(f'Size of our base vocabulary: {len(base_vocab)}')
print(f'First element: `{base_vocab[0]}`, last element: `{base_vocab[-1]}`')
```

7 P. Gage, "A New Algorithm for Data Compression," *The C Users Journal* 12, no. 2 (1994): 23–38, *https://dx.doi.org/10.14569/IJACSA.2012.030803*.

```
Size of our base vocabulary: 256
First element: `!`, last element: `Ń`
```

And we can take a look at some common values of bytes and associated mapped Unicode characters in Table 10-1.

Table 10-1. Examples of character mappings in BPE

Description	Character	Bytes	Mapped bytes
Regular characters	\`a\` and \`?\`	97 and 63	\`a\` and \`?\`
A nonprintable control character (carriage return)	\`U+000D\`	13	\`č\`
A space	\` \`	32	\`Ġ\`
A nonbreakable space	\`\xa0\`	160	\`ł\`
A newline character	\`\n\`	10	\`Ċ\`

We could have used a more explicit conversion, like mapping newlines to a `NEWLINE` string, but BPE algorithms are typically designed to work on characters. For this reason, keeping one Unicode character for each byte character is easier to handle with an out-of-the-box BPE algorithm. Now that we have been introduced to the dark magic of Unicode encodings, we can understand our tokenization conversion a bit better:

```
print(tokenizer.backend_tokenizer.pre_tokenizer.pre_tokenize_str(python_code))
```

```
[('def', (0, 3)), ('Ġsay', (3, 7)), ('_', (7, 8)), ('hello', (8, 13)), ('():',
(13, 16)), ('ĊĠĠĠ', (16, 20)), ('Ġprint', (20, 26)), ('("', (26, 28)), ('Hello',
(28, 33)), (',', (33, 34)), ('ĠWorld', (34, 40)), ('!")', (40, 43)), ('Ġ#', (43,
45)), ('ĠPrint', (45, 51)), ('Ġit', (51, 54)), ('Ċ', (54, 55)), ('Ċ', (55, 56)),
('say', (56, 59)), ('_', (59, 60)), ('hello', (60, 65)), ('()', (65, 67)), ('Ċ',
(67, 68))]
```

We can recognize the newlines, which as we now know are mapped to Ċ, and the spaces, mapped to Ġ. We also see that:

- Spaces, and in particular consecutive spaces, are conserved (for instance, the three spaces in `'ĊĠĠĠ'`).
- Consecutive spaces are considered as a single word.
- Each space preceding a word is attached to and considered a part of the subsequent word (e.g., in `'Ġsay'`).

Let's now experiment with the BPE model. As we've mentioned, it's in charge of splitting the words into subunits until all subunits belong to the predefined vocabulary.

The vocabulary of our GPT-2 tokenizer comprises 50,257 words:

- The base vocabulary with the 256 values of the bytes

- 50,000 additional tokens created by repeatedly merging the most commonly co-occurring tokens
- A special character added to the vocabulary to represent document boundaries

We can easily check that by looking at the length attribute of the tokenizer:

```
print(f"Size of the vocabulary: {len(tokenizer)}")
```

```
Size of the vocabulary: 50257
```

Running the full pipeline on our input code gives us the following output:

```
print(tokenizer(python_code).tokens())
```

```
['def', 'Ġsay', '_', 'hello', '():', 'Ċ', 'Ġ', 'Ġ', 'Ġ', 'Ġprint', '("',
'Hello', ',', 'ĠWorld', '!"', ')', 'Ġ#', 'ĠPrint', 'Ġit', 'Ċ', 'Ċ', 'say', '_',
'hello', '()', 'Ċ']
```

As we can see, the BPE tokenizer keeps most of the words but will split the multiple spaces of our indentation into several consecutive spaces. This happens because this tokenizer is not specifically trained on code, but mostly on texts where consecutive spaces are rare. The BPE model thus doesn't include a specific token in the vocabulary for indentation. This is a case where the tokenizer model is poorly suited for the dataset's domain. As we discussed earlier, the solution is to retrain the tokenizer on the target corpus. So let's get to it!

Training a Tokenizer

Let's retrain our byte-level BPE tokenizer on a slice of our corpus to get a vocabulary better adapted to Python code. Retraining a tokenizer provided by 🤗 Transformers is simple. We just need to:

- Specify our target vocabulary size.
- Prepare an iterator to supply lists of input strings to process to train the tokenizer's model.
- Call the `train_new_from_iterator()` method.

Unlike deep learning models, which are often expected to memorize a lot of specific details from the training corpus, tokenizers are really just trained to extract the main statistics. In a nutshell, the tokenizer is just trained to know which letter combinations are the most frequent in our corpus.

Therefore, you don't necessarily need to train your tokenizer on a very large corpus; the corpus just needs to be representative of your domain and big enough for the tokenizer to extract statistically significant measures. But depending on the vocabulary size and the exact texts in the corpus, the tokenizer can end up storing unexpected words. We can see this, for instance, when looking at the longest words in the vocabulary of the GPT-2 tokenizer:

```
tokens = sorted(tokenizer.vocab.items(), key=lambda x: len(x[0]), reverse=True)
print([f'{tokenizer.convert_tokens_to_string(t)}' for t, _ in tokens[:8]]);
```

```
['ÃÂÃÂÃÂÃÂÃÂÃÂÃÂÃÂÃÂÃÂÃÂÃÂÃÂÃÂÃÂÃÂÃÂÃÂÃÂÃÂÃÂÃÂÃÂÃÂÃÂÃÂÃÂÃÂÃÂÃÂÃÂÃÂ', '
================================================================', '
----------------------------------------------------------------
',
'................................................................',
'ÃÂÃÂÃÂÃÂÃÂÃÂÃÂÃÂÃÂÃÂÃÂÃÂÃÂÃÂÃÂÃÂ',
'

----------------------------------------------------------------
',
'================================================================',
'________________________________________________________________']
```

These tokens look like separator lines that are likely to be used on forums. This makes sense since GPT-2 was trained on a corpus centered around Reddit. Now let's have a look at the last words that were added to the vocabulary, and thus the least frequent ones:

```
tokens = sorted(tokenizer.vocab.items(), key=lambda x: x[1], reverse=True)
print([f'{tokenizer.convert_tokens_to_string(t)}' for t, _ in tokens[:12]]);
```

```
['<|endoftext|>', ' gazed', ' informants', ' Collider', ' regress', 'ominated',
 ' amplification', 'Compar', '..."', ' (/', 'Commission', ' Hitman']
```

The first token, `<|endoftext|>`, is the special token used to specify the end of a text sequence and was added after the BPE vocabulary was built. For each of these tokens our model will have to learn an associated word embedding, and we probably don't want the embedding matrix to contain too many noisy words. Also note how some very time- and space-specific knowledge of the world (e.g., proper nouns like `Hitman` and `Commission`) is embedded at a very low level in our modeling approach by these words being granted separate tokens with associated vectors in the vocabulary. The creation of such specific tokens by a BPE tokenizer can also be an indication that the target vocabulary size is too large or that the corpus contains idiosyncratic tokens.

Let's train a fresh tokenizer on our corpus and examine its learned vocabulary. Since we just need a corpus reasonably representative of our dataset statistics, let's select about 1–2 GB of data, or about 100,000 documents from our corpus:

```
from tqdm.auto import tqdm

length = 100000
dataset_name = 'transformersbook/codeparrot-train'
dataset = load_dataset(dataset_name, split="train", streaming=True)
iter_dataset = iter(dataset)

def batch_iterator(batch_size=10):
```

```
    for _ in tqdm(range(0, length, batch_size)):
        yield [next(iter_dataset)['content'] for _ in range(batch_size)]

new_tokenizer = tokenizer.train_new_from_iterator(batch_iterator(),
                                                  vocab_size=12500,
                                                  initial_alphabet=base_vocab)
```

Let's investigate the first and last words created by our BPE algorithm to see how relevant our vocabulary is. We skip the 256 byte tokens and look at the first tokens added thereafter:

```
tokens = sorted(new_tokenizer.vocab.items(), key=lambda x: x[1], reverse=False)
print([f'{tokenizer.convert_tokens_to_string(t)}' for t, _ in tokens[257:280]]);
```

```
['  ', '    ', '   ', '        ', 'se', 'in', '       ', 're', 'on', 'te', '\n
', '\n        ', 'or', 'st', 'de', '\n   ', 'th', 'le', ' =', 'lf', 'self',
'me', 'al']
```

Here we can see various standard levels of indentation and whitespace tokens, as well as short common Python keywords like `self`, `or`, and `in`. This is a good sign that our BPE algorithm is working as intended. Now let's check out the last words:

```
print([f'{new_tokenizer.convert_tokens_to_string(t)}' for t,_ in tokens[-12:]]);
```

```
[' capt', ' embedded', ' regarding', 'Bundle', '355', ' recv', ' dmp', ' vault',
' Mongo', ' possibly', 'implementation', 'Matches']
```

Here there are still some relatively common words, like `recv` (*https://oreil.ly/tliPP*), as well as some more noisy words probably coming from the comments.

We can also tokenize our simple example of Python code to see how our tokenizer is behaving on a simple example:

```
print(new_tokenizer(python_code).tokens())
```

```
['def', 'Ġs', 'ay', '_', 'hello', '():', 'ĊĠĠĠ', 'Ġprint', '("', 'Hello', ',',
'ĠWor', 'ld', '!")', 'Ġ#', 'ĠPrint', 'Ġit', 'Ċ', 'Ċ', 's', 'ay', '_', 'hello',
'()', 'Ċ']
```

Even though they are not code keywords, it's a little annoying to see common English words like `World` or `say` being split by our tokenizer, since we'd expect them to occur rather frequently in the corpus. Let's check if all the Python reserved keywords are in the vocabulary:

```
import

print(f'There are in total {len(keyword.kwlist)} Python keywords.')
for keyw in keyword.kwlist:
    if keyw not in new_tokenizer.vocab:
        print(f'No, keyword `{keyw}` is not in the vocabulary')
```

```
There are in total 35 Python keywords.
No, keyword `await` is not in the vocabulary
```

```
No, keyword `finally` is not in the vocabulary
No, keyword `nonlocal` is not in the vocabulary
```

It appears that several quite frequent keywords, like `finally`, are not in the vocabulary either. Let's try building a larger vocabulary using a larger sample of our dataset. For instance, we can build a vocabulary of 32,768 words (multiples of 8 are better for some efficient GPU/TPU computations) and train the tokenizer on a twice as large slice of our corpus:

```
length = 200000
new_tokenizer_larger = tokenizer.train_new_from_iterator(batch_iterator(),
    vocab_size=32768, initial_alphabet=base_vocab)
```

We don't expect the most frequent tokens to change much when adding more documents, but let's look at the last tokens:

```
tokens = sorted(new_tokenizer_larger.vocab.items(), key=lambda x: x[1],
                reverse=False)
print([f'{tokenizer.convert_tokens_to_string(t)}' for t, _ in tokens[-12:]]);
```

```
['lineEdit', 'spik', ' BC', 'pective', 'OTA', 'theus', 'FLUSH', ' excutils',
'00000002', ' DIVISION', 'CursorPosition', ' InfoBar']
```

A brief inspection doesn't show any regular programming keywords here, which is promising. Let's try tokenizing our sample code example with the new larger tokenizer:

```
print(new_tokenizer_larger(python_code).tokens())
```

```
['def', 'Ġsay', '_', 'hello', '():', 'ĊĠĠĠ', 'Ġprint', '("', 'Hello', ',',
'ĠWorld', '!")', 'Ġ#', 'ĠPrint', 'Ġit', 'Ċ', 'Ċ', 'say', '_', 'hello', '()',
'Ċ']
```

Here also the indents are conveniently kept in the vocabulary, and we see that common English words like `Hello`, `World`, and `say` are also included as single tokens. This seems more in line with our expectations of the data the model may see in the downstream task. Let's investigate the common Python keywords, as we did before:

```
for keyw in keyword.kwlist:
    if keyw not in new_tokenizer_larger.vocab:
        print(f'No, keyword `{keyw}` is not in the vocabulary')
```

```
No, keyword `nonlocal` is not in the vocabulary
```

We are still missing the `nonlocal` keyword (*https://oreil.ly/IHAMu*), but it's also rarely used in practice as it makes the syntax more complex. Keeping it out of the vocabulary seems reasonable. After this manual inspection, our larger tokenizer seems well adapted for our task—but as we mentioned earlier, objectively evaluating the performance of a tokenizer is a challenging task without measuring the model's performance. We will proceed with this one and train a model to see how well it works in practice.

You can easily verify that the new tokenizer is about twice as efficient than the standard GPT-2 tokenizer by comparing the sequence lengths of tokenized code examples. Our tokenizer uses approximately half as many tokens as the existing one to encode a text, which gives us twice the effective model context for free. When we train a new model with the new tokenizer on a context window of size 1,024 it is equivalent to training the same model with the old tokenizer on a context window of size 2,048, with the advantage of being much faster and more memory efficient.

Saving a Custom Tokenizer on the Hub

Now that our tokenizer is trained, we should save it. The simplest way to save it and be able to access it from anywhere later is to push it to the Hugging Face Hub. This will be especially useful later, when we use a separate training server.

To create a private model repository and save our tokenizer in it as a first file, we can directly use the `push_to_hub()` method of the tokenizer. Since we already authenticated our account with `huggingface-cli login`, we can simply push the tokenizer as follows:

```
model_ckpt = "codeparrot"
org = "transformersbook"
new_tokenizer_larger.push_to_hub(model_ckpt, organization=org)
```

If you don't want to push to an organization, you can simply omit the `organization` argument. This will create a repository in your namespace named `codeparrot`, which anyone can then load by running:

```
reloaded_tokenizer = AutoTokenizer.from_pretrained(org + "/" + model_ckpt)
print(reloaded_tokenizer(python_code).tokens())
```

```
['def', 'Ġsay', '_', 'hello', '():', 'ĊĠĠĠ', 'Ġprint', '("', 'Hello', ',',
'ĠWorld', '!")', 'Ġ#', 'ĠPrint', 'Ġit', 'Ċ', 'Ċ', 'say', '_', 'hello', '()',
'Ċ']
```

The tokenizer loaded from the Hub behaves exactly as we just saw. We can also investigate its files and saved vocabulary on the Hub (*https://oreil.ly/vcLeo*). For reproducibility, let's save our smaller tokenizer as well:

```
new_tokenizer.push_to_hub(model_ckpt+ "-small-vocabulary", organization=org)
```

This was a deep dive into building a tokenizer for a specific use case. Next, we will finally create a new model and train it from scratch.

Training a Model from Scratch

Here's the part you've probably been waiting for: the model training. In this section we'll decide which architecture works best for the task, initialize a fresh model without pretrained weights, set up a custom data loading class, and create a scalable training loop. In the grand finale we will train small and large GPT-2 models with 111 million and 1.5 billion parameters, respectively! But let's not get ahead ourselves. First, we need to decide which architecture is best suited for code autocompletion.

In this section we will implement a longer than usual script to train a model on a distributed infrastructure. Therefore, you should not run each code snippet independently, but instead download the script provided in the 🤗 Transformers repository (*https://oreil.ly/ZyPPR*). Follow the accompanying instructions to execute the script with 🤗 Accelerate on your hardware.

A Tale of Pretraining Objectives

Now that we have access to a large-scale pretraining corpus and an efficient tokenizer, we can start thinking about how to pretrain a transformer model. With such a large codebase consisting of code snippets like the one shown in Figure 10-1, we can tackle several tasks. Which one we choose will influence our choice of pretraining objectives. Let's have a look at three common tasks.

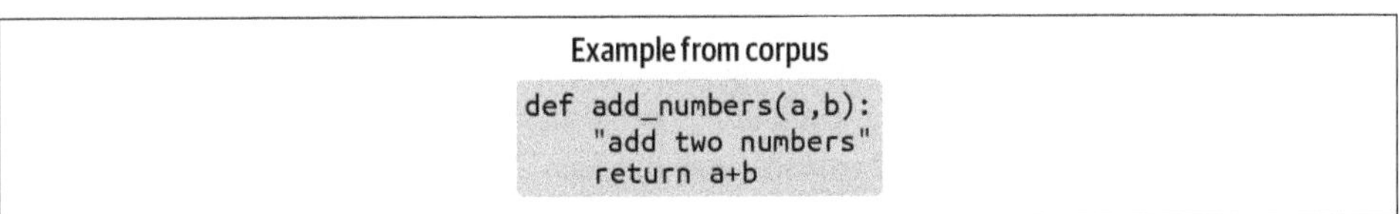

Example from corpus
def add_numbers(a,b):
"add two numbers"
return a+b

Figure 10-1. An example of a Python function that could be found in our dataset

Causal language modeling

A natural task with textual data is to provide a model with the beginning of a code sample and ask it to generate possible completions. This is a self-supervised training objective in which we can use the dataset without annotations. This should ring a bell: it's the *causal language modeling* task we encountered in Chapter 5. A directly related downstream task is code autocompletion, so we'll definitely put this model on the shortlist. A decoder-only architecture such as the GPT family of models is usually best suited for this task, as shown in Figure 10-2.

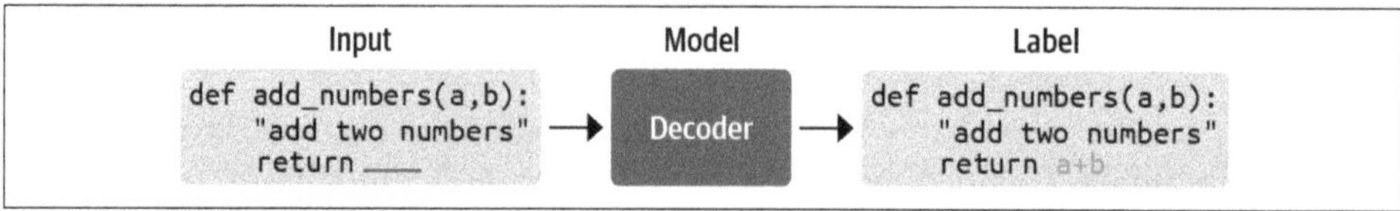

Figure 10-2. In causal language modeling, the future tokens are masked and the model has to predict them; typically a decoder model such as GPT is used for such a task

Masked language modeling

A related but slightly different task is to provide a model with a noisy code sample, for instance with a code instruction replaced by a random or masked word, and ask it to reconstruct the original clean sample, as illustrated in Figure 10-3. This is also a self-supervised training objective and is commonly called *masked language modeling* or the *denoising objective*. It's harder to think about a downstream task directly related to denoising, but denoising is generally a good pretraining task to learn general representations for later downstream tasks. Many of the models that we have used in the previous chapters (like BERT and XLM-RoBERTa) are pretrained in that way. Training a masked language model on a large corpus can thus be combined with fine-tuning the model on a downstream task with a limited number of labeled examples.

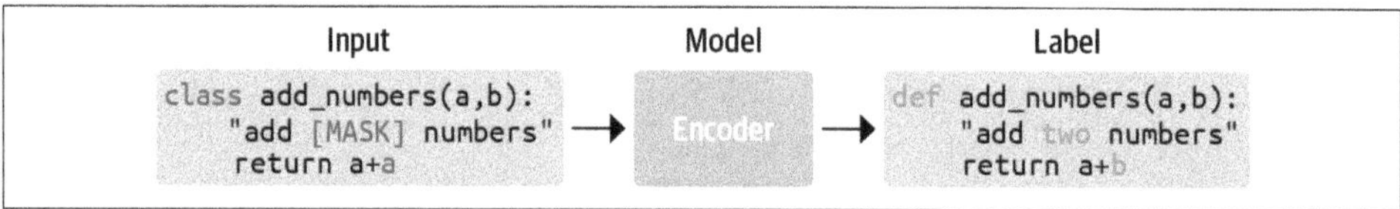

Figure 10-3. In masked language modeling some of the input tokens are either masked or replaced, and the model's task is to predict the original tokens; this is the architecture underlying the encoder branch of transformer models

Sequence-to-sequence training

An alternative task is to use a heuristic like regular expressions to separate comments or docstrings from code and build a large-scale dataset of (code, comments) pairs that can be used as an annotated dataset. The training task is then a supervised training objective in which one category (code or comment) is used as input for the model and the other category (comment or code) is used as labels. This is a case of *supervised learning* with (input, labels) pairs, as highlighted in Figure 10-4. With a large, clean, and diverse dataset as well as a model with sufficient capacity, we can try to train a model that learns to transcript comments in code or vice versa. A downstream task directly related to this supervised training task is then documentation generation from code or code generation from documentation, depending on how we set our input/outputs. In this setting a sequence is translated into another sequence, which is where encoder-decoder architectures such as T5, BART, and PEGASUS shine.

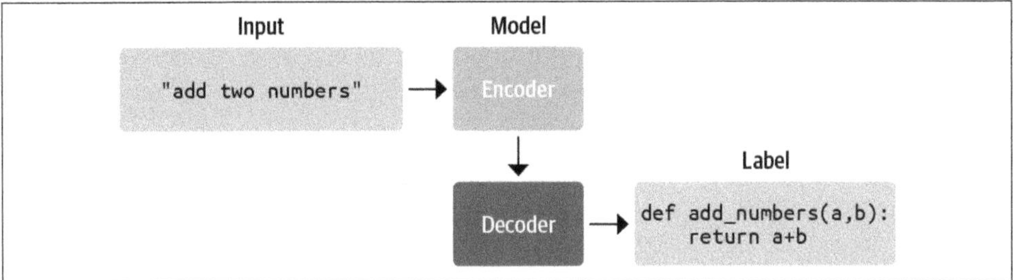

Figure 10-4. Using an encoder-decoder architecture for a sequence-to-sequence task where the inputs are split into comment/code pairs using heuristics: the model gets one element as input and needs to generate the other one

Since we want to build a code autocompletion model, we'll select the first objective and choose a GPT architecture for the task. So let's initialize a fresh GPT-2 model!

Initializing the Model

This is the first time in this book that we won't use the `from_pretrained()` method to load a model but initialize the new model. We will, however, load the configuration of `gpt2-xl` so that we use the same hyperparameters and only adapt the vocabulary size for the new tokenizer. We then initialize a new model with this configuration with the `from_config()` method:

```
from transformers import AutoConfig, AutoModelForCausalLM, AutoTokenizer

tokenizer = AutoTokenizer.from_pretrained(model_ckpt)
config = AutoConfig.from_pretrained("gpt2-xl", vocab_size=len(tokenizer))
model = AutoModelForCausalLM.from_config(config)
```

Let's check how large the model actually is:

```
print(f'GPT-2 (xl) size: {model_size(model)/1000**2:.1f}M parameters')
```

```
GPT-2 (xl) size: 1529.6M parameters
```

This is a 1.5B parameter model! This is a lot of capacity, but we also have a large dataset. In general, large language models are more efficient to train as long as the dataset is reasonably large. Let's save the newly initialized model in a *models/* folder and push it to the Hub:

```
model.save_pretrained("models/" + model_ckpt, push_to_hub=True,
                      organization=org)
```

Pushing the model to the Hub may take a few minutes given the size of the checkpoint (> 5 GB). Since this model is quite large, we'll also create a smaller version that we can train to make sure everything works before scaling up. We will take the standard GPT-2 size as a base:

```
tokenizer = AutoTokenizer.from_pretrained(model_ckpt)
config_small = AutoConfig.from_pretrained("gpt2", vocab_size=len(tokenizer))
model_small = AutoModelForCausalLM.from_config(config_small)
```

```
print(f'GPT-2 size: {model_size(model_small)/1000**2:.1f}M parameters')
```

```
GPT-2 size: 111.0M parameters
```

And let's save it to the Hub as well for easy sharing and reuse:

```
model_small.save_pretrained("models/" + model_ckpt + "-small", push_to_hub=True,
                            organization=org)
```

Now that we have two models we can train, we need to make sure we can feed them the input data efficiently during training.

Implementing the Dataloader

To be able to train with maximal efficiency, we will want to supply our model with sequences filling its context. For example, if the context length of our model is 1,024 tokens, we always want to provide 1,024-token sequences during training. But some of our code examples might be shorter or longer than 1,024 tokens. To feed batches with full sequences of `sequence_length` to our model, we should thus either drop the last incomplete sequence or pad it. However, this will render our training slightly less efficient and force us to take care of padding and masking padded token labels. We are much more compute- than data-constrained, so we'll take the easy and efficient way here. We can use a little trick to make sure we don't lose too many trailing segments: we can tokenize several examples and then concatenate them, separated by the special end-of-sequence token, to get a very long sequence. Finally, we split this sequence into equally sized chunks as shown in Figure 10-5. With this approach, we lose at most a small fraction of the data at the end.

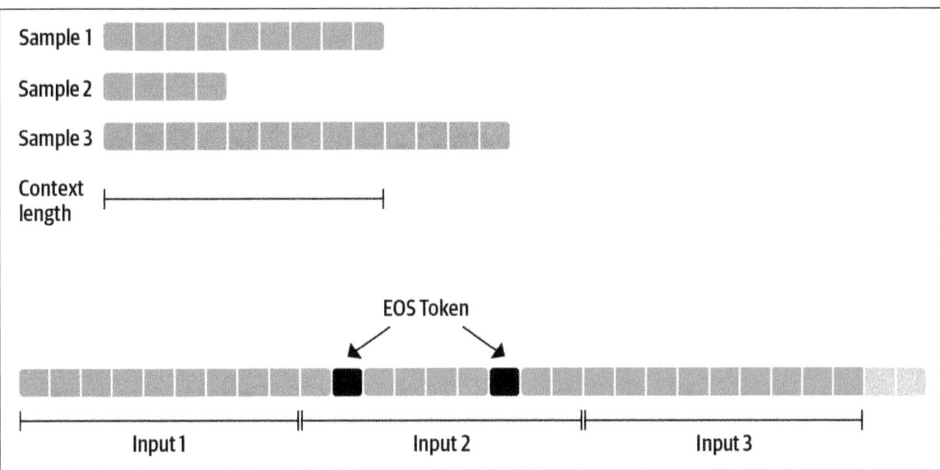

Figure 10-5. Preparing sequences of varying length for causal language modeling by concatenating several tokenized examples with an EOS token before chunking them

We can, for instance, make sure we have roughly one hundred full sequences in our tokenized examples by defining our input string character length as:

```
input_characters = number_of_sequences * sequence_length * characters_per_token
```

where:

- `input_characters` is the number of characters in the string input to our tokenizer.
- `number_of_sequences` is the number of (truncated) sequences we would like from our tokenizer, (e.g., 100).
- `sequence_length` is the number of tokens per sequence returned by the tokenizer, (e.g., 1,024).
- `characters_per_token` is the average number of characters per output token that we first need to estimate.

If we input a string with `input_characters` characters we will thus get on average `number_of_sequences` output sequences, and we can easily calculate how much input data we are losing by dropping the last sequence. If `number_of_sequences=100` it means that we stack roughly 100 sequences and at most lose the last element, which might be too short or too long. This corresponds to at most losing 1% of our dataset. At the same time, this approach ensures that we don't introduce a bias by cutting off the majority of file endings.

Let's first estimate the average character length per token in our dataset:

```
examples, total_characters, total_tokens = 500, 0, 0
dataset = load_dataset('transformersbook/codeparrot-train', split='train',
                       streaming=True)

for _, example in tqdm(zip(range(examples), iter(dataset)), total=examples):
    total_characters += len(example['content'])
    total_tokens += len(tokenizer(example['content']).tokens())

characters_per_token = total_characters / total_tokens
```

```
print(characters_per_token)
```

```
3.6233025034779565
```

With that we have all that's needed to create our own `IterableDataset` (which is a helper class provided by PyTorch) for preparing constant-length inputs for the model. We just need to inherit from `IterableDataset` and set up the `__iter__()` function that yields the next element with the logic we just walked through:

```
import torch
from torch.utils.data import IterableDataset

class ConstantLengthDataset(IterableDataset):

    def __init__(self, tokenizer, dataset, seq_length=1024,
                 num_of_sequences=1024, chars_per_token=3.6):
        self.tokenizer = tokenizer
        self.concat_token_id = tokenizer.eos_token_id
        self.dataset = dataset
        self.seq_length = seq_length
        self.input_characters = seq_length * chars_per_token * num_of_sequences

    def __iter__(self):
        iterator = iter(self.dataset)
        more_examples = True
        while more_examples:
            buffer, buffer_len = [], 0
            while True:
                if buffer_len >= self.input_characters:
                    m=f"Buffer full: {buffer_len}>={self.input_characters:.0f}"
                    print(m)
                    break
                try:
                    m=f"Fill buffer: {buffer_len}<{self.input_characters:.0f}"
                    print(m)
                    buffer.append(next(iterator)["content"])
                    buffer_len += len(buffer[-1])
                except StopIteration:
                    iterator = iter(self.dataset)

            all_token_ids = []
```

```
            tokenized_inputs = self.tokenizer(buffer, truncation=False)
            for tokenized_input in tokenized_inputs["input_ids'"]:
            for tokenized_input in tokenized_inputs:
                all_token_ids.extend(tokenized_input + [self.concat_token_id])

            for i in range(0, len(all_token_ids), self.seq_length):
                input_ids = all_token_ids[i : i + self.seq_length]
                if len(input_ids) == self.seq_length:
                    yield torch.tensor(input_ids)
```

The `__iter__()` function builds up a buffer of strings until it contains enough characters. All the elements in the buffer are tokenized and concatenated with the EOS token, then the long sequence in `all_token_ids` is chunked in `seq_length`-sized slices. Normally, we need attention masks to stack padded sequences of varying length and make sure the padding is ignored during training. We have taken care of this by only providing sequences of the same (maximal) length, so we don't need the masks here and only return the `input_ids`. Let's test our iterable dataset:

```
shuffled_dataset = dataset.shuffle(buffer_size=100)
constant_length_dataset = ConstantLengthDataset(tokenizer, shuffled_dataset,
                                                num_of_sequences=10)
dataset_iterator = iter(constant_length_dataset)

lengths = [len(b) for _, b in zip(range(5), dataset_iterator)]
print(f"Lengths of the sequences: {lengths}")
```

```
Fill buffer: 0<36864
Fill buffer: 3311<36864
Fill buffer: 9590<36864
Fill buffer: 22177<36864
Fill buffer: 25530<36864
Fill buffer: 31098<36864
Fill buffer: 32232<36864
Fill buffer: 33867<36864
Buffer full: 41172>=36864
Lengths of the sequences: [1024, 1024, 1024, 1024, 1024]
```

Nice, this works as intended and we get constant-length inputs for the model. Now that we have a reliable data source for the model, it's time to build the actual training loop.

Notice that we shuffled the raw dataset before creating a `ConstantLengthDataset`. Since this is an iterable dataset, we can't just shuffle the whole dataset at the beginning. Instead, we set up a buffer with size `buffer_size` and shuffle the elements in this buffer before we get elements from the dataset.

Defining the Training Loop

We now have all the elements to write our training loop. One obvious limitation of training our own language model is the memory limits on the GPUs we will use. Even on a modern graphics card you can't train a model at GPT-2 scale in reasonable time. In this tutorial we will implement *data parallelism*, which will help us utilize several GPUs for training. Fortunately, we can use 🤗 Accelerate to make our code scalable. The 🤗 Accelerate library is designed to make distributed training—and changing the underlying hardware for training—easy. We can also use the `Trainer` for distributed training but 🤗 Accelerate gives us full control over the training loop, which is what we want to explore here.

🤗 Accelerate provides an easy API to make training scripts run with mixed precision and in any kind of distributed setting (single GPU, multiple GPUs, and TPUs). The same code can then run seamlessly on your local machine for debugging purposes or your beefy training cluster for the final training run. You only need to make a handful of changes to your native PyTorch training loop:

```
  import
  import                    as
  from          import load_dataset
+ from             import Accelerator

- device = 'cpu'
+ accelerator = Accelerator()

- model = torch.nn.Transformer().to(device)
+ model = torch.nn.Transformer()
  optimizer = torch.optim.Adam(model.parameters())
  dataset = load_dataset('my_dataset')
  data = torch.utils.data.DataLoader(dataset, shuffle=True)
+ model, optimizer, data = accelerator.prepare(model, optimizer, data)

  model.train()
  for epoch in range(10):
      for source, targets in data:
-         source = source.to(device)
-         targets = targets.to(device)
          optimizer.zero_grad()
          output = model(source)
          loss = F.cross_entropy(output, targets)
-         loss.backward()
+         accelerator.backward(loss)
          optimizer.step()
```

The core part of the changes is the call to `prepare()`, which makes sure the model, optimizers, and dataloaders are all prepared and distributed on the infrastructure. These minor changes to the PyTorch training loop enable you to easily scale training across different infrastructures. With that in mind, let's start building up our training script and define a few helper functions. First we set up the hyperparameters for training and wrap them in a `Namespace` for easy access:

```
from argparse import Namespace

# Commented parameters correspond to the small model
config = {"train_batch_size": 2, # 12
          "valid_batch_size": 2, # 12
          "weight_decay": 0.1,
          "shuffle_buffer": 1000,
          "learning_rate": 2e-4, # 5e-4
          "lr_scheduler_type": "cosine",
          "num_warmup_steps": 750, # 2000
          "gradient_accumulation_steps": 16, # 1
          "max_train_steps": 50000, # 150000
          "max_eval_steps": -1,
          "seq_length": 1024,
          "seed": 1,
          "save_checkpoint_steps": 50000} # 15000

args = Namespace(**config)
```

Next, we set up logging for training. Since we are training a model from scratch, the training run will take a while and require expensive infrastructure. Therefore, we want to make sure that all the relevant information is stored and easily accessible. The `setup_logging()` method sets up three levels of logging: using a standard Python `Logger` (*https://oreil.ly/P9Xrm*), TensorBoard (*https://oreil.ly/kY5ri*), and Weights & Biases (*https://oreil.ly/BCC3k*). Depending on your preferences and use case, you can add or remove logging frameworks here:

```
from torch.utils.tensorboard import SummaryWriter
import logging
import wandb

def setup_logging(project_name):
    logger = logging.getLogger(__name__)
    logging.basicConfig(
        format="%(asctime)s - %(levelname)s - %(name)s - %(message)s",
        datefmt="%m/%d/%Y %H:%M:%S", level=logging.INFO, handlers=[
        logging.FileHandler(f"log/debug_{accelerator.process_index}.log"),
        logging.StreamHandler()])
    if accelerator.is_main_process: # We only want to set up logging once
        wandb.init(project=project_name, config=args)
        run_name = wandb.run.name
        tb_writer = SummaryWriter()
        tb_writer.add_hparams(vars(args), {'0': 0})
        logger.setLevel(logging.INFO)
        datasets.utils.logging.set_verbosity_debug()
        transformers.utils.logging.set_verbosity_info()
    else:
        tb_writer = None
```

```
        run_name = ''
        logger.setLevel(logging.ERROR)
        datasets.utils.logging.set_verbosity_error()
        transformers.utils.logging.set_verbosity_error()
    return logger, tb_writer, run_name
```

Each worker gets a unique `accelerator.process_index`, which we use with the `FileHandler` to write the logs of each worker to an individual file. We also use the `accelerator.is_main_process` attribute, which is only `true` for the main worker. We make sure we don't initialize the TensorBoard and Weights & Biases loggers several times, and we decrease the logging levels for the other workers. We return the autogenerated, unique `wandb.run.name`, which we use later to name our experiment branch on the Hub.

We'll also define a function to log the metrics with TensorBoard and Weights & Biases. We again use the `accelerator.is_main_process` here to ensure that we only log the metrics once and not for each worker:

```
def log_metrics(step, metrics):
    logger.info(f"Step {step}: {metrics}")
    if accelerator.is_main_process:
        wandb.log(metrics)
        [tb_writer.add_scalar(k, v, step) for k, v in metrics.items()]
```

Next, let's write a function that creates the dataloaders for the training and validation sets with our brand new `ConstantLengthDataset` class:

```
from torch.utils.data.dataloader import DataLoader

def create_dataloaders(dataset_name):
    train_data = load_dataset(dataset_name+'-train', split="train",
                              streaming=True)
    train_data = train_data.shuffle(buffer_size=args.shuffle_buffer,
                                    seed=args.seed)
    valid_data = load_dataset(dataset_name+'-valid', split="validation",
                              streaming=True)

    train_dataset = ConstantLengthDataset(tokenizer, train_data,
                                          seq_length=args.seq_length)
    valid_dataset = ConstantLengthDataset(tokenizer, valid_data,
                                          seq_length=args.seq_length)

    train_dataloader=DataLoader(train_dataset, batch_size=args.train_batch_size)
    eval_dataloader=DataLoader(valid_dataset, batch_size=args.valid_batch_size)
    return train_dataloader, eval_dataloader
```

At the end we wrap the dataset in a `DataLoader`, which also handles the batching. 🤗 Accelerate will take care of distributing the batches to each worker.

Another aspect we need to implement is optimization. We will set up the optimizer and learning rate schedule in the main loop, but we define a helper function here to differentiate the parameters that should receive weight decay. In general, biases and LayerNorm weights are not subject to weight decay:

```
def get_grouped_params(model, no_decay=["bias", "LayerNorm.weight"]):
    params_with_wd, params_without_wd = [], []
    for n, p in model.named_parameters():
        if any(nd in n for nd in no_decay):
            params_without_wd.append(p)
        else:
            params_with_wd.append(p)
    return [{'params': params_with_wd, 'weight_decay': args.weight_decay},
            {'params': params_without_wd, 'weight_decay': 0.0}]
```

Finally, we want to evaluate the model on the validation set from time to time, so let's add an evaluation function we can call that calculates the loss and perplexity on the evaluation set:

```
def evaluate():
    model.eval()
    losses = []
    for step, batch in enumerate(eval_dataloader):
        with torch.no_grad():
            outputs = model(batch, labels=batch)
        loss = outputs.loss.repeat(args.valid_batch_size)
        losses.append(accelerator.gather(loss))
        if args.max_eval_steps > 0 and step >= args.max_eval_steps: break
    loss = torch.mean(torch.cat(losses))
    try:
        perplexity = torch.exp(loss)
    except OverflowError:
        perplexity = torch.tensor(float("inf"))
    return loss.item(), perplexity.item()
```

The perplexity measures how well the model's output probability distributions predict the targeted tokens. So a lower perplexity corresponds to a better performance. Note that we can compute the perplexity by exponentiating the cross-entropy loss which we get from the model's output. Especially at the start of training when the loss is still high, it is possible to get a numerical overflow when calculating the perplexity. We catch this error and set the perplexity to infinity in these instances.

Before we put it all together in the training script, there is one more additional function that we'll use. As you know by now, the Hugging Face Hub uses Git under the hood to store and version models and datasets. With the `Repository` class from the *huggingface_hub* library you can programmatically access the repository and pull, branch, commit, or push. We'll use this in our script to continuously push model checkpoints to the Hub during training.

Now that we have all these helper functions in place, we are ready to write the heart of the training script:

```
set_seed(args.seed)

# Accelerator
accelerator = Accelerator()
samples_per_step = accelerator.state.num_processes * args.train_batch_size

# Logging
logger, tb_writer, run_name = setup_logging(project_name.split("/")[1])
logger.info(accelerator.state)

# Load model and tokenizer
if accelerator.is_main_process:
    hf_repo = Repository("./", clone_from=project_name, revision=run_name)
model = AutoModelForCausalLM.from_pretrained("./", gradient_checkpointing=True)
tokenizer = AutoTokenizer.from_pretrained("./")

# Load dataset and dataloader
train_dataloader, eval_dataloader = create_dataloaders(dataset_name)

# Prepare the optimizer and learning rate scheduler
optimizer = AdamW(get_grouped_params(model), lr=args.learning_rate)
lr_scheduler = get_scheduler(name=args.lr_scheduler_type, optimizer=optimizer,
                             num_warmup_steps=args.num_warmup_steps,
                             num_training_steps=args.max_train_steps,)
def get_lr():
    return optimizer.param_groups[0]['lr']

# Prepare everything with our `accelerator` (order of args is not important)
model, optimizer, train_dataloader, eval_dataloader = accelerator.prepare(
    model, optimizer, train_dataloader, eval_dataloader)

# Train model
model.train()
completed_steps = 0
for step, batch in enumerate(train_dataloader, start=1):
    loss = model(batch, labels=batch).loss
    log_metrics(step, {'lr': get_lr(), 'samples': step*samples_per_step,
                       'steps': completed_steps, 'loss/train': loss.item()})
    loss = loss / args.gradient_accumulation_steps
    accelerator.backward(loss)
    if step % args.gradient_accumulation_steps == 0:
        optimizer.step()
        lr_scheduler.step()
        optimizer.zero_grad()
        completed_steps += 1
    if step % args.save_checkpoint_steps == 0:
        logger.info('Evaluating and saving model checkpoint')
        eval_loss, perplexity = evaluate()
        log_metrics(step, {'loss/eval': eval_loss, 'perplexity': perplexity})
        accelerator.wait_for_everyone()
        unwrapped_model = accelerator.unwrap_model(model)
        if accelerator.is_main_process:
```

```
            unwrapped_model.save_pretrained("./")
            hf_repo.push_to_hub(commit_message=f'step {step}')
        model.train()
    if completed_steps >= args.max_train_steps:
        break

# Evaluate and save the last checkpoint
logger.info('Evaluating and saving model after training')
eval_loss, perplexity = evaluate()
log_metrics(step, {'loss/eval': eval_loss, 'perplexity': perplexity})
accelerator.wait_for_everyone()
unwrapped_model = accelerator.unwrap_model(model)
if accelerator.is_main_process:
    unwrapped_model.save_pretrained("./")
    hf_repo.push_to_hub(commit_message=f'final model')
```

This is quite a code block, but remember that this is all the code you need to train a fancy, large language model on a distributed infrastructure. Let's deconstruct the script a little bit and highlight the most important parts:

Model saving
: We run the script from within the model repository, and at the start we check out a new branch named after the `run_name` we get from Weights & Biases. Later, we commit the model at each checkpoint and push it to the Hub. With that setup each experiment is on a new branch and each commit represents a model checkpoint. Note that we need to call `wait_for_everyone()` and `unwrap_model()` to make sure the model is properly synchronized when we store it.

Optimization
: For the model optimization we use `AdamW` with a cosine learning rate schedule after a linear warming-up period. For the hyperparameters, we closely follow the parameters described in the GPT-3 paper for similar-sized models.[8]

Evaluation
: We evaluate the model on the evaluation set every time we save—that is, every `save_checkpoint_steps` and after training. Along with the validation loss we also log the validation perplexity.

Gradient accumulation and checkpointing
: The required batch sizes don't fit in a GPU's memory, even when we run on the latest GPUs. Therefore, we implement gradient accumulation, which gathers gradients over several backward passes and optimizes once enough gradients are accumulated. In Chapter 6, we saw how we can do this with the `Trainer`. For the large model, even a single batch does not quite fit on a single GPU. Using a

8 T. Brown et al., "Language Models Are Few-Shot Learners" (*https://arxiv.org/abs/2005.14165*), (2020).

method called *gradient checkpointing* we can trade some of the memory footprint for an approximately 20% training slowdown.[9] This allows us to fit even the large model in a single GPU.

One aspect that might still be a bit obscure is what it means to train a model on multiple GPUs. There are several approaches to train models in a distributed fashion depending on the size of your model and volume of data. The approach utilized by 🤗 Accelerate is called `DataDistributedParallelism` (DDP) (*https://oreil.ly/m4iNm*). The main advantage of this approach is that it allows you to train models faster with larger batch sizes that wouldn't fit into any single GPU. The process is illustrated in Figure 10-6.

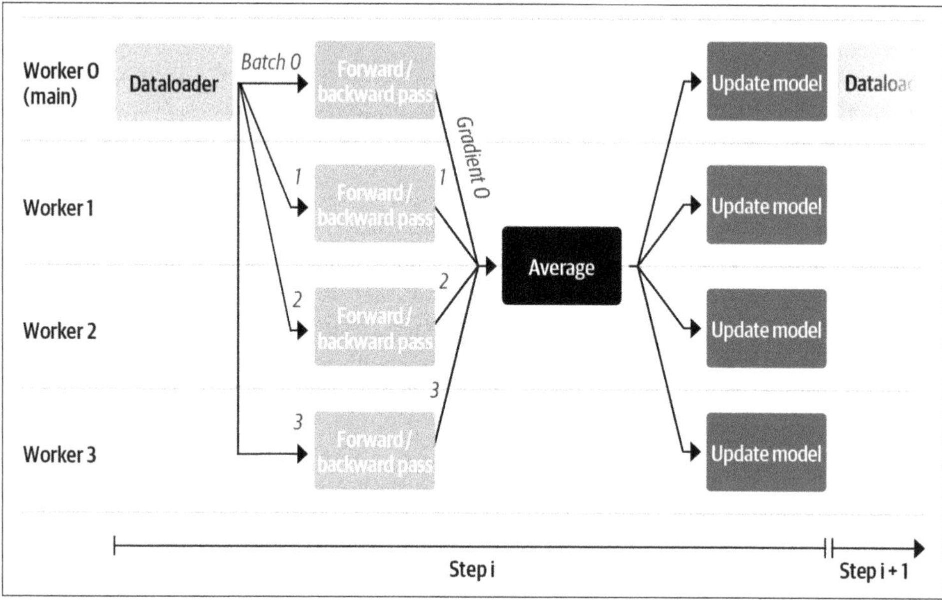

Figure 10-6. Illustration of the processing steps in DDP with four GPUs

Let's go through the pipeline step by step:

1. Each worker consists of a GPU. In 🤗 Accelerate, there is a dataloader running on the main process that prepares the batches of data and sends them to all the workers.
2. Each GPU receives a batch of data and calculates the loss and respective accumulated gradients from forward and backward passes with a local copy of the model.

9 You can read more about gradient checkpointing on OpenAI's release post (*https://oreil.ly/94oj1*).

3. The gradients from each node are averaged with a *reduce* pattern, and the averaged gradients are sent back to each worker.
4. The gradients are applied using the optimizer on each node individually. Although this might seem like redundant work, it avoids transferring copies of the large models between nodes. We'll need to update the model at least once, and without this approach the other nodes would each need to wait until they'd received the updated version.
5. Once all models are updated we start all over again, with the main worker preparing new batches.

This simple pattern allows us to train large models extremely fast by scaling up to the number of available GPUs without much additional logic. Sometimes, however, this is not enough. For example, if the model does not fit on a single GPU you might need more sophisticated parallelism strategies (*https://oreil.ly/3uhfq*). Now that we have all the pieces needed for training, it's time to launch a job! As you'll see in the next section, this is quite simple to do.

The Training Run

We'll save the training script in a file called *codeparrot_training.py* so that we can execute it on our training server. To make life even easier, we'll add it along with a *requirements.txt* file containing all the required Python dependencies to the model repository on the Hub (*https://oreil.ly/ndqSB*). Remember that the models on the Hub are essentially Git repositories so we can just clone the repository, add any files we want, and then push them back to the Hub. On the training server, we can then spin up training with the following handful of commands:

```
$ git clone https://huggingface.co/transformersbook/codeparrot
$ cd codeparrot
$ pip install -r requirements.txt
$ wandb login
$ accelerate config
$ accelerate launch codeparrot_training.py
```

And that's it—our model is now training! Note that `wandb login` will prompt you to authenticate with Weights & Biases for logging. The `accelerate config` command will guide you through setting up the infrastructure; you can see the settings used for this experiment in Table 10-2. We use an `a2-megagpu-16g` instance (*https://oreil.ly/ZJIG3*) for all experiments, which is a workstation with 16 A100 GPUs with 40 GB of memory each.

Table 10-2. Configuration used to train the CodeParrot models

Setting	Value
Compute environment?	multi-GPU
How many machines?	1
DeepSpeed?	No
How many processes?	16
Use FP16?	Yes

Running the training script with these settings on that infrastructure takes about 24 hours and 7 days for the small and large models, respectively. If you train your own custom model, make sure your code runs smoothly on smaller infrastructure in order to make sure that expensive long run goes smoothly as well. After the full training run completes successfully, you can merge the experiment branch on the Hub back into the main branch with the following commands:

```
$ git checkout main
$ git merge <RUN_NAME>
$ git push
```

Naturally, *RUN_NAME* should be the name of the experiment branch on the Hub you would like to merge. Now that we have a trained model, let's have a look at how we can investigate its performance.

Results and Analysis

After anxiously monitoring the logs for a week, you will probably see loss and perplexity curves that look like those shown in Figure 10-7. The training loss and validation perplexity go down continuously, and the loss curve looks almost linear on the log-log scale. We also see that the large model converges faster in terms of processed tokens, although the overall training takes longer.

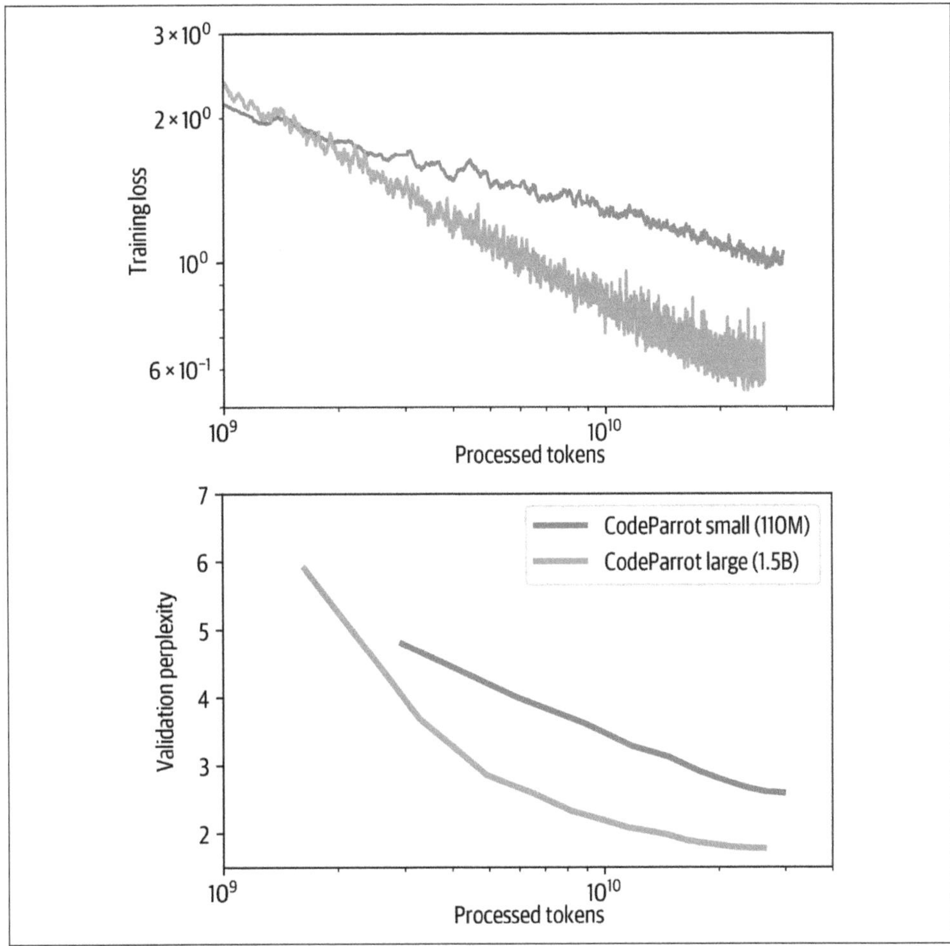

Figure 10-7. Training loss and validation perplexity as a function of processed tokens for the small and large CodeParrot models

So what can we do with our freshly baked language model, straight out of the GPU oven? Well, we can use it to write some code for us. There are two types of analyses we can conduct: qualitative and quantitative. In the former, we look at concrete examples and try to better understand in which cases the model succeeds and where it fails. In the latter case, we evaluate the model's performance statistically on a large set of test cases. In this section we'll explore how we can use our model. First we'll have a look at a few examples, and then we'll briefly discuss how we could evaluate the model systematically and more robustly. First, let's wrap the small model in a pipeline and use it to continue some code inputs:

```
from transformers import pipeline, set_seed
```

```
model_ckpt = 'transformersbook/codeparrot-small'
generation = pipeline('text-generation', model=model_ckpt, device=0)
```

Now we can use the generation pipeline to generate candidate completions from a given prompt. By default, the pipeline will generate code until a predefined maximum length, and the output could contain multiple functions or classes. So, to keep the outputs concise, we'll implement a `first_block()` function that uses regular expressions to extract the first occurrence of a function or class. The `complete_code()` function below applies this logic to print out the completions generated by CodeParrot:

```
import
from              import set_seed

def first_block(string):
    return re.split('\nclass|\ndef|\n#|\n@|\nprint|\nif', string)[0].rstrip()

def complete_code(pipe, prompt, max_length=64, num_completions=4, seed=1):
    set_seed(seed)
    gen_kwargs = {"temperature":0.4, "top_p":0.95, "top_k":0, "num_beams":1,
                  "do_sample":True,}
    code_gens = generation(prompt, num_return_sequences=num_completions,
                           max_length=max_length, **gen_kwargs)
    code_strings = []
    for code_gen in code_gens:
        generated_code = first_block(code_gen['generated_text'][len(prompt):])
        code_strings.append(generated_code)
    print(('\n'+'='*80 + '\n').join(code_strings))
```

Let's start with a simple example and have the model write a function for us that calculates the area of a rectangle:

```
prompt = '''def area_of_rectangle(a: float, b: float):
    """Return the area of the rectangle."""'''
complete_code(generation, prompt)
```

```
    return math.sqrt(a * b)
================================================================================

    return a * b / 2.0
================================================================================

    return a * b
================================================================================

    return a * b / a
```

That looks pretty good! Although not all the generations are correct, the right solution is in there. Now, can the model also solve a more complex task of extracting URLs from an HTML string? Let's see:

```
prompt = '''def get_urls_from_html(html):
    """Get all embedded URLs in a HTML string."""'''
complete_code(generation, prompt)
```

```
    if not html:
        return []
    return [url for url in re.findall(r'<a href="(/[^/]+/[^"]+?)">', html)]
================================================================================

    return [url for url in re.findall(r'<a href="(.*?)"', html)
            if url]
================================================================================

    return [url for url in re.findall(r'<a href="(/.*)",', html)]
================================================================================

    return re.findall(r'<a href="(.*?)" class="url"[^>]*>', html)
```

Although it didn't quite get it right in the second attempt, the other three generations are correct. We can test the function on the Hugging Face home page:

```
import requests

def get_urls_from_html(html):
    return [url for url in re.findall(r'<a href="(.*?)"', html) if url]

print(" | ".join(get_urls_from_html(requests.get('https://hf.co/').text)))
```

```
https://github.com/huggingface/transformers | /allenai | /facebook |
/asteroid-team | /google | /amazon | /speechbrain | /microsoft | /grammarly |
/models | /inference-api | /distilbert-base-uncased |
/dbmdz/bert-large-cased-finetuned-conll03-english |
https://huggingface.co/transformers | https://arxiv.org/abs/1811.06031 |
https://arxiv.org/abs/1803.10631 | https://transformer.huggingface.co/ | /coref
| https://medium.com/huggingface/distilbert-8cf3380435b5
```

We can see that all the URLs starting with `https` are external pages, whereas the others are subpages of the main website. That's exactly what we wanted. Finally, let's load the large model and see if we can use it to translate a function from pure Python to NumPy:

```
model_ckpt = 'transformersbook/codeparrot'
generation = pipeline('text-generation', model=model_ckpt, device=0)

prompt = '''# a function in native python:
def mean(a):
    return sum(a)/len(a)

# the same function using numpy:
import numpy as np
def mean(a):'''
complete_code(generation, prompt, max_length=64)
```

```
Setting `pad_token_id` to `eos_token_id`:0 for open-end generation.


    return np.mean(a)
================================================================================

    return np.mean(a)
================================================================================

    return np.mean(a)
================================================================================

    return np.mean(a)
```

That worked! Let's see if we can also use the CodeParrot model to help us build a Scikit-learn model:

```
prompt = '''X = np.random.randn(100, 100)
y = np.random.randint(0, 1, 100)

# fit random forest classifier with 20 estimators'''
complete_code(generation, prompt, max_length=96)
```

```
Setting `pad_token_id` to `eos_token_id`:0 for open-end generation.


reg = DummyRegressor()

forest = RandomForestClassifier(n_estimators=20)

forest.fit(X, y)
================================================================================

clf = ExtraTreesClassifier(n_estimators=100, max_features='sqrt')
clf.fit(X, y)
================================================================================

clf = RandomForestClassifier(n_estimators=20, n_jobs=n_jobs, random_state=1)
clf.fit(X, y)
================================================================================

clf = RandomForestClassifier(n_estimators=20)
clf.fit(X, y)
```

Although in the second attempt it tried to train an extra-trees classifier (*https://oreil.ly/40Uy7*), it generated what we asked in the other cases.

In Chapter 5 we explored a few metrics to measure the quality of generated text. Among these was the BLEU score, which is frequently used for that purpose. While this metric has limitations in general, it is particularly badly suited for our use case. The BLEU score measures the overlap of *n*-grams between the reference texts and the generated texts. When writing code we have a lot of freedom in terms of variables and classes, and the success of a program does not depend on the naming scheme as long as it is consistent. However, the BLEU score would punish a generation that deviates from the reference naming, which might in fact be almost impossible to predict (even for a human coder).

In software development there are much better and more reliable ways to measure the quality of code, such as unit tests. This is how all the OpenAI Codex models were evaluated: by running several code generations for coding tasks through a set of unit tests and calculating the fraction of generations that pass the tests.[10] For a proper performance measure we should apply the same evaluation regimen to our models but this is beyond the scope of this chapter. You can find details on how CodeParrot performs on the HumanEval benchmark in the model's accompanying blog post (*https://oreil.ly/hKOP8*).

Conclusion

Let's take a step back for a moment and contemplate what we have achieved in this chapter. We set out to create a code autocomplete function for Python. First we built a custom, large-scale dataset suitable for pretraining a large language model. Then we created a custom tokenizer that is able to efficiently encode Python code with that dataset. Finally, with the help of 🤗 Accelerate we put everything together and wrote a training script to train small and large versions of a GPT-2 model from scratch on a multi-GPU infrastructure, in under two hundred lines of code. Investigating the model outputs, we saw that it can generate reasonable code continuations, and we discussed how the model could be systematically evaluated.

You now not only know how to fine-tune any of the many pretrained models on the Hub, but also how to pretrain a custom model from scratch when you have enough data and compute resources available. You are now prepared to tackle almost any NLP use case with transformers. So the question is: where to next? In the next and last chapter, we'll have a look at where the field is currently moving and what new exciting applications and domains beyond NLP transformer models can tackle.

10 M. Chen et al., "Evaluating Large Language Models Trained on Code" (*https://arxiv.org/abs/2107.03374*), (2021).

CHAPTER 11

Future Directions

Throughout this book we've explored the powerful capabilities of transformers across a wide range of NLP tasks. In this final chapter, we'll shift our perspective and look at some of the current challenges with these models and the research trends that are trying to overcome them. In the first part we explore the topic of scaling up transformers, both in terms of model and corpus size. Then we turn our attention toward various techniques that have been proposed to make the self-attention mechanism more efficient. Finally, we explore the emerging and exciting field of *multimodal transformers*, which can model inputs across multiple domains like text, images, and audio.

Scaling Transformers

In 2019, the researcher Richard Sutton (*https://oreil.ly/119br*) wrote a provocative essay entitled "The Bitter Lesson" (*https://oreil.ly/YtD3V*) in which he argued that:

> The biggest lesson that can be read from 70 years of AI research is that general methods that leverage computation are ultimately the most effective, and by a large margin.... Seeking an improvement that makes a difference in the shorter term, researchers seek to leverage their human knowledge of the domain, but the only thing that matters in the long run is the leveraging of computation. These two need not run counter to each other, but in practice they tend to.... And the human-knowledge approach tends to complicate methods in ways that make them less suited to taking advantage of general methods leveraging computation.

The essay provides several historical examples, such as playing chess or Go, where the approach of encoding human knowledge within AI systems was ultimately outdone by increased computation. Sutton calls this the "bitter lesson" for the AI research field:

> We have to learn the bitter lesson that building in how we think we think does not work in the long run.... One thing that should be learned from the bitter lesson is the great power of general purpose methods, of methods that continue to scale with increased computation even as the available computation becomes very great. The two methods that seem to scale arbitrarily in this way are *search* and *learning*.

There are now signs that a similar lesson is at play with transformers; while many of the early BERT and GPT descendants focused on tweaking the architecture or pretraining objectives, the best-performing models in mid-2021, like GPT-3, are essentially basic scaled-up versions of the original models without many architectural modifications. In Figure 11-1 you can see a timeline of the development of the largest models since the release of the original Transformer architecture in 2017, which shows that model size has increased by over four orders of magnitude in just a few years!

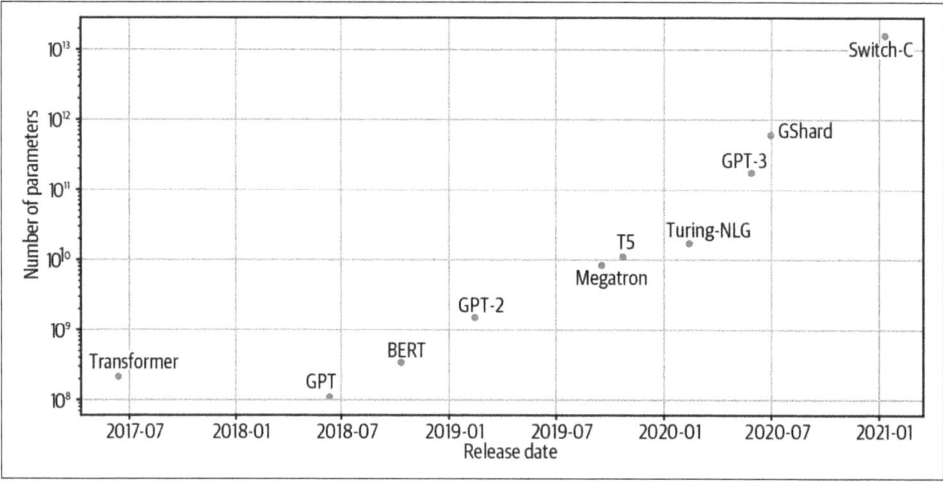

Figure 11-1. Parameter counts over time for prominent Transformer architectures

This dramatic growth is motivated by empirical evidence that large language models perform better on downstream tasks and that interesting capabilities such as zero-shot and few-shot learning emerge in the 10- to 100-billion parameter range. However, the number of parameters is not the only factor that affects model performance; the amount of compute and training data must also be scaled in tandem to train these monsters. Given that large language models like GPT-3 are estimated to cost $4.6 million (*https://oreil.ly/DUVcq*) to train, it is clearly desirable to be able to estimate the model's performance in advance. Somewhat surprisingly, the performance of language models appears to obey a *power law relationship* with model size and other factors that is codified in a set of scaling laws.[1] Let's take a look at this exciting area of research.

Scaling Laws

Scaling laws allow one to empirically quantify the "bigger is better" paradigm for language models by studying their behavior with varying compute budget *C*, dataset size *D*, and model size *N*.[2] The basic idea is to chart the dependence of the cross-entropy loss *L* on these three factors and determine if a relationship emerges. For autoregressive models like those in the GPT family, the resulting loss curves are shown in Figure 11-2, where each blue curve represents the training run of a single model.

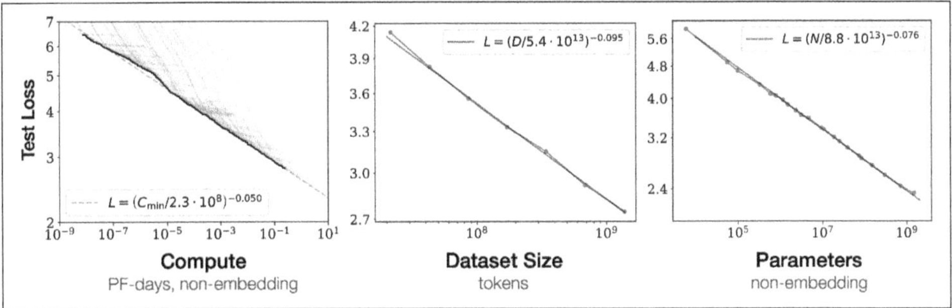

Figure 11-2. Power-law scaling of test loss versus compute budget (left), dataset size (middle), and model size (right) (courtesy of Jared Kaplan)

From these loss curves we can draw a few conclusions about:

The relationship of performance and scale
: Although many NLP researchers focus on architectural tweaks or hyperparameter optimization (like tuning the number of layers or attention heads) to improve performance on a fixed set of datasets, the implication of scaling laws is that a more productive path toward better models is to focus on increasing *N*, *C*, and *D* in tandem.

Smooth power laws
: The test loss *L* has a power law relationship with each of *N*, *C*, and *D* across several orders of magnitude (power law relationships are linear on a log-log scale). For $X = N, C, D$ we can express these power law relationships as $L(X) \sim 1/X^{\alpha}$, where α is a scaling exponent that is determined by a fit to the loss curves shown

1 J. Kaplan et al., "Scaling Laws for Neural Language Models" (*https://arxiv.org/abs/2001.08361*), (2020).

2 The dataset size is measured in the number of tokens, while the model size excludes parameters from the embedding layers.

in Figure 11-2.[3] Typical values for α_X lie in the 0.05–0.095 range, and one attractive feature of these power laws is that the early part of a loss curve can be extrapolated to predict what the approximate loss would be if training was conducted for much longer.

Sample efficiency
: Large models are able to reach the same performance as smaller models with a smaller number of training steps. This can be seen by comparing the regions where a loss curve plateaus over some number of training steps, which indicates one gets diminishing returns in performance compared to simply scaling up the model.

Somewhat surprisingly, scaling laws have also been observed for other modalities, like images, videos, and mathematical problem solving, as illustrated in Figure 11-3.

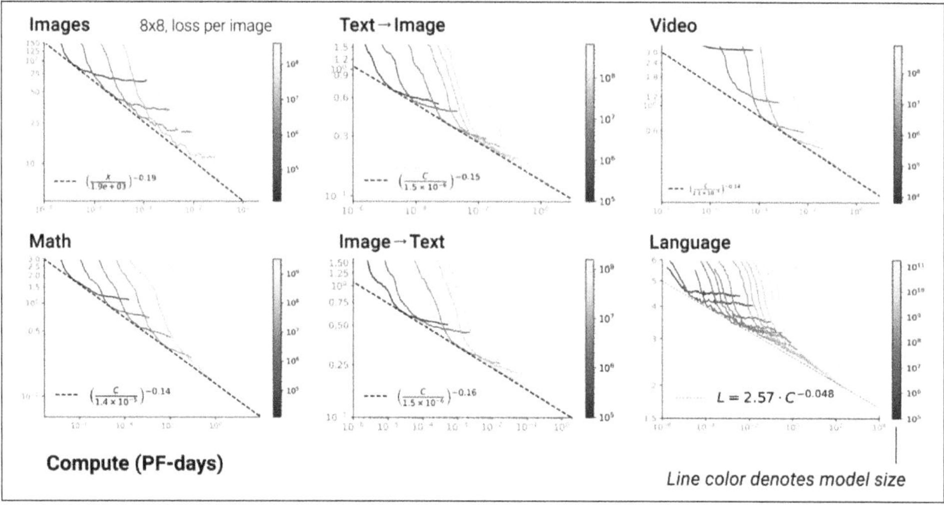

Figure 11-3. Power-law scaling of test loss versus compute budget across a wide range of modalities (courtesy of Tom Henighan)

Whether power-law scaling is a universal property of transformer language models is currently unknown. For now, we can use scaling laws as a tool to extrapolate large, expensive models without having to explicitly train them. However, scaling isn't quite as easy as it sounds. Let's now look at a few challenges that crop up when charting this frontier.

3 T. Henighan et al., "Scaling Laws for Autoregressive Generative Modeling" (*https://arxiv.org/abs/2010.14701*), (2020).

Challenges with Scaling

While scaling up sounds simple in theory ("just add more layers!"), in practice there are many difficulties. Here are a few of the biggest challenges you're likely to encounter when scaling language models:

Infrastructure
: Provisioning and managing infrastructure that potentially spans hundreds or thousands of nodes with as many GPUs is not for the faint-hearted. Are the required number of nodes available? Is communication between nodes a bottleneck? Tackling these issues requires a very different skill set than that found in most data science teams, and typically involves specialized engineers familiar with running large-scale, distributed experiments.

Cost
: Most ML practitioners have experienced the feeling of waking up in the middle of the night in a cold sweat, remembering they forgot to shut down that fancy GPU on the cloud. This feeling intensifies when running large-scale experiments, and most companies cannot afford the teams and resources necessary to train models at the largest scales. Training a single GPT-3-sized model can cost several million dollars, which is not the kind of pocket change that many companies have lying around.[4]

Dataset curation
: A model is only as good as the data it is trained on. Training large models requires large, high-quality datasets. When using terabytes of text data it becomes harder to make sure the dataset contains high-quality text, and even preprocessing becomes challenging. Furthermore, one needs to ensure that there is a way to control biases like sexism and racism that these language models can acquire when trained on large-scale webtext corpora. Another type of consideration revolves around licensing issues with the training data and personal information that can be embedded in large text datasets.

Model evaluation
: Once the model is trained, the challenges don't stop. Evaluating the model on downstream tasks again requires time and resources. In addition, you'll want to probe the model for biased and toxic generations, even if you are confident that you created a clean dataset. These steps take time and need to be carried out thoroughly to minimize the risks of adverse effects later on.

4 However, recently a distributed deep learning framework has been proposed that enables smaller groups to pool their computational resources and pretrain models in a collaborative fashion. See M. Diskin et al., "Distributed Deep Learning in Open Collaborations" (*https://arxiv.org/abs/2106.10207*), (2021).

Deployment
Finally, serving large language models also poses a significant challenge. In Chapter 8 we looked at a few approaches, such as distillation, pruning, and quantization, to help with these issues. However, this may not be enough if you are starting with a model that is hundreds of gigabytes in size. Hosted services such as the OpenAI API (*https://beta.openai.com*) or Hugging Face's Accelerated Inference API (*https://oreil.ly/E4q3b*) are designed to help companies that cannot or do not want to deal with these deployment challenges.

This is by no means an exhaustive list, but it should give you an idea of the kinds of considerations and challenges that go hand in hand with scaling language models to ever larger sizes. While most of these efforts are centralized around a few institutions that have the resources and know-how to push the boundaries, there are currently two community-led projects that aim to produce and probe large language models in the open:

BigScience
This is a one-year-long research workshop that runs from 2021 to 2022 and is focused on large language models. The workshop aims to foster discussions and reflections around the research questions surrounding these models (capabilities, limitations, potential improvements, bias, ethics, environmental impact, role in the general AI/cognitive research landscape) as well as the challenges around creating and sharing such models and datasets for research purposes and among the research community. The collaborative tasks involve creating, sharing, and evaluating a large multilingual dataset and a large language model. An unusually large compute budget was allocated for these collaborative tasks (several million GPU hours on several thousands GPUs). If successful, this workshop will run again in the future, focusing on involving an updated or different set of collaborative tasks. If you want to join the effort, you can find more information at the project's website (*https://oreil.ly/13xfb*).

EleutherAI
This is a decentralized collective of volunteer researchers, engineers, and developers focused on AI alignment, scaling, and open source AI research. One of its aims is to train and open-source a GPT-3-sized model, and the group has already released some impressive models like GPT-Neo (*https://oreil.ly/ZVGaz*) and GPT-J (*https://oreil.ly/Kup60*), which is a 6-billion-parameter model and currently the best-performing publicly available transformer in terms of zero-shot performance. You can find more information at EleutherAI's website (*https://eleuther.ai*).

Now that we've explored how to scale transformers across compute, model size, and dataset size, let's examine another active area of research: making self-attention more efficient.

Attention Please!

We've seen throughout this book that the self-attention mechanism plays a central role in the architecture of transformers; after all, the original Transformer paper is called "Attention Is All You Need"! However, there is a key challenge associated with self-attention: since the weights are generated from pairwise comparisons of all the tokens in a sequence, this layer becomes a computational bottleneck when trying to process long documents or apply transformers to domains like speech processing or computer vision. In terms of time and memory complexity, the self-attention layer of the Transformer architecture naively scales like $\mathcal{O}(n^2)$, where n is the length of the sequence.[5]

As a result, much of the recent research on transformers has focused on making self-attention more efficient. The research directions are broadly clustered in Figure 11-4.

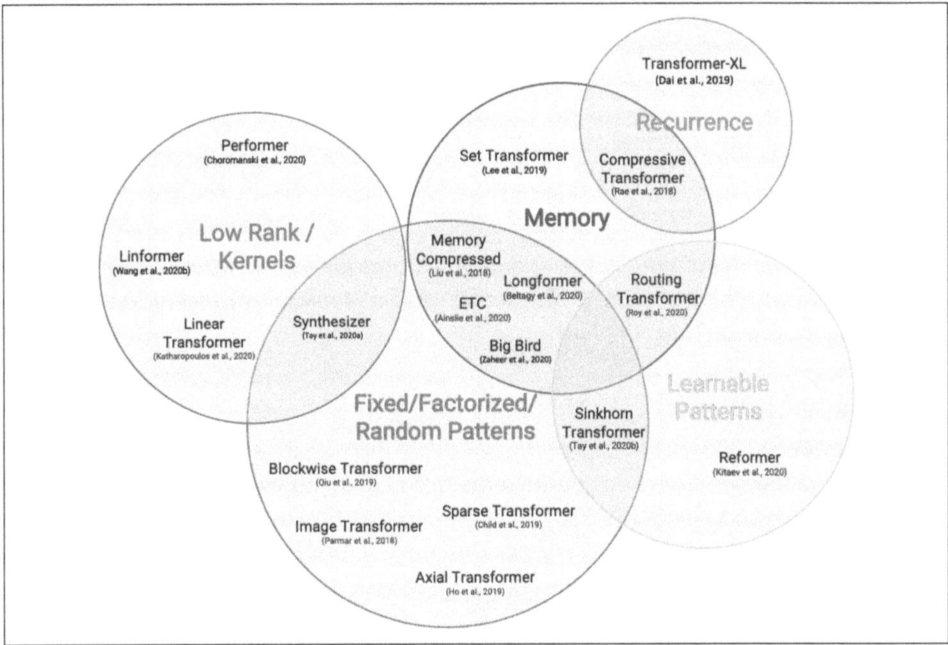

Figure 11-4. A summarization of research directions to make attention more efficient (courtesy of Yi Tay et al.)[6]

5 Although standard implementations of self-attention have $O(n^2)$ time and memory complexity, a recent paper by Google researchers (*https://arxiv.org/abs/2112.05682*) shows that the memory complexity can be reduced to $O(\log n)$ via a simple reordering of the operations.

6 Yi Tay et al., "Efficient Transformers: A Survey" (*https://arxiv.org/abs/2009.06732*), (2020).

A common pattern is to make attention more efficient by introducing sparsity into the attention mechanism or by applying kernels to the attention matrix. Let's take a quick look at some of the most popular approaches to make self-attention more efficient, starting with sparsity.

Sparse Attention

One way to reduce the number of computations that are performed in the self-attention layer is to simply limit the number of query-key pairs that are generated according to some predefined pattern. There have been many sparsity patterns explored in the literature, but most of them can be decomposed into a handful of "atomic" patterns illustrated in Figure 11-5.

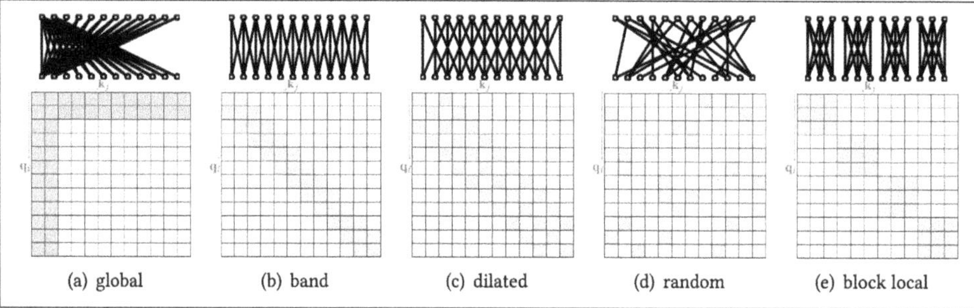

Figure 11-5. Common atomic sparse attention patterns for self-attention: a colored square means the attention score is calculated, while a blank square means the score is discarded (courtesy of Tianyang Lin)

We can describe these patterns as follows:[7]

Global attention
: Defines a few special tokens in the sequence that are allowed to attend to all other tokens

Band attention
: Computes attention over a diagonal band

Dilated attention
: Skips some query-key pairs by using a dilated window with gaps

Random attention
: Randomly samples a few keys for each query to compute attention scores

7 T. Lin et al., "A Survey of Transformers" (*https://arxiv.org/abs/2106.04554*), (2021).

Block local attention
: Divides the sequence into blocks and restricts attention within these blocks

In practice, most transformer models with sparse attention use a mix of the atomic sparsity patterns shown in Figure 11-5 to generate the final attention matrix. As illustrated in Figure 11-6, models like Longformer (*https://oreil.ly/F7xCY*) use a mix of global and band attention, while BigBird (*https://oreil.ly/yFPyj*) adds random attention to the mix. Introducing sparsity into the attention matrix enables these models to process much longer sequences; in the case of Longformer and BigBird the maximum sequence length is 4,096 tokens, which is 8 times larger than BERT!

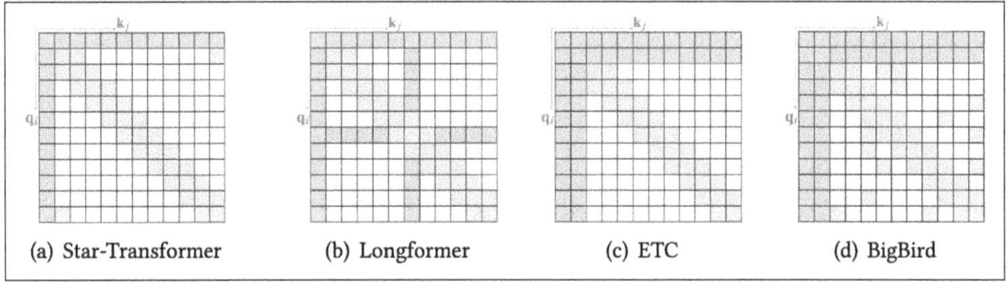

Figure 11-6. Sparse attention patterns for recent transformer models (courtesy of Tianyang Lin)

It is also possible to *learn* the sparsity pattern in a data-driven manner. The basic idea behind such approaches is to cluster the tokens into chunks. For example, Reformer (*https://oreil.ly/yIVvX*) uses a hash function to cluster similar tokens together.

Now that we've seen how sparsity can reduce the complexity of self-attention, let's take a look at another popular approach based on changing the operations directly.

Linearized Attention

An alternative way to make self-attention more efficient is to change the order of operations that are involved in computing the attention scores. Recall that to compute the self-attention scores of the queries and keys we need a similarity function, which for the transformer is just a simple dot product. However, for a general similarity function $\text{sim}(q_i, k_j)$ we can express the attention outputs as the following equation:

$$y_i = \sum_j \frac{\text{sim}(Q_i, K_j)}{\sum_k \text{sim}(Q_i, K_k)} V_j$$

The trick behind linearized attention mechanisms is to express the similarity function as a *kernel function* that decomposes the operation into two pieces:

$$\text{sim}\left(Q_j, K_j\right) = \varphi\left(Q_i\right)^T \varphi\left(K_j\right)$$

where φ is typically a high-dimensional feature map. Since $\varphi\left(Q_i\right)$ is independent of j and k, we can pull it under the sums to write the attention outputs as follows:

$$y_i = \frac{\varphi\left(Q_i\right)^T \Sigma_j \varphi\left(K_j\right) V_j^T}{\varphi\left(Q_i\right)^T \Sigma_k \varphi\left(K_k\right)}$$

By first computing $\Sigma_j \varphi\left(K_j\right) V_j^T$ and $\Sigma_k \varphi\left(K_k\right)$, we can effectively linearize the space and time complexity of self-attention! The comparison between the two approaches is illustrated in Figure 11-7. Popular models that implement linearized self-attention include Linear Transformer and Performer.[8]

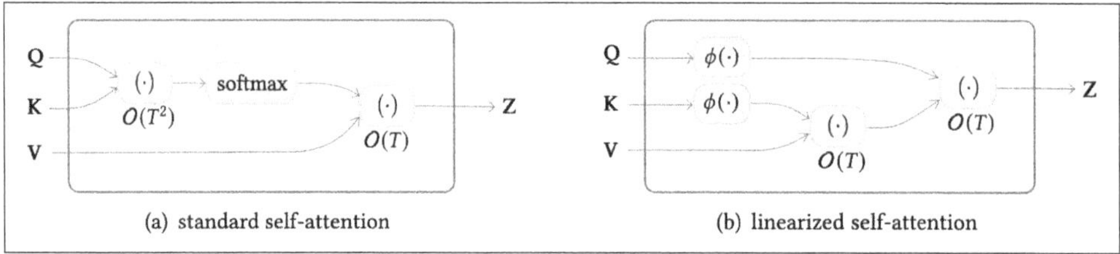

Figure 11-7. Complexity difference between standard self-attention and linearized self-attention (courtesy of Tianyang Lin)

In this section we've seen how Transformer architectures in general and attention in particular can be scaled up to achieve even better performance on a wide range of tasks. In the next section we'll have a look at how transformers are branching out of NLP into other domains such as audio and computer vision.

Going Beyond Text

Using text to train language models has been the driving force behind the success of transformer language models, in combination with transfer learning. On the one hand, text is abundant and enables self-supervised training of large models. On the other hand, textual tasks such as classification and question answering are common,

8 A. Katharopoulos et al., "Transformers Are RNNs: Fast Autoregressive Transformers with Linear Attention" (*https://arxiv.org/abs/2006.16236*), (2020); K. Choromanski et al., "Rethinking Attention with Performers" (*https://arxiv.org/abs/2009.14794*), (2020).

and developing effective strategies for them allows us to address a wide range of real-world problems.

However, there are limits to this approach, including:

Human reporting bias
: The frequencies of events in text may not represent their true frequencies.[9] A model solely trained on text from the internet might have a very distorted image of the world.

Common sense
: Common sense is a fundamental quality of human reasoning, but is rarely written down. As such, language models trained on text might know many facts about the world, but lack basic common-sense reasoning.

Facts
: A probabilistic language model cannot store facts in a reliable way and can produce text that is factually wrong. Similarly, such models can detect named entities, but have no direct way to access information about them.

Modality
: Language models have no way to connect to other modalities that could address the previous points, such as audio or visual signals or tabular data.

So, if we could solve the modality limitations we could potentially address some of the others as well. Recently there has been a lot of progress in pushing transformers to new modalities, and even building multimodal models. In this section we'll highlight a few of these advances.

Vision

Vision has been the stronghold of convolutional neural networks (CNNs) since they kickstarted the deep learning revolution. More recently, transformers have begun to be applied to this domain and to achieve efficiency similar to or better than CNNs. Let's have a look at a few examples.

iGPT

Inspired by the success of the GPT family of models with text, iGPT (short for image GPT) applies the same methods to images.[10] By viewing images as sequences of pixels, iGPT uses the GPT architecture and autoregressive pretraining objective to predict

9 J. Gordon and B. Van Durme, "Reporting Bias and Knowledge Extraction" (*https://openreview.net/pdf?id=AzxEzvpdE3Wcy*), (2013).

10 M. Chen et al., "Generative Pretraining from Pixels," *Proceedings of the 37th International Conference on Machine Learning* 119 (2020):1691–1703, *https://proceedings.mlr.press/v119/chen20s.html*.

the next pixel values. Pretraining on large image datasets enables iGPT to "autocomplete" partial images, as displayed in Figure 11-8. It also achieves performant results on classification tasks when a classification head is added to the model.

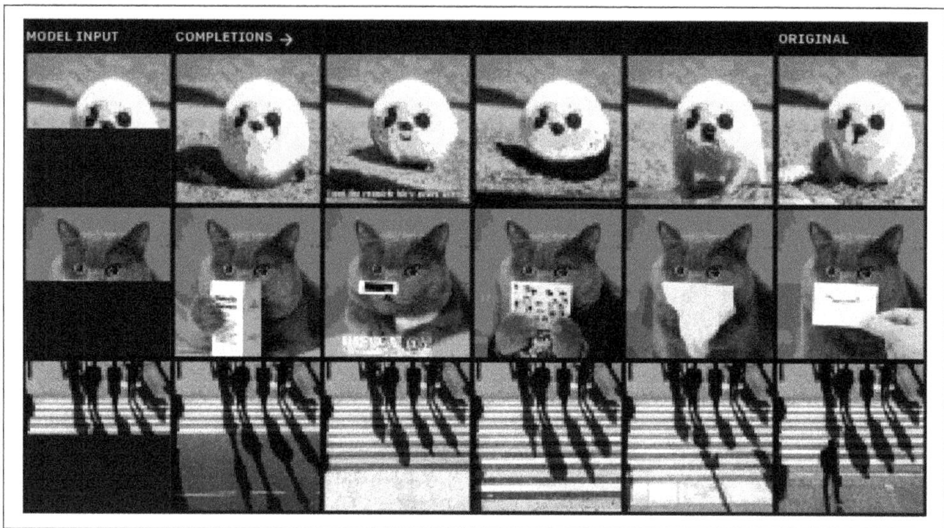

Figure 11-8. Examples of image completions with iGPT (courtesy of Mark Chen)

ViT

We saw that iGPT follows closely the GPT-style architecture and pretraining procedure. Vision Transformer (ViT)[11] is a BERT-style take on transformers for vision, as illustrated in Figure 11-9. First the image is split into smaller patches, and each of these patches is embedded with a linear projection. The results strongly resemble the token embeddings in BERT, and what follows is virtually identical. The patch embeddings are combined with position embeddings and then fed through an ordinary transformer encoder. During pretraining some of the patches are masked or distorted, and the objective is to predict the average color of the masked patch.

11 A. Dosovitskiy et al., "An Image Is Worth 16x16 Words: Transformers for Image Recognition at Scale" (*https://arxiv.org/abs/2010.11929*), (2020).

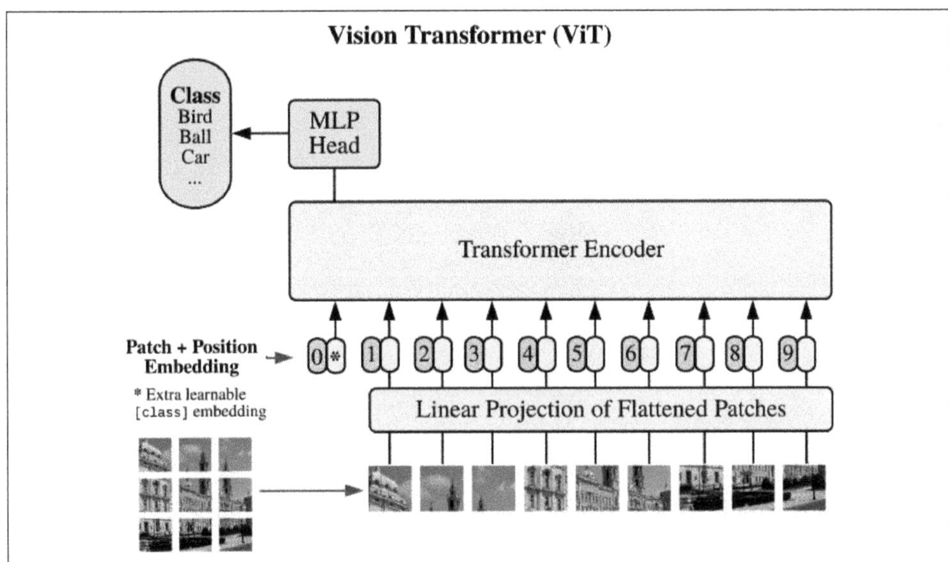

Figure 11-9. The ViT architecture (courtesy of Alexey Dosovitskiy et al.)

Although this approach did not produce better results when pretrained on the standard ImageNet dataset, it scaled significantly better than CNNs on larger datasets.

ViT is integrated in 🤗 Transformers, and using it is very similar to the NLP pipelines that we've used throughout this book. Let's start by loading the image of a rather famous dog:

```
from PIL import Image
import matplotlib.pyplot as plt

image = Image.open("images/doge.jpg")
plt.imshow(image)
plt.axis("off")
plt.show()
```

To load a ViT model, we just need to specify the `image-classification` pipeline, and then we feed in the image to extract the predicted classes:

```
import        as
from                import pipeline

image_classifier = pipeline("image-classification")
preds = image_classifier(image)
preds_df = pd.DataFrame(preds)
preds_df
```

	score	label
0	0.643599	Eskimo dog, husky
1	0.207407	Siberian husky
2	0.060160	dingo, warrigal, warragal, Canis dingo
3	0.035359	Norwegian elkhound, elkhound
4	0.012927	malamute, malemute, Alaskan malamute

Great, the predicted class seems to match the image!

A natural extension of image models is video models. In addition to the spatial dimensions, videos come with a temporal dimension. This makes the task more challenging as the volume of data gets much bigger and one needs to deal with the extra dimension. Models such as TimeSformer introduce a spatial and temporal attention mechanism to account for both.[12] In the future, such models can help build tools for a wide range of tasks such as classification or annotation of video sequences.

12 G. Bertasius, H. Wang, and L. Torresani, "Is Space-Time Attention All You Need for Video Understanding?" (*https://arxiv.org/abs/2102.05095*), (2021).

Tables

A lot of data, such as customer data within a company, is stored in structured databases instead of as raw text. We saw in Chapter 7 that with question answering models we can query text with a question in natural text. Wouldn't it be nice if we could do the same with tables, as shown in Figure 11-10?

Table

Rank	Name	No. of reigns	Combined days
1	Lou Thesz	3	3,749
2	Ric Flair	8	3,103
3	Harley Race	7	1,799
4	Dory Funk Jr.	1	1,563
5	Dan Severn	2	1,559
6	Gene Kiniski	1	1,131

Example questions

#	Question	Answer	Example Type
1	*Which wrestler had the most number of reigns?*	Ric Flair	Cell selection
2	*Average time as champion for top 2 wrestlers?*	AVG(3749,3103)=3426	Scalar answer
3	*How many world champions are there with only one reign?*	COUNT(Dory Funk Jr., Gene Kiniski)=2	Ambiguous answer
4	*What is the number of reigns for* Harley Race?	7	Ambiguous answer
5	*Which of the following wrestlers were ranked in the bottom 3?*	{Dory Funk Jr., Dan Severn, Gene Kiniski}	Cell selection
	Out of these, who had more than one reign?	Dan Severn	Cell selection

Figure 11-10. Question answering over a table (courtesy of Jonathan Herzig)

TAPAS (short for Table Parser)[13] to the rescue! This model applies the Transformer architecture to tables by combining the tabular information with the query, as illustrated in Figure 11-11.

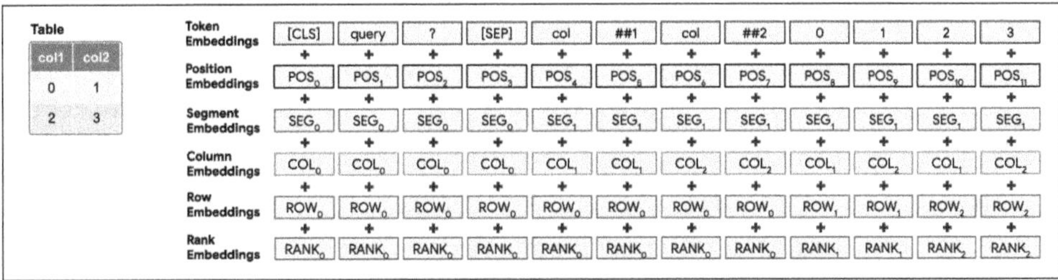

Figure 11-11. Architecture of TAPAS (courtesy of Jonathan Herzig)

Let's look at an example of how TAPAS works in practice. We have created a fictitious version of this book's table of contents. It contains the chapter number, the name of the chapter, as well as the starting and ending pages of the chapters:

```
book_data = [
    {"chapter": 0, "name": "Introduction", "start_page": 1, "end_page": 11},
    {"chapter": 1, "name": "Text classification", "start_page": 12,
     "end_page": 48},
    {"chapter": 2, "name": "Named Entity Recognition", "start_page": 49,
     "end_page": 73},
```

13 J. Herzig et al., "TAPAS: Weakly Supervised Table Parsing via Pre-Training" (*https://arxiv.org/abs/2004.02349*), (2020).

```
    {"chapter": 3, "name": "Question Answering", "start_page": 74,
     "end_page": 120},
    {"chapter": 4, "name": "Summarization", "start_page": 121,
     "end_page": 140},
    {"chapter": 5, "name": "Conclusion", "start_page": 141,
     "end_page": 144}
]
```

We can also easily add the number of pages each chapter has with the existing fields. In order to play nicely with the TAPAS model, we need to make sure that all columns are of type `str`:

```
table = pd.DataFrame(book_data)
table['number_of_pages'] = table['end_page']-table['start_page']
table = table.astype(str)
table
```

	chapter	name	start_page	end_page	number_of_pages
0	0	Introduction	1	11	10
1	1	Text classification	12	48	36
2	2	Named Entity Recognition	49	73	24
3	3	Question Answering	74	120	46
4	4	Summarization	121	140	19
5	5	Conclusion	141	144	3

By now you should know the drill. We first load the `table-question-answering` pipeline:

```
table_qa = pipeline("table-question-answering")
```

and then pass some queries to extract the answers:

```
table_qa = pipeline("table-question-answering")
queries = ["What's the topic in chapter 4?",
           "What is the total number of pages?",
           "On which page does the chapter about question-answering start?",
           "How many chapters have more than 20 pages?"]
preds = table_qa(table, queries)
```

These predictions store the type of table operation in an `aggregator` field, along with the answer. Let's see how well TAPAS fared on our questions:

```
for query, pred in zip(queries, preds):
    print(query)
    if pred["aggregator"] == "NONE":
        print("Predicted answer: " + pred["answer"])
    else:
        print("Predicted answer: " + pred["answer"])
    print('='*50)
```

```
What's the topic in chapter 4?
Predicted answer: Summarization
==================================================
What is the total number of pages?
Predicted answer: SUM > 10, 36, 24, 46, 19, 3
==================================================
On which page does the chapter about question-answering start?
Predicted answer: AVERAGE > 74
==================================================
How many chapters have more than 20 pages?
Predicted answer: COUNT > 1, 2, 3
==================================================
```

For the first chapter, the model predicted exactly one cell with no aggregation. If we look at the table, we see that the answer is in fact correct. In the next example the model predicted all the cells containing the number of pages in combination with the sum aggregator, which again is the correct way of calculating the total number of pages. The answer to question three is also correct; the average aggregation is not necessary in that case, but it doesn't make a difference. Finally, we have a question that is a little bit more complex. To determine how many chapters have more than 20 pages we first need to find out which chapters satisfy that criterion and then count them. It seem that TAPAS again got it right and correctly determined that chapters 1, 2, and 3 have more than 20 pages, and added a count aggregator to the cells.

The kinds of questions we asked can also be solved with a few simple Pandas commands; however, the ability to ask questions in natural language instead of Python code allows a much wider audience to query the data to answer specific questions. Imagine such tools in the hands of business analysts or managers who are able verify their own hypotheses about the data!

Multimodal Transformers

So far we've looked at extending transformers to a single new modality. TAPAS is arguably multimodal since it combines text and tables, but the table is also treated as text. In this section we examine transformers that combine two modalities at once: audio plus text and vision plus text.

Speech-to-Text

Although being able to use text to interface with a computer is a huge step forward, using spoken language is an even more natural way for us to communicate. You can see this trend in industry, where applications such as Siri and Alexa are on the rise and becoming progressively more useful. Also, for a large fraction of the population, writing and reading are more challenging than speaking. So, being able to process and understand audio is not only convenient, but can help many people access more information. A common task in this domain is *automatic speech recognition* (ASR), which converts spoken words to text and enables voice technologies like Siri to answer questions like "What is the weather like today?"

The wav2vec 2.0 (*https://oreil.ly/tPpC7*) family of models are one of the most recent developments in ASR: they use a transformer layer in combination with a CNN, as illustrated in Figure 11-12.[14] By leveraging unlabeled data during pretraining, these models achieve competitive results with only a few minutes of labeled data.

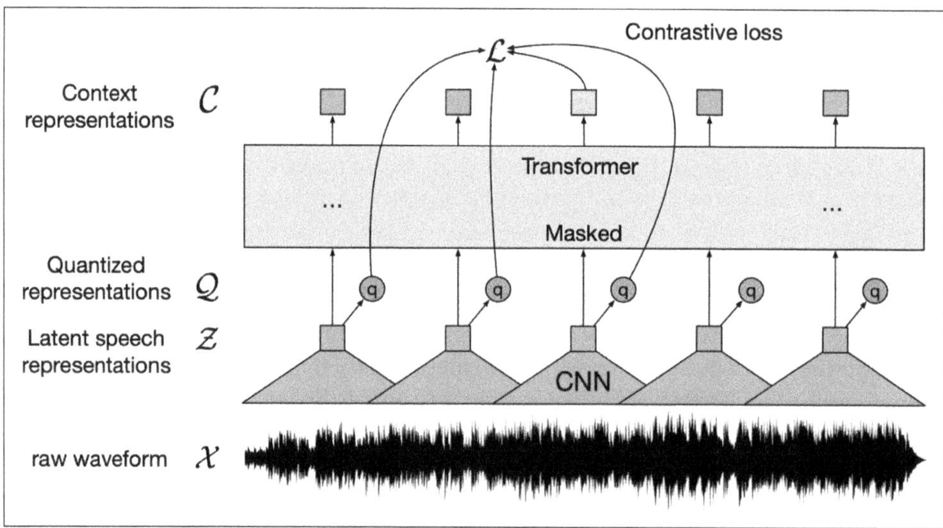

Figure 11-12. Architecture of wav2vec 2.0 (courtesy of Alexei Baevski)

The wav2vec 2.0 models are integrated in 🤗 Transformers, and you won't be surprised to learn that loading and using them follows the familiar steps that we have seen throughout this book. Let's load a pretrained model that was trained on 960 hours of speech audio:

```
asr = pipeline("automatic-speech-recognition")
```

To apply this model to some audio files we'll use the ASR subset of the SUPERB dataset (*https://oreil.ly/iBAK8*), which is the same dataset the model was pretrained on. Since the dataset is quite large, we'll just load one example for our demo purposes:

```
from datasets import load_dataset

ds = load_dataset("superb", "asr", split="validation[:1]")
print(ds[0])
```

14 A. Baevski et al., "wav2vec 2.0: A Framework for Self-Supervised Learning of Speech Representations" (*https://arxiv.org/abs/2006.11477*), (2020).

```
{'chapter_id': 128104, 'speaker_id': 1272, 'file': '~/.cache/huggingf
ace/datasets/downloads/extracted/e4e70a454363bec1c1a8ce336139866a39442114d86a433
6014acd4b1ed55e55/LibriSpeech/dev-clean/1272/128104/1272-128104-0000.flac',
'id': '1272-128104-0000', 'text': 'MISTER QUILTER IS THE APOSTLE OF THE MIDDLE
CLASSES AND WE ARE GLAD TO WELCOME HIS GOSPEL'}
```

Here we can see that the audio in the `file` column is stored in the FLAC coding format, while the expected transcription is given by the `text` column. To convert the audio to an array of floats, we can use the *SoundFile* library (*https://oreil.ly/eo106*) to read each file in our dataset with `map()`:

```
import soundfile as sf

def map_to_array(batch):
    speech, _ = sf.read(batch["file"])
    batch["speech"] = speech
    return batch

ds = ds.map(map_to_array)
```

If you are using a Jupyter notebook you can easily play the sound files with the following `IPython` widgets:

```
from IPython.display import Audio

display(Audio(ds[0]['speech'], rate=16000))
```

Finally, we can pass the inputs to the pipeline and inspect the prediction:

```
pred = asr(ds[0]["speech"])
print(pred)
```

```
{'text': 'MISTER QUILTER IS THE APOSTLE OF THE MIDDLE CLASSES AND WE ARE GLAD TO
WELCOME HIS GOSPEL'}
```

This transcription seems to be correct. We can see that some punctuation is missing, but this is hard to get from audio alone and could be added in a postprocessing step. With only a handful of lines of code we can build ourselves a state-of-the-art speech-to-text application!

Building a model for a new language still requires a minimum amount of labeled data, which can be challenging to obtain, especially for low-resource languages. Soon after the release of wav2vec 2.0, a paper describing a method named wav2vec-U was published.[15] In this work, a combination of clever clustering and GAN training is used to build a speech-to-text model using only independent unlabeled speech and unlabeled text data. This process is visualized in detail in Figure 11-13. No aligned speech and text data is required at all, which enables the training of highly performant speech-to-text models for a much larger spectrum of languages.

15 A. Baevski et al., "Unsupervised Speech Recognition" (*https://arxiv.org/abs/2105.11084*), (2021).

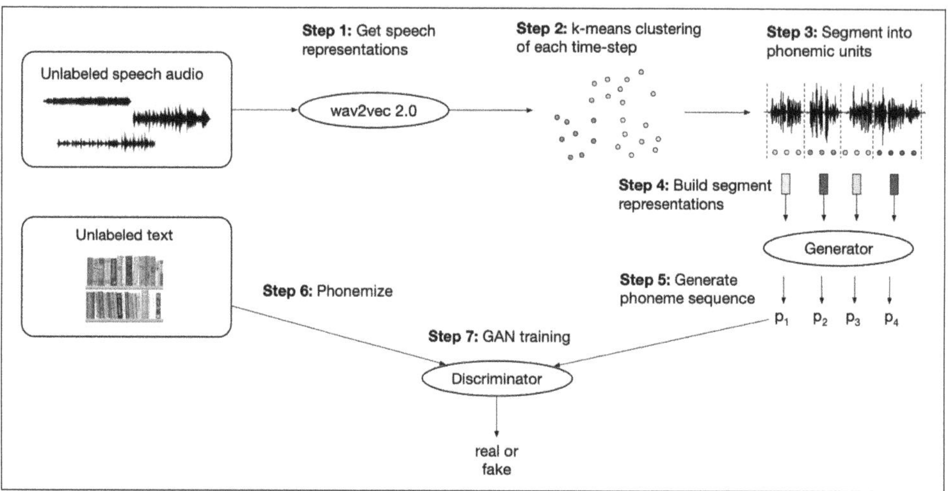

Figure 11-13. Training scheme for wav2vec-U (courtesy of Alexsei Baevski)

Great, so transformers can now "read" text and "hear" audio—can they also "see"? The answer is yes, and this is one of the current hot research frontiers in the field.

Vision and Text

Vision and text are another natural pair of modalities to combine since we frequently use language to communicate and reason about the contents of images and videos. In addition to the vision transformers, there have been several developments in the direction of combining visual and textual information. In this section we will look at four examples of models combining vision and text: VisualQA, LayoutLM, DALL·E, and CLIP.

VQA

In Chapter 7 we explored how we can use transformer models to extract answers to text-based questions. This can be done ad hoc to extract information from texts or offline, where the question answering model is used to extract structured information from a set of documents. There have been several efforts to expand this approach to vision with datasets such as VQA,[16] shown in Figure 11-14.

16 Y. Goyal et al., "Making the V in VQA Matter: Elevating the Role of Image Understanding in Visual Question Answering" (*https://arxiv.org/abs/1612.00837*), (2016).

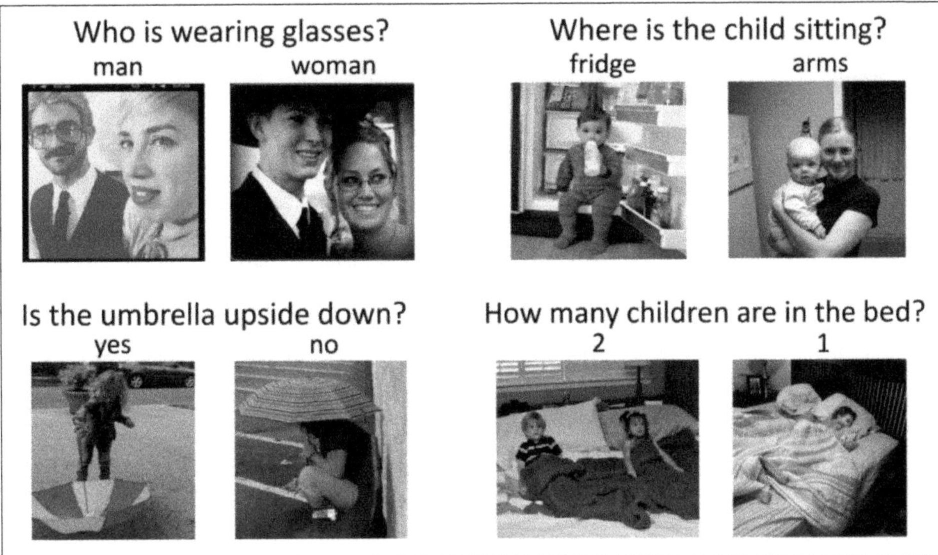

Figure 11-14. Example of a visual question answering task from the VQA dataset (courtesy of Yash Goyal)

Models such as LXMERT and VisualBERT use vision models like ResNets to extract features from the pictures and then use transformer encoders to combine them with the natural questions and predict an answer.[17]

LayoutLM

Analyzing scanned business documents like receipts, invoices, or reports is another area where extracting visual and layout information can be a useful way to recognize text fields of interest. Here the LayoutLM (*https://oreil.ly/uQc5t*) family of models are the current state of the art. They use an enhanced Transformer architecture that receives three modalities as input: text, image, and layout. Accordingly, as shown in Figure 11-15, there are embedding layers associated with each modality, a spatially aware self-attention mechanism, and a mix of image and text/image pretraining objectives to align the different modalities. By pretraining on millions of scanned documents, LayoutLM models are able to transfer to various downstream tasks in a manner similar to BERT for NLP.

17 H. Tan and M. Bansal, "LXMERT: Learning Cross-Modality Encoder Representations from Transformers" (*https://arxiv.org/abs/1908.07490*), (2019); L.H. Li et al., "VisualBERT: A Simple and Performant Baseline for Vision and Language" (*https://arxiv.org/abs/1908.03557*), (2019).

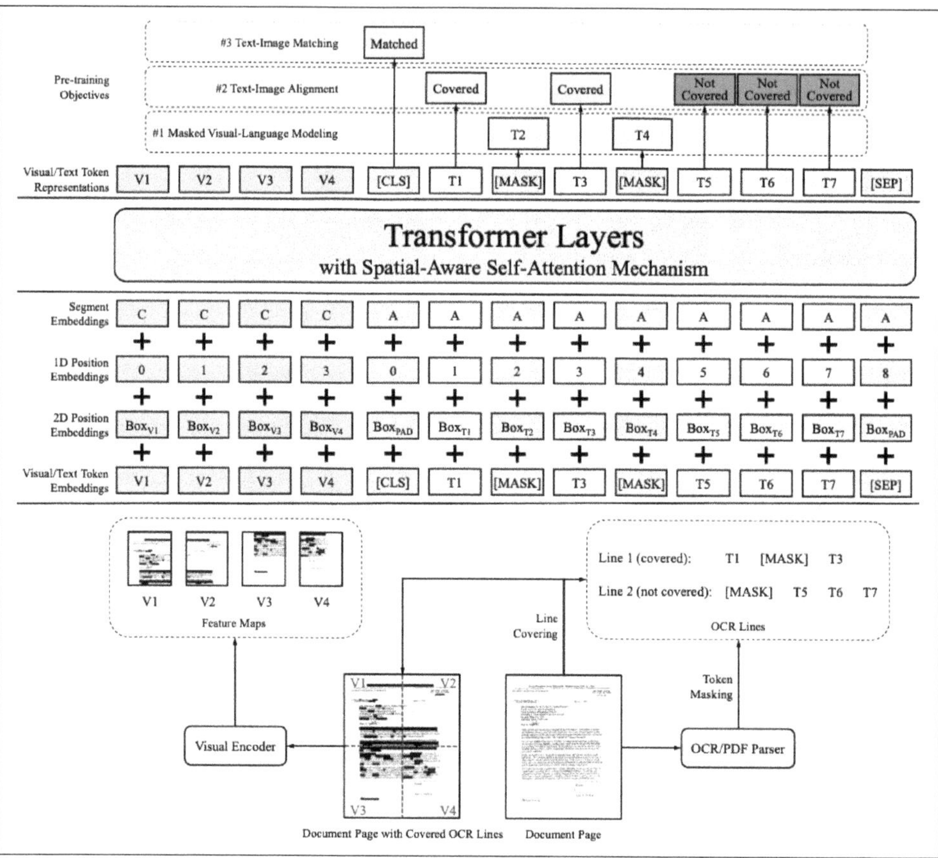

Figure 11-15. The model architecture and pretraining strategies for LayoutLMv2 (courtesy of Yang Xu)

DALL·E

A model that combines vision and text for *generative* tasks is DALL·E.[18] It uses the GPT architecture and autoregressive modeling to generate images from text. Inspired by iGPT, it regards the words and pixels as one sequence of tokens and is thus able to continue generating an image from a text prompt, as shown in Figure 11-16.

18 A. Ramesh et al., "Zero-Shot Text-to-Image Generation" (*https://arxiv.org/abs/2102.12092*), (2021).

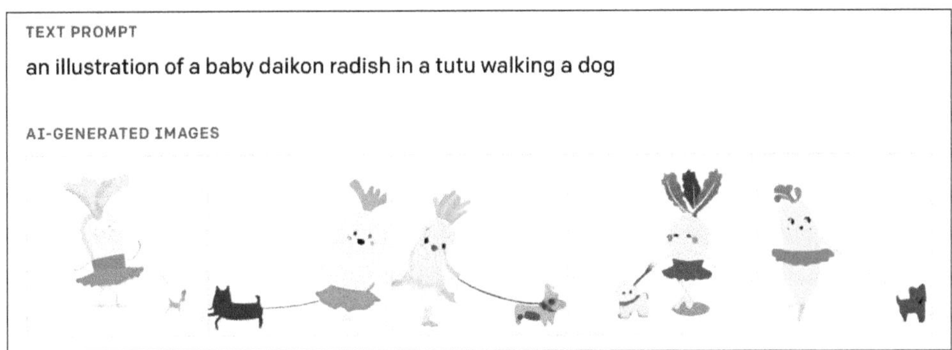
TEXT PROMPT
an illustration of a baby daikon radish in a tutu walking a dog
AI-GENERATED IMAGES

Figure 11-16. Generation examples with DALL·E (courtesy of Aditya Ramesh)

CLIP

Finally, let's have a look at CLIP,[19] which also combines text and vision but is designed for supervised tasks. Its creators constructed a dataset with 400 million image/caption pairs and used contrastive learning to pretrain the model. The CLIP architecture consists of a text and an image encoder (both transformers) that create embeddings of the captions and images. A batch of images with captions is sampled, and the contrastive objective is to maximize the similarity of the embeddings (as measured by the dot product) of the corresponding pair while minimizing the similarity of the rest, as illustrated in Figure 11-17.

In order to use the pretrained model for classification the possible classes are embedded with the text encoder, similar to how we used the zero-shot pipeline. Then the embeddings of all the classes are compared to the image embedding that we want to classify, and the class with the highest similarity is chosen.

19 A. Radford et al., "Learning Transferable Visual Models from Natural Language Supervision" (*https://arxiv.org/abs/2103.00020*), (2021).

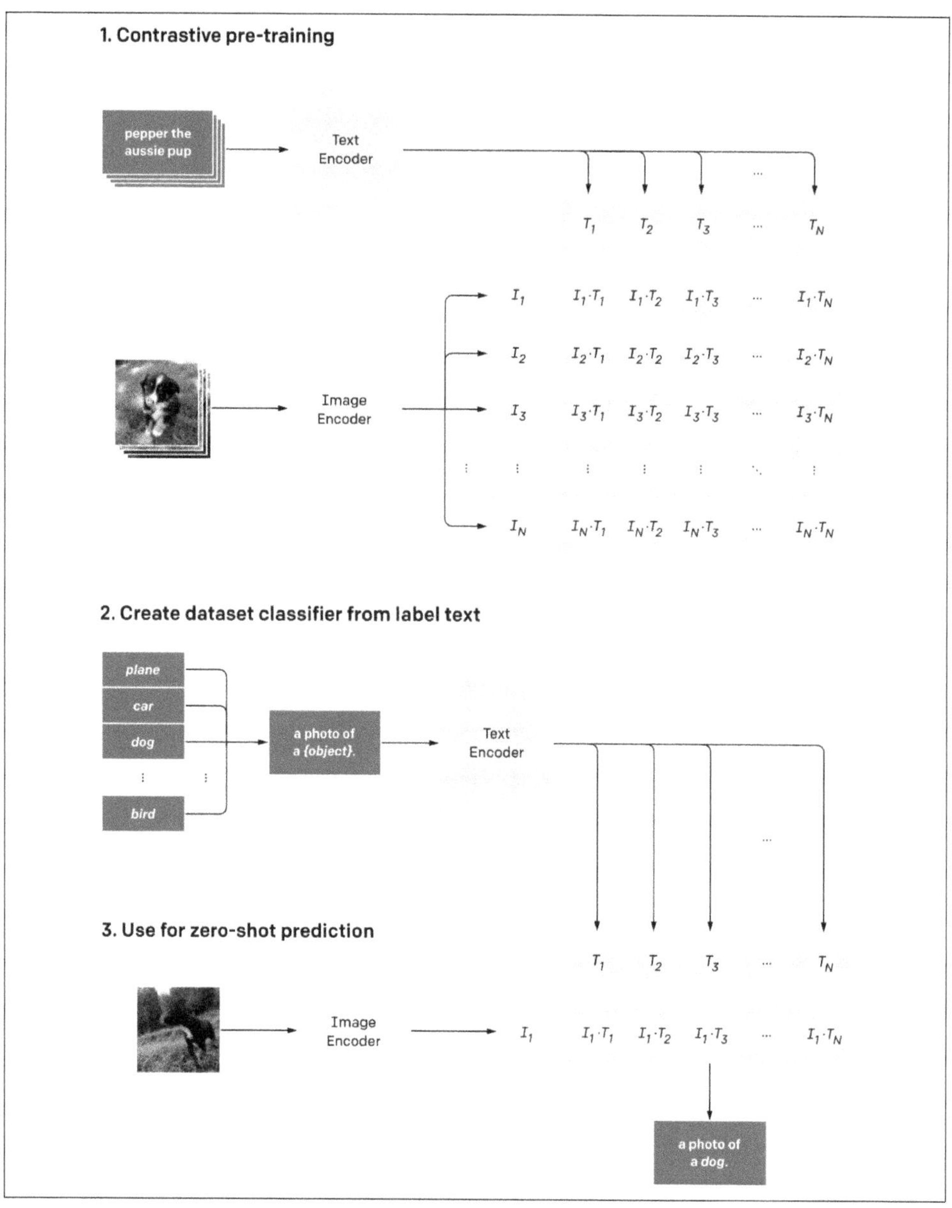

Figure 11-17. Architecture of CLIP (courtesy of Alec Radford)

The zero-shot image classification performance of CLIP is remarkable and competitive with fully supervised trained vision models, while being more flexible with regard to new classes. CLIP is also fully integrated in 🤗 Transformers, so we can try it out. For image-to-text tasks, we instantiate a *processor* that consists of a *feature extractor* and a tokenizer. The role of the feature extractor is to convert the image into a form suitable for the model, while the tokenizer is responsible for decoding the model's predictions into text:

```
from transformers import CLIPProcessor, CLIPModel

clip_ckpt = "openai/clip-vit-base-patch32"
model = CLIPModel.from_pretrained(clip_ckpt)
processor = CLIPProcessor.from_pretrained(clip_ckpt)
```

Then we need a fitting image to try it out. What would be better suited than a picture of Optimus Prime?

```
image = Image.open("images/optimusprime.jpg")
plt.imshow(image)
plt.axis("off")
plt.show()
```

Next, we set up the texts to compare the image against and pass it through the model:

```
import torch

texts = ["a photo of a transformer", "a photo of a robot", "a photo of agi"]
inputs = processor(text=texts, images=image, return_tensors="pt", padding=True)
with torch.no_grad():
    outputs = model(**inputs)
logits_per_image = outputs.logits_per_image
probs = logits_per_image.softmax(dim=1)
probs
```

```
tensor([[0.9557, 0.0413, 0.0031]])
```

Well, it almost got the right answer (a photo of AGI of course). Jokes aside, CLIP makes image classification very flexible by allowing us to define classes through text instead of having the classes hardcoded in the model architecture. This concludes our tour of multimodal transformer models, but we hope we've whetted your appetite.

Where to from Here?

Well that's the end of the ride; thanks for joining us on this journey through the transformers landscape! Throughout this book we've explored how transformers can address a wide range of tasks and achieve state-of-the-art results. In this chapter we've seen how the current generation of models are being pushed to their limits with scaling and how they are also branching out into new domains and modalities.

If you want to reinforce the concepts and skills that you've learned in this book, here are a few ideas for where to go from here:

Join a Hugging Face community event
: Hugging Face hosts short sprints focused on improving the libraries in the ecosystem, and these events are a great way to meet the community and get a taste for open source software development. So far there have been sprints on adding 600+ datasets to 🤗 Datasets, fine-tuning 300+ ASR models in various languages, and implementing hundreds of projects in JAX/Flax.

Build your own project
: One very effective way to test your knowledge in machine learning is to build a project to solve a problem that interests you. You could reimplement a transformer paper, or apply transformers to a novel domain.

Contribute a model to 🤗 Transformers
: If you're looking for something more advanced, then contributing a newly published architecture to 🤗 Transformers is a great way to dive into the nuts and bolts of the library. There is a detailed guide to help you get started in the 🤗 Transformers documentation (*https://oreil.ly/3f4wZ*).

Blog about what you've learned
: Teaching others what you've learned is a powerful test of your own knowledge, and in a sense this was one of the driving motivations behind us writing this book! There are great tools to help you get started with technical blogging; we recommend *fastpages* (*https://oreil.ly/f0L9u*) as you can easily use Jupyter notebooks for everything.

Index

A

B

C

D

E

F

G

H

I

J

K

L

M

N

O

P

Q

R

S

T

U

V

W

X

Z

About the Authors

Lewis Tunstall is a machine learning engineer at Hugging Face. He has built machine learning applications for startups and enterprises in the domains of NLP, topological data analysis, and time series. Lewis has a PhD in theoretical physics and has held research positions in Australia, the USA, and Switzerland. His current work focuses on developing tools for the NLP community and teaching people to use them effectively.

Leandro von Werra is a machine learning engineer in the open source team at Hugging Face. He has several years of industry experience bringing NLP projects to production by working across the whole machine learning stack, and is the creator of a popular Python library called TRL, which combines transformers with reinforcement learning.

Thomas Wolf is chief science officer at and cofounder of Hugging Face. His team is on a mission to catalyze and democratize NLP research. Prior to cofounding Hugging Face, Thomas earned a PhD in physics and later a law degree. He has worked as a physics researcher and a European patent attorney.

Colophon

The bird on the cover of *Natural Language Processing with Transformers* is a coconut lorikeet (*Trichoglossus haematodus*), a relative of parakeets and parrots. It is also known as the green-naped lorikeet and is native to Oceania.

The plumage of coconut lorikeets blends into their colorful tropical and subtropical surroundings; their green nape meets a yellow collar beneath a deep dark blue head, which ends in an orange-red bill. Their eyes are orange and the breast feathers are red. Coconut lorikeets have one of the longest, pointed tails of the seven species of lorikeet, which is green from above and yellow underneath. These birds measure 10 to 12 inches long and weigh 3.8 to 4.8 ounces.

Coconut lorikeets have one monogamous partner and lay two matte white eggs at a time. They build nests over 80 feet high in eucalyptus trees and live 15 to 20 years in the wild. This species suffers from habitat loss and capture for the pet trade. Many of the animals on O'Reilly's covers are endangered; all of them are important to the world.

The cover illustration is by Karen Montgomery, based on a black and white engraving from *English Cyclopedia*. The cover fonts are Gilroy Semibold and Guardian Sans. The text font is Adobe Minion Pro; the heading font is Adobe Myriad Condensed; and the code font is Dalton Maag's Ubuntu Mono.

Milton Keynes UK
Ingram Content Group UK Ltd.
UKHW051052011024
449063UK00001B/2

9 781098 136796